# Economic Forecasting

Nicolas Carnot

Vincent Koen

and

Bruno Tissot

First published in 2005 by
PALGRAVE MACMILLAN
Houndmills, Basingstoke, Hampshire RG21 6XS and
175 Fifth Avenue, New York, N.Y. 10010
Companies and representatives throughout the world.

PALGRAVE MACMILLAN is the global academic imprint of the Palgrave
Macmillan division of St. Martin's Press, LLC and of Palgrave Macmillan Ltd.
Macmillan® is a registered trademark in the United States, United Kingdom
and other countries. Palgrave is a registered trademark in the European
Union and other countries.

ISBN-13: 978–1–4039–3653–0 hardback
ISBN-13: 978–1–4039–3654–7 paperback
ISBN-10: 1–4039–3653–6 hardback
ISBN-10: 1–4039–3654–4 paperback

This book is printed on paper suitable for recycling and made from fully
managed and sustained forest sources. Logging, pulping and manufacturing
processes are expected to conform to the environmental regulations of the
country of origin.

A catalogue record for this book is available from the British Library.

Library of Congress Cataloging-in-Publication Data
Carnot, Nicolas.
    Economic forecasting / by Nicolas Carnot, Vincent Koen and Bruno Tissot.
        p. cm.
    Includes bibliographical references and index.
        ISBN 1–4039–3653–6 (cloth : alk. paper) – ISBN 1–4039–3654–4 (pbk. : alk. paper)
        1. Economic forecasting. I. Koen, Vincent. II. Tissot, Bruno. III. Title.
HB3730.C35 2005
330'.01'12—dc22                                                      2004063677

Printed and bound in Great Britain by
CPI Antony Rowe, Chippenham and Eastbourne

# Contents

# List of Figures

# List of Tables

# List of Boxes

# Foreword

While macroeconomic and economic policy handbooks abound, they rarely dwell on the important question of economic forecasting. Many even bypass it altogether. Yet, scores of economists, both in the private and in the public sector, spend their working days constructing forecasts, and worry at night whether they got them right. The techniques they use blend traditional macroeconomic analysis, statistical and econometric tools, microeconomic insights and a fair dose of eclectic judgement. Granted, some of them are described in journal articles but few if any books pull these various strands of knowledge and expertise together in a comprehensive survey. Bruno, Nicolas and Vincent aptly fill the void, drawing on their experience built up first-hand, in particular at the International Monetary Fund, the Bank for International Settlements and the Organisation for Economic Co-operation and Development.

*Economic Forecasting* is accessible to anyone with a general background in economics, yet nuanced and state-of-the-art. It provides the complete toolkit needed by forecasters, with clear presentations of the technicalities and numerous up-to-date real-life exhibits. It covers a broad set of areas, including national accounting, business cycle analysis, macroeconomic model-building and usage, long-term projections and fiscal forecasting.

But this book also steps back from the nitty-gritty of day-to-day forecasting cuisine to put things in perspective. It sets out the theoretical underpinnings of forecasting models. It vividly shows how forecasts feed into policy-making or private agents' decisions. It discusses forecasting (in)accuracy, convincingly arguing that forecasts are essential even if forecasters are almost inevitably bound to be off the mark. It candidly points out the shortcomings of the existing analytical frameworks and gives readers a glimpse of forthcoming developments on the frontier of national accounting, economic analysis and forecasting. Last but not least, it offers a unique round-the-world tour of the institutions producing forecasts – a precious roadmap for what has become a crowded jungle.

A preliminary version of this book was first published in French in 2002 and received the prize of the best economic policy book from the French Academy of Moral and Political Sciences. I trust that the English version, which adopts a more global perspective and incorporates relevant recent developments, will be equally successful and will rapidly become popular with students, academics and practitioners alike.

Jean-Philippe Cotis
*OECD Chief Economist*

# Acknowledgements

This book owes a lot to what we learnt from colleagues as we built up fore-casting experience as economists at the International Monetary Fund, the Bank for International Settlements and the Organisation for Economic Co-operation and Development, but also in national policy-making bodies, as government and central bank staffers in Paris. A number of colleagues are actually quoted along the way in the book, but attempting an exhaustive thank you list would be as fastidious as it would be vain. We would nonetheless like to single out those who most directly supported our efforts: Professor Olivier Blanchard, at the Massachusetts Institute of Technology; Frédéric Bobay, at the French Ministry of Finance; Jean-Philippe Cotis, as head of the Economic Forecasting Department of the French Ministry of Finance and subsequently as head of the OECD's Economics Department; François Lequiller, head of the OECD's National Accounts Division; and Bill White, head of the Monetary and Economic Department at the BIS. Our gratitude also extends to Jean Pavlevski at Economica Editions who published an earlier version of this book in French, and to our families, who bore with us during a long march.

While grateful for all the wisdom and backing, we take full responsibility for the views expressed in this book as well as for any residual shortcomings, which should not be ascribed to the aforementioned institutions or individuals.

NICOLAS CARNOT
VINCENT KOEN
BRUNO TISSOT

# Acronyms

| | |
|---|---|
| ADB | African Development Bank |
| ADB | Asian Development Bank |
| AGE | applied general equilibrium (model) |
| AIDS | acquired immune deficiency syndrome |
| AR | auto-regressive |
| ARIMA | auto-regressive integrated moving average |
| ARMA | auto-regressive moving average |
| BEA | Bureau of Economic Analysis (United States) |
| BEER | behavioural equilibrium exchange rate |
| BIPE | Bureau d'Informations et de Prévisions Économiques (France) |
| BIS | Bank for International Settlements |
| BLS | Bureau of Labor Statistics (United States) |
| CAE | Conseil d'Analyse Économique (France) |
| CBI | Confederation of British Industry (United Kingdom) |
| CBO | Congressional Budget Office (United States) |
| CEA | Council of Economic Advisors (United States) |
| CEPII | Centre d'Études Prospectives et d'Informations Internationales (France) |
| CEPR | Centre for Economic Policy Research (Europe) |
| CES | constant elasticity of substitution |
| CGE | computable general equilibrium (model) |
| c.i.f. | cost of insurance and freight |
| CLI | composite leading indicator |
| CPB | Central Planning Bureau (Netherlands, renamed Bureau for Economic Policy Analysis) |
| CPI | consumer price index |
| DEER | desired equilibrium exchange rate |
| DGTPE | Direction Générale du Trésor et de la Politique Économique (France) |
| DIR | Daiwa Institute of Research (Japan) |
| DIW | Deutsche Institut für Wirtschaftsforschung (Berlin) |
| EBRD | European Bank for Reconstruction and Development |
| EC | European Commission |
| ECB | European Central Bank |
| ECM | error-correction model |
| ECOFIN | Economic and Financial Affairs Council (European Union) |
| ECRI | Economic Cycle Research Institute |
| ESA | European System of Accounts |
| ESRI | Economic and Social Research Institute (Ireland) |
| ESRI | Economic and Social Research Institute (Japan) |
| ETLA | Research Institute of the Finnish Economy (Finland) |
| EU | European Union |

| | |
|---|---|
| FDI | foreign direct investment |
| FEER | fundamental equilibrium exchange rate |
| f.o.b. | free on board |
| FOMC | Federal Open Market Committee (United States) |
| FY | fiscal year |
| GDP | gross domestic product |
| GNI | gross national income |
| GNP | gross national product |
| HDI | human development index |
| HICP | harmonised index of consumer prices |
| HP | Hodrick-Prescott (filter) |
| HPI | human poverty index |
| HWWA | Hamburgische Welt-Wirtschafts-Archiv (Hamburg) |
| IADB | Interamerican Development Bank |
| IBRD | International Bank for Reconstruction and Development |
| ICSID | International Centre for Settlement of Investment Disputes |
| IDA | International Development Association |
| IEA | International Energy Agency |
| IFC | International Finance Corporation |
| IFL | Instituto Flores de Lemus (Madrid University) |
| IFO | Institut für Wirtschaftsforschung (Munich) |
| IFS | Institut for Fiscal Studies (London) |
| IfW | Institut für Weltwirtschaft (Kiel) |
| IGIER | Innocenzo Gasparini Institute for Economic Research (Bocconi University) |
| ILO | International Labour Organisation |
| IMF | International Monetary Fund |
| INSEE | Institut National de la Statistique et des Études Économiques (France) |
| IRR | internal rate of return |
| ISAE | Istituto di Studi e Analisi Economica (Italy) |
| ISIC | International Standard Industrial Classification |
| ISM | Institute for Supply Management (United States) |
| ISTAT | Istituto Nazionale di Statistica (Italy) |
| IVCCA | inventory valuation and capital consumption adjustments |
| IWH | Institut für Wirtschaftsforschung (Halle) |
| JCER | Japan Center for Economic Research |
| LFS | Labour Force Survey |
| MA | moving average |
| MAE | mean absolute error |
| MCI | monetary conditions index |
| METI | Ministry of Economy, Trade and Industry (Japan) |
| MFCI | monetary and financial conditions index |
| MIGA | Multilateral Investment Guarantee Agency |
| MPC | Monetary Policy Committee |
| MSE | mean square error |
| NACE | Statistical Classification of Economic Activities in the European Community |

| | |
|---|---|
| NAICS | North American Industry Classification System |
| NAIRU | non-accelerating inflation rate of unemployment |
| NAPM | National Association of Purchasing Management (United States) |
| NATREX | natural real exchange rate |
| NBER | National Bureau of Economic Research |
| NDP | net domestic product |
| NIESR | National Institute of Economic and Social Research (United Kingdom) |
| NIPA | National Income and Product Accounts |
| NPI | non-profit institutions |
| NPISH | non-profit institutions serving households |
| NPV | net present value |
| OECD | Organisation for Economic Co-operation and Development |
| OEEC | Organisation for European Economic Co-operation (now OECD) |
| OEF | Oxford Economic Forecasting |
| OFCE | Observatoire Français des Conjonctures Économiques (France) |
| OLS | ordinary least squares |
| OMB | Office of Management and Budget (United States) |
| ONS | Office for National Statistics (United Kingdom) |
| OPEC | Organisation of the Petroleum Exporting Countries |
| PEER | permanent equilibrium exchange rate |
| PER | price–earnings ratio |
| PMI | purchasing managers' index |
| PPP | purchasing power parity |
| RBNZ | Reserve Bank of New Zealand |
| R&D | research and development |
| RMSE | root mean square error |
| RPI | retail price index |
| RPIX | retail price index excluding mortgage interest payments |
| RWI | Rheinisch-Westfälisches Institut für Wirtschaftsforschung (Essen) |
| SARS | severe acute respiratory syndrome |
| SEATS | signal extraction in ARIMA time series |
| SEEA | integrated environmental and economic accounting |
| SNA | system of national accounts |
| STAR | smooth transition auto-regressive (model) |
| TFP | total factor productivity |
| UIP | uncovered interest parity |
| UN | United Nations |
| UNCTAD | United Nations Conference on Trade and Development |
| UNDP | United Nations Development Programme |
| VAR | vector auto-regressive (model) |
| VAT | value-added tax |
| VECM | vector error-correction model |
| WEO | *World Economic Outlook* (IMF) |
| WIFO | Österreichisches Institut für Wirtschaftsforschung (Austria) |
| WTO | World Trade Organisation |

# Introduction

All human errors are impatience, a premature breaking off of methodical procedure, an apparent fencing-in of what is apparently at issue.

F. Kafka

Man approaches the unattainable truth through a succession of errors.

A. Huxley

In recent decades, economic forecasting has taken on an increasingly important role. Expected future economic developments are discussed daily, both in specialised fora and more broadly. News carrying risks for the economic outlook can send financial markets into jitters at any time. Hence, an articulated assessment of economic prospects is now widely seen as an indispensable ingredient in economic policy-making, as well as for private-sector decisions. To cope with uncertainty and anticipate the implications of their behaviour, nearly every agent or collective entity has to rely on some description of how the economy is likely to evolve, that is, on an economic forecast.

## What is economic forecasting?

This book focuses mainly on the forecasting of macroeconomic phenomena, pertaining to the evolution of overall economic magnitudes. From a formal standpoint, economic forecasting can be defined as a set of hypothetical statements about future macroeconomic developments, such as the evolution of overall activity or price levels. As a rule, economic forecasting involves:

- A view of the economic future, consisting of quantitative estimates for the main macroeconomic variables at different horizons.
- An underlying analytical 'story', which includes an exposition of the assumptions underpinning the forecast, and an investigation of the risks that could materialise if some of them turned out to be wrong.
- A discussion of the implied options for the user of the forecast.

Economic forecasting is basically a structured way to peer into the future using all available information, including recent outcomes, survey data on agents' mood and plans, prior knowledge of economic relationships, and so forth. Obviously, forecasting requires economic and econometric expertise, and in particular a specialised knowledge of several techniques. But it also draws on history as well as on political and social science, while the forecaster's own judgement plays a crucial role.

## The book's aims

This book covers all aspects of economic forecasting. It is aimed both at the non-specialists wishing to understand this field better and at forecasters looking for a comprehensive and up-to-date compendium on the subject. It thus fills the void between specialised textbooks with a heavy statistical content and more general economic textbooks. The perspective here is that of practitioners presenting their profession's contribution to analysis and decision-making, in particular economic policymaking.

The book describes and discusses most current forecasting techniques. It tries to be comprehensive, but with an emphasis on those techniques that are most commonly used in practice. The mathematical material is kept to a minimum and can be understood by any reader with a general, undergraduate level, background in economics. The forecasting tools are not presented in isolation. They are motivated by empirical observations and theoretical considerations, and as much intuition as possible is provided. In addition, they are accompanied by important advice on practical implementation.

The book further explains the role of economic forecasts. Granted, any economic forecast is inherently shrouded in uncertainty. But when properly prepared and used, it helps improve the quality of decision-making. Indeed, the value of any particular forecast has less to do with specific numbers than with its ability to structure public debate in a simple yet rigorous fashion. Forecasters therefore have a pedagogical and advisory role.

## Outline

The book reviews both the methods and the uses of economic forecasting. It is structured as follows. The first chapter deals with the principles of economic forecasting and answers three basic questions: what to forecast, why forecast and how to forecast? It also serves as an introduction to the main topics covered in the book. Chapter 2 goes over the economic data, and in particular the national accounts, which constitute the general framework for economic forecasting.

The book then turns to the forecaster's usual tools. Chapter 3 focuses on macroeconomic monitoring and business cycle analysis for the purpose of very near-term forecasting. Chapter 4 presents the time series methods used in forecasting. Chapters 5 and 6 are devoted to the so-called structural approaches, and respectively discuss the modelling of economic behaviour and macroeconomic models. The next four chapters introduce the techniques used in medium- and long-run projections (Chapter 7), financial forecasting (Chapter 8), budget forecasting (Chapter 9) and sectoral forecasting (Chapter 10).

The following chapters offer perspectives on the contribution of economic forecasts to decision-making. Chapter 11 discusses forecasting accuracy. Chapter 12 explains how forecasts are used in practice by economic policymakers and other agents. Chapter 13 examines the communication of economic forecasts, and includes some discussion of forecasting ethics. Lastly, Chapter 14 tours the institutions producing forecasts.

Each chapter is relatively self-contained, allowing readers to go explore them in the order that best suits their needs.

# 1
# First Principles

This chapter provides an overview of the main themes covered in the book. It revolves around three basic questions:

- First, what is being forecast? In this book, the focus is on forecasting macroeconomic variables. Aggregate changes are thus primarily of concern, with sectoral developments being considered only insofar as they have a significant impact at a more global level. These forecasts are underpinned by traditional macroeconomic analysis, especially as it relates to cyclical fluctuations and long-run growth theory (Section 1.1).
- Second, why forecast these variables? Forecasting as a specific professional activity has emerged for both intellectual and practical reasons. The latter have become increasingly important with the growing sophistication of modern economies. Indeed, forecasts constitute a convenient framework to bring together assessments of the future and to evaluate the consequences of possible decisions (Section 1.2).
- Third, how are forecasts produced? As a rule, a forecast combines informed judgement and model-based predictions. Well-digested information is key: the best forecaster is often the one with the most documented and sharpest reading of the facts. But the role of the model(s) is also essential: models impart a healthy dose of discipline and help draw lessons for the future from observations of the past. Finally, it is important to note that forecasting involves much more than merely coming up with a set of numbers. The forecaster must be able to explain how the numbers hang together, to weave a compelling story around them, to identify the risks surrounding the central scenario and to map out alternative courses of action (Section 1.3).

## 1.1   What to forecast?

The main variables forecasters try to pin down include output growth, inflation, unemployment, interest rates, exchange rates, international trade flows, fiscal balances and public debt. This section defines the scope of economic forecasting, starting with a few basic facts.

1

### 1.1.1   Rehearsing some basic facts: growth trends and business cycles

When looking at growth in advanced economies, two features stand out. First, over a period of several decades, economic activity as measured by real gross domestic product (GDP) expands steadily (Figure 1.1). On this measure, the US economy was over four times as large in 2003 as it was in the early 1960s, the euro area economy almost four times as large and the Japanese economy over seven times as large. In general, economic expansion has far exceeded demographic growth, implying a substantial improvement in GDP per capita and thus in individual living standards.[1] Second, over shorter periods, growth rates fluctuate, as economies are hit by shocks (Figure 1.2). At times, growth can even turn negative and countries experience recessions. Growth in the advanced economies was generally rapid from the late 1940s to the mid-1970s, when the first oil shock occurred and many

*Figure 1.1*   **Real GDP levels since the 1960s**

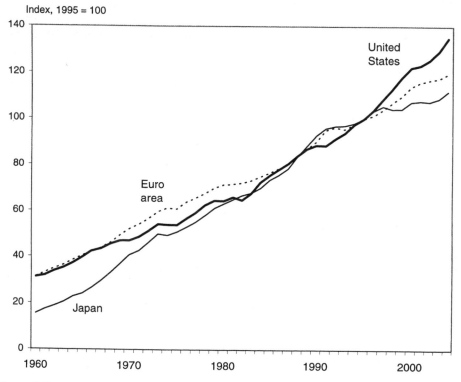

*Source*: OECD.

---

[1] Over the very long run, the increase in output has been even more enormous. Estimates suggest that real GDP per capita has been multiplied by 15 or so since 1820 in Western countries (Maddison, 2001). Some regions tend to grow faster than others, however, even over long periods (with Africa for instance standing out as a low-growth area).

*Figure 1.2*　Real GDP growth rates since the 1960s

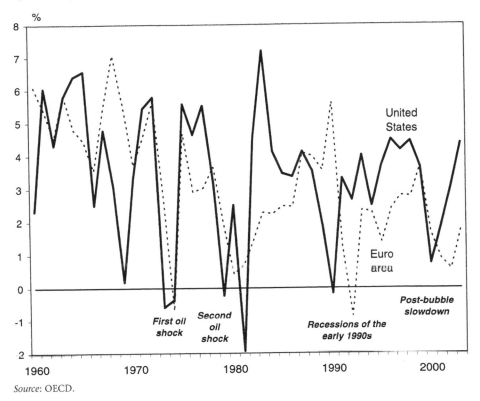

*Source*: OECD.

countries entered a recession. A few years later, the second oil shock heralded another sharp slowdown. For a variety of reasons, including a brief geopolitically induced spike in oil prices as well as idiosyncratic shocks in some major countries, the early 1990s saw a number of economies slowing down again, although this time the recessions were far from synchronised. More recently, and following a spell of rapid growth in the latter part of the 1990s, the bursting of the 'new economy' bubble translated into a shallow but nonetheless significant slowdown. These phases of acceleration and deceleration in activity point to the existence of economic cycles. Four different types of cycles are usually distinguished, depending on the horizon under consideration:

- Kondratieff cycles (or waves), which last about half a century, correspond to the transition from one set of dominant technologies to the next (steam power and railways, electricity, information technology);
- Kuznets cycles, spanning about two decades, were mainly associated with the US construction industry before the First World War; they are derived looking at population changes, capital formation and incomes;

- Kitchin cycles, which are much shorter (two to four years), are primarily related to fluctuations in inventories and wholesale prices;
- Juglar cycles, lasting five to ten years, are what is usually understood under the generic term 'cycle', when it is not further specified. This is also referred to as the 'business cycle' or the 'conjunctural cycle'.

### 1.1.2 Horizons

The concepts of trend growth and cycles play a key role in macroeconomic analysis as well as in forecasting. Trend growth refers to long-run tendencies. Cyclical fluctuations are temporary departures from the longer-run trend. Against this backdrop, four different forecasting horizons are traditionally distinguished:

- The very short run, from the latest observations to two quarters ahead;
- The short run, from six months to two years down the road;
- The medium run, generally understood as two to five years ahead (sometimes ten);
- The long run, beyond the five- or ten-year horizon.

As regards the very short run, the objective of what is widely called 'business cycle analysis' is first to pin down recent developments. Indeed, since indicators of economic activity are published with a lag, there is a need to 'forecast', or estimate, the recent past (unlike in weather forecasting). On the basis of this tentative assessment, a forecast is built for the next few months, which itself then serves as the starting point for longer-run forecasts. Routine forecasting exercises usually look at the short run, which implicitly encompasses the very short run. Typically, published forecasts cover the current year and the following one.

Medium and long-run projections are produced less frequently, albeit still quite regularly, in particular by government bodies. Occasionally, large firms also prepare such projections, for example when they need to evaluate a big investment project.

### 1.1.3 Basic mechanisms

Forecasting relies on the analysis of economic facts in the light of economic theory, with the exact combination depending on the time horizon.

Over the short run, stock variables, such as the productive capital that is in place, are more or less fixed. Therefore, the analysis focuses on flow variables, with most forecasters sharing relatively similar assumptions. Specifically:

- The conventional wisdom is that the business cycle is shaped first and foremost by changes in aggregate demand. Of particular importance in this respect are changes in fixed investment and inventories, as well as changes in foreign demand. Some components of household consumption, particularly purchases of durables, are also rather volatile.
- But aggregate demand may meet a supply constraint, notably when factors of production are already fully used or when enterprise profitability is deemed too

weak to warrant new investment. Then, prices increase and/or domestic buyers turn to foreign suppliers.

- Macroeconomic policies act on aggregate demand. Fiscal policy operates directly via public spending and indirectly via taxation. Monetary policy influences financial variables, including interest rates, exchange rates, credit and stock prices (see Chapter 8).
- Employment usually follows the ups and downs in output with a bit of a lag and in a more subdued fashion. As a result, labour productivity is normally pro-cyclical. The same holds for the productivity of capital and for the usual indicators of economic slack (capacity utilisation rate, duration of the equipment's use, overtime).
- In the short run, prices and wages do not react directly to real disequilibria. But over time, and with a lag, they do. In contrast, exchange rate shifts and changes in the price of imported goods (in particular oil) affect domestic inflation fairly rapidly. Changes in domestic prices in turn affect the real side, via competitiveness, which influences foreign trade flows; via real balances, which influence household consumption (the so-called 'Pigou effect'); and via the impact of changes in costs on factor demand. Overall, however, these various feedback effects play a minor role in explaining cyclical turnarounds.
- Lastly, the shares of wages and profits in total income fluctuate over the business cycle. The profit share tends to increase when exiting recession and in the early stages of an expansion, and vice versa for the wage share. This affects investment and consumption patterns.

These stylised features of the business cycle are not always observed in practice, and forecasters differ on the relative importance of the various mechanisms (see Chapter 5). Moreover, each cycle has its idiosyncrasies, and may come with its own set of effects.

Looking several years ahead, the degree of uncertainty is such that the term 'projections' is generally preferred to that of 'forecast'. Strictly speaking, a projection is an extrapolation of past trends, while a forecast can include *ad hoc* modifications which are thought to improve accuracy. In practice, this distinction is less clear-cut. Instead, the horizon typically determines the choice of the term.

Over the medium run, economic structures are not deemed to change much. Therefore, a natural approach to medium-run projections is to examine what happens when the trends that are forecasted at an 18-month or two-year horizon are prolonged. If the economy is seen to be close to its steady-state path at the end of the short-run projection period, then the usual approach is to forecast a continuation of its trend. But if this is not the case, it suggests that some of the short-run trends are unlikely to be sustained because they translate into ever-larger disequilibria, for example an inflationary spiral or a protracted recession. Such disequilibria may be related to unsustainable macroeconomic policies (say, excessive fiscal deficits) or to exuberant private-agent behaviour (say, in the case of a stock or housing market bubble). The projections would then suggest that a correction has to take place. But it is difficult to predict when. There are then two ways to proceed:

- One is to present a projection that simply extrapolates current trends. This may not be realistic, but it can serve to raise awareness of their unsustainability and thereby prompt some reactions, especially on the part of policymakers.
- The other is to introduce an assumption as to when and how adjustment will come about which will steer the economy back to equilibrium by the end of the projection period. This is what is often done, implicitly, when the projection is constructed around a gradual closing of the output gap and the unwinding of other imbalances (see Chapter 7).

In this context, however, there is no point in fine-tuning by trying to foresee cyclical fluctuations three or four years in advance, as they are inherently unpredictable.

Over the long run, that is beyond the five- to ten-year horizon, economies can undergo substantial structural transformations. These are difficult to forecast. But one way to look at the long run is to use growth models, which focus on the supply side and disregard cyclical fluctuations. In this context, labour force resources and technical progress are the two key determinants of future trend growth. The latter can thus be estimated by combining demographic assumptions and their implications for labour force growth with assumptions on total factor productivity growth, based on what has been observed in the past.

Going into more detail is tricky. Indeed, when looking at long-run phenomena, causes and effects are difficult to disentangle. For example, progress in education unquestionably boosts growth prospects, but higher growth in turn allows more resources to be devoted to education. More generally, over the long run, each variable depends on all the others, and there are no truly 'exogenous' ones left which could anchor a forecast.[2]

In a nutshell, and whatever the time horizon, any forecast thus revolves around two questions: where is the economy in the cycle and what is the underlying growth trend? Forming a view on both is at the heart of any forecasting endeavour. It is also a prerequisite in order to proceed with more specific forecasts, such as forecasts of tax revenues (see Chapter 9) or of a particular sector (see Chapter 10).

## 1.2  Why forecast?

Forecasting began around the time of the Second World War, as a way to test economic theories, but it also has very concrete uses and has played an increasing role as an input in decision-making.

### 1.2.1  Intellectual and practical reasons

Economic forecasting emerged in the late 1930s and 1940s, when researchers built the first forecasting models (Tinbergen, 1939; Klein, 1950), for intellectual as well

---

[2] There is also a literature that goes beyond economics *stricto sensu* and tries to foresee changes in technology, social structures or the environment. This type of so-called 'prospective' analysis goes well beyond the aim of this book.

as practical reasons. The scientific objective was to test the empirical relevance of economic theories, in particular the Keynesian synthesis which was taking off at the time, using statistical data generated by the fledgling national accounts systems. The forecasts were intended to play the role experiments play in the hard sciences: invalidate the underlying model if unreliable or corroborate it when on the mark. The practical objective was to provide new economic tools to policymakers, in the form of instruments to assess the cyclical situation and to gauge the impact on aggregate activity of their potential decisions. This concern was obviously sharpened by the painful experience of the Great Depression of the 1930s.

Subsequently, it appeared that economic forecasts could also fulfil other needs than macroeconomic stabilisation and help agents in the private sector as well – for instance, a firm deciding to invest or a household wishing to anticipate its future earnings. As a result, forecasts started to be used more widely and in a growing number of specialised areas. Another related consequence is that practical objectives have gained in importance, with a rising recognition that forecasts have to be useful and to address well-defined issues. As a result, forecasting is nowadays more a practitioner's than a researcher's activity, even if the intellectual impetus has not disappeared.[3]

### 1.2.2   The need for forecasts

The demand for forecasts stems from a need to form an educated view of the future before taking decisions. More precisely, in the economic sphere, it arises from two basic constraints (see Chapter 12):

- Lags: economic relationships are complex and the impact of actions initiated today may not materialise for some time. It is therefore necessary to anticipate these effects somehow.
- Uncertainty: the future is inherently uncertain. Forecasts cannot eliminate the uncertainty but they can help assess risks, thereby enabling agents to deal with them better.

Prior to making choices for the future, agents simply need a better understanding of the environment in which their actions will unfold. That said, the required degree of sophistication and detail of the forecast depends on the circumstances. In some cases, informal or even implicit assessments may suffice. In others, specific and well-reasoned assumptions are called for, and quantitative methods must be brought to bear. The forecasts then constitute a useful framework drawing together all the relevant information and spelling out the costs, benefits and risks associated with economic agents' behaviour.

---

[3] Academics are generally not inclined to engage in forecasting, and only a few large-scale research efforts are under way that are specifically aimed at improving forecasts.

### 1.2.3   Impact of the forecasts

Forecasts affect agents' behaviour in two, non-mutually-exclusive, ways:

- Adaptation: agents will seize an opportunity, or try to protect themselves against the consequences of an adverse event. For example, faced with a forecasted decline in demand for its products, a firm will adjust its production schedule and its budget accordingly, not unlike an individual who is informed that rain is on the way and then chooses to take along an umbrella or to stay at home.
- Retroaction: when agents can influence what is forecasted, they might act on it. For example, governments and central banks can take initiatives to alter the course of macroeconomic events. Of course, some adaptation remains in order even then, since the authorities' powers are limited.

This leads to the distinction between 'conditional' and 'unconditional' forecasts. Conditional forecasts are based on specific and possibly somewhat unrealistic assumptions regarding economic agents' behaviour. The idea is to explore their implications for the shape of the forecast, often by trying out an alternative set of hypotheses. The results can help agents decide which course of action is preferable. Unconditional forecasts are closer to what is commonly understood by 'forecasts': they attempt to describe the most likely scenario. Implicitly, they rest on assumptions concerning the most plausible behaviour of all agents, including policymakers. Unconditional forecasts are typically destined to agents who adapt rather than retroact.

### 1.2.4   Forecasting and decision-making

While forecasting plays an important and sometimes decisive role in decision-making,[4] decisions may depart from what the forecast would suggest. For one thing, individuals' objectives go far beyond the variables usually included in the forecast. For example, a government may care at least as much about its own popularity as about the country's economic performance, and may therefore prefer not to take the painful measures that a forecast might call for. Moreover, even if decision-makers acted only on strictly 'economic' grounds, disagreements could arise on the forecast itself. And agents may weigh policy objectives differently, for example when considering the trade-off between more inflation and more growth or their degree of risk aversion. Hence, it is best for forecasters to stick to a clear division of labour. They should lay out the various plausible scenarios and quantify the associated costs and benefits. Decision-makers then have to take responsibility for their actions, based on this information and on their objectives (see Chapter 13).

### 1.2.5   Why is the short run important?

In practice, institutions producing forecasts devote much more resources to short-run and very short-run forecasts than to medium- and long-run projections, which are

---

[4] Elections have been triggered or lost on the basis of erroneous forecasts.

done less frequently and receive less publicity (see Chapter 14).[5] This is a paradox, given that growth is somewhat erratic in the short run, and given that in the end structural trends are what matters most. Indeed, classical economists cared mainly about the expansion of the supply side, viewing cycles as no more than temporary disturbances. Until the 1930s and the advent of Keynes' ideas, this meant that cyclical analysis was confined to some very specific phenomena, such as the hog cycle in agriculture for instance, or to a narrowly descriptive approach, limited to recording the ups and downs of the stock market and of inflation to characterise the cycle.

In fact, there are three sets of reasons why short-run prospects matter. First, business cycle fluctuations are important in and of themselves, and may have consequences going beyond mere disturbances. Slowdowns and recessions aggravate social problems, not least through the rise in unemployment. And macroeconomic statistics may understate the pain because they mask disparities between sectors or groups of individuals. Moreover, some slowdowns are far worse than average, notably the Great Depression in the 1930s, but also – albeit to a lesser extent – the sluggish growth rate in Germany and Italy since the 1990s, as well as the recent period of deflation in Japan. The fact that eventually economies recover is cold comfort: 'in the long run, we are all dead', as Keynes famously put it.

Second, the ground lost during downturns may not be offset by higher growth later on. On the contrary, short-run macroeconomic instability may undermine investment, and thereby lead to lower growth over the long run. Therefore, improving short-run stability is important from a long-run perspective.

Lastly, assessing short-run prospects is crucial for economic policy purposes, especially as regards fiscal and monetary policy. The forecasts provide an indispensable framework for the preparation of budgets and their quality affects that of macroeconomic stabilisation policy (see Chapters 9 and 12).

## 1.3   How to forecast

Economic forecasting draws on a variety of methods. Each of them hinges on some specific theoretical or statistical assumptions, with their pros and cons. There is no single optimal way to proceed, if only because reality is so complex and ever in flux. In practice, a variety of methods are therefore brought to bear. To the extent that they can be combined, they provide for a more robust forecast.

The preparation of a forecast involves three steps: observing the facts, selecting a model (or models) to interpret them, and using this model (or these models) to forecast the future. In practice, these steps tend to overlap somewhat.

### 1.3.1   Deciphering the facts

Any forecast rests on an understanding of past developments. Hence, it is conditioned by a phase of active observation, devoted to measuring and interpreting the facts.

---

[5] In recent years, longer-run projections have gained in prominence, however, as public finance sustainability issues have come to the fore, notably the future of pension and health-care systems.

The usefulness of proper measurement has become obvious. Economic indicators nowadays receive intense media coverage, but this was not always so. For example, the economic information and understanding of European citizens in the 1930s was extremely poor, and this led to serious policy mistakes (Sauvy, 1984). The production and dissemination of economic data has made considerable progress since, and national statistical systems now offer a wealth of information. At their core lie the national accounts, which offer a rich and coherent summary picture (see Chapter 2). In addition, there are numerous administrative and survey data, some of which are published well ahead of the national accounts.

While the profusion of measures allows for more rigorous and sophisticated interpretations, far greater efforts than in the past are needed to sift through the maze of indicators and make sense of the data (see Chapter 3). A good understanding of economic history is also necessary to read the facts properly. Quantitative tools, such as the macroeconomic models discussed below, can help store this knowledge and facilitate the interpretation of new observations by offering benchmarks. For example, when abnormal fluctuations seem to occur (such as surges in investment or sharp drops in consumption), it is useful to compare them to average past movements. This then helps characterise and explain these fluctuations, and says something about their likely future developments.

This task of interpreting the incoming information is the challenge faced daily by business cycle analysts. A certain degree of urgency as well as the volatility of short-term indicators, coupled with sometimes considerable publication lags, tend to obscure underlying trends. Getting the recent past right is thus in itself quite difficult.

### 1.3.2   The various approaches

Broadly speaking, four types of quantitative approaches are used in economic forecasting: subjective methods, indicator-based methods, time series models and structural models.

Subjective methods call exclusively upon the forecasters' common sense, intuition or experience, without bringing in any explicit model. Such forecasts are not necessarily inaccurate, but they can only take into account a limited information set while resting on implicit assumptions. Hence, they are difficult to interpret and discuss.

Indicator-based methods exploit the information provided by 'advance' indicators that are published before the forecasted variables, so as to anticipate the latter. Such methods are mainly used in business cycle analysis, in particular for the early detection of turning points. One example of such advance indicators is export orders in small open economies, which often foreshadow activity trends.

Most indicators used in this context come from business cycle surveys, such as surveys of investment plans, or from administrative records, for example customs data on foreign trade flows. Composite indicators can also be constructed, combining several indicators so as to gauge trends better. A well-known case in point is the IFO indicator in Germany.[6]

---

[6] See www.ifo-business-climate-index.info/.

The predictive power of any single indicator is limited, and in practice business cycle analysts tend to look at a whole range of indicators. However, these often diverge: what if, say, business sentiment and household confidence move in opposite directions? Both intuition and past experience may be of help when gauging the respective merits of each indicator, but it is sometimes hard to reconcile such divergences.

Time series models are solely based on the statistical properties of the series under consideration, irrespective of any interpretation or causal relationships informed by economic theory (see Chapter 4). Generally, the only assumption needed in this approach is that the probabilistic model describing the past behaviour of the series remains valid going forward. There are two types of time series methods:

- Univariate methods: in this case, the forecast of a variable only depends on its past realisations. These methods encompass so-called 'naïve' forecasts (say, forecasted growth equals average past growth), simple techniques such as moving averages or smoothing algorithms, but also more general approaches such as ARIMA models, which combine auto-regressive and moving average models. These methods are well suited for dealing with variables subject to random disturbances.
- Multivariate methods: these jointly forecast several variables based on their past behaviour. This makes it possible to take into account the correlations between series. Vector auto-regressive (VAR) models are the most popular among such methods, being very simple to use.

Time series methods offer clear advantages: they are simple, require few data, and can be relatively successful even if the analyst knows little about the phenomenon under consideration. Therefore, they can be used to obtain quickly a quantitative forecast for a small number of variables.

A drawback, however, is that these methods fail to explain how they reach their conclusions: the forecast is generated by simply prolonging past correlations. The results cannot be interpreted in the sense that the forecast cannot be decomposed to show the contributions of various explanatory factors. Hence, these methods are ill suited for the construction of scenarios based on alternative assumptions or for the analysis of the sensitivity of the forecast to changes in structural parameters.

Structural models try to explain as much as to forecast.[7] They feature causal relationships among variables and distinguish between 'endogenous' ones, which are determined by the model, and 'exogenous' ones, which are treated as given (see Chapter 6). The model delivers a forecast of the endogenous variables based on assumptions made, outside the model, on the evolution of the exogenous variables.[8]

---

[7] These methods are sometimes referred to as 'econometric'. This is confusing, however, insofar as econometric techniques are also used for time series analysis and in indicator-based approaches.

[8] These assumptions can themselves be established using one of the forecast approaches described here, or they may be set more judgementally.

Building a structural model involves three stages: design, estimation and testing. First, the model is written up in the form of a set of equations spelling out the relationships between variables, based on some theoretical priors and a clear distinction between endogenous and exogenous variables. Second, values of the parameters appearing in these equations are estimated using econometric regressions, calibration techniques and the like. Then, the validity of the model is tested to see whether it accurately describes observed past behaviour, whether the simulations it generates are plausible, and so forth. In practice, these three stages are interdependent and require going back and forth.

The size of structural models ranges from the very small to the enormous. At one extreme, single-equation models are often estimated to assess a particular behavioural pattern. At the other extreme, so-called macroeconomic (or 'macroeconometric') models contain up to hundreds of equations. Their purpose is to provide an overall picture of the economy, showing its main interdependencies. The endogenous variables typically include such key economic indicators as GDP, inflation, employment, the fiscal deficit, exports and imports, and so on. The exogenous variables tend to relate to demography, technical progress, the international environment (including the price of raw materials) and economic policy decisions.

A main advantage of macroeconomic models is that they bring together in a common framework a vast quantity of information. They allow for a coherent forecast of all the variables that are traditionally taken into account to appraise economic developments, including growth and its main components, prices, jobs and incomes, public finance aggregates and flows of funds among economic agents. They are useful to compare alternative scenarios and to evaluate the impact of policy measures. But such models do require a high degree of expertise, are costly to set up and to maintain, and sometimes produce relatively poor value for money in terms of forecast accuracy (on the latter, see Chapter 11).

### 1.3.3   Building a forecast

In practice, forecasts are rarely based on the mechanical implementation of any single one of the above methods. Rather, different approaches are usually combined and raw model outputs are adjusted in order to take outside judgements into consideration. Moreover, the numbers normally have to come with a story spelling out the underlying assumptions, the main driving forces of the forecast, the risks surrounding the central scenario and the room for manoeuvre.

Fundamentally, economic forecasting is an attempt to anticipate the future using a large variety of information sources. In so doing, it would not be sensible to rely on only one model, whatever its merits. As far as possible, it is advisable to test different methods so as to obtain a more robust forecast.

One way to proceed is to carry out separate experimental forecasts using various tools, such as advance indicators, simple or more sophisticated extrapolations and structural models. Divergences typically surface when the results are laid side by side, highlighting the problems associated with this or that forecasting approach. Such problems do not necessarily disqualify the tool used, since it is often possible to adjust the results: for instance, methodological shortcomings associated with a given approach may be spotted at this stage, leading to technical refinements and more robust evaluations.

In the end, one central method has undoubtedly to be selected for the practical purpose of structuring the forecast. But it is of great importance that the forecast take into account the weaknesses of the chosen method that have been brought to light by other approaches. At the same time, judgement will typically have to be incorporated, to reflect information or knowledge that is not precisely embodied in the model. In that sense, the science of forecasting may require some degree of craftsmanship.

Exercising judgement is done using an array of techniques designed to amend 'spontaneous' model results that are only partly satisfactory. For example, one technique is the use, at the margin, of add-on factors or of multiplicative corrections (see Chapter 6). It may be surmised that such judgemental adjustments denote a lack of rigour. In fact, they are a rational response to the known limitations of models. The latter can only be simplified representations of reality. Corrections may thus be appropriate and legitimate when there are compelling reasons to believe that in some ways the model lacks realism. However, these corrections are best done transparently, if possible on the basis of quantifications undertaken outside the model.

As judgement often has the last word, the forecast should be viewed as the economist's more than the model's. What then is the role of the model? The following chapters will shed light on this but three aspects can be underlined here:

- The model imposes discipline. It obliges the forecaster to think about the underlying assumptions and greatly facilitates the discussion on the forecast with other economists and with users.
- The model memorises the past. Its structure and parameters reflect the behavioural patterns that have been observed so far. Thus, the forecast has a historical anchor. The model also allows keeping a track-record of past forecasting errors and the associated lessons.
- As noted earlier, the model, especially if it is a macroeconomic one, constitutes a tool to assemble lots of information into a coherent and common framework.

In sum, the model needs to be complemented by the economist's judgement, but conversely, judgement is better exercised when underpinned by a model. The model instils discipline and transparency into the forecasting process even if, in the end, the forecast is served by the model rather than the other way round.

When a forecast is presented, it is usually described in terms of raw economic figures. However, users also need an explanation of the economic mechanisms at work, a review of the underlying assumptions, and a description of the associated risks. For this purpose, the traditional macrodynamic interactions listed above (in Section 1.1) have to be presented, showing in particular how they unfold in the specific context of the period under consideration. The forecast thus comes across as a story articulated around some key behavioural relationships (investment accelerator, consumption and saving, impact of the international environment and of economic policies, wage–price setting, and so on). The coherence and plausibility of that story contribute to the credibility of the forecast.

The story has to start somehow with a rationale for the assumptions that have been chosen. Their nature differs according to the type of model used. Indicator-based and time series approaches rest on the premise that historical statistical regularities will endure. Structural methods rely on a greater variety of hypotheses, both related to exogenous variables and to the validity of the model used, so that it can be difficult to define them concisely. A good forecaster understands his/her own assumptions well.

In practice, experts are often asked about the main risks associated with their forecast. This is closely linked to the identification of the assumptions. One answer is to elaborate model-based 'variants' around the central scenario, using a different set of assumptions and quantifying the resulting impact on the forecast. Another way to characterise the risks is to provide confidence intervals for the key variables, which can convey a sense of the overall uncertainty surrounding the forecast.

# 2
# The Data

Measuring and interpreting economic developments requires a set of statistical standards as well as a coherent overall framework. By and large, forecasters around the world use a common language and refer to the same key macroeconomic variables. However, there are differences across time and space regarding the specific empirical content of some of the concepts used. For most practical purposes, at least in forecasting, these differences are relatively minor, but they ought to be borne in mind when laying side by side national forecasts or comparing performance across countries.

The framework underpinning forecasting is that of the national accounts, which describe the economy at an aggregate level (Section 2.1). Economic activity as captured in the national accounts can be seen from three different angles: supply, demand and income. Economic agents are grouped into so-called institutional sectors, whose operations are quantified in a standard set of tables. A key and tricky issue is the split of nominal magnitudes between volumes and prices.

The most comprehensive national accounts are constructed at an annual frequency. But forecasters typically reason at higher frequencies, and therefore rely heavily on quarterly national accounts, especially for short-term forecasts (Section 2.2). Quarterly accounts are now routinely produced in most countries, albeit with varying degrees of detail and rigour. They are not just a simplified replica of the annual ones and raise specific technical issues.

While the national accounts provide a coherent analytical ensemble, the quality of the data feeding into this framework is uneven, and methodological problems abound (Section 2.3). Statistical observation is art as much as science and some headline variables – say, employment, unemployment or inflation – can be and are measured in a variety of ways, with sometimes very different results. Even when one and the same approach is used, there are problems of data heterogeneity. The split between prices and volumes, which is so central, is not devoid of complications. Last but not least, as better information trickles in and as methods improve, the national accounts data are subject to substantial revisions, which need to be properly factored in.

Stepping back somewhat from run-of-the-mill forecasting, the depiction of economies raises conceptual challenges, some of which are being addressed in the course of ongoing revisions to the internationally agreed national accounts frame-work (Section 2.4). Others are more fundamental and are difficult to deal with through mere amendments to the framework, in particular those concerning the definition and measurement of welfare.

## 2.1   The national accounts framework

### 2.1.1   Historical background

The roots of today's national accounts frameworks go back a very long way. For centuries, political authorities have tried to measure the creation of wealth in the territories they controlled. Over 4000 years ago, in Ancient Egypt, people and property were registered for tax purposes and a census of raw materials, cattle, and produce took place regularly. In the seventeenth century, interest in raising revenue and in assessing England's war potential as against that of France and Holland led William Petty and later Gregory King to try and estimate national income as the sum of factor incomes or of expenditures (Stone, 1986). They were soon followed by Pierre de Boisguillebert and Marshal Vauban, who used similar approaches to estimate France's national income (but Louis XIV disapproved, and their books were suppressed). The eighteenth-century French Physiocrats took a step backwards by restricting the concept of national income to agriculture and the extractive industries, on the grounds that other activities were not productive. But in his *Tableau économique*, Quesnay, one of the Physiocrats, inaugurated the analysis of intersectoral flows.

It is only with the coming of age of classical economic theory, however, that two key insights came to the fore. First, production became a central concept, under-stood as a flow of newly created value, as opposed to stocks of wealth; however, the notion that services, and not just goods, were also part of value added only emerged in the late nineteenth century. Second, the idea that overall income stem-ming from production is distributed amongst the parties involved and then on to other agents gained prominence, and subsequently gave rise to the concept of integrated economic accounts and to synoptic representations of the economic dealings between agents.

A number of obstacles stood in the way of the development of national accounts frameworks. Governments and private agents proved reluctant to reveal informa-tion about their activities, and there were doubts about the merits of state inter-ventionism, even when the latter only had to do with statistical observation. Cyclical crises in the late nineteenth and early twentieth century were the focus of much attention, and indicators were designed to assess economies' position in the cycle and to try and anticipate cyclical swings. But the need for an overall frame-work had not yet become obvious at the time. Budgets were prepared on a purely financial basis, with little if any regard for the cycle: outlays and receipts were programmed on the basis of the outcomes of the past year and of any discretionary changes to spending or taxes, ignoring the impact of the cycle.

The experience of the 1930s, when policies to combat the Great Depression were based on such data as stock price indices, freight car loadings, and sketchy indices of industrial production, cruelly underlined the problems of incomplete information and spurred the development both of national accounts and of a greater economic role for government.

In the United States, the Department of Commerce commissioned Kuznets of the National Bureau of Economic Research to develop a set of national economic accounts, the first version of which was presented in 1937 in a report to Congress. In 1942, annual estimates of gross national product were introduced to complement the national income estimates and to facilitate war-time planning. The war also helped stimulate the development of input–output tables, which following Leontief's work became an integral part of the national accounts.

Meanwhile, in the United Kingdom Meade and Stone put together a new survey of the country's economic and financial situation, consisting of three tables relating to national income and expenditure, personal income, spending and saving, and the net amount of funds required by, and available from, private sources for government purposes. Thanks to Keynes, who was then a member of the Chancellor's Consultative Council at the Treasury, they were published as part of a White Paper which accompanied the 1941 Budget.

This early work led to the development of systems of national accounts (SNAs) in a number of countries after the Second World War. Over time, these SNAs have been improved and harmonised, under the aegis of what is now the Inter-secretariat Working Group on National Accounts, which brings together experts from the United Nations, the Organisation for Economic Co-operation and Development (OECD), Eurostat, the International Monetary Fund (IMF) and the World Bank. The first international standard saw the light of day in 1953. It has gone through two revisions since, with a second vintage in 1968 and a third one in 1993. A number of changes to the 1993 SNA are currently under discussion. A European Union version of the SNA was derived under the label of European System of Accounts (ESA), with a first vintage in 1970 and a second one in 1995. It imposes stricter harmonisation, which is required for policy purposes, for instance for the calculation of budgetary transfers within the European Union or for the assessment of macroeconomic convergence in the context of monetary union. The US system, called the National Income and Product Accounts (NIPA), differs somewhat from the international SNA, for example in the way household disposable income is defined or in the way some types of spending are classified as consumption or investment.

### 2.1.2 Three ways to slice up GDP

National accounting focuses first and foremost on measuring the production of goods and services, which is generally referred to as gross domestic product (GDP). To start with, this requires to delineate the boundaries of GDP and to define which activities fall within its scope and which are excluded. GDP encompasses the production of goods and services that are sold at an 'economically significant' price, but also some other activities which do not lead to a sale on a market at commercial terms, plus an estimate of 'black market' activity (see Box 2.1). GDP excludes some activities, such as domestic services produced and consumed within households (cleaning, preparing meals, and child care).

---

*Box 2.1*  **GDP: a mixed bag**

Viewed from the production side, GDP encompasses three types of activity:

- Market output: this is the value added by private entities but also the services provided by the public sector when their price is 'economically significant', a term many national accountants define as a price sufficiently high to cover more than half of their costs. In addition to goods and services, including those rendered by the distribution and transport sectors, market output encompasses the services provided by banks and other financial institutions, measured indirectly by subtracting interest paid to depositors from interest earned on loans and other revenue.
- Non-market output: this includes most of the services (and less importantly goods) provided by the public sector or non-profit institutions (NPIs) free of charge or at an economically non-significant price. They are valued at their cost of production. Non-market output also includes imputed values for the production of some other goods and services by economic agents for their own usage, which are not sold in the marketplace but for which the implied national transaction can be valued, notably: the services provided by owner-occupied dwellings (home-owners are assumed to rent their homes, as owners, to themselves, as occupants); the food and other goods produced by households for their own final consumption (farmers who eat some of the food they have grown are assumed to sell it, as producers, to themselves, as consumers); and the services provided by owner-builders in the construction or alteration of dwellings (same type of assumption). The latter two categories are especially significant in developing countries.
- Output produced in the informal, 'shadow', 'hidden', 'underground' or 'non-observed' sector: this relates to economic activities that are not reported to the tax authorities and government statisticians either through ignorance or deliberate intent on the part of producers or through incompetence or deliberate choice on the part of the authorities. This sector is estimated to represent around 4 per cent of GDP in Belgium, 15 per cent in Italy and well over 20 per cent in many emerging market or developing economies (Blades and Roberts, 2002). A variety of methods are used to guesstimate the size of this sector (OECD, 2002), including the comparison of tax control files with statistical sources to derive an average rate of fraud (in France for example) or detailed studies of the labour market (in Italy for instance). Careful estimation is time-consuming and is usually carried out for some base year, with the results being extrapolated for subsequent years.

A separate category of activities are the outright illegal ones. The 1993 SNA recommends including productive illegal activities in GDP for two main reasons. First, the associated incomes tend to be spent mostly on legal goods and services, implying that ignoring illegal activity would entail a mismatch between output and expenditure-based GDP. Second, legislation differs across countries and the borderlines between legal and illegal activities shift over time, so that abstracting from the latter would be detrimental to the comparability between countries and over time. Not all illegal activities are deemed productive, however, only those which involve an exchange of goods and services between willing buyers and sellers. Protection rackets and most kinds of theft or fraud involve forcible transfers but do not add to GDP, hence they are not productive in this sense. Currently, very few countries incorporate explicit estimates of illegal activities in GDP although most of them have made experimental estimates.

GDP can be compiled from three sides:

- On the production side (resources):
  *GDP = gross value added generated in the economy + taxes net of subsidies on products*
- On the expenditure side (uses):
  *GDP = final consumption + gross capital formation + exports − imports*
- On the income side:
  *GDP = compensation of employees + gross operating surplus (including mixed income received by the self-employed) + taxes net of subsidies on production and imports*

In practice, summing up the components from each side, which use different sources of information, does not lead to exactly the same total. Some countries hide the discrepancy by adjusting one or several components. Others prefer not to (Wilson, 2005). Thus, in the United States, a discrepancy between income and expenditure-side GDP is explicitly shown (Table 2.1).

*Supply side*

In the first approach, also called the supply-side approach, GDP is obtained as the sum of value added produced by all the economic agents residing in the country during a given period of time, where value added is total output minus the inputs used in production. Value added is measured at basic prices, that is the prices effectively received by producers.[1] When indirect taxes apply, such as the value-added tax (VAT), or when the product is subsidised so as to lower its price, the basic price differs from the market price, which is the one paid by the purchaser. GDP is computed at market prices, hence the adjustment for taxes and subsidies above. The difference between the basic price and the market price also includes trading margins and transport costs, which correspond to the value added by the trading and transport sectors.

The production of goods and services generally requires physical capital (buildings and equipment in particular), which gradually wears out or becomes technologically obsolescent, implying that it needs to be replaced after a number of years. This erosion of the capital stock is called consumption of fixed capital. When subtracting the latter from 'gross' value added (as calculated above), 'net' value added obtains.

Units producing similar goods or services are grouped in the same activity branch (or 'industry'), regardless of ownership. Since by definition value added excludes intermediate consumption, it can be added across units or branches. A branch's value added is the sum of the value added by each of the units in that branch, and nation-wide value added is the sum of value added across branches of activity. Each unit is classified in one and only one branch, in accordance with the International Standard Industrial Classification (ISIC), which provides for several

---

[1] This is the 1993 SNA rule. In the United States, however, value added is compiled at market prices.

*Table 2.1*   **Main national account aggregates in the United States**
(for the year 2003, NIPA presentation)

| | $ billion | % of GDP | | $ billion | % of GDP |
|---|---|---|---|---|---|
| **DOMESTIC INCOME AND PRODUCT ACCOUNT** | | | | | |
| Employee compensation | 6295 | 57.2 | Personal consumption expenditures | 7761 | 70.5 |
| Wages and salaries | 5109 | 46.4 | Durable goods | 951 | 8.6 |
| Supplements | 1186 | 10.8 | Non-durable goods | 2200 | 20.0 |
| + Taxes on production and imports | 798 | 7.3 | Services | 4610 | 41.9 |
| - Subsidies | 47 | 0.4 | + Gross private domestic investment | 1666 | 15.1 |
| + Net operating surplus of enterprises | 2579 | 23.4 | Fixed investment | 1667 | 15.1 |
| + Consumption of fixed capital | 1354 | 12.3 | Nonresidential | 1095 | 9.9 |
| **= Gross domestic income** | 10979 | 99.8 | Structures | 262 | 2.4 |
| | | | Equipment and software | 833 | 7.6 |
| + Statistical discrepancy | 26 | 0.2 | Residential | 572 | 5.2 |
| | | | Change in private inventories | -1 | 0.0 |
| | | | + Net exports of goods and services | -498 | -4.5 |
| | | | Exports | 1046 | 9.5 |
| | | | Imports | 1544 | 14.0 |
| | | | + Government consumption and investment | 2075 | 18.9 |
| | | | Federal | 752 | 6.8 |
| | | | National defence | 496 | 4.5 |
| | | | Non-defence | 256 | 2.3 |
| | | | State and local | 1323 | 12.0 |
| **= GDP** | 11004 | 100.0 | **= GDP** | 11004 | 100.0 |
| | | | | | |
| **FOREIGN TRANSACTIONS CURRENT ACCOUNT** | | | | | |
| Exports of goods and services | 1046 | 9.5 | Imports of goods and services | 1544 | 14.0 |
| + Income receipts from the rest of the world | 329 | 3.0 | Income payments to the rest of the world | 274 | 2.5 |
| Wages and salary receipts | 3 | 0.0 | Wages and salaries | 9 | 0.1 |
| Income receipts on assets | 326 | 3.0 | Income payments on assets | 265 | 2.4 |
| Interest | 75 | 0.7 | Net current taxes and transfers to the rest of the world | 68 | 0.6 |
| Dividend | 82 | 0.7 | | | |
| Reinvested earnings on US direct investment abroad | 169 | 1.5 | **Balance on current account** | -511 | -4.6 |
| = Current receipts from abroad | 1375 | 12.5 | Current payments to the rest of the world plus balance | 1375 | 12.5 |
| | | | | | |
| **DOMESTIC CAPITAL ACCOUNT** | | | | | |
| Gross domestic investment | 2024 | 18.4 | **Net saving** | 134 | 1.2 |
| Private fixed investment | 1667 | 15.1 | Personal saving | 111 | 1.0 |
| Government fixed investment | 359 | 3.3 | Undistributed corporate profits with IVCCA | 391 | 3.6 |
| Change in private inventories | -1 | 0.0 | Nondisbursed accrued wages | 0 | 0.0 |
| Net capital account transactions | 3 | 0.0 | Net government saving | -368 | -3.3 |
| **Net lending (+) or net borrowing (-)** | -514 | -4.7 | + Consumption of fixed capital | 1354 | 12.3 |
| | | | **= Gross saving** | 1488 | 13.5 |
| Gross domestic investment, capital account transactions | | | Statistical discrepancy | 26 | 0.2 |
| and net lending | 1513 | 13.8 | Gross saving and statistical discrepancy | 1513 | 13.8 |
| | | | | | |
| **FOREIGN TRANSACTIONS CAPITAL ACCOUNT** | | | | | |
| Balance on current account, national income | | | Net capital account transactions | 3 | 0.0 |
| and product accounts | -511 | -4.6 | Net lending (+) or net borrowing (-) | -514 | -4.7 |

*Source*: US Bureau of Economic Analysis.

levels of disaggregation: at a broad level, the economy is divided into 17 branches (of which for instance manufacturing would be one), which are in turn subdivided (there are 23 manufacturing branches at the next level), and each of the subdivisions may be split up itself at the so-called 'four-digit' level into even more specific branches. In the United States and Canada, a slightly different classification is used, the North American Industry Classification System (NAICS). In the European Union, the statistical Classification of Economic Activities in the European Community (NACE) is used.

At any given level of disaggregation in the classification, the relationships between branches can be described in an input–output table. It is a matrix which for each pair of branches $(i,j)$ shows how much branch $j$ uses up of branch $i$'s output as intermediate consumption, which depends on technology and on prices (see Section 10.2 for further discussion).

*Demand side*

Turning to the demand side, GDP equals the sum of final uses of goods and services by residents plus exports less imports. This does not include intermediate consumption, which pertains to the goods and services used or consumed in production. It only refers to the purchases by or for the ultimate user, so as to avoid double counting. This breaks down into:

- Final consumption expenditure $C$ by households, non-profit institutions serving households (NPISH) and government;
- Gross capital formation $I$ by enterprises, households (for which investment is mainly residential) and government, which comprises:
  - Gross fixed capital formation, that is capital expenditure on tangible and intangible fixed assets. It differs from intermediate consumption in that the goods involved are not used up within the production process in an accounting period. One can also look at net investment, which corresponds to the increase in the capital stock and is obtained by subtracting the consumption of fixed capital from gross fixed capital formation.
  - Changes in inventories. Inventories are what has been produced or imported but not yet consumed, invested or exported. Changes in inventories, or stockbuilding, can be positive or negative. Hence, referring to their rate of growth is unhelpful. When decomposing GDP growth into its components on the expenditure side, it is the change in the change in inventories that comes into play, and the convention is to compute the contribution of stockbuilding to GDP growth as the change in stockbuilding in per cent of the past period's GDP.
  - Acquisitions less disposals of valuables;
- Net exports (that is, exports $X$ minus imports $M$) or 'trade balance'. For the same reason as in the case for inventories, the focus is on the contribution of net exports to GDP growth and not on their rate of growth. Exports include all sales to non-residents, and are regarded as final spending, since they are final as far as the domestic economy is concerned (although they can be used as intermediate consumption in a foreign economy). Imports are subtracted from demand to obtain GDP because while they are included directly or indirectly in final expenditure they are not part of domestic production.

Hence the demand-side approach can be summarised as:

$$GDP = C + I + X - M$$

or, equivalently, in supply-equals-demand terms:

$$GDP + M = C + I + X$$

Demand is valued at purchasers' prices, including trade and transport margins, VAT and other taxes on products. Exports are valued 'free on board' (f.o.b.), that is at the price fetched at the border of the exporting country. In the case of imports, which are part of aggregate supply, flows are also valued f.o.b. The cost of insurance and freight (c.i.f.) is therefore subtracted from the price paid for imports. Total demand excluding changes in inventories is referred to as 'final demand'.

*Income side*

Turning to the income side, GDP equals the sum of all income earned by resident individuals or corporations in the production of goods and services, plus net taxes on supply. Some types of income are not included, for example transfer payments like unemployment benefit, child benefit or state pensions, since they are a redistribution of existing income via taxes and national insurance contributions. To avoid double counting, these payments and other current transfers (for example taxes on income and wealth) are excluded. GDP on the income side thus breaks down into firms' gross operating surplus, the self-employed's gross mixed income, compensation of employees (wages plus employee as well as employer social contributions), and taxes on production and imports less subsidies on production. The operating surplus and mixed income are measures of profit excluding any holding gains. Mixed income is the operating surplus of unincorporated enterprises owned by households, which implicitly includes remuneration for work done by the owner or other members of the household. This remuneration cannot be identified separately from the return to the owner as entrepreneur.

Some income is not declared to the tax authorities, and to take this into account adjustments are typically made to the GDP income measure. For instance, in 2002 the adjustment for undeclared income in the United Kingdom amounted to a bit over 1.5 per cent of GDP.

### 2.1.3   Institutional sectors

At an elementary level, economic activity and wealth can be attributed to institutional units, which are the basic transactor units. The SNA groups economic agents with similar economic functions into institutional sectors and sub-sectors. The economy as a whole consists of the entire set of resident institutional units. The operations carried out by the various institutional sectors are described in a set of integrated economic accounts which includes production accounts, income accounts, capital accounts, financial accounts, balance sheet accounts and external accounts. The following institutional sectors are distinguished: households, non-financial corporations, financial corporations, general government, NPISH and the rest of the world.

The households sector consists of all resident households, defined as small groups of persons who share accommodation, pool some or all of their income and wealth and collectively consume goods and services, mainly housing and food. Households also engage in other forms of economic activity as producers of dwelling rental services (including as owner-occupiers) and through their operation of unincorporated enterprises. The latter are included in the households sector because the owners of ordinary partnerships and sole proprietorships will frequently combine their business and personal transactions, so that complete sets of accounts disentangling these operations will often be unavailable.

Households' gross disposable income principally includes wage earnings, remuneration in kind received from enterprises, mixed income of the self-employed (partly wages, partly profits), property income and social benefits net of taxes and social contributions paid, and other payments. Gross disposable income minus consumption equals saving. The saving rate is saving divided by gross disposable income. The financial saving rate is the ratio of households' net lending over gross disposable income, where net lending is saving minus households' investment outlays, which mainly consists of residential investment and investment by unincorporated enterprises.

Household consumption is defined in one of two ways:

- Final consumption expenditure, which encompasses all purchases of goods and services by resident households, except housing but including imputed expenditure (notably imputed rents in the case of owner-occupied housing) as well as benefits in kind received from employers.
- Actual final consumption of households, which is final consumption expenditure plus consumption by NPISH and general government that can be attributed to households individually. These transfers are non-market output, produced for instance by public authorities, as well as goods and services bought from market producers, and are delivered to households free of charge or at a subsidised price. In practice, they include such spending as health and education but not spending on collective services, such as legislation and regulation, defence, police and environmental protection.

The first of the two concepts of consumption is best suited to study the relationship between household income and consumption, and is often the one referred to in economic forecasting. The second one is useful for international comparisons, as the share of social transfers in kind in actual final consumption varies considerably across countries. For example, in 2002, this share amounted to 21 per cent in France and 19 per cent in the United Kingdom (see Table 2.2) versus 15 per cent in Japan, reflecting the greater importance of the welfare state in Europe.

The non-financial corporations sector consists of resident corporations mainly engaged in the production of market goods and non-financial services (irrespective of the residence of their shareholders). They are mostly private but can also be government-owned or controlled. Their value added can be decomposed into wages and gross operating surplus. The margin ratio, defined as gross operating surplus divided by value added, is a broad measure of profitability.[2] Gross corporate saving is defined as the profit that is left after deducting the remuneration of

---

[2] In the United States, profits (defined as the operating surplus minus interest payments and business current transfer payments) rather than the gross operating surplus are usually the focus of attention.

*Table 2.2*  **Main national account aggregates in the United Kingdom**
(for the year 2002, in accordance with the 1993 SNA)

| | £ million | % of GDP |
|---|---:|---:|
| **GOODS AND SERVICES ACCOUNT** | | |
| **GDP (production side)** | | |
| Output of goods and services | 1959103 | 187.7 |
| - Intermediate consumption | 1033519 | 99.0 |
| = Gross value added, at basic prices | 925584 | 88.7 |
| + VAT and other taxes on products | 125248 | 12.0 |
| - Subsidies on products | 6887 | 0.7 |
| = GDP at market prices | **1043945** | **100.0** |
| **GDP (expenditure side)** | | |
| Household final consumption expenditure | 666877 | 63.9 |
| + NPISH final consumption expenditure | 26009 | 2.5 |
| + Individual government final consumption expenditure | 129043 | 12.4 |
| = Total actual individual consumption | 821929 | 78.7 |
| + Collective government final consumption expenditure | 79953 | 7.7 |
| = Total final consumption expenditure (1) | 901882 | 86.4 |
| Gross fixed capital formation | 169972 | 16.3 |
| + Changes in inventories | 1584 | 0.2 |
| + Acquisition less disposals of valuables | 213 | 0.0 |
| = Total gross capital formation (2) | 171769 | 16.5 |
| Exports of goods and services | 272727 | 26.1 |
| - Imports of goods and services | 304016 | 29.1 |
| = External balance of goods and services (3) | -31289 | -3.0 |
| Statistical discrepancy (4) | 1583 | 0.2 |
| GDP: (1) + (2) + (3) + (4) | **1043945** | **100.0** |
| **GDP (income side)** | | |
| Gross operating surplus | 256247 | 24.5 |
| *of which*: Corporations | 184387 | 17.7 |
| Households and NPISH | 62558 | 6.0 |
| + Mixed income | 63957 | 6.1 |
| + Compensation of employees | 587488 | 56.3 |
| + Taxes on production and imports | 145380 | 13.9 |
| - Subsidies | 8980 | 0.9 |
| + Statistical discrepancy | -147 | 0.0 |
| = GDP at market prices | **1043945** | **100.0** |
| **CURRENT AND CAPITAL ACCOUNT** | | |
| GDP | **1043945** | **100.0** |
| + Net employee compensation from abroad (receipts minus payments) | 67 | 0.0 |
| + Net subsidies from abroad (receipts minus payments) | -1974 | -0.2 |
| + Property and entrepreneurial income receipts from abroad | 121954 | 11.7 |
| - Property and entrepreneurial income payments to the rest of the world | 100902 | 9.7 |
| = **Gross national income (GNI)** | 1063090 | 101.8 |
| + Current transfers from abroad (receipts minus payments) | -6822 | -0.7 |
| = **Gross national disposable income** | 1056268 | 101.2 |
| - Total final consumption expenditure | 901882 | 86.4 |
| = **Gross saving** | 154386 | 14.8 |
| + Net capital transfers from abroad (receipts minus payments) | 1162 | 0.1 |
| - Gross capital formation | 171769 | 16.5 |
| - Acquisition less disposals of non-produced non-financial assets | 117 | 0.0 |
| - Statistical discrepancy (4) | 1583 | 0.2 |
| = **Net lending (+) or net borrowing (-)** | -17920 | -1.7 |
| **FINANCIAL ACCOUNT** | | |
| Net acquisition of financial assets | 548121 | 52.5 |
| - Net acquisition of financial liabilities | 551657 | 52.8 |
| - Statistical discrepancy between financial and non-financial accounts | 14384 | 1.4 |
| = **Net lending (+) or net borrowing (-)** | -17920 | -1.7 |

*Source*: National Statistics, *Blue Book*, London, 2003.

capital and taxes on corporate income. The extent to which investment can be financed by these retained earnings is measured by the self-financing ratio, which is gross corporate saving divided by gross fixed capital formation.

The financial corporations sector consists of resident corporations mainly engaged in financial intermediation or in auxiliary financial activities. Financial corporations principally conduct financial market transactions: borrowing and lending money; providing life, health or other insurance; financial leasing; and investing in financial assets. Financial auxiliaries include stockbrokers, insurance brokers, investment advisers, trustees, custodians, mortgage originators and other entities providing services closely related to financial intermediation even though they do not intermediate themselves.

The general government sector consists of central, state and local government as well as public social security funds. It includes all departments, offices and other bodies mainly engaged in the production of goods and services outside the normal market mechanism and for consumption by the general public. Their costs of production are mainly financed from public revenues enabling them to provide goods and services free of charge or at a nominal price well below production cost. The tax burden (or compulsory levies ratio), defined as the sum of all taxes and social contributions financing general government divided by GDP, is a key measure of fiscal pressure broadly defined.

The NPISH sector includes non-market entities that are not controlled or mainly financed by government and provide goods or services to their members or other households without charge or at nominal prices. This sector includes trade unions, professional societies, consumer associations, political parties, churches, sports clubs and charities. In some countries, this sector is not recognised separately in the national accounts (for instance, in Australia).

In addition to accounts for the resident sectors, the 1993 SNA includes external, or rest-of-the-world, accounts, which summarise the transactions of residents with non-resident persons, businesses and governments. The rest of the world can conveniently be thought of as a separate sector. Its accounts are broadly consistent with the balance of payments (Table 2.3).[3] In the latter, transactions on goods and services are recorded in the current account, which includes exports and imports, income flows (for example interest on loans) and current transfers (for example remittances by migrant workers or inter-governmental grants). The current account balance is the nation's (or region's) net saving, that is, the difference between saving and investment. The capital account encompasses transactions on non-financial assets, such as sales of patents or debt relief operations. The sum of the current plus the capital account is the nation's net lending (or net borrowing). The balance of payments is always 'balanced' in the sense that the aggregate position of the current and capital accounts is always matched, or 'financed', by the financial

---

[3] The US balance of payments is presented by the BEA in a somewhat different format. For expositional purposes, it is translated in Table 2.3 into the format used in the euro area and Japan.

*Table 2.3*  Balance of payments
(for the year 2003, in per cent of GDP)

| | United States | Euro area | Japan |
|---|---|---|---|
| **Current account** | -4.8 | 0.4 | 3.2 |
| Exports of goods | 6.5 | 14.3 | 10.4 |
| Imports of goods | 11.5 | 12.8 | 8.0 |
| Balance on goods | -5.0 | 1.5 | 2.5 |
| Services (net) | 0.5 | 0.2 | -0.8 |
| Income (net) | 0.3 | -0.6 | 1.7 |
| Current transfers (net) | -0.6 | -0.8 | -0.2 |
| **Capital account (net)** | 0.0 | 0.2 | -0.1 |
| **Financial account\*** | 5.0 | -0.6 | -2.6 |
| Direct investment (net) | -1.2 | -0.1 | -0.5 |
| Portfolio investment (net) | 4.4 | 0.3 | -2.3 |
| Financial derivatives (net) | .. | -0.2 | 0.1 |
| Other investment (net) | 1.7 | -1.0 | 4.4 |
| Change in reserve assets (net) | 0.0 | 0.4 | -4.3 |
| **Errors and omissions** | -0.1 | 0.1 | -0.5 |

*Note:*
\* A negative sign denotes a positive outflow and vice versa.

*Sources*: US BEA, ECB, Japanese Ministry of Finance.

account (except for the discrepancy arising from errors and omissions). In the case of a net lending position, for instance, the financial account position will be negative: the sum of total net capital outflows plus the change in the central bank's foreign exchange reserves is then positive.[4] In this context, capital flows include foreign direct investment (FDI, when a significant share – generally over 10 per cent – of a firm's capital is bought by non-residents), portfolio investment, bank lending and the like.

Two additional concepts are often used. Firstly, the balance of 'capital flows' represents the net long-term capital flows into a country, namely the sum of FDI, bonds and equity flows. This aggregate is useful to assess the quality of the financing of a current account deficit, insofar as these flows are perceived to be less volatile than other capital flows. Secondly, the 'basic balance' is defined as the sum of the current account balance and net long-term capital flows.

Gross national income (GNI) – formerly known as gross national product (GNP) – is defined as GDP less incomes payable to non-resident units plus incomes receivable from non-resident units. In other words, GNI equals GDP less net taxes on production and imports, less compensation of employees and property income payable to the rest of the world, plus the corresponding items receivable from the rest of the world. GNI is thus the total income accruing to national residents regardless of the country where their services were supplied. Net national income is GNI minus fixed capital consumption.

---

[4] By convention, albeit somewhat counter-intuitively, the sign for these lines of the balance of payments is reversed: for example, accumulation of foreign exchange reserves by the Bank of Japan will be shown as a negative entry.

### 2.1.4   Key accounts

The national accounts seek to provide a coherent overview of the economic situation capturing all relevant physical quantities, incomes and financial positions. A sequence of accounts or tables are used to this effect:

- The goods and services accounts present a comprehensive picture of the supply and use of goods and services (referred to generically as 'products') in the economy and of the incomes generated from production. They ensure that in value terms the flows in each sector and between sectors are consistent. In volume terms, consistency is also ensured but is only approximate when chain linking is used, as discussed in Box 2.4 on page 38.
- A second set of accounts trace the distribution and use of income. The allocation of primary income account shows how the income generated in production is distributed. The secondary distribution of income account shows how primary income is redistributed via taxes, social contributions, benefits and other transfers, and hence the income really received in the end by each category of agents. The use of disposable income account shows how disposable income is used in consumption or saved. The capital account then shows what part of saving is mainly invested in non-financial assets, the remainder being net lending or net borrowing.
- The financial and balance sheet accounts record transactions in financial assets and liabilities and show how net worth (total assets minus total liabilities) increases or decreases. Net worth typically rises when net lending is positive, though its exact variation also depends on fixed capital consumption, on revaluations of assets or liabilities and on other changes (disappearance or emergence of assets or liabilities, say, when oil is discovered underground). This third set of accounts is often referred to as the 'flows of funds'.

In principle, the national accounts record transactions on an accrual basis (as opposed to a cash or a payment due basis), reflecting the time when economic value is transferred rather than when cash relating to the transaction is paid or falls due for payment. For example, interest flows are recorded as interest accrues, irrespective of payment schedules. The same holds for taxes. In practice, however, some operations may be observable and recorded only on a cash basis, calling for statistical corrections.

The above sequence of accounts can be built for each of the institutional sectors, and summarised in a comprehensive table of integrated economic accounts. All these accounts are double-entry, so that they balance for each sector. For example, the balance of the income account matches the change in net lending, which in turn is reflected in the financial account.

At the national level, net worth is the sum of the net worth of all residents, namely their stock of physical assets plus their net financial claims on the rest of the world (since financial assets and liabilities held amongst residents cancel out).

In practice, the income and the financial accounts are often less developed than the goods and services account. An important reason is that the producers of the requisite statistical information often differ, with national statistics institutes usually in charge of the 'real sector' while flows of funds are frequently elaborated by central banks. All in all, national balance sheets are difficult to put together, and in many countries they are rough or non-existent. For example, the assets should include valuables and intangible non-produced assets, but often those lines are left empty due to a lack of suitable data sources.

### 2.1.5   The split between prices and volumes

Transactions between economic agents take place and are recorded at current prices. But for analytical purposes, when looking at these transactions over time, it is necessary to distinguish volumes and prices. In this context, volume refers to all factors other than price that affect valuation at current prices, including sheer quantity but also the quality of the product.

The national accounts provide a description of supply and uses in volume terms. The accounts depicting the distribution of income and the balance sheet accounts are presented only at current prices, even if many of the aggregates involved are then deflated by a relevant price index in order to assess their evolution in real, as opposed to nominal, terms. This is the case for instance for disposable income and net worth.

Moving from current prices to volumes is not straightforward, as will be discussed in greater detail in Section 2.3. Suffice it to stress here that first, adequate price indices are needed for each component of the account under consideration, which is not always easy. Then, the volumes obtained for the components need to be aggregated, which raises a host of problems as soon as relative prices shift over time, as they generally do.

## 2.2   Quarterly national accounting

In practice, it would be unthinkable to wait for the release of last year's annual accounts before updating economic forecasts. Moreover, exclusive reliance on annual data would make it impossible to properly capture the dynamic relationships or leads and lags between key economic variables. In addition, there has been an increasing need for having a general framework allowing the collection and the analysis of short-term economic indicators in a coherent way, as in the case of annual data. Therefore, quarterly national accounts have gradually been developed in most OECD countries and in a growing number of emerging market economies. Their coverage and timeliness have improved over time. A first estimate of the quarterly accounts is now usually published within the two months following the end of the quarter they relate to (and within one month in the United States and the United Kingdom). In a few countries, such as Canada and Finland, partial monthly national accounts are even available. This can be useful, although there is a trade-off between frequency and quality of the accounts. Constructing quarterly national accounts requires some specific techniques, to control for seasonal variations (as discussed in Section 3.4) and to ensure consistency with the annual accounts, which draw on a richer information set.

For some variables, the quarterly accounts are derived in the same way as the annual accounts. But for many components, there are often no intra-annual source data similar to the annual ones, for instance when dealing with investment or tax data. Econometric techniques then need to be used to build 'notional' quarterly accounts. The idea is to exploit the information provided by available higher-frequency series related to the missing national account observations. In effect, the higher-frequency indicators are benchmarked on the actual annual data to construct the quarterly accounts. For the sake of illustration, suppose that household consumption is not observed quarterly but only annually, but that some of its components, such as retail sales and car registrations, are. Then a regression of consumption on retail sales and car registrations can be run on annual data and the estimated equation can serve to produce an estimate of quarterly consumption. This can be refined if needed by explicitly taking into account special factors or known trends in some of the components of consumption. In practice, such benchmarking is hard to get right (Box 2.2), not least because of the appearance of econometric residuals that need to be adequately taken into account.

The challenge is compounded by the fact that as some key data are missing at the quarterly frequency, not least as regards corporations, some hazardous shortcuts are taken. For example, an estimate of stockbuilding will often be derived as the difference between the sum of estimated value added across branches and the estimated components of final demand. It will therefore be polluted by the errors made in each estimation (to the extent that they do not offset each other). This is done separately at current prices and in volume terms, and sometimes adjustments for seasonality are not carried out consistently. Hence, the implied quarterly deflators often behave somewhat erratically, in particular the one derived for stockbuilding. In addition, the first quarterly accounts estimates rely on incomplete monthly information. For example, the foreign trade data for the last month of the quarter will often not be known yet. Hence, subsequent versions of the quarterly accounts often involve substantial revisions, especially if the initial estimates are published rapidly.

Other problems also arise. In some countries, a price–volume split is not provided for all components of the quarterly accounts, or only with long lags. Moreover, there are usually no accounts for all institutional sectors at the quarterly frequency, so that some key indicators have to be proxied somehow. For example, in Germany, the level of the household saving rate published by the Bundesbank in its seasonally adjusted quarterly accounts is very different from the one shown in the annual national accounts data. Another gap is the absence of quarterly financial data, although there are a few exceptions, notably the United States, where the Federal Reserve publishes fairly comprehensive quarterly flow-of-funds statistics.

## 2.3 Technical hurdles

Although the national accounts provide a consistent framework, the forecaster faces a number of practical problems having to do with statistical observation itself, data heterogeneity, the price–volume split and revisions of the source data.

---

**Box 2.2   Benchmarking the quarterly national accounts**

Benchmarking can serve two purposes. One, dubbed 'quarterisation' or interpolation, is to build a quarterly series $X_{t,a}$ (where $t = 1, \ldots, 4$ stands for the quarter and $a$ for the year) when an annual series $A_a$ of better statistical quality exists. The second one, extrapolation, is to estimate $X_{t,a}$ when $A_a$ is not yet available. Denote $I_{t,a}$ the quarterly series observed for the indicator used to estimate $X_{t,a}$. In practice, the choice of $I$ depends on its availability and on how closely it mirrors the variations of $A_a$ at the annual frequency.

The simplest way to proceed would be to assume proportionality, namely that:

$$X_{t,a} = A_a I_{t,a} \Big/ \sum_t I_{t,a} \text{ subject to constraint (1)}: \sum_t X_{t,a} = A_a \qquad \text{(interpolation)}$$

or that

$$X_{t,a+1} = X_{4,a} \, I_{t,a+1}/I_{4,a} \qquad \text{(extrapolation beyond the last known year for } A_a)$$

But if $I$ does not rise as fast as $A$, there will be a catch-up in the form of a jump in the $X_{t,a}$ series in the first quarter of each year, because of the need to meet constraint (1). This is called the 'step problem'.

For this reason, the pro rata distribution technique is generally not advisable. There are several ways to overcome the problem. The best known is the so-called proportional Denton (1971) method, which is recommended by the IMF. In its basic version, it keeps $X_{t,a}$ as proportional as possible to the indicator by minimising (in a least square sense) the difference in relative adjustment to neighbouring quarters subject to the constraint provided by the annual benchmarks. Mathematically, this amounts to minimising over all quarters the expression: $\sum_i [(X_i/I_i) - (X_{i-1}/I_{i-1})]^2$.

When the annual data are later released, the whole quarterly series constructed in this way has to be re-estimated, since the adjustment for the errors in the indicator is distributed smoothly over a number of years, not just within a given year.

A number of other benchmarking techniques exist (discussed in greater detail by Bloem *et al.*, 2001). They can be grouped in two categories:

- Numerical methods similar to Denton's, but based on the minimisation of somewhat different expressions, with a view to better incorporate information on past systematic movements in the indicator's bias (whose magnitude may for example depend on the business cycle).
- Statistical methods, which try to gauge the foreseeable evolution of the indicator's bias, for example using ARIMA or multivariate models. Such methods are quite heavy to implement and may at times result in over-corrections.

---

### 2.3.1   Statistical observation

Statistical coverage of the economy is very uneven, including in advanced market economies. A key reason is that national accounts have usually been constructed using a pre-existing and heterogeneous set of statistical data, rather than the other way round. Agriculture, which in these countries represents only a tiny share of GDP, is graced with a wealth of data. Conversely, data on the service sector, which is by far the largest one in advanced economies, are typically wanting. Partly, this is due to history, but it also stems from the fact that measuring value added in services is more difficult than in agriculture or industry. Even in the industrial sector, where many data are available, some crucial elements are not adequately captured in the statistics, notably stockbuilding and investment behaviour, or work-in-progress. These problems are even more acute in the case of higher-frequency data. Industrial production is usually monitored on a monthly basis, but in gross rather than value-added terms. Since the latter is not a constant proportion of the former, this is an extra complication. In addition, relatively few monthly data are available for service sector activities.

Another difficulty is that economic data are released with a lag, and sometimes with huge lags. In the meantime, the forecaster has to make do with other indicators, which are designed for different purposes (for instance, administrative purposes). It also happens that two series exist for one variable, which send conflicting messages. Controversies surrounding the employment and unemployment data in a number of countries illustrate the confusion that may ensue (see Box 2.3).

---

*Box 2.3*　**Capturing labour market trends**

In the case of labour markets, the problem is less the lack of data than the contradictory signals sent by alternative employment or unemployment series.

Consider the case of the US employment data. The series that the Federal Reserve trusts most is the payroll statistic, which is based on a monthly survey of some 400 000 business establishments conducted by the Bureau of Labor Statistics (BLS). This measure showed a decline in US employment by over 0.8 million persons in the two years following the November 2001 cyclical trough in real GDP, leading to the description of the recovery as 'jobless', or even 'job-loss'. In contrast, the monthly household survey, conducted by the BLS and the Bureau of the Census on a sample of about 60 000 households, showed that over the same period employment had risen by over 1.5 million. To some extent, this startling dissonance can be explained by differences in coverage between the two surveys: employment in the household survey includes unincorporated self-employed workers, unpaid family workers and farm workers, none of whom are covered in the payroll survey; at the same time, a person holding two jobs counts once in the household survey but twice in the payroll survey. Controlling for these differences, the gap between the two measures narrowed somewhat (partly because of unusually strong growth in the number of self-employed after the 2001 downturn), but it remained huge. Another possible explanation might have been that the payroll survey failed to catch newly formed businesses, but the BLS adjusts the raw data to take this into account and posterior benchmark revisions to the series did not show any systematic bias in this respect. In Canada as well, a similar difference was observed in 2002–03, but the most reliable source in that country is the household survey, and little attention is paid to the payroll survey data. As depicted in Figure 2.1 for the United States, the choice of the data source matters tremendously over the short run, but it is less important when the focus is on long-run trends, since the two series tend to move much more closely together over a ten-year period.

Considerable scope for confusion also exists regarding unemployment statistics, mainly because the number of people claiming unemployment benefits and the number of those strictly defined as unemployed (who, according to the internationally agreed definition of the International Labour Organisation (ILO), are people without jobs who are actively looking for work and are immediately available) can greatly differ. For instance, a person receiving a benefit may not be looking for a new job and would thus be considered as inactive. Conversely, a job-seeker may not receive any benefit at all if his rights have expired but would be considered as unemployed. In addition, the way these populations are measured is often quite different. Information on people receiving unemployment benefits is often produced on an exhaustive basis by public administrations, at a relatively high frequency (usually each month or even each week in the United States). By contrast, determining the total number of people unemployed can be a difficult exercise, requiring the conduct of surveys, and is therefore subject to a certain degree of uncertainty and time lags.

In the United Kingdom for example, two series compete for attention. One is the Labour Force Survey (LFS) series, conducted using the internationally agreed ILO definition of unemployment. The other is the claimant count series, which measures how many are claiming unemployment-related benefits. In late 2004, the LFS measure stood at 4.7 per cent of the labour force, whereas the claimant count was only 2.6 per cent. The divergence between the two measures has increased since the mid-1990s, as improving labour market conditions encouraged people who had left the labour force to actively resume job searching. These people were new LFS unemployed, but since they did not qualify for benefits, they did not appear among the claimants. Likewise, in France and Germany as well, there are two very different series for unemployment.

*Figure 2.1*   **Elusive trends**

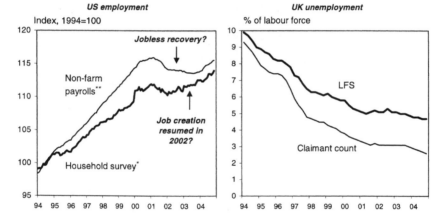

Notes:
* Data affected by changes in population controls in January 2000, January 2003 and January 2004.
** Establishment-based data.

*Sources*: US BLS and UK National Statistics.

In practice, data limitations may mislead analysts. For example, they may put more weight than is warranted by its share in GDP on developments in industry, simply because the data for this sector are much more complete. Consider the Asian crisis in 1997–98: the industrial sector in the United States went through a soft patch, as evidenced by high frequency indicators such as output and capacity utilisation, but the economy at large as measured by GDP continued to expand, benefiting in particular from gains in the terms of trade and the flight of capital away from emerging markets towards safer US shores (see Figure 2.2). The somewhat alarmist high frequency information probably spurred the Federal Reserve to adopt a more stimulatory monetary stance than would otherwise have been the case.

*Figure 2.2* US GDP and industrial output during the Asian crisis

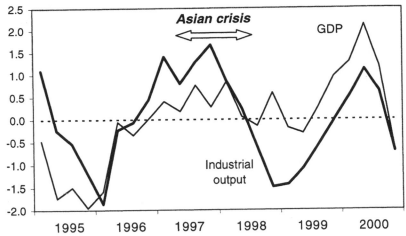

Note:
* Observed growth rate minus trend growth, divided by the standard deviation of growth.
Source: US BEA and Federal Reserve.

With the benefit of hindsight, the push provided by the Federal Reserve may thus have been pro-cyclical.

While forecasters' conclusions are conditioned by data availability, the converse also holds, as some data tend to create a diagnosis. For example, data on industrial orders in Germany receive enormous attention. The press and analysts await them eagerly, as if they conveyed precious information about the outlook of the German economy. In reality, they are a coincident more than a leading indicator, and often appear less informative than the qualitative opinions expressed by respondents in the smaller sample of industrial firms surveyed by Munich's IFO Institute. Likewise, the publication of household confidence indicators gives rise to many comments and analyses, despite the fact that they can be of limited value for forecasting purposes.

### 2.3.2 Data heterogeneity

The data used in forecasting are very heterogeneous, as they were developed for a variety of reasons and not necessarily to facilitate economic analysis. For example, foreign trade data originally stem from the need to raise taxes at the border while data on the registered unemployed primarily serve administrative purposes. In addition, data frequency ranges from intra-day or daily (for exchange rates) to annual or multi-annual (some surveys or censuses are conducted only once in so many years). Another difficulty pertains to data presentation, which differs across countries. For instance, in the United States the quarterly national accounts are presented in annualised format. In contrast, they are traditionally presented in quarter-on-quarter terms in Europe.

Practices regarding deseasonalisation also vary. Price data, for example, tend to be presented in seasonally adjusted form in the United States (with some exceptions, however, notably in the case of foreign trade deflators) but not in Europe. In emerging markets, data are often presented on the basis of the 12-month rate of change, even when seasonally adjusted series exist. This can be misleading, as 12-month rates are a lagging indicator: thus, in 1999, following the devaluation of Brazil's real, many observers announced a recession, even though the country was already experiencing a recovery. Another example of confusion is the contradictory comments surrounding the release of inflation data, when some analysts describe inflation in terms of the month-on-month increase in the consumer price index, ignoring seasonal factors, whilst others focus on the 12-month rate of change, which essentially controls for these factors but may not adequately portray the latest price developments. Most national statistical offices have developed measures of core inflation (which exclude certain volatile items) to offer a better gauge of underlying inflation trends. This is useful but compounds data heterogeneity, as the list of excluded items varies.

The diversity of data used has also increased as globalisation, financial market development and diversification of public-sector activities have prompted forecasters to try to factor in information that is not part and parcel of the standard national accounts. Examples include capital flows, intra-firm trade across borders, microeconomic balance sheet data and governments' off-balance sheet operations.

### 2.3.3 Measuring inflation

Proper estimation of transaction volumes requires reliable deflators. Depending on the specific purpose, different indices may be used, which are sometimes not adequately kept separate in public commentary. For example, in the case of household consumption, one can use a retail price index (with weights based on retail trade turnover), a consumer price index (CPI) (with weights based on the average consumer's basket), or a national accounts deflator (which also takes into account items that are not directly purchased by households but nonetheless consumed by them). Moreover, in the case of the CPI, some countries monitor it only for the typical urban household, whose consumption patterns may differ significantly from the nation-wide average.

Different measures of inflation at times send conflicting signals, not least for the central bank. In the United Kingdom for example, no less than three very different indices make headlines on inflation (Figure 2.3): the old retail price index (RPI), a truncated version thereof (RPIX, which strips out mortgage interest payments) and the European harmonised index of consumer prices (HICP), which is now referred to simply as the CPI. In late 2003, the Bank of England's $2\frac{1}{2}$ per cent RPIX inflation target was replaced by a 2 per cent CPI inflation target. In early 2004, the first two measures of inflation suggested that inflationary pressures might warrant an interest rate hike, but CPI inflation was running well below target, pointing in the opposite direction.

Finding sound measures of real output or reliable deflators is challenging in large sectors of the economy, especially in most services. Wheat production is easy enough to measure, but the real value of lawyer services for instance is harder to

*Figure 2.3* Three measures of UK inflation

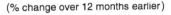
(% change over 12 months earlier)

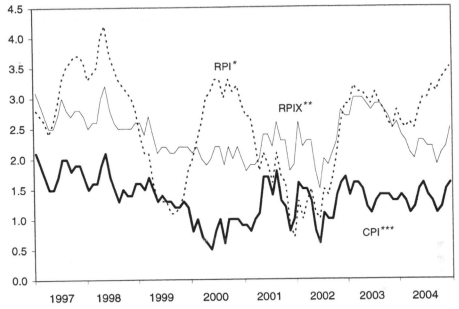

*Notes*:
  * Retail price index, all items.
  ** Retail price index, excluding mortgage interest payments.
  *** Consumer price index (previously called the harmonised index of consumer prices).

*Source*: UK National Statistics.

pin down. Moreover, as emphasized by Griliches (1994), the share in GDP of 'reasonably measurable' sectors, which include agriculture and manufacturing activities, tends to decline over time as services expand.

Measuring prices in foreign trade is also notoriously complicated. In general, customs statistics fail to capture illegal trade flows, and in the European single market they have been altogether overtaken by institutional developments. Insofar as they record actual quantities (tonnes or number of items), the implied unit value indices are useful only if this is done at a very disaggregated level. There is also the aforementioned difference between f.o.b. (for exports) and c.i.f. (for imports) prices and sometimes much larger differences still between the price of a given good in the importing and in the exporting country. And although cross-border trade in services is expanding rapidly, they are hard to price. Furthermore, emerging market and developing countries often monitor foreign trade in US dollar terms only, neglecting the price–volume split. This led to some diagnosis errors during the 1997–98 Asian crisis, when the sharp depreciation of a number of currencies translated into steep drops in measured exports, even though actual export volumes were by no means plummeting.

Equally if not even more tricky is the pricing of inventories, which as explained in Section 5.1 matters a lot to assess cyclical conditions accurately. Firms often value inventories at historical cost, that is, at the price they purchased the goods (but using a variety of methods, in particular 'first in, first out' or 'last in, first out'). The standard national accounts convention instead is to value addition to or exit from inventories at the market price prevailing at the exact time of the movement.

Lastly, there is also an issue of consistency in valuation. If, for example, imports of computer equipment are valued in a certain way, one should use the same method for the valuation of these items as components of final demand. In practice, this is not always the case.

### 2.3.4 Dealing with relative price shifts

How aggregation is carried out matters a lot for the estimation of inflation and changes in volume. Consider a national accounts aggregate in periods 0 and 1, with $V$ standing for values at current prices, $p^i$ for the price of elementary item $i$ and $q^i$ for its quantity. Then:

$$V_1/V_0 = \sum p_1^i q_1^i / \sum p_0^i q_0^i = \underbrace{\left( \sum p_0^i q_1^i / \sum p_0^i q_0^i \right)}_{(1)} \times \underbrace{\left( \sum p_1^i q_1^i / \sum p_0^i q_1^i \right)}_{(2)}$$

$$= \underbrace{\left( \sum p_1^i q_1^i / \sum p_1^i q_0^i \right)}_{(3)} \times \underbrace{\left( \sum p_1^i q_0^i / \sum p_0^i q_0^i \right)}_{(4)}$$

Here, (1) shows the change in volumes holding prices constant at their levels in period 0, which is called a Laspeyres volume index. The weights are the relative values in the base period, which is period 0 in this case. Symmetrically, (2) shows the change in prices holding quantities constant at their levels in period 1, which is called a Paasche price index.

Alternatively, the change in value can be expressed as the product of a Paasche quantity index (3) by a Laspeyres price index (4). In practice, however, the first decomposition is preferred since it leads to additive volumes.

The following simple numerical example illustrates the importance of the choice of index. Suppose that production of good A has doubled and that its price has increased by 50 per cent, so that the value of the production of A rose three-fold, from 1 to 3 (using the price of good A in period 0 as the *numéraire*). At the same time, suppose that the production and price of good B remained unchanged at 1 in both periods. Now consider the basket initially including one unit of A and one unit of B. Its value $V$ has doubled since $V_1/V_0 = 4/2 = 2$. The increase in volume is 50 per cent if period 0 prices are used as weights: $[(1 \times 2) + (1 \times 1)]/[(1 \times 1) + (1 \times 1)] = 1.5$. However, it is 60 per cent if period 1 prices are used: $[(1 \times 3) + (1 \times 1)]/[(0.5 \times 3) + (1 \times 1)] = 1.6$. Correspondingly, inflation is 33 per cent in the first case and 25 per cent in the second case.

Hence, changes in the volume of a given national accounts aggregate depend on the weights of its components and on the date used to estimate their relative prices. This can make for large effects when relative prices change substantially. Consider the case of computers, whose price in the United States dropped ninefold between 1996 and 2003 and whose sales soared: at 1996 prices, the contribution of computer purchases to growth in consumption in 2003 would be enormous compared with their contribution at 2003 prices. More generally, using a fixed-weight measure of real GDP based on 1996 prices would considerably overstate growth in the early 2000s. This substitution bias led to the adoption of chained indices (see Box 2.4).

### 2.3.5   Revisions

Adding to an already lengthy list of technical hurdles are the revisions to earlier estimates carried out routinely or exceptionally by statistical offices, which in effect alter economic history, in some cases going back several decades (as with the 2003 comprehensive revision of the US NIPA, which affected data all the way from 1929 to 2003). Large-scale revisions may be required when better data, based for example on more thorough survey evidence, are released or when methodological changes occur. In practice, comprehensive revisions are only conducted once every few years and are often associated with a change in the base year of the national accounts. The aim is to improve the representation of the economy, by refining the definition of some concepts, using more statistical information, and/or updating relative prices. Though to a much lesser extent, annual national accounts are also routinely revised in order to incorporate the emergence of new information, such as tax rolls, which only become available two or three years after the period to which they relate.

Quarterly national accounts are revised even more frequently. First, they are naturally affected by the regular revisions of the annual national accounts as well as by the more infrequent revisions. Second, quarterly national accounts are produced rapidly, sometimes before the release of some of the underlying monthly data themselves, and therefore based on preliminary and often partial statistical information (for instance, the first estimate of quarterly GDP will be published when trade flows are only available for the first two months). Given that more information will progressively become available, at least three or four vintages of quarterly national accounts data are produced for any single quarter: 'advance' estimates shortly (one to two months for the major economies) after the end of the quarter, then preliminary estimates, and then 'final' estimates. Even if they complicate forecasters' task, revisions are desirable insofar as they significantly improve data quality, provided of course they are well planned, properly documented and not overly frequent.[5]

The size of the revisions depends on the aggregate: revisions to GDP tend to be smaller than revisions to its components (York and Atkinson, 1997). Investment and the public sector accounts in particular are subject to sizeable revisions. Even so, GDP estimates change substantially over time: the average absolute revision to quarterly real GDP growth in the United States over the last three decades of the twentieth century amounted to 1.7 percentage points (at an annualised rate).

---

[5] Against the background of criticism leveled at the UK statistical office following repeated substantial revisions of the national accounts, its head defended the merits of revisions, underlining in particular the trade-off between timeliness and reliability, the United Kingdom putting more weight on timeliness than most continental European countries (Cook, 2004).

*Box 2.4*   Base-year versus chained indices*

Prior to the 1993 SNA, the tradition was to compile volume national account estimates using fixed base-year constant-price estimates, and to shift the base year forward every five or ten years. One major drawback was that the weights used in this approach were the same for the base year, when they reflected actual relative prices and spending patterns, and for periods before or after the base year, when they lost their relevance and biased volume estimates, especially in times of rapid change in the structure of the economy. Moreover, the periodical rebasing often led to uncomfortably large revisions to previously published estimates. Therefore, the 1993 SNA recommended abandoning this approach and moving to chain-linked volume measures, which provide for an annual updating of the weights. The growth rates obtained with these chain-linked indices are no longer dependent on the base year. This was implemented in 1996 in the United States by the Bureau of Economic Analysis (BEA) and in 2003 in the United Kingdom. Many other OECD countries have also adopted chain linking in recent years.

While chain-linked indices largely overcome the bias problem and mean that henceforth the revisions associated with rebasing will mostly result from improvements in the quality of source data or methodological changes, they do come with costs. One is greater computational complexity. The 1993 SNA recommends that Fisher indices be used, which are the geometric average of a Laspeyres and a Paasche index for two adjacent years.** The chain-type quantity index $I$ is obtained by multiplying, or 'chaining', together the Fisher indices $F$ for each successive pair of periods. If the reference year is 0, the index for year $t$ is $I_{t,0} = F_{t,t-1} \times F_{t-1,t-2} \times \cdots \times F_{1,0}$. The term 'reference', rather than 'base' year is used to highlight that the choice of the period 0 does not affect the weights used in the calculation.

Another drawback of chain-linked indices is that because the weights shift over time GDP components expressed in volume terms are no longer strictly additive, unlike the constant-price data of yore, and are indeed expressed as indices rather than values computed at base year prices. In order to assist users in making comparisons across components of GDP for periods away from the reference year, the US BEA publishes so-called chained-dollar indices which are derived by multiplying the above chain-weighted indices by the current-dollar values of a specific reference year (currently the year 2000). Nevertheless, the problem of non-additivity remains and these tables expressed in chained 2000 dollars include a residual line showing the discrepancy between the sum of the components of GDP and total GDP. Furthermore, the growth contributions of the main components of GDP based on chain-type indices cannot be calculated easily. They have therefore to be published by the BEA in specific tables. Statistical offices in other countries proceed likewise. For the broad components of GDP, and for periods close to the reference year, this provides a reasonable approximation of their contribution to GDP growth and of their relative importance as a share of GDP. For some sub-components, however – notably computers and other high-tech equipment with rapid growth in the volume of sales and falling prices – as well as for periods further away from the reference year, chained-dollar levels misrepresent their relative importance.

One further question is how to compute quarterly changes. In the United States, this is done using a Fisher formula incorporating the weights from two adjacent quarters, but before per cent changes are calculated, the quarterlies are adjusted so as to make them consistent with the annual indices. In general, it is advisable to keep relative prices constant during the course of a year, as quarterly updates would lead to excessive volatility. Table 2.4 provides a numerical illustration in the case of chained Laspeyres volume indices, and using a one-quarter overlap with the fourth quarter as linking quarter: estimates for the overlap quarter are compiled at the average prices of the current year as well as at the average prices of the previous year, and the ratio of the former on the latter is the linking factor used to rescale the quarterly data.*** More details and tips on how to use chained indices for analytical and forecasting purposes are provided by Bloem *et al.* (2001) in generic terms, and by Landefeld *et al.* (2003) for the United States.

*Table 2.4* **Annual chain-linking and quarterly data**
(hypothetical economy with two quantities $q_1$ and $q_2$ and respectively two prices $p_1$ and $p_2$)

| | $q_1$ | $q_2$ | $p_1$ | $p_2$ | Total at current prices | At constant prices of 1997 | | At constant prices of 1998 | | At constant prices of 1999 | | Chain-linked index 1997 = 100 | |
|---|---|---|---|---|---|---|---|---|---|---|---|---|---|
| | | | | | | Level | Index 1997 = 100 | Level | Index 1998Q4 = 100 | Level | Index 1999Q4 = 100 | Level | q-on-q % rate of change |
| 1997 | 251.0 | 236.0 | 7.0 | 6.0 | 3 173.0 | 3 173.0 | 100.00 | | | | | 100.00 | |
| 1998Q1 | 67.4 | 57.6 | | | | 817.4 | 103.04 | | | | | 103.04 | |
| 1998Q2 | 69.4 | 57.1 | | | | 828.4 | 104.43 | | | | | 104.43 | 1.3 |
| 1998Q3 | 71.5 | 56.5 | | | | 839.5 | 105.83 | | | | | 105.83 | 1.3 |
| 1998Q4 | 73.7 | 55.8 | | | | 850.7 | 107.24 | 907.55 | 100.00 | | | 107.24 | 1.3 |
| 1998 | 282.0 | 227.0 | 5.5 | 9.0 | 3 594.0 | 3 336.0 | 105.14 | 3 594.00 | | | | 105.14 | |
| 1999Q1 | 76.0 | 55.4 | | | | | | 916.60 | 101.00 | | | 108.31 | 1.0 |
| 1999Q2 | 78.3 | 54.8 | | | | | | 923.85 | 101.80 | | | 109.17 | 0.8 |
| 1999Q3 | 80.6 | 54.2 | | | | | | 931.10 | 102.59 | | | 110.03 | 0.8 |
| 1999Q4 | 83.1 | 53.6 | | | | | | 939.45 | 103.51 | 948.80 | 100.00 | 111.01 | 0.9 |
| 1999 | 318.0 | 218.0 | 4.0 | 11.5 | 3 779.0 | | | 3 711.00 | | 3 779.00 | | 109.63 | |
| 2000Q1 | 85.5 | 53.2 | | | | | | | | 953.80 | 100.53 | 111.60 | 0.5 |
| 2000Q2 | 88.2 | 52.7 | | | | | | | | 958.85 | 101.06 | 112.19 | 0.5 |
| 2000Q3 | 90.8 | 52.1 | | | | | | | | 962.35 | 101.43 | 112.60 | 0.4 |
| 2000Q4 | 93.5 | 52.0 | | | | | | | | 972.00 | 102.45 | 113.73 | 1.0 |
| 2000 | 358.0 | 210.0 | 3.0 | 13.5 | 3 909.0 | | | | | 3 847.00 | | 112.53 | |

*Steps involved:*
1. Compile estimates for each quarter at annual average prices of previous year; annual data obtained as sum of quarters.
2. Compile estimates for the fourth quarter of each year, at annual average price of the same year, for instance: 1998Q4: 5.5 * 73.7 + 9.0 * 55.8 = 907.55.
3. Convert constant price estimates for the quarters of the first year following the reference year (here 1997) into a volume index with the average of the reference year set at 100. For instance: 1998Q1: 817.4/(3173.00/4) * 100 = 103.04.
4. Convert the constant price estimates for each of the other quarters into a volume index with the fourth quarter of last year set at 100. For instance: 1999Q1: 916.60/907.55 * 100 = 101.00.
5. Link together the quarterly volume indices with shifting base using the fourth quarter of each year as the link. For instance: 1999Q1: 101.00 * 107.24/100 = 108.31.

*Notes:*
* The exposition in this box pertains to volume indices, but it applies symmetrically to price indices.
** This is the SNA recommendation, but it is implemented only in the United States and Canada. Other countries use chained annual Laspeyres indices, in particular in the European Union, where this is a Eurostat requirement.
*** Alternatively, an annual overlap could be used.

*Source:* Bloem *et al.* (2001).

The magnitude and sign of the revisions also depend on the business cycle: as they are partly based on trends in preceding quarters, early GDP estimates tend to overstate activity when activity is decelerating and to understate it when it is accelerating, as documented for the US case by Dynan and Elmendorf (2001). That said, revisions are hard to predict, although they are somewhat more predictable in Italy, Japan and the United Kingdom than in the United States (Faust *et al.*, 2000).

The difference between preliminary and final estimates in the G7 countries is shown in Table 2.5, which shows them to be particularly large in Japan, Germany

*Table 2.5*   **Mean revision to preliminary GDP estimates in the G7 countries**
(based on quarter-on-quarter real GDP growth rates, in per cent, to end-1997)*

| | Canada | France | Germany | Italy | Japan | United Kingdom | United States |
|---|---|---|---|---|---|---|---|
| Arithmetic mean | 0.18 | 0.01 | 0.11 | 0.11 | −0.07 | 0.30 | 0.10 |
| Mean of absolute value | 0.58 | 0.28 | 0.69 | 0.59 | 0.64 | 0.84 | 0.40 |

*Note*:
* The sample starts respectively in 1965Q1, 1987Q4, 1979Q4, 1979Q4, 1970Q1, 1965Q1 and 1965Q1.
*Source*: Faust *et al.* (2000).

and the United Kingdom.[6] The fact that revisions are relatively limited in a specific country does not necessarily imply that the initial estimates are of good quality, and could simply reflect the fact that 'final' national account estimates fail to take sufficient subsequent statistical information into account. That said, a few historical examples can serve to illustrate that some revisions can be disconcerting, while others have fairly limited implications:

- In the case of the US recession of the early 1990s, monetary policy would probably have been different if the final numbers had been known at the time. When the Federal Open Market Committee (FOMC) of the Federal Reserve met in November 1990, real GDP was estimated to have risen 1.7, 0.4 and 1.8 per cent respectively in the first three quarters of the year (in annualised terms). This suggested that the economy was muddling through a period of slow but positive growth. With the benefit of hindsight, activity was in fact already contracting substantially: after more than half a dozen revisions, the data for this period now show a clear deceleration in economic activity in the course of 1990, from a 4.7 per cent increase in the first quarter to a 1.0 per cent gain in the second, turning into 0.0 per cent in the third and −3.0 in the fourth quarter.
- In contrast, the comprehensive revisions implemented in late 2003 by the US BEA were relatively innocuous. One difference compared with the data published earlier was that the 2001 downturn was milder than previously thought, but Figure 2.4 shows that the total revision to the GDP series over the past 15 years was relatively small, with its two components offsetting each other to a large extent: statistical adjustments stemming from improved data and methodologies pushed nominal GDP up by as much as one per cent, but changes in definition and classification worked in the opposite direction, and were on average of a broadly similar order of magnitude.
- In early 2004, the Bank of Korea (which in South Korea is responsible for the compilation of the national accounts) adopted most of the provisions of the 1993 SNA, thus extending the coverage of GDP to a wider range of economic

---

[6] See Faust *et al.* (2000) for the exact meaning of the terms 'preliminary' and 'final' in the context of Table 2.5.

activity, and updated the base year. As a result, the estimates for the level of nominal GDP in 2001–03 were raised by over 10 per cent on average, and the new real GDP series displayed less volatility.

- In late 2004, the Japanese statistical authorities released a new set of national accounts, introducing chain linking, with retropolation back to 1994. This translated into much lower GDP growth estimates for recent years without altering those for earlier years very much, so that Japan's economic recovery had to be reassessed and no longer appeared that robust compared to previous ones.

*Figure 2.4* **Sources of 2003 revisions to nominal US GDP**

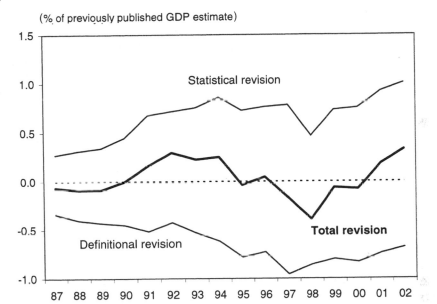

*Source*: BEA, December 2003 Comprehensive Revision.

## 2.4 Open questions and limitations

While the national accounts framework is extremely useful, it does raise a number of questions and has some serious limitations. For instance, in an era where quite a few multinational firms operating in dozens of different national economies each generate more value added than the GDP produced by some of the world's small economies, 'national' accounts may fail to fully capture some of the economic mechanisms at work. More fundamentally perhaps, national accounts reflect implicit assumptions or economic theories with which one may be more or less comfortable: for instance, they are based on the assumption that in any given period, an economic equilibrium obtains. Furthermore, the SNA is almost continuously under review as new problems emerge, calling for adjustments to the framework.

### 2.4.1   Conundrums

A first limitation has to do with the fact that the focus of the national accounts is more on flows than on stocks, even if the latter dwarf quarterly or even annual flows. As agents' behaviour obviously depends heavily on their balance sheets, this is a serious problem, and in recent times more effort has gone into measuring stocks. Even so, agents' assets and liabilities are often not well quantified. Some assets are not always recognised as such, notably automobiles, which are treated as a consumer rather than an investment good. Another difficulty is valuation. The valuation of existing fixed assets is uncertain. In principle, it should be carried out at replacement or market prices. In practice, however, businesses record assets at historic acquisition costs in their balance sheet and replacement costs are often derived from bankruptcy procedures and therefore possibly biased downwards. Hence, statisticians have to use an indirect method (called the 'perpetual inventory method') to estimate the market value of assets, based on the application of adequate price index numbers to cumulated flows of gross fixed capital formation (net of depreciation). Turning to financial assets, only some of them are priced in markets on a continuous basis. Even those assets may turn out to be worth little when they actually are disposed of, for instance if sold in a context of generalised financial distress. Other assets are only infrequently valued, for example only when they change hands. As a result, price information on the main household asset, houses, is notoriously shaky. Some assets are never explicitly valued at all, for instance in the case of human or ecological capital. The depreciation coefficients are only rough approximations. Furthermore, there is the problem of implicit assets and liabilities, which are not recorded as such but do influence consumption and investment decisions, for example in the case of the accrual of pension rights in a pay-as-you-go system but also more generally (see Box 2.5).

Price measurement is another conundrum. In theory, prices should reflect equilibrium between supply and demand for each good and service, an assumption that is unlikely to be verified in each market at every point in time. In practice, as

---

*Box 2.5*   **Generational accounting**

The fiscal deficit and public debt as recorded in the standard government accounts ignore future demographic and other pressures on revenue and spending, even when they are relatively predictable. Hence, these measures are not sufficient to assess fully the public finance situation, especially long-term fiscal sustainability and inter-generational equity. One possible tool is the so-called generational accounts, inspired by overlapping generations, general-equilibrium models. Such accounts are now compiled more or less regularly in many countries (see Bonin and Patxot, 2004 and, for country-by-country overviews, Auerbach *et al.*, 1999 and European Commission, 1999). In a nutshell, the idea is to calculate the net tax burden (taxation minus government transfers) that cohorts of individuals will pay over their remaining lifetime, assuming unchanged policy parameters. By comparing the net tax burden faced by the current generation with that of future generations it is possible to examine the extent to which current policy settings imply transfers between generations.

More specifically, generational accounting addresses the following related questions:

- What is the implicit public debt, namely the net government liabilities stemming from current policy?
- How heavy a fiscal burden do current tax and expenditure arrangements imply across generations?
- Is fiscal policy sustainable without increases in net tax on current or future generations or cutbacks in government spending?
- What policy measures would restore generational balance, in the sense that generations face the same fiscal burden – as a share of their lifetime earnings?
- How would such measures affect the remaining lifetime fiscal burdens of those now alive?

Generational accounts compute the present value of net taxes that individuals of different age cohorts are expected, under current policy, to pay over their remaining lifetimes. The sum of the generational accounts of those now alive is their collective contribution towards paying the government's bills, defined as the present value of its current and future purchases of goods and services plus its net debt (financial liabilities minus financial and real assets, including public-sector enterprises). The share of the bill left unpaid by current generations must be paid by future generations.

Comparing the generational accounts of current newborns with those of future newborns, adjusting for intervening economic growth, provides a measure of generational imbalance. If future newborns face a higher burden than do current ones, today's policy set-up is generationally imbalanced, calling for tax increases or spending cuts today. If instead future newborns face a smaller lifetime net tax burden than do current ones, generational balance can be restored by reducing the fiscal burden facing the current generation. A summary measure of the size of the adjustment required to achieve generational balance is the generational balance gap, defined as the ratio to GDP of the difference between the present value of the government's bills and the net taxes it is set to collect under unchanged policies.

In practice, the calculation of generational accounts is far from straightforward. The measurement of the net tax burden of a generation is not easy, not least because of the difficulty of deciding on who benefits from some of the public transfers (does government spending on education represent a transfer in favour of the young generations or to their parents?). Moreover, it should be borne in mind that generational accounting calculations assume that the fiscal burden of current generations is set by current policies, even when they will get older, and that the rest of the burden will be faced by future generations; in reality, this is unlikely to be the case, as illustrated by ongoing reforms of public pensions in OECD economies. Furthermore, besides a good understanding of the intricacies of the tax and benefit system, generational accounting also necessitates making assumptions about future demographic developments, the growth of real GDP and the discount rate, to which the results are very sensitive. A final limitation is that in practice the accounting often disregards the general equilibrium feedback effects associated with the interaction between tax rates, public spending and growth.

illustrated above, there are various ways to quantify price developments. One prominent difficulty pertains to new goods and services. They are introduced in the price basket only with a lag, meaning that in the meantime the price index is incomplete. This was the case of cell phone services, which in France, for example, entered the consumer price index eight years after their commercial launch. In addition, some of the new items are very difficult to price. In the case of cell-phone services, there is a great and ever-changing variety of tarification packages. Similarly, for several other products, such as computers and automobiles, taking into account the quality of the good is a major challenge. A technique to do so is hedonic pricing, which involves regressing the price of items, say cars, computers or even clothing, on a number of technical characteristics (in the case of computers, speed, memory, card type and so on). But hedonic price indices themselves raise a host of new problems, not least because differences in approach across countries hamper international comparability (Triplett, 2001). House prices are also often mismeasured, as many house price indices ignore changes in the physical characteristics of housing.

A third difficulty is the treatment of interest payments in income flows. To some extent, interest is compensation for inflation. In theory, one might therefore prefer to count as income for the creditors (or as expenditure in the case of debtors) only the difference between nominal interest payments and the inflationary erosion of the loan or deposit.

A fourth and more general problem is that national account aggregates subsume a bewildering diversity of microeconomic transactions. Hence, the relationships between these aggregates are artificial constructs and may not correspond to any single agent's actual behaviour. How disaggregated the analysis should be to make most economic sense is an open question.

A fifth complication is that a given seemingly well-defined national accounts measure may have a different meaning in two countries depending on institutional arrangements. Consider the case of the household saving rate as a share of disposable income, which is far higher in Continental Europe (where it approaches or is in the double digits) than in the United States or the United Kingdom (where it is in the low single digits). In Continental Europe, a larger share of education and health services is provided by the government. This may not affect saving itself, yet it increases the saving rate to the extent that financing of these services through higher taxes diminishes disposable income. The definition of households may also differ, in particular regarding the treatment of the self-employed. Another important institutional factor influencing measured saving rates is differences in pension systems, as transactions relating to private pension schemes are treated as financial operations, whereas those related to social security schemes are considered as current operations.

Lastly, one should beware of spurious precision. Even abstracting from the complications listed above, national accounts are no more than estimates, and as such they are subject to error margins. The level of GDP in particular is measured with a statistical error reflecting coverage, sampling, processing, non-response and modelling errors (Akritidis, 2002). The size of the overall error is hard to establish, given that the notional true value is by definition unknown. But the likely error, expressed in per cent of GDP, is far larger for the level of GDP than for its growth rate, and much larger still when countries are compared, due to differences in concepts and techniques. For example, measured GDP growth in Europe would be significantly higher, possibly by as much as half a percentage point annually in certain years, if statistical methods were more similar to those used in the United

States – especially regarding the use of hedonic prices and the measurement of spending on software (Sakellaris and Vijselaar, 2004).

### 2.4.2 Ongoing revisions to the SNA

Although the 1993 SNA has not yet been implemented worldwide, it has already been overtaken in some respects by changes in the economic environment, advances in methodological research and efforts to further harmonise macroeconomic statistics. The national accounts manual – as well as the balance of payments and government statistics manuals published by the IMF – is being revised, and an update is scheduled for publication in 2008. It will take a number of years, however, before the new guidelines are implemented by all countries. By early 2005, agreement had been reached on:

- The treatment of employee stock options, which took off as a form of remuneration during the 1990s but on which the 1993 SNA was silent: they will be treated as part of employee compensation.
- Military expenditures: the 1993 SNA recommended that outlays on weapons be expensed, irrespective of their expected service lives. In other words, they were not to be treated as investment, unless they could be used for civilian purposes. In the future, all military assets deemed to provide an ongoing capability to achieve their objective for more than a year will have to be capitalised.
- Provisions for termination costs (say for nuclear plants): they will be included by anticipation in depreciation calculations.
- The measurement of output in the non-life insurance sector, which was an issue in particular following the 11 September 2001 terrorist attacks, when it had significant effects on GDP and on the balance of payments. Under the 1993 SNA guidelines, recorded output in this sector (which reflects premia minus claims) drops when disasters hit, which is unfortunate as it is in these circumstances that the insurance service is activated, and because it entails volatility in the output series for this sector, which after some catastrophes even becomes negative. The new SNA will redefine output using expected rather than observed claims (as already is the case in US accounts) so that it reflects actual insurance activity and becomes much smoother.

Several other points still open for discussion were:

- The treatment of pension schemes: the 1993 SNA makes a distinction between social-security schemes and employer-insurance schemes, and among the latter between funded and unfunded schemes, but in several cases it does not recognise pension obligations as liabilities of the schemes and financial assets of the beneficiaries, notably for unfunded pension schemes set up by government units; some countries (including Australia and Canada) have already departed from the 1993 SNA, recognising government liabilities as they accrue as well as the corresponding assets of households.
- The treatment of R&D spending: a recurring concern among national accountants is whether, unlike what is prescribed in the 1993 SNA, R&D outlays

should be capitalised to build up to an intangible produced asset called 'knowledge'. However, this raises difficult questions regarding the treatment of unsuccessful R&D, the choice of the rate of depreciation, the calculation of the R&D expenditure deflator as well as the value of the 'knowledge' asset.

- The contours and transactions of the general government sector: given the growing emphasis on public finance monitoring, notably in Europe in the context of the Stability and Growth Pact, recommendations regarding the delineation of the general government sector and the treatment of specific transactions such as capital injections, securitisation, public-private partnerships and so forth are being developed for inclusion in the SNA.

Nevertheless, some important issues remain unresolved:

- The treatment of business spending on software: while the 1993 SNA recommends the capitalisation of software, statistical offices follow different practices. Some treat their purchases as intermediate consumption and others (notably in the United States) as investment, which distorts comparisons of GDP (Lequiller, 2001).
- The pre-eminence of GDP versus net domestic product (NDP, equal to GDP minus depreciation): the 1993 SNA does note that NDP is theoretically superior, since NDP takes into account the capital consumed in the course of production, but at the same time it mentions practical reasons to favour GDP.

### 2.4.3   Measuring welfare

The national accounts focus on the production and exchange of marketed goods and services. They do extend to public services, but value them in a rather crude way, as a sum of costs, ignoring any notional profit and therefore potentially underestimating the associated value added (a problem which is also being revisited in the context of the aforementioned review). As noted in Section 2.1, the national accounts simply exclude a whole range of activities undertaken at home, which in theory could be included as services provided to other members of the household or to oneself, and on some estimates would then account for a substantial chunk of GDP. In that sense, the coverage of the national accounts is somewhat incomplete, reflecting statistical hurdles but also underlying normative views on the relative value of various human occupations.

There are also other reasons why GDP per capita is a poor measure of welfare. One is that GDP increases when some undesirable events occur: car accidents, for example, add to GDP since they generate business in car manufacturing and repair, and so do traffic jams, which increase spending on transportation. More generally, GDP is recorded without netting out the induced environmental impoverishment in the form of pollution and exhaustion of finite natural resources. That said, attempts have been made to factor in such costs, particularly in the form of satellite systems gravitating around the core SNA such as the integrated environmental and economic accounting system (see Box 2.6).

*Box 2.6* **Greening the national accounts**

In recent years, methods have been developed to combine economic and environmental information so as to measure the contribution of the environment to the economy, and the impact of the economy on the environment. The handbook *Integrated Environmental and Economic Accounting 2003*, referred to as SEEA 2003, presents a satellite system of the 1993 SNA allowing monitoring of these interactions. It comprises:

- Flow accounts for pollution, energy and materials, which provide information at the industry level about the use of energy and materials as inputs to production and the generation of pollutants and solid waste.
- Environmental protection and resource management expenditure accounts, which identify expenditures incurred by industry, government and households to protect the environment or to manage natural resources. They build on the elements of the 1993 SNA which are relevant to the management of the environment to show how environment-related transactions can be made more explicit.
- Non-market valuation techniques, including calculation of macroeconomic aggregates adjusted for depletion and degradation costs.
- Natural resource asset accounts, which record stocks and changes in stocks of natural resources such as land, fish, forest, water and minerals (Table 2.6).

*Table 2.6* **Illustrative natural resource asset account**

Opening stock
    + Increases during the year
        New discoveries of minerals
        Natural growth of plants and animals
        Land reclamation
    − Decreases during the year
        Extraction of minerals
        Soil erosion
        Loss of capacity of reservoirs due to silting
        Harvesting of plants and animals
        Natural death of plants and animals
        Loss of animals due to drought
= Closing stock

*Source:* SEEA 2003.

Environmentally modified aggregates can be compiled along the following lines (Bartelmus, 1999):

- Supply-use identity: $GDP + M = EC + C + (I - EC) + X$, where GDP stands for output, and $EC$ for environmental depletion and degradation costs associated with production and consumption.
- Value-added identity for industry $i$: $EVA_i = O_i - IC_i - CC_i - EC_i = VA_i - EC_i$, where $EVA$ stands for environmentally adjusted value added, $O$ for gross output, $IC$ for intermediate consumption, $CC$ for fixed capital consumption and $VA$ for value added.
- Domestic-product identity for the whole economy: $EDP = \Sigma_i EVA_i - EC^h = NDP - EC$, where $EDP$ stands for environmentally-adjusted net domestic product and $EC^h$ for the environmental costs generated by households.

- Alternatively: $EDP = C + I - CC - EC + X - M$, where $I - CC - EC$ can be viewed as environmentally adjusted net capital formation, an indicator that can be used to assess the sustainability of economic performance.

To compute such identities and indicators, a monetary value must be put on natural assets, even if they are not traded in markets. A variety of valuation techniques can be used. In some cases, there are market prices, for instance for traded pollution permits, the price of which represents a market value for environmental waste absorption capacities. Market prices may also allow indirect estimation of pollution costs, say, in the case of two similar housing units, one of which is in a polluted area and the other not. In other cases, hypothetical maintenance costs can in principle be calculated, defined as what it would have taken to keep the environment unaffected, although in practice such calculations are very challenging, if not impossible. Yet another approach is contingent valuation, namely estimating what agents would have been ready to pay to avoid environmental costs, which is also difficult to implement.

Yet another limitation of GDP as a measure of welfare is that it ignores important dimensions of well-being other than monetary income, such as life expectancy and literacy. The United Nations Development Programme (UNDP) thus monitors a broad set of human development indicators of which GDP per capita is only one component (Box 2.7). Their headline human development index (HDI) is positively correlated with GDP per capita but not perfectly (Figure 2.5). Moreover,

*Figure 2.5*   **GDP per capita and the human development index** (observations for 2002)

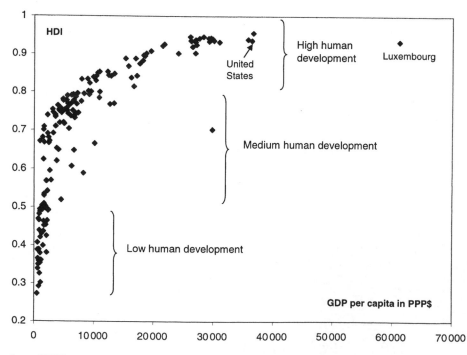

*Source*: UNDP.

---

*Box 2.7*  **Human development indicators**

In the spirit of Sen's work on welfare (Anand and Sen, 1994), the UNDP publishes a head-line HDI as well as a number of derivative versions thereof. The HDI measures a country's average achievement in basic human capabilities, indicating whether its citizens lead long and healthy lives, are educated and knowledgeable and enjoy a decent standard of living. These three basic components of human development – longevity, knowledge and standard of living – enter the HDI with equal weights. They are measured respectively by life expectancy, by a combination of adult literacy (with a weight of $\frac{2}{3}$) and mean years of schooling (with a weight of $\frac{1}{3}$), and by real GDP per capita adjusted for the local cost of living (that is, in purchasing power parity (PPP) terms).

The HDI sets a minimum and a maximum for each dimension and then locates each country in relation to these scales expressed as a value between 0 and 1. Since the mini-mum adult literacy rate is 0 and the maximum is 100 per cent, the literacy component of knowledge for a country where the literacy rate is 80 per cent would be 0.8. Similarly, the minimum for life expectancy is 25 and the maximum 85 years, so the longevity compo-nent for a country where life expectancy is 55 years would be 0.5. For income, the mini-mum is $100 (in PPP terms) and the maximum (ignoring Luxembourg) is $40 000. The log of income is used rather than income itself, consistent with the notion that achieving a respectable level of human development does not require unlimited income (although this treatment may look somewhat arbitrary). The arithmetic average of the scores for the three dimensions constitutes the HDI, which by construction also ranges between 0 and 1. In 2002, Norway had the highest HDI, and the United States was ranked eighth.

Other indicators have been developed by the UNDP to capture inequality and poverty. The HPI-1 (Human Poverty Index for developing countries) measures deprivations in the same three aspects of human development as the HDI. The HPI-2 (Human Poverty Index for industrialised countries) includes, in addition to these dimensions, social exclusion. For the HPI-1, deprivations in longevity are measured by the percentage of newborns not expected to survive to age 40, deprivations in knowledge by the percentage of illiterate adults, and deprivations in a decent standard of living by the percentage of people with-out access to safe water and the percentage of underweight children below the age of five. For the HPI-2, deprivations in longevity are measured by the percentage of newborns not expected to survive to age 60, deprivations in knowledge by the percentage of people who are functionally illiterate and deprivations in a decent standard of living by the per-centage of people living below the income poverty line (set at 50 per cent of the median disposable household income). Social exclusion is measured by the rate of long-term (12 months or more) unemployment of the labour force. The United States stands out with a comparatively high GDP per capita coupled with a high level of deprivations.

Lastly, the Gender-related Development Index measures the same variables as the HDI but adjusting for gender inequalities.

---

the relationship is non-linear, with income gains at the bottom of the interna-tional scale increasing the HDI much more than similarly sized income gains in rich countries. In some cases, the evolution of GDP per capita and the HDI diverge dramatically, for instance in African countries beset by the AIDS epidemic, where the narrowly economic indicator holds up well or continues to rise even as the HDI collapses.

This strand of analysis further includes work on inequality and poverty indica-tors: the average welfare level associated with a given level of per capita GDP may not be the same depending on the distribution of income, the presumption being that a very uneven distribution will make for lower welfare. In recent years, increasing attention has also been paid to the role of social capital, namely the idea that social relationships play a critical role, alongside individual attributes, in economic activity and human well-being: social networks coupled with shared reciprocity norms, values and understandings favour mutual trust and facilitate cooperation, including in economic pursuits (Healy and Côté, 2001). While they would generally have positive spillover effects on the rest of society, some forms of social capital can have a detrimental impact, for instance in the case of mafias. Social capital and its contribution are, however, difficult to measure (Durlauf and Fafchamps, 2004).

Lastly, a somewhat different approach to welfare has been developed at the World Bank (Dixon and Hamilton, 1996), looking at well-being from the angle of sustainable development. The focus here is on the stocks of assets broadly defined, both natural and man-made, that support well-being: the present value of natural wealth (minerals and fossil fuels, timber, non-timber benefits of forests, cropland, pastureland and protected areas), produced assets (calculated using a perpetual inventory model based on investment data and assumed lifetimes for the different types of assets) and human resources (derived residually, based on gross national income minus natural resource rents and the depreciation of produced assets). The estimates carried out in the mid-1990s using this approach showed that the gap between poor and rich countries was several times larger for human than for natural resources.

# 3

# Incoming News and Near-Term Forecasting

The first step in economic forecasting is to establish where the economy actually is. This constitutes a prerequisite for a proper forecast of where it is heading (Section 3.1). The starting point is therefore the collection of a great variety of economic information with a view to assessing the state of the economy before national accounts data become available, weeks or months down the road (Section 3.2). In this regard, survey data can provide precious insights, almost in 'real time', and usefully complement the 'hard data' due to be released later on (Section 3.3). Once reasonably comprehensive information has been gathered, the challenge is to make sense of it, by adjusting the raw data in various ways and combining some of them to build summary indicators (Section 3.4). In this context, bridge models are especially useful for near-term forecasting purposes (Section 3.5). Even so, macroeconomic monitoring involves difficult trade-offs between abundant but often seemingly inconsistent bits of information (Section 3.6).

## 3.1 Monitoring the ups and downs

Understanding recent economic developments is the first building block for longer-run forecasts.

### 3.1.1 Capturing ongoing trends

Gauging where the economy is at present is difficult, since many of the key data come out with considerable lags. In fact, even the recent past has to be estimated, or 'forecasted'. This is important in many settings. Policymakers in particular need to assess the state of the economy in order to take decisions long before the statistical office renders its *ex post* verdict. Thus, central banks spend considerable resources monitoring incoming data. Governments also scrutinise them, for example to check whether budget execution is on track and to take measures if it is not. Financial market participants, whose trades are quintessentially forward-looking, are equally eager to find out where things stand and where the next economic turn lies. Bond market 'vigilantes', in particular, closely follow all the ups and downs, trying to anticipate whatever comes next. And, in turn, reactions in financial markets are closely monitored by decision-makers, be they public authorities or business leaders, and at times influence their own behaviour.

### 3.1.2   Laying the basis for longer-run forecasts

Understanding the recent past offers clues about the immediate future. For example, an acceleration of output is likely to translate into a pick-up in hires a few months or quarters ahead, which itself will boost household income and therefore consumption. Conversely, some phenomena may foreshadow a subsequent correction. For instance, involuntary stockbuilding signals future destocking.

More mechanically, recent developments have direct near-term implications, since the way the data have evolved in the past will to some extent shape future statistical releases. Consider a strong increase in activity at the beginning of year $t$. This will have a major impact on average annual growth in year $t$, but not much of an impact on growth in year $t + 1$. But if activity rises sharply towards the end of year $t$, average annual growth in year $t$ will not be affected much, while average annual growth in year $t + 1$ will typically be significantly higher (see Box 3.1). In that sense,

---

**Box 3.1   Carry-over effects**

Carry-over effects can be thought of as 'what's in the bag' going forward, assuming that the variable under consideration (usually GDP, but also the price level or other variables) stays flat. Take US real GDP as from the start of 2004, once the advance estimate for the last quarter of 2003 was published. The carry-over effect is the average annual growth rate that would have obtained in 2004 had real GDP remained flat throughout 2004 at its end-2003 level. Since real GDP grew substantially in the course of 2003, its average level in 2004 would have been around 2 per cent higher than its average level in 2003 even in the absence of any further growth in the course of 2004 (Figure 3.1).

Arithmetically, let $g^1_{-1}$, $g^2_{-1}$, $g^3_{-1}$ and $g^4_{-1}$ be the quarter-on-previous-quarter (non-annualised) growth rates of real GDP in year $t - 1$ and $g^1$, $g^2$, $g^3$ and $g^4$ be the ones in year $t$. Let $Y^i_{-1}$ be the level of real GDP in quarter $i$ of year $t - 1$, $Y^i$ its level in quarter $i$ of year $t$ and $g$ the average annual growth rate of real GDP in year $t$ over year $t - 1$. Then:

$$g = (Y^1 + Y^2 + Y^3 + Y^4)/(Y^1_{-1} + Y^2_{-1} + Y^3_{-1} + Y^4_{-1}) - 1$$
$$= Y^1 [1 + (1 + g^2) + (1 + g^2)(1 + g^3) + (1 + g^2)(1 + g^3)(1 + g^4)]$$
$$/ \{Y^1 [1/(1 + g^1) + 1/(1 + g^1)(1 + g^4_{-1}) + 1/(1 + g^1)(1 + g^4_{-1})(1 + g^3_{-1})$$
$$+ 1/(1 + g^1)(1 + g^4_{-1})(1 + g^3_{-1})(1 + g^2_{-1})]\} - 1$$

Given that quarter-on-previous-quarter growth rates are typically small, one can use first-order approximations of the type $(1 + x)(1 + y) \approx 1 + x + y$, $1/(1 + x) \approx 1 - x$ and $(1 + x)/(1 + z) \approx 1 + x - z$. Thus, simplifying by $Y^1$:

$$g \approx [1 + (1 + g^2) + (1 + g^2 + g^3) + (1 + g^2 + g^3 + g^4)]$$
$$/ [(1 - g^1) + (1 - g^1 - g^4_{-1}) + (1 - g^1 - g^4_{-1} - g^3_{-1}) + (1 - g^1 - g^4_{-1} - g^3_{-1} - g^2_{-1})] - 1$$
$$\approx (4 + 3g^2 + 2g^3 + g^4)/(4 - 4g^1 - 3g^4_{-1} - 2g^3_{-1} - g^2_{-1}) - 1$$
$$\approx (1 + 0.75g^2 + 0.5g^3 + 0.25g^4)/(1 - g^1 - 0.75g^4_{-1} - 0.5g^3_{-1} - 0.25g^2_{-1}) - 1$$
$$\approx g^1 + 0.75(g^2 + g^4_{-1}) + 0.5(g^3 + g^3_{-1}) + 0.25(g^4 + g^2_{-1})$$

Hence, the average annual growth rate of real GDP in year $t$ over year $t - 1$ can be approximated as a weighted average of quarterly growth rates, with the weights being 1 for the first quarter of year $t$, $\frac{3}{4}$ for the second quarter of year $t$ and the fourth quarter of year $t - 1$, $\frac{1}{2}$ for the third quarter of year $t$ and the third quarter of year $t - 1$ and $\frac{1}{4}$ for the fourth quarter of year $t$ and the second quarter of year $t - 1$. It is influenced far more by developments towards the end of year $t - 1$ than by what happens towards the end of year $t$.

Going back to the numerical example, the US advance estimate for the fourth quarter of 2003 published in early 2004 showed that US GDP had been growing by respectively 3.1, 8.2 and 4.0 per cent in the second, third and fourth quarter of 2003 at annual rates (and by 0.8, 2.0 and 1.0 per cent at quarter-on-quarter rates). Hence, one can calculate the carry-over effect for the average annual growth rate in 2004 at the end of 2003 using the above formula, with $g^2_{-1} = 0.8$, $g^3_{-1} = 2$, $g^4_{-1} = 1$ and $g^1 = g^2 = g^3 = g^4 = 0$: $g \approx 0.75 \times 1 + 0.5 \times 2 + 0.25 \times 0.8 \approx 2$ per cent.

*Figure 3.1* **Inherited growth**

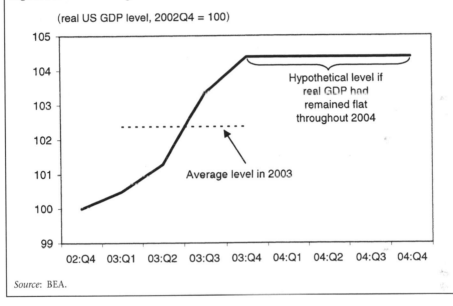

(real US GDP level, 2002Q4 = 100)

*Source*: BEA.

average annual growth in 2005 is almost a done deal once the GDP data for the third quarter of 2005 are out, and already a lot is known about average annual growth in 2006 once the GDP data for the last quarter of 2005 are published. In sum, short-term monitoring lays the foundation for forecasting in two ways: by drawing lessons from recent developments, not least to understand why past forecasts were off the mark; and by using fresh information to anticipate near-term evolutions.

## 3.2 Collecting economic information

Recent economic information typically consists of bits and pieces of variable quality, many of which are subject to substantial revisions later on, and some of which are only loosely related to a proper national accounts framework. Sifting the incoming data is a heavy job, with no end in sight. In addition, it requires making tricky judgement calls given the trade-off between timeliness and reliability. Yet, it is an indispensable and crucial step.

Broadly speaking, the data that need to be collected can be grouped into five categories: domestic production, the international environment, economic policy variables, prices and private demand. They are analysed using a number of standard statistical descriptors (Box 3.2).

Monitoring supply-side developments in 'real time' is difficult, since the quarterly national accounts data come out with a lag and sometimes do not even provide a

---

**Box 3.2   Statistical workhorses**

Let $A_a$ denote the value observed in year $a$ for some economic variable, $Q_{a,q}$ its value observed in quarter $q$ of year $a$, and $M_{a,m}$ its value in month $m$ of year $a$ (or $M_{q,m}$ its value in month $m$ of quarter $q$). When frequency does not matter, the variable is simply called $X_t$. The following concepts are commonly used in forecasting.

*Summary statistics*

- The mean $M$ of the series $X_t$ between $t = 1$ and $t = T$ is its 'first moment': $M = (\Sigma_t X_t)/T$.
- The median of $X_t$ is another measure of central tendency, namely the dividing point such that half of the observations of $X_t$ are above and half below.
- The standard deviation $\sigma$ is a measure of dispersion such that $\sigma^2 = [\Sigma_t (X_t - M)^2]/T$. Note that $\sigma^2$ is also known as the variance or 'second moment'. When $M$ is not known but estimated based on the observations $X_t$, the sum of squares has to be divided by $(T - 1)$ instead of $T$ to obtain an unbiased estimator of $\sigma^2$.
- The skewness $S$ or 'third moment' characterizes the degree of asymmetry of a distribution around its mean: $S = \{\Sigma_t [(X_t - M)/\sigma]^3\}/T$. A curve is said to be skewed to the right, or positively skewed, if it tails off toward the high end of the scale. While the mean and standard deviation are dimensional quantities, that is, have the same units as $X_t$, the skewness is non-dimensional. It is a pure number that describes only the shape of the distribution.
- The kurtosis $K$ or 'fourth moment', which is also a pure number, measures the heaviness of the tails of a distribution, compared with a normal distribution: $K = \{\Sigma_t [(X_t - M)/\sigma]^4\}/T$. For a normal distribution, $K = 3$. If $K > 3$, the distribution is said to be leptokurtic and if $K < 3$, it is said to be platykurtic.

*Values and volumes*

- Let $N_t$ denote the nominal value of a variable, that is its value at the prices prevailing in period or at date $t$.
- Let $V_t$ be the corresponding volume, that is its value at the prices of some base period or date: $V_t$ is obtained by deflating $N_t$ by the change in the relevant price index since that time.
- Let $I_t$ denote the index value of a series $X_t$, be it a nominal value, a volume or a price. Often $I_t$ is set at 100 for the base period: $I_0 = 100$. Then $I_t = X_t/X_0 \times 100$.
- If $I_t$ is the relevant price index, the following relationship must hold: $N_t/N_{t-1} = V_t/V_{t-1} \times I_t/I_{t-1}$.

*Growth rates*

- Growth of $X_t$ between $t = 1$ and $t = 2$, in per cent: $(X_2 - X_1)/X_1 \times 100$. 'Growth' is often implicitly referring to the change in real GDP (which can be negative of course).

- Year-average growth refers to $A_a/A_{a-1}$, or $(Q_{a,1} + \cdots + Q_{a,4})/(Q_{a-1,1} + \cdots + Q_{a-1,4})$ for quarterly observations, or $(M_{a,1} + \cdots + M_{a,12})/(M_{a-1,1} + \cdots + M_{a-1,12})$ for monthly observations.
- Year-on-year growth generally refers to growth over the past four quarters or 12 months in quarter $q$ or month $m$ of year $a$, that is to $Q_{a,q}/Q_{a-1,q}$ or $M_{a,m}/M_{a-1,m}$.
- Within-year growth, or growth over the four quarters of year $a$, is growth observed in the course of the elapsed year, when standing at the end of year $a$, that is $Q_{a,4}/Q_{a-1,4}$ with quarterly data and $M_{a,12}/M_{a-1,12}$ with monthly data.
- Quarter-on-quarter growth typically refers to $Q_{a,q}/Q_{a,q-1}$, month-on-month growth to $M_{a,m}/M_{a,m-1}$ and within-quarter growth to $M_{q,3}/M_{q-1,3}$ (where 3 stands for the latest month of the quarter).
- Intra-annual rates of growth are often corrected for seasonal oscillations (see Section 3.4). In this context, they can sometimes be annualised (as it is often the case in the United States), to get a sense of what the pace of change would be if growth continued for four quarters or 12 months at the same rate: $[(Q_q/Q_{q-1})^4 - 1] \times 100$ for quarterly data,* $[(M_m/M_{m-1})^{12} - 1] \times 100$ for monthly data, or $[(M_m/M_{m-3})^4 - 1] \times 100$ for the annualised rate of change over the past three months.
- The contribution of a variable $X_t$ to the growth of a variable $Y_t$ is defined as $(X_t - X_{t-1})/Y_{t-1} \times 100$, and is thus expressed in percentage points of $Y_{t-1}$.
- The base effect refers to an evolution of $X_t$ that reflects what happened one year earlier. For example, suppose that month-on-month inflation is 0.1 per cent (or approximately 1.2 per cent annualised) at all times except in January 2005, when owing to a hike in value-added tax, the consumer price level in addition shifts upwards by 5 per cent. Then year-on-year inflation jumps from 1.2 to 6.3 per cent in January 2005 and stays there for one year, falling back to 1.2 per cent in January 2006. The fall in January 2006 is then attributed to a base effect (due to what happened one year earlier).

*Figure 3.2* **The base effect**
(impact of a one-time price level shift on inflation)

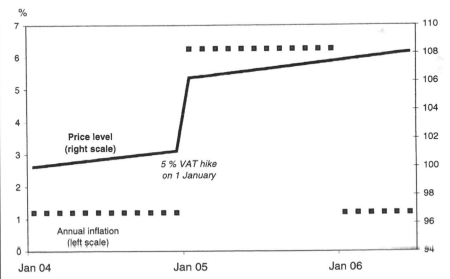

Note:
\* This will often be characterised as quarterly growth 'in annualised terms' or, as in the United States, 'at annual rates' (not be confused with year-on-year growth).

detailed decomposition by sector (notably in the United States). Hence, one needs to work from gross output data, making assumptions about intermediate consumption to derive estimates of value added. Supply-side indicators are readily available for industry (output, orders), agriculture, construction (housing starts and completions) and trade (turnover), but less so for services, which account for the lion's share of GDP. In Japan, however, an indicator of service sector output has been developed analogous to the industrial output index, and efforts are under way in a number of OECD countries to monitor service sector output better.

The incompleteness of the supply-side statistics can be remedied in two ways. One is by using sectoral labour market data and, in particular, statistics on hours worked (for instance, the very detailed monthly reports released by the US Bureau of Labour Statistics). The other is by exploiting survey information (see Section 3.3). In addition, comparing the supply-side information with that obtained on the demand side is key, although the latter is often also incomplete at the monthly frequency. In principle, data on the income side too can serve as useful checks, but they tend to be even less complete, even at the annual frequency.

On the external side, forecasters need to take into account:

- World demand for the output produced by the country under consideration, that is, the imports of that country's trading partners. This information is available at current prices for almost all countries (and easily accessible in the IMF's Direction of Trade Statistics), and in volume terms – though only for a number of them and with significant lags and uncertainty.
- The evolution of the country's competitiveness, which depends on exchange rate, price and cost developments in that country and in its trading partners. Relatively sophisticated indicators such as cost-competitiveness in manufacturing are available for almost all OECD countries and CPI-based real effective exchange rates are available for virtually all economies.
- Financial variables, such as interest rates and equity prices in the major countries (see Sections 8.2 and 8.3).
- Commodity price developments, in particular as regards oil (see Section 8.5).

One problem is that these data are not strictly comparable across countries and come out at different times. To some extent, using OECD, IMF or BIS statistics allows this difficulty to be overcome, but at the expense of delays. In practice, therefore, there is a trade-off between data timeliness and consistency.

Turning to fiscal data, a wealth of information is generally released by governments on budgetary developments at the monthly, quarterly and annual frequency. Some of it is useful to gauge the evolution of private sector demand, for instance value-added tax receipts. But its heterogeneity and pitfalls make it difficult to exploit effectively. Among the complications associated with this type of data are the following:

- Some of the most important fiscal variables are available only at an annual frequency, and with delay.

- There are important differences between the budget and the national accounts. For instance, in the case of investment, outlays by the military, which are considered as investment in the budget, are generally not treated as such in the national accounts, where they show up as intermediate consumption (except for dual-use investments). Another example are privatisation receipts, which are treated as revenue in the budget accounts but not in the national accounts (where they are the counterpart of an asset transfer). Moreover, budgets are often drawn up in cash terms, whereas the national accounts are based on accrual accounting.
- There is usually a whole range of public sector entities: besides the central government, there are subnational governments and social security bodies, which publish less information and less frequently. This is particularly problematic in federal countries, such as the United States or Germany. In practice, analysts thus often focus on central government data, even though they typically represent less or even far less than half of the general government sector.

In contrast, monetary and financial variables are more readily available. However, this information is not that easy to factor into a short-run forecast, since these variables tend to influence activity and spending with lags and through complex channels. For instance, monetary aggregates are available on a monthly basis but they are at best correlated with inflation two or three years down the road. That said, some financial variables are more relevant for short-run monitoring, for example credit aggregates and interest rate spreads.

Price data are usually very abundant, as most countries publish numerous monthly and quarterly indices. However, the relevance and quality of this type of data varies, as underlined in Section 2.3. Moreover, information on asset prices (especially for housing) is often not readily available from one and the same source. Besides prices, a number of other variables are indicative of the tensions between supply and demand: capacity utilisation rates, margins, the unemployment rate or job offers.

As concerns household demand, data on purchases of goods and some services are available rapidly (car registrations, retail sales), as are data on housing investment. But they are very volatile, and highly sensitive to special factors such as the weather, promotions and so forth. Household purchases are also difficult to relate to their incomes, as the saving rate often displays considerable short-run variation. In addition, incomes themselves are not captured that precisely: while headline wage series are often available, information on benefits is scarcer; in addition, labour compensation is an imperfect proxy of households' total income, since the share of non-wage incomes may fluctuate significantly (partly but not exclusively as a function of the cycle). Furthermore, many of the data are at current prices and on a cash basis, rather than in volume terms and on an accruals basis.

Enterprise investment and stockbuilding is even harder to monitor. Investment indicators come out with long lags and some of them are not aligned on national account concepts or refer to longer-run horizons (multi-year projects). Two specific problems are that a substantial chunk of capital spending is undertaken by new firms, whose activities are not captured well, and that investment outlays tend to be concentrated in time, as they take place at discrete intervals rather than on a continuous basis. While investment in transportation capital goods is relatively well measured, spending on other types of equipment is often estimated indirectly (as a residual based on output and international trade data). In some cases (notably in the United States and Germany), it can be monitored through statistics on orders of durable goods. Regarding investment in buildings, data on the delivery of permits can be used based on some assumptions as to average construction times (as for households' residential investment). Data on stockbuilding are usually very poor, even taking into account the information available on the inventories of certain goods (raw materials, agricultural products), the enterprise-level data and the survey data. Given that investment and especially stockbuilding are very volatile and contribute far more than proportionately to fluctuations in GDP (see Section 5.1), these data problems are very serious.

## 3.3   Business and consumer surveys

Against the backdrop of the shortcomings of the 'hard' high-frequency data, survey evidence, which describes many facets of economic activity, can be extremely helpful – provided it is used properly.

### 3.3.1   How surveys are carried out

Business and consumer surveys have become very important tools for short-run forecasting purposes. They are conducted regularly by public or private bodies, who ask economic agents how they perceive the current situation and near-term outlook, be it in general or as far as their own prospects are concerned. Though a few are quantitative, the questions are mostly of a qualitative nature. Indeed, qualitative questions (for instance, is production up, stable or down?) allow for faster answers and, in the case of firms, they make it possible for managers rather than subordinates to reply. The information is then presented in the form of balances of opinions – also called diffusion indices – which broadly speaking can be thought of as the difference between percentages of respondents giving favourable and unfavourable answers, and measure to what extent the indicated change is prevalent throughout the sample population.

The samples are usually quite small and stable, so as to increase speed and enhance consistency over time: having the same person answer the questionnaire facilitates prompt replies and means that the questions, especially the qualitative ones, will be understood in the same way from one month or quarter to the next. Small samples, however, imply that the results will be particularly sensitive to the methods used to aggregate individual replies – an issue for firms more than for households, though, since there are a variety of ways to weigh the former (usually by taking into account both the relative size of the firm and the economic importance of its sector) whilst the latter all receive the same weight. Another tricky issue is how to deal with missing replies: one technique is to retain only those respondents who answered in both months when computing month-on-month changes.

In the European Union (EU) the European Commission has long published EU-wide business and consumer survey results, putting a lot of effort into ensuring that the underlying data are as comparable as possible across countries (Box 3.3).

---

*Box 3.3* **European Commission surveys**

Since the early 1960s, the European Commission coordinates and publishes the results of harmonised business surveys across member countries and since the early 1970s it does so for consumer surveys as well. At present, 110 000 firms are surveyed during the first fortnight of every month in the industry, construction, retail trade, and service sectors and so are 33 000 consumers. In addition, 42 000 industrial firms are polled twice a year in an investment survey. The answers are used as such but also summarised in synthetic confidence indicators, typically defined as arithmetic means of seasonally adjusted balances of the answers to questions closely related to the reference variable they track. EU-wide and euro-area-wide indicators are calculated as weighted averages of the country-aggregate replies, and the weights are updated annually.

More specifically, the balances are computed as the difference (in percentage points of total answers) between positive and negative options. If a question has three alternative options, 'positive' (the exact wording varies and may also be 'up', 'more', 'more than sufficient', 'good', 'too large', 'increase', 'improve', and so forth), 'neutral' ('unchanged', 'as much', 'sufficient', 'satisfactory', 'adequate', and so forth) and 'negative' ('down', 'less', 'not sufficient', 'too small', 'decline', and so forth), and if $P$, $E$ and $M$ stand for the shares of respondents having chosen respectively the positive, neutral, and negative option, the balance is $B = P - M$. A similar type of calculation applies for questions with a richer menu of options. Hence, balance values range from $-100$ (all respondents choose the (most) negative option) to $+100$ (all respondents choose the (most) positive option). Though in theory the questions explicitly refer to a 'normal' situation for a given period of time, the opinions recorded may still be influenced by events taking place at the same time every year, for example Christmas or certain public holidays. This is filtered through seasonal adjustment procedures.

The broadest survey indicator published by the European Commission is the EU economic sentiment indicator, which combines judgements and perceptions of firms and consumers by aggregating the opinion balances of the confidence indicators for industry (with a weight of 40 per cent), services (30 per cent), consumers (20 per cent), construction (5 per cent) and retail trade (5 per cent).

The industrial confidence indicator for instance (shown in Figure 3.3. below) is the arithmetic average of the balances of the answers to the following questions (the last one with an inverted sign):

- Do you consider your current overall order books to be more than sufficient (above normal), sufficient (normal for the season) or not sufficient (below normal)?
- Do you expect your production over the next three months to increase, to remain unchanged or to decrease?
- Do you consider your current stock of finished products to be too large (above normal), adequate (normal for the season) or too small (below normal)?

The institutions providing inputs for this purpose are typically leading public or private bodies, such as national statistical institutes (in the case of France) or prominent think tanks which conduct surveys that are well known in their own right (such as IFO in Germany).

Other prominent European indices include Reuters' purchasing managers' index (PMI), published on the first working day of each month for manufacturing and on the third day for services, both for (almost all) individual countries and for the euro area as a whole. These series are based on surveys conducted by UK-based NTC Research in conjunction with national members of the purchasing associations and cover over 5000 companies altogether. The Reuters PMIs are diffusion indices, with a reading above 50 suggesting growth and a reading below contraction (just like the ISM's PMI in the United States, described below). They reflect 'hard' evidence only ('is your output up, stable or down?'), and not 'softer' opinions about the future, and are therefore less forward-looking than business sentiment measures. They are highly regarded but started only in 1998.

The United States has an even longer-standing tradition of surveying businesses and households. The most prominent surveys include the ones conducted by the Institute for Supply Management (ISM), the University of Michigan and the New York-based Conference Board (Box 3.4). The ISM's PMI for manufacturing is available on a monthly basis since 1948. The one for services is more recent, starting in 1998. The monthly series for the consumer confidence indices published by the University of Michigan and the Conference Board go back to the late 1970s (and much earlier for lower-frequency data).

In Japan, the most prominent business survey is the Bank of Japan's Tankan (Box 3.5). One of its limitations is that it is quarterly. Monthly surveys include NTC Research's manufacturing PMI, based on a sample of 300 companies, which is internationally comparable and is also released on the first working day of each month. However, it only started in 2001, so that its performance is difficult to assess. Consumer and business confidence surveys are also conducted by the government, with the Economic and Social Research Institute (ESRI).

Finally, it should be noted that NTC Research also publishes a global PMI aggregating the main economies (Williamson, 2002).

### 3.3.2   Interpreting survey results

Paradoxically, qualitative questions tend to be more informative than quantitative ones, despite the fact that it is difficult to summarise their answers using simple averages. This is because firm managers have an overall sense of how the enterprise is doing but less of a precise knowledge of detailed numbers. It also reflects problems of comparability across firms and sectors, which render aggregation more hazardous. The quantitative surveys on investment conducted under the aegis of the European Commission are a good illustration: expectations and outcomes often differ radically (as shown for the case of France in Table 3.1). Likewise, the quantitative information provided by managers on prices and wages does not add much to what is already known from the detailed price and wage statistics. One exception relates to capacity utilisation rates, for which respondents are asked for

*Box 3.4* **Some leading US surveys**

The ISM was formerly known as the National Association of Purchasing Management (NAPM). Issued on the first business day of each month, its manufacturing PMI is one of the most closely watched near-term economic barometers. On the third business day of the month, the ISM releases its non-manufacturing PMI, which covers the service sector. Respondents to ISM surveys (around 350 purchasing agents in both sectors) indicate each month whether particular activities for their organisation have increased, decreased, or remained unchanged from the previous month. This allows to compute diffusion indices for each activity, calculated as the percentage of respondents reporting 'positive' (for instance that activity has increased) plus $\frac{1}{2}$ of the percentage reporting 'no change'. The composite manufacturing PMI index is compiled on the basis of the seasonally adjusted diffusion indices for the following five indicators, with the weights in parentheses: new orders (30 per cent), production (25 per cent), employment (20 per cent), supplier deliveries (15 per cent) and inventories (10 per cent). According to the ISM, a PMI index above 50 denotes expansion compared with the prior month, whilst a reading under 50 suggests contraction. Other indicators are computed (especially for price developments and export orders) but they do not enter the composite PMI index.

The University of Michigan publishes a widely monitored monthly index of consumer sentiment. It comes out relatively early in the month but is revised later in the month. It is based on a sample of about 500 telephone interviews. The overall index is based on five questions:

1. Are you (and your family living there) better off or worse off financially than a year ago?
2. A year from now, will you (and your family living there) be better off or worse off financially than now, or just about the same?
3. Turning to business conditions in the country as a whole, will the next 12 months be good or bad financially, or what?
4. Will the next five years more likely see continuous good times, periods of widespread unemployment or depression, or what?
5. Is now a good or a bad time for people to buy major household items?

In addition, an index of current economic conditions is compiled, averaging the scores for the first and last question, as well as an index of consumer expectations, averaging those for the other questions.

The Conference Board also publishes a monthly consumer confidence index, based on a survey of some 5 000 households. It is usually released on the last Tuesday of the month. The five underlying questions relate to respondents' appraisal of:

1. Current business conditions.
2. Expected business conditions six months hence.
3. Current employment conditions.
4. Expected employment conditions six months hence.
5. Expected total family income six months hence.

For each question, they can reply positive, negative or neutral. The response proportions to each question are seasonally adjusted. For each question, the positive figure is divided by the sum of the positive and negative to yield a proportion, the 'relative value'. The average relative for 1985 is then used as a benchmark to yield the index value for that question. The consumer confidence index is the average of all five indices. A present situation index is also compiled, as the average of the indices for the first and third question, as well as an expectations index, which averages the indices for the other questions.

---

**Box 3.5    The Tankan survey**

The Tankan is a short-term economic survey of Japanese enterprises carried out in March, June, September and December. Firm coverage has varied somewhat over time, with about 10 500 enterprises in the sample in early 2004. They are divided into three groups, based since 2004 on capitalisation rather than employment: large, medium-sized and small. The survey also provides a sectoral decomposition: manufacturing is divided into 16 categories and non-manufacturing into 14, following the Japan Standard Industrial Classification introduced in 2002. Hence, the results are decomposed in 90 strata (30 industries times three sizes). In addition, a sample of financial institutions is also surveyed (divided into 18 strata).

The survey contains some 40 questions, grouped in four types: judgemental questions, quarterly data, annual projections and number of new graduates hired (the latter only in June and December). Financial institutions are subject only to a subset of these questions. The qualitative judgements (favourable, not so favourable or unfavourable for business conditions; excessive, balanced/adequate or insufficient for demand conditions, inventory levels, production capacity and employment; easy, not so tight or tight for corporate finance; accommodative, not so severe or severe for the lending attitude of financial institutions) are used to calculate diffusion indexes, obtained as the balance of responses with a positive tone minus those with a negative tone (thus ignoring the intermediate answers).

---

*Table 3.1*    **Investment intention surveys: fickle animal spirits**
(investment by French industrial firms, annual per cent change, in value terms)

|  | 1998 | 1999 | 2000 | 2001 | 2002 | 2003 |
|---|---|---|---|---|---|---|
| Business expectations in October of the previous year | 3 | 1 | 3 | 5 | −4 | 4 |
| Outcome as measured in April of the following year | 6 | 5 | 9 | 0 | −13 | −5 |

*Source*: INSEE, *Survey of Investment in Industry.*

a point estimate: this sort of information is usually not available elsewhere and is very useful.[1]

As indicated above, qualitative surveys are conducted somewhat differently across countries and sectors. For purposes of comparability, it is useful to normalise them, that is to translate the results into departures from a long-run average, divided by the standard deviation of the series (Figure 3.3). This also allows control for any structural bias in the responses (for instance, if for some reason

---

[1] There is more than one way to define capacity utilisation. For instance, the US Federal Reserve's measure of capacity utilisation assumes the availability of additional labour, if needed, as is standard practice in most other countries. In contrast, the Institute of Supply Management measures the capacity of plants to produce with their current labour force. Following a significant cyclical contraction in manufacturing employment, as witnessed in the latest US downturn, a definition of capacity relying on workers in place will indicate much less slack than one that does not consider current employees as a limiting factor.

*Figure 3.3*   **Business confidence**
(deviation from long-run average, in units of standard deviation)

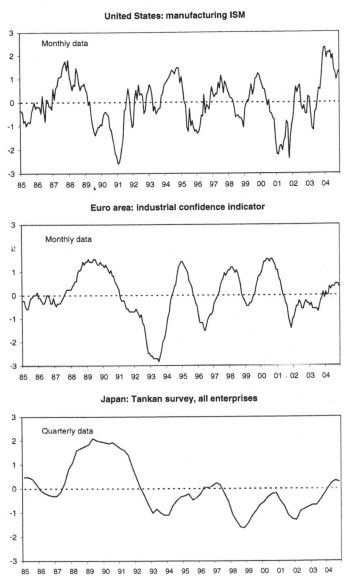

**United States: manufacturing ISM**

**Euro area: industrial confidence indicator**

**Japan: Tankan survey, all enterprises**

*Sources:* Institute for Supply Management; European Commission; Bank of Japan.

there is a propensity to err on the pessimistic side). But even then, a number of caveats ought to be borne in mind:

- Depending on the period within the month when the survey is actually conducted, it may reflect the previous calendar month more than the current month, or vice versa.

- The horizon over which respondents actually reason may not be the one stated in the question: French businesses asked about their own production prospects are supposed to indicate what they expect over the next three months, as opposed to six months in Germany, although in practice they tend to implicitly look at a similar horizon.
- Answers to questions about firms' own situation are generally more informative than those about their perception of the economy-wide outlook.
- The vaguer questions posed to households about their view of overall economic conditions may be coloured by political or other non-economic news. In fact, consumer confidence is less closely correlated with actual economic trends than business confidence (Santero and Westerlund, 1996) and, based on the information available at the time of the forecast, consumer confidence fails to improve forecasts of consumer spending (Croushore, 2004).[2] Similarly, business surveys of the trade sector are less reliable than surveys of industry.
- A given balance of responses may have a different meaning depending on the cyclical context: for some questions, there may be a tendency to overreact when the cycle turns sour but to underreact when prospects take a turn for the better. And a given balance value might have different implications depending on the relative importance of the 'neutral' responses. Questions on inventories are also difficult to interpret: the rule is that inventories are deemed to be on the low side the more orders increase, but by how much depends on the level of activity.
- With the expansion of multinational firms and globalisation of activity, the replies to questions on their own situation by a respondent in establishment X of firm Y increasingly tend to reflect the overall situation rather than just their own. This should serve to nuance the results region by region or sector by sector. Likewise, surveys conducted in small open economies may be less informative about these economies themselves than about the situation more broadly: for instance, industrial confidence in Belgium is more useful as a bellwether of the situation in the euro area at large than as an early indicator of developments in that country (also because Belgian industry is relatively specialised in cyclically upstream intermediate goods).
- Since any balance value is limited on the down- and the upside, both its level and its change have to be considered when assessing the state of the business cycle.

For all these reasons, normalising the responses may not be enough, and more sophisticated techniques may be needed to exploit survey information properly (see Section 3.5).

## 3.4  Making sense of the data

Once the raw data have been collected, they need to be processed. First, they need to be adjusted for seasonality and working days if they are not already. Then, they

---

[2] This finding, however, may at least partly reflect the shortcomings of the models used to forecast consumer spending.

can be combined to form synthetic indicators characterising overall cyclical conditions, or turning-point indicators which signal possible inflections in the cycle.

### 3.4.1 Adjusting the raw data

*Smoothing*

The raw data, especially at high frequencies, may be very volatile, reflecting short-run shocks of various kinds (strikes or extreme weather for instance) and/or measurement problems. One way to smooth the series – if indeed the view is that it is unduly bumpy – is then simply to remove the outliers. For this solution to be warranted, however, truly exceptional factors have to be identifiable, and, even then, outright removal may be unsatisfactory.

A more common technique is to use moving averages. Let $X_t$ be the variable under consideration. The centred and uniformly weighted moving average is then:

$$(X_{t-k} + X_{t-k+1} + \cdots + X_{t-1} + X_t + X_{t+1} + X_{t+2} + \cdots + X_{t+k})/p$$

where $p = 2k + 1$ and $k$ is chosen as a function of the desired degree of smoothness. Depending on how forward or backward-looking the moving average is to be, it can be computed asymmetrically. For example, if it is intended to capture recent trends, it can be computed as:

$$(X_{t-k} + X_{t-k+1} + \cdots + X_{t-1} + X_t)/(k + 1)$$

The drawback of this formulation is that it overstates past data developments and tends to lag actual data. Alternatively, it is possible to assign smaller weights to periods further away from time $t$. For example, one could define the moving average as:

$$(X_{t-2} + 2X_{t-1} + 3X_t + 2X_{t+1} + X_{t+2})/9$$

All in all, many different types of specifications can be used. The Bundesbank for instance uses three-month moving averages of seasonally adjusted two-month averages for purposes of cyclical analysis, but smoothes the raw data over six years when looking at long-term trends. The choice of the averaging method can matter greatly, especially around turning points, as illustrated by the case of US industrial output: the centred moving average shows the downturn in 2000 before the lagged one (Figure 3.4). *A priori*, symmetric averaging seems preferable, but of course, in real time, the analyst does not know the forthcoming observations that enter the moving average. In practice therefore, asymmetric averaging is often used. Alternaltively, one can estimate the required $X_{t+1}, \cdots, X_{t+k}$ (for example by using the methods presented in Sections 4.1 and 4.2)

*Seasonal adjustment*

One reason for the bumpiness of the raw data may be seasonal variations, when these are not already controlled for. A simple way to remove their impact – or at

**Figure 3.4**   **Alternative ways to average**
(month-on-month rate of change in US industrial output, seasonally adjusted)

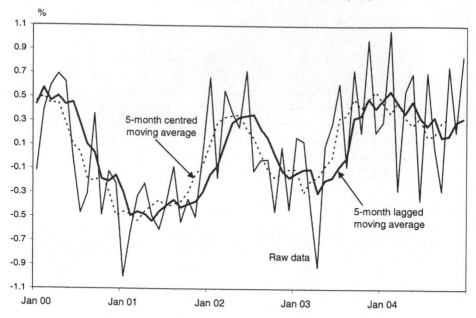

*Source*: Federal Reserve.

least most of it – is to look at cumulative data or changes over the past 12 months rather than at monthly or month-on-month or quarterly or quarter-on-quarter data.[3] One drawback, however, is that this amounts to focus on a lagging variable. Consider a variable that is steadily increasing, then suddenly drops, and then starts growing again but at a slower pace (Figure 3.5). If the focus is on year-on-year changes, the analyst will initially perceive less of a slowdown than is actually occurring. Subsequently, he or she will measure a further slowdown even though growth has already resumed, and will be almost one year late in identifying the upturn.

Alternatively, the series itself can be deseasonalised (when appropriate – some series, such as certain financial data, are not obviously subject to significant seasonal oscillations).This can be done in multiplicative or additive fashion. The former amounts to decomposing the series as the product of a trend $T_t$, a seasonal coefficient $S_t$ (which in the absence of seasonality equals 1) and a random or irregular component $I_t$:

$$X_t = T_t \times S_t \times I_t$$

---

[3] Seasonality may not be removed entirely, for example when Easter matters for the series under consideration and falls in a different month from one year to the next (see below). And even if seasonality is removed, the analyst needs to be fully aware of the nature of the corrections that have been implemented.

*Figure 3.5* Year-on-year versus quarter-on-quarter changes
(hypothetical economy)

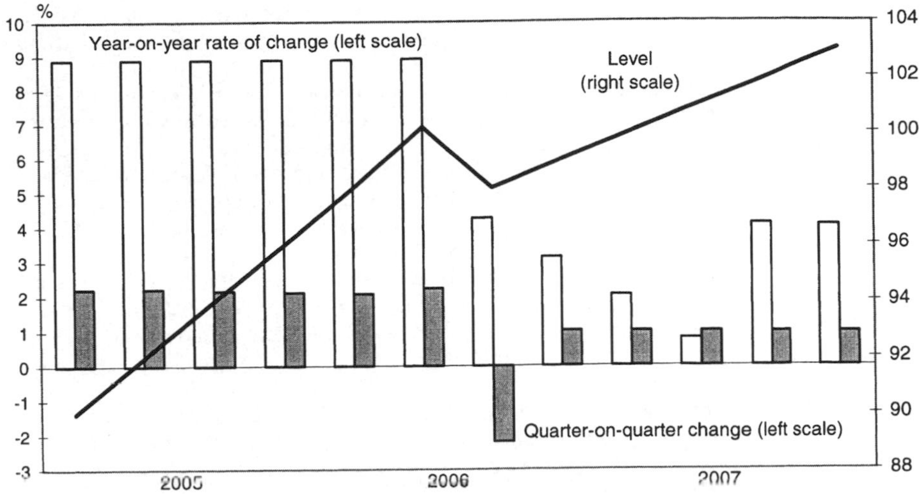

Alternatively, the decomposition can be carried out additively, with:

$$X_t = T_t + S_t + I_t$$

The seasonally adjusted series, respectively $X_t/S_t$ or $X_t - S_t$, will not be smooth if $I_t$ moves around significantly. Moreover, what is called trend here is in fact the combination of cyclical movement and a long-run trend (the latter being presented at length in Section 4.3). The choice between the multiplicative and additive approach depends on whether $T$, $S$ and $I$ are roughly proportional or not. If they are, as is often the case, the multiplicative formula is advisable. If not, the additive one is to be preferred. Also, when $X$ takes on negative values, only the additive formula can be used.

In both cases, the aim of deseasonalisation is essentially to derive $S_t$, by comparing developments in a given month (quarter) with those in the same month (quarter) of other years. In this respect, it is first necessary to have sufficient data – say five years worth. In addition, one has to extend the available series by at least a few months so as to be able to smooth the latest observations using centred moving averages or similar procedures implemented by seasonal-adjustment software. Another reason is the need to derive seasonal adjustment coefficients that can be applied to future raw data. These coefficients are usually not stable over time, as the impact of seasonal factors evolves: in France for example, August used to be a 'dead month' when a large portion of the population was on vacation, implying a large seasonal adjustment, but as the French have tended to spread out their holidays more over the year, the size of the adjustment has declined.

In practice, there exist several deseasonalisation software packages. A widely used programme is X-12 (see Box 3.6), which was developed by the US Bureau of Census and replaced the long-standing X-11 package (see Findley *et al.*, 1998).

---

*Box 3.6*   **Seasonal-adjustment software: X-12**

The X-12 programme, like its X-11 predecessor, follows an iterative estimation procedure, based on a series of moving averages. The user has numerous choices as to the length of the averages.

To start with, the user is given the option to 'preadjust' the series for outliers, level shifts, known irregular events and calendar-related effects using adjustment factors he or she supplies or that can be estimated using built-in estimation procedures. The so-called RegARIMA part of the programme then allows the user to extend the series by backcasts and forecasts so that less asymmetric filters can be used at the beginning and the end of the series than in the original X-11 programme (this drawback was so significant that an intermediate X11-ARIMA version had to be implemented).

The preadjusted series subsequently goes through three rounds of filtering. This represents the core of the programme and has not changed that much compared with X-11, even if X-12 does provide some enhancements. In the case of a multiplicative decomposition of the time series, the three rounds unfold as follows:

1. The trend $T_t$ is calculated as a moving average, providing an estimate for $S_t \times I_t$; the latter is smoothed for the same months of several years so as to derive a set of seasonal coefficients $S$, which are normalised so that their product equals one; an initial seasonally-adjusted series thus falls out.
2. A new trend is computed based on this initial seasonally adjusted series, which is subjected to the same treatment as in the first round.
3. The same procedure is then repeated once more.

Lastly, various diagnostics and quality control statistics are computed, tabulated, and graphed. This is an important step in the procedure, not least to assess whether the user made the right choices amongst the many options offered along the way.

In practice, the seasonal adjustment coefficients are refreshed once a year rather than after each new high-frequency observation. The programme provides the extrapolated coefficients needed for the coming year, which are applied to the incoming raw data.

Research on seasonal adjustment continues and recent work explores how X-12 can be combined with other procedures such as SEATS (signal extraction in ARIMA time series, developed by the Bank of Spain and promoted by Eurostat), or how heavy-tailed distributions for the disturbances can better be taken into account (Monsell *et al.*, 2003).

---

There are other packages, notably those based on the spectral decomposition of time series, such as the so-called BV4 method or the Baxter and King filter (see Section 4.3). Different methods can yield very different results, as is evident when comparing the GDP growth estimates published in Germany by the Bundesbank (using X-12) and the DIW institute (using BV4), which at times diverge quite dramatically (Figure 3.6).

Deseasonalisation is important to properly assess the shape of the cycle, including possible turning points. It also facilitates international comparisons, given that seasonal oscillations differ from country to country. Three complications deserve to be underlined, however:

- The usual procedures rely on smoothing techniques which typically suffer from end-point problems. More generally, deseasonalisation is a statistical procedure which, by its very nature, is subject to uncertainty.

- Standard push-button procedures ignore idiosyncratic irregularities, such as a drop in output due to a strike. Proper deseasonalisation requires an intimate knowledge of the series.
- Some seasonal oscillations vary over time, for instance in the case of Germany, where school holiday dates change from one year (and one *Länder*) to the next, causing seasonally adjusted industrial production to move rather erratically over the summer months.

*Figure 3.6* **Two incarnations of German real GDP**
(quarter-on-quarter growth, seasonally and working-day adjusted rate of change)

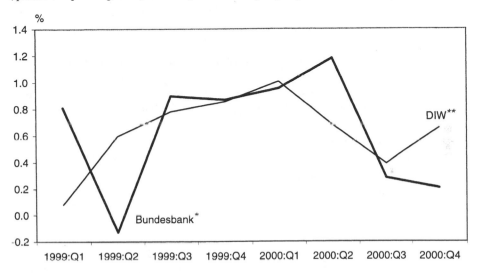

Notes:
 * Seasonally-adjusted using X-12.
** Seasonally-adjusted using the BV4 method.

Sources: Bundesbank, *Saisonbereinigte Wirtschaftszahlen*, March 2001; DIW, *Wochenbericht*, 8/01.

### Working-day adjustment

Another important factor that needs to be taken into account when 'cleaning up' the raw data is that the number of working (or 'trading') days varies from one month, one quarter or one year to the next (in the case of annual data leap years are a well-known problem in this respect).[4] How many of those there are in a given period may not matter for the consumption of food or for rents, but it does for retail sales, for example. In the case of industrial output, one extra working day can mechanically push up monthly production by as much as 5 per cent or so (given that there are around 20 working days per month).

---

[4] For instance, 2004 was a leap year and in addition several public holidays fell on weekends, leading to 2.8 more working days than average in the euro area. The European Central Bank (ECB) estimated the implied calendar effect on GDP growth to around $\frac{1}{4}$ per cent, albeit with considerable differences across countries, ranging from $\frac{1}{2}$ per cent in Germany to $\frac{1}{4}$ per cent in France and even less in some other euro area members (ECB, 2004).

Correcting for the number of working days is particularly tricky, however. To some extent, working-day effects are seasonal and deseasonalisation therefore already takes them into account. Christmas, for example, always falls in December. However, it does not always fall on a Sunday. In fact, only once every 28 years is the calendar identical in terms of dates and days of the week. Moreover, some holidays are set according to the lunar cycle, which is not synchronised with the (solar) calendar of economic activity. This is the case for a few celebrations in Europe and North America (Easter in particular). It is more of a problem in Asia, as well as in Muslim countries, owing to the length of Ramadan. Furthermore, the elasticity of economic variables with respect to the number of working days is not necessarily fixed. It may depend in particular on the economy's position in the cycle.[5] Hence, fully correcting for working-day effects can be an impossible task and might only be feasible on a qualitative basis.

In practice, working-day correction starts with the identification of the series that are likely to be affected by this problem, such as industrial output, exports and imports (customs offices are not open seven days a week), retail sales and so forth. Four different types of methods can then be applied to these series:

- The first one is to adjust the individual components of the relevant series directly, for example production industry by industry, drawing on specialised knowledge of the practices in each one. The raw data are then adjusted proportionately based on a standardised number of working days.
- Alternatively, one can test econometrically whether the number of Mondays, Tuesdays and so on in a month has a statistically significant influence on the raw monthly series. If so, the latter can be adjusted accordingly. To some extent, this type of test is in fact embedded in most deseasonalisation packages.
- The third approach is to count for each month the number of working days in excess or below the long-run average, and to adjust the raw data proportionately. De facto, however, this tends to lead to overcorrections.
- Yet another approach is to first identify and adjust for the working-day effects that are controlled for by the deseasonalisation procedure, and then to deal with the residual irregular component to see if it still contains some working-day effects. This type of treatment of the data can be applied iteratively.

*Caveats*

Users should of course be careful to establish whether the series they work with are seasonally and/or working-day adjusted or not and what sort of corrections were indeed implemented, and try to avoid mixing genres. In practice though, this can be difficult: in Germany for example, the quarterly series for private consumption

---

[5] See Lin and Liu (2002), who note that the date of the three most important Chinese holidays are determined by a lunar calendar and move between two solar months, strongly affecting consumption and production in countries with large Chinese populations. They also document that when unemployment rises, the magnitude of holiday and seasonal factors declines.

embodies both corrections but the household saving rate is only adjusted for seasonality. Several presentational problems may also arise. For instance annual growth rates may differ when using adjusted quarterly figures and raw data, not least for leap years. Or the balance between two adjusted series may not match the adjusted raw balance.

A last note of caution is in order: even when the raw data are not or no longer revised, the seasonally and/or working-day adjusted series can continue to change as new observations lead to the re-estimation of adjustment coefficients, which are then applied retroactively to the historical raw data. This is referred to as the 'wagging tail' problem.

### 3.4.2   Synthetic indicators

The raw data can be combined or used in a variety of ways to produce synthetic leading, coincident or lagging indicators of the business cycle. The confidence indices and the composite PMIs described above are in effect one example of such synthetic indicators and are intuitively appealing for broader audiences in that they seem to capture prevalent moods. However, they are rather *ad hoc* and to the extent that they do move with the cycle, the leads or lags vary across countries and over time. Hence, while they do help identify major swings and are a useful tool to characterise economic agents' psychological condition, other indicators may in some cases more adequately signal changes in activity.

One possible shortcut of sorts to try and anticipate cyclical developments is to focus on financial variables, specifically on equity prices (which in principle embody future profits and therefore reflect growth prospects), interest rate spreads between riskier and less risky bonds (with a presumption that a smaller spread denotes a lower probability of default, and hence a more favourable outlook for activity) and the difference between long and short-term interest rates, the so-called 'yield curve', or 'term spread' (Box 3.7).

A more comprehensive approach is to use a much broader range of variables to construct synthetic cyclical indicators. This approach was already quite popular a century ago, when some crude 'business barometers' were computed. At the time of the Great Depression, the National Bureau of Economic Research (NBER), having dated the US cycle, developed a more rational approach, by classifying economic statistics distinguishing leading, coincident and lagging series (Burns and Mitchell, 1946). The series were then combined into composite indicators correlated with the cycle, in order to depict the economic situation in real time. Aggregating a variety of series reduced the risk that noise in any individual one would send incorrect signals. To be considered, the series had to have sufficient coverage, time-liness, correlation with the cycle, and economic relevance. Other important selection criteria included their susceptibility to revisions and short-run variability.

Since 1987, the OECD publishes this type of synthetic indicators, in the form of monthly composite leading indicators (CLIs).[6] These are constructed to predict

---

[6] Leading indicators have also been developed by others for non-OECD countries. Dua and Banerji (2001), for instance, propose one for India.

---

**Box 3.7   What does the yield curve say about future growth?**

A number of analysts put considerable emphasis on the yield curve alone, based on the striking empirical correlation between the term spread and GDP growth several quarters down the road, both in the main advanced economies and more globally (C. Harvey, 1991). The canonical linear regression used in this context is $g = \alpha + \beta s$, where $g$ stands for real GDP growth over some future period, $s$ for the current yield spread and $\alpha$ for the expected growth rate when short and long-term interest rates are identical. Indeed, every US recession (as defined by the National Bureau of Economic Research) since the late 1960s has been preceded by a negative (or 'inverted') term spread, albeit with a variable lag ranging from two to six quarters (Ang *et al.*, 2004). Moreover, every yield curve inversion has been followed by a recession (suggesting that this indicator does not send 'false signals'). Hence, the yield curve seems to provide useful early warnings of business cycle turning points and, in practice, many forecasters closely monitor the yield curve.

Several types of economic rationale tend to be invoked to explain this pattern. The first one pertains to agents' portfolio choices: if they expect a recession, they will adjust their portfolio today away from short-term bonds and towards longer-term ones with a view to earn interest later to cushion future income losses; this pushes short-term yields up and longer-term yields down, flattening or even inverting the yield curve. The second rationale is that, during recessions, short-term interest rates are low, as the central bank tries to counter the downturn, while long-term interest rates are high, since agents expect future short-term interest rates to rise. Hence, an upward-sloping yield curve is associated with bad times today but better times tomorrow. The converse holds during economic expansions. A third rationale is that a falling term spread discourages banks (inasmuch as they borrow short and lend long) from engaging in new lending, thus leading to lower credit creation and activity – and vice versa.

However, the situation is far from clear-cut. These explanations often rely on the assumption that private agents can anticipate future developments relatively well, which is far from obvious, not least when compared to monetary authorities. Moreover, interest rates are quite volatile and the lags between changes in term spreads and activity vary (Estrella *et al.*, 2003) and can be relatively long – at least for those forecasters who look mainly at the very short run. Therefore, the yield curve should not be seen as more than one useful advance indicator among others.

---

cycles in a reference series which is chosen as a proxy measure for aggregate economic activity. Industrial (or in a few cases manufacturing) output is used as the reference series as it correlates fairly well with GDP, constitutes the most cyclical subset of economy-wide activity and – unlike GDP – is available at a monthly frequency for most OECD countries.

The CLIs combine five to eleven series which are selected on the basis of their economic relationship with the reference series, their cyclical behaviour (their cycle should lead that of the reference series, with no missing or extra cycles and the lead at turning points should not vary too much over time) and data quality (coverage, frequency, availability, absence of breaks, limited revisions). For most countries, variables such as share prices, interest rates, car registrations and business/consumer survey data will be included, as well as variables for a key foreign country in a few cases. The list of component series is regularly revised, if only because over time some components are suspended by the national source, but also because they may gradually lose relevance. Each component of the CLIs is equally weighted in the aggregation process. Before they are aggregated, however, they are deseasonalised, smoothed and normalised. If needed, quarterly components are converted into a monthly series by linear interpolation.

In addition, these data have to be detrended. This is done using a modified version of the NBER's phase-average-trend method. In a nutshell, this procedure requires an initial list of turning points which define the cyclical phases. These turning points are calculated using the so-called Bry-Boschan routine, which estimates a trend using a 75-month moving average (requiring backward and forward extrapolation at the beginning and end of the series respectively). Tests are then carried out on the deviation from the estimated trend so as to eliminate extreme values. The minimum duration imposed for each phase is five months and for cycles 15 months. Finally, an OECD expert validates the list of turning points from an economic point of view, and discards what are deemed to be minor cycles. As this approach rests on the concept of 'growth cycles', defined as recurrent fluctuations in the series of deviations from trend, it produces different results from the 'classical' approach (say, the NBER's) of cycles: growth cycle contractions include slowdowns as well as absolute declines in activity, as opposed to classical contractions, which include only absolute declines (recessions). The difference is illustrated in Figure 3.7, which shows that growth peaks tend to precede level peaks, whereas growth troughs tend to occur after level troughs. To purge irregularities, the component series are also smoothed according to their 'months for cyclical dominance' values (see R. Nilsson, 1987 for details). They are further normalised so as to make cyclical amplitudes directly comparable, by subtracting the mean from the observed value and then dividing by the mean of the absolute values of the difference from the mean.

*Figure 3.7*   **Activity versus growth cycle: turning points**

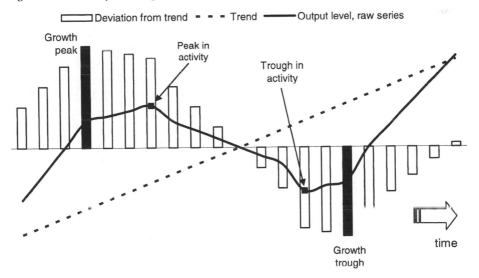

In turn, once its components have been assembled, the CLI itself is adjusted to ensure that its cyclical amplitude on average matches that of the detrended reference series. The OECD presents information on CLIs in two different forms:

- The 'trend-restored' CLI – reincorporating the trend component – allows direct comparisons with the evolution of the reference series. However, given that component series are not selected according to strict statistical criteria regarding their correlation with the reference series, this indicator cannot be used for forecasting the reference series on a proper quantitative basis. Furthermore, it is difficult to interpret the movement of the trend-restored CLI over short periods, due to its volatility.
- The 'annualised six-month rate of change' of the CLI smoothes out the volatility and provides turning-point signals with a significant lead (of about 9 months before the reference series according to the OECD).

This information needs nonetheless to be handled with care. In particular, a turning point in the CLI needs to be sufficiently marked and durable – not least with respect to its past developments – and widely shared among its components before inferring that a turning point in the reference series is imminent. Moreover, the ability of the CLI to predict turning points may vary over time and across countries.

In addition, the OECD CLIs suffer from a number of shortcomings. Publication of timely CLIs generally entails the use of an incomplete set of component series, with the minimum percentage of component series required ranging from 40 to 60 per cent depending on the country. Hence, the real degree of advance of the CLIs is smaller than the theoretical lead. Moreover, these indicators are substantially revised over time, which makes it difficult, when looking at the latest observations, to distinguish turning-point signals from erratic CLI fluctuations. Furthermore, industrial production accounts for a shrinking share of GDP, yet is one of its more volatile building blocks. In addition, the various data processing steps described above are all rather *ad hoc* and there exist theoretically sounder filters than those used for the OECD CLIs. In particular, one might wish to take more properly into account the nature of the relationships between variables (for example through cointegration analysis), as it would help the forecaster present an 'economic story' when pointing to the arrival of a turning point. Unfortunately, this story is all the harder to tell, as many components entering the CLIs are financial series (for instance their weight in the US leading indicator of the Conference Board exceeds 60 per cent), for which the relationship with business cycle developments is difficult to assess, as already noted. Also, these CLIs are built symmetrically, whereas business cycles tend to be asymmetric, with expansions lasting longer than contractions. Last but not least, the composition of the CLIs is often significantly modified *ex post* to improve tracking of past cycles. Nevertheless, as a practical matter, the OECD's CLI for the United States evolves in tandem with the leading indicators developed by the Conference Board (Box 3.8), and with others (Marcellino, forthcoming).

*Box 3.8*  **The Conference Board's composite indicators**

Every month, the Conference Board releases a widely watched set of composite leading, coincident and lagging indicators for the United States and several other large economies. The weight of each component is inversely related to the standard deviation of its month-to-month change over the past few decades and the weights are normalised to sum to one (Table 3.2). When one or more components are missing, the other weights are adjusted proportionately to ensure that the total still sums to one. To address the problem of lags in data availability, those indicators that are not out at the time of publication are estimated using an auto-regressive model. The resulting indices thus incorporate actual and estimated data, and are subsequently revised as the data unavailable at the time of publication are released.

One interpretation of the Conference Board's leading index, due to Vaccara and Zarnowitz (1978), is that if it declines during three months in a row, it signals an impending downturn. While crude, this type of rule of thumb is not necessarily outperformed by more sophisticated methods (Filardo, 2004).

*Table 3.2*  **Leading, coincident and lagging indices for the US economy**

|  | *Weight* |
|---|---|
| **Leading Index** |  |
| Average weekly working hours in manufacturing | 0.1965 |
| Average weekly initial claims for unemployment insurance | 0.0252 |
| Manufacturers' new orders (consumer goods and materials) | 0.0588 |
| Vendor performance (slower deliveries diffusion index) | 0.0292 |
| Manufacturers' new orders (non-defence capital goods) | 0.0146 |
| Building permits for new private housing units | 0.0202 |
| Stock prices (500 common stocks) | 0.0291 |
| Money supply (M2) | 0.2774 |
| Interest rate spread (10-year Treasury bonds less federal funds) | 0.3303 |
| Index of consumer expectations | 0.0188 |
| Total | 1 |
| **Coincident Index** |  |
| Employees on non-agricultural payrolls | 0.5235 |
| Personal income less transfer payments | 0.2141 |
| Industrial production | 0.1467 |
| Manufacturing and trade sales | 0.1157 |
| Total | 1 |
| **Lagging Index** |  |
| Average duration of unemployment | 0.0378 |
| Inventories-to-sales ratio (manufacturing and trade) | 0.1249 |
| Labour cost per unit of output in manufacturing | 0.0648 |
| Average prime rate charged by banks | 0.2788 |
| Commercial and industrial loans | 0.0968 |
| Ratio of consumer instalment credit to personal income | 0.2019 |
| Consumer price index for services | 0.1950 |
| Total | 1 |

*Source*: Conference Board.

### 3.4.3   More advanced techniques

Techniques have been developed since the late 1980s – in particular following an influential contribution by Stock and Watson (1989) – to overcome some of the problems highlighted above, in the form of more rigorous statistical procedures and the replacement of judgemental characterisations of the current situation by more formal and probabilistic ones (quantifying the likelihood to be in a recession or an expansion, or to face one). These new tools are quite sophisticated, however, and some of them are still somewhat experimental.

*Dynamic factor analysis*

One avenue is dynamic factor analysis, which builds on the insight that when a set of macroeconomic time series clearly tend to move together, the evolution of each one can be represented as a linear combination of the evolution of a small number of common latent variables which drive the co-movements (the so-called common factors), and of an uncorrelated residual term (the idiosyncratic component). More specifically, if $X_t^i$ is the $i^{\text{th}}$ series being observed:

$$X_t^i = a^i C_t + \varepsilon_t^i$$

where $C_t$ is the $(k \times 1)$ vector of $k$ common factors, $a^i$ a $(1 \times k)$ vector of parameters and $\varepsilon^i$ is white noise. The model is then written in so-called state-space form, as the variables are unobservable, and the parameters are estimated through a maximum likelihood procedure, using a Kalman filter. This allows to derive a relatively smooth synthetic indicator. It also sheds light on the contribution of each series to the overall outlook: for instance, if in a recovery order books in industry are buoyant, they may at first glance seem to be one of the drivers of the upturn, but once the common factor is taken into account, it may well appear that they are in fact a drag.

This type of analysis can be carried out on a relatively limited number of time series, as done by Doz and Lenglart (2001) for the six largest euro area countries (which represent about 90 per cent of total euro area GDP) and five questions from the monthly harmonised industrial business surveys. They find one common factor and posit that it follows an ARMA(2,1) process, and that the idiosyncratic components are AR(1) (the definition of such processes is given in Section 4.2). The estimated common factor can be used as a synthetic index to analyse the evolution of euro area industrial output over the short run.

Alternatively, and based on a generalised version of this type of model, dynamic factor analysis can be conducted on a much larger number of series, with the cross-section dimension potentially exceeding the time dimension. A prominent example is the coincident EuroCOIN index, which is constructed as the cyclical, common component of euro area GDP. It is based on some 250 monthly time series (chosen amongst an initial set of 3000 series) for the same six largest euro area economies.[7] This index takes into account cross-correlations across and

---

[7] The variables cover industrial production, producer prices, consumer prices, monetary aggregates, interest rates, financial markets and exchange rates, European Commission

within countries. The approach also allows characterisation of the degree of synchronisation of national business cycles and the leading or lagging properties of various sectors across European countries. In addition, it provides a dating of the euro area cycle (in growth cycle terms). The cross-correlations also permit identification of the leading variables in each of the economies, which can be aggregated to construct a euro-area leading indicator (Forni *et al.*, 2001). These include orders, capacity utilisation and energy consumption.

This approach has the advantage of taking into account a very large information set. Moreover, it does not require, unlike earlier work, to identify a set of coincident variables prior to estimation using heuristic criteria: here, all available variables – leading, coincident and lagging – are used, without any *a priori* classification. That said, the gains associated with complex dynamic factor models, compared with cruder approaches, are not necessarily large (Banerjee *et al.*, 2003). More parsimonious dynamic factor models, using a far smaller number of variables, can lead to very similar results. Azevedo *et al.* (2003), for instance, derive a coincident index for the euro area resembling EuroCOIN but pooling information from only nine key economic variables.

### Turning-point indicators and regime switches

Another class of studies has focused on the probability of facing a cyclical turning point. Artis *et al.* (1995) followed this route, setting up a framework that treats turning-point prediction as a problem of pattern recognition, based on a variant of the Bayesian forecasting method developed by Neftçi (1982). First, a business cycle chronology is constructed to describe the past as an oscillation between two regimes, downturns and upturns.[8] A turning point is said to occur when the regime shifts. Then, a leading indicator is scrutinised to try and recognise early on that a turning point in the reference series lies ahead. In addition to the statistical delay for obtaining the leading data, two types of lags come into play: the time needed to realise that a turning point in the leading series has been reached (the 'recognition lag'), and the lead time between turning points of the leading and the reference series (the 'signal lead time'). They involve a trade-off: attempting to increase the signal lead time by reducing the recognition lag runs the risk of issuing false signals. This risk, however, can be reduced by exploiting the cumulative information provided as observations come in, taking into account the distributions observed in past regimes. This allows derivation of a probabilistic indicator of being in one regime or the other that varies in intensity, rather than simply

---

surveys, national institute surveys, trade and labour markets (Altissimo *et al.*, 2001). EuroCOIN is updated monthly on www.cepr.org/data/eurocoin. For further information on this class of models, see www.dynfactors.org/, and for papers on the euro area business cycle, see www.eabcn.org/.

[8] It is also possible to use existing chronologies, such as those produced by the Business Cycle Dating Committee of the NBER or the CEPR for classical cycles in the United States and the euro area respectively, or the ones published by the Economic Cycle Research Institute (ECRI) for growth cycles in several countries.

flashing 'on' or 'off'. Yet, the user still has to decide on a threshold value for the probabilistic indicator at which to issue a turning-point call. Moreover, the choice of the indicator as well as the pre-determination of the cycles leave some room for discretion.

One of the key elements in predicting the turning point is the assumption made regarding the expected lifetime of the reference series' regime: is a regime more likely to end as it ages? More formally, is the conditional probability or 'hazard' of a regime ending at time $t$, given that it has survived up to that time, increasing, decreasing or constant? If it is increasing (decreasing) within a regime, there is said to be positive (negative) duration dependence in that regime; if it is constant, there is said to be duration independence. The empirical studies quoted in Artis *et al.* (1995) suggest, perhaps somewhat counter-intuitively, that in practice the latter can be assumed. Indeed, duration independence is compatible with the notion that the longer a regime persists, the rarer it is.

More recent work in the probabilistic vein (albeit with a different functional set-up) has emphasised cross-country links. Sensier *et al.* (2004) have looked at classical business cycles in Germany, France, Italy and the United Kingdom, with regimes defined as binary variables (recessions, expansions), and Osborn *et al.* (2005) have done the same for growth cycles. In both cases, foreign variables enter significantly into the national leading indicators. In this context, it is worth noting that growth cycles typically exhibit more frequent regime changes than classical cycles. This is not surprising, since a spell of slow growth may be sufficient to define a growth recession even in the absence of the output decline that defines a classical recession. Growth cycles are also closer to being symmetric, in the sense of approximately the same number of observations falling in recessions and expansions.

A somewhat different approach to turning points is based on the so-called hidden Markov switching models, a statistical tool originally developed in the 1960s for speech recognition purposes (see also Section 4.3). The idea is again that the economy moves back and forth between two regimes, with a probability that varies over time, depending on the evolution of an unobserved 'state' variable. Observed statistical series (say, business confidence) are characterised by two different probability distributions, depending on the type of regime and thus on the unobserved state variable. Each new data point is treated as a 'surprise' compared to the assumed probability distribution of the observed series. It will therefore give some information regarding the probability of the unobserved variable to be in one state or another. A sudden change in this probability will signal that a turning point is imminent. This methodology is applied to French business survey data by Gregoir and Lenglart (2000), to UK data by Simpson *et al.* (2001), and to German data by Bandholz and Funke (2003). Andersson *et al.* (2004) evaluate the merits of this and related approaches using the Swedish recession of the early 1990s as an example. While Markov-switching non-linear effects have some intuitive appeal, Harding and Pagan (2002) argue that this approach actually fails to outperform simpler, linear models.

Lastly, another non-linear approach has been recently explored, known as neural network models, developed initially in computer science half a century ago and widely used in medical science and engineering, which have powerful pattern recognition abilities (Kaashoek and van Dijk, 2003). This approach is also premised on the view that linear, constant-parameter models are not adequate to forecast turning points. In principle, this class of models offers a very general framework which can approximate any type of non-linearity in the data. Qi (2001) applies this methodology with some success to US data, and Heravi *et al.* (2004) to European data. However, because of their very flexibility in approximating different functional forms, neural network models run the risk of 'overfitting': despite a near-perfect in-sample fit, the representation of the data-generation process might be incorrect, leading to poor out-of-sample predictions.

In a nutshell, these advanced techniques present several advantages, not least the estimation of various 'signals' that nicely complement more traditional monitoring exercises. There are, however, two drawbacks. First, the emergence of any signal often appears to come from a 'black box', implying that it is difficult to turn it into a convincing economic story. A second, and related, problem is that communicating this information to forecast users is often challenging.

## 3.5 Bridge models

Business and consumer surveys provide the earliest economic information but it is mostly of a qualitative nature, whereas forecasters aim for quantification. One way to bridge this gap is to use econometric techniques to pin down the relationship between 'soft' survey evidence and 'hard' economic indicators, so as to extrapolate it over the forecast period. Generally, such bridge models are estimated equation by equation, but joint estimation is also possible, as in the European Commission's BUSY model (Biart and Praet, 1986). The interpretation of this type of equations, however, is not straightforward. Survey data are imperfect measures of agents' expectations, owing to sampling errors and the phrasing of the questions, and expectations themselves may be wrong (Nardo, 2003). Also, how does causality run? It is not clear, for example, whether business managers' views determine future production or whether their answers to survey questions are shaped by the outlook but do not explain it.

The first step is to select the most relevant survey indicators. Usually, balances of opinion are used, both in level terms and in first difference. The choice amongst survey questions is based on the forecaster's experience, but can also be informed by elaborate statistical testing along the lines discussed in Section 3.4, or drawing on vector auto-regression (see Section 4.4). In practice, most of the useful information for forecasting is often embodied in a small subset of questions and answers.

Before linking up soft and hard variables, a few checks are in order, including:

- Sectoral coverage, which may not be similar. In some countries, statistical coverage differs in the monthly and in the quarterly data for what at first sight may look like one and the same indicator.
- The period under consideration. While it is fairly unambiguous for hard data, it is sometimes less so for soft data. For instance, it is not obvious whether firm

managers' answers are more reflective of the ongoing month or quarter, the last one or the next. This partly depends on when during the period they are polled. In the case of the German IFO survey for example, the answers for month $m$ are provided before mid-month and can be influenced by the outcome in the previous month rather than developments in month $m$.

- Possible working-day distortions: in principle, firms' answers should not be influenced by the number of working days, but in practice, they sometimes are, for example in the retail sector. Also, in some cases, the hard series is itself not adjusted for working days.

- The statistical properties of the series: opinion balances are typically stationary and bounded whereas quantitative variables are often integrated of order one (see Section 4.4), implying that their rate of growth rather than their level is stationary and has to be related to the survey data.

- Frequencies, which may differ. Surveys are often, albeit not always, monthly, whilst the hard data used in bridge models are generally quarterly, so as to ensure consistency with the quarterly national accounts data.

The canonical equation used in this context is of the form:

$$\Delta \log Y_t = \sum_{i \geq 1} (a_i X_{t+1-i} + b_i \Delta \log Y_{t-i}) + c$$

where $X$ is the qualitative exogenous variable (opinion balance), assumed to be leading other variables, $Y$ the quantitative endogenous variable, $\Delta \log Y$ the growth rate of $Y$ and $c$ a parameter reflecting the systematic bias in respondents' answers (which can be zero).

This general formulation can be amended in various ways depending on circumstances:

- Some lags may be eliminated if the associated parameter values are unstable.
- The lagged values of the endogenous variable may be excluded. Then only the survey data appear on the right hand side, which can be welcome, for example when there are doubts as to how accurately the latest values of the endogenous variables are measured (say, if the preliminary estimate of GDP looks awkward). Hence, $Y$ will be determined only by current and past values of the exogenous qualitative variable. But recent developments (exceptional weather for instance) might have caused $Y$ to deviate from this underlying trajectory; ignoring the information provided by $Y_{t-i}$ might therefore affect the equation's forecasting power.
- Conversely, it may be appropriate to add other exogenous variables.
- *A priori*, the change in the opinion balance is more important than its level to explain the growth in $Y$, especially around turning points. But taking its level into account may serve to amplify or dampen the estimated impact. One can easily switch from a formulation in level terms to a hybrid one, as $\Delta \log Y_t = a_1 X_t + a_2 X_{t-1} + c$ can be rewritten as $\Delta \log Y_t = a_1 \Delta X_t + (a_1 + a_2) X_{t-1} + c$.
- In principle, these growth rates can be expressed in year-on-year or in quarter-on-quarter terms. Practices differ across institutions and depend in part on how survey questions are put (for instance on whether the survey is explicitly comparing one time period to another).

The forecaster has an incentive to try and have the largest possible lag between survey data and the hard indicators required, so as to extend the forecasting horizon. But the best fit for the above equations is for short lags, so there is a trade-off.

In practice, the following steps can be distinguished, assuming output is the variable under consideration ($Y_t$):

- The coincident variables are first used, so as to estimate output in the current quarter, $T$, say, by benchmarking it on the latest balance of opinion on produced output in $T$.
- Then the forecast is extended directly, by benchmarking – more tentatively – production in quarter $T + 1$ on the latest balance of opinion on firms' own output prospects (ideally, opinions expressed in $T$ regarding output in $T + 1$).
- Or the forecast is extended more indirectly, by extrapolating the latest balance of opinion on firms' own output prospects in $T + 1$ and expressed in $T$ to derive an estimate of the balance of opinion that will be expressed in $T + 1$ on produced output in quarter $T + 1$, and then benchmarking output in quarter $T + 1$ on this estimate. When the balance of opinion on produced output for the first month or two of quarter $T + 1$ is already known, or when extraneous information on the likely results of the coming surveys is somehow available, it may be better to try to proceed along such lines (adjusting the extrapolation accordingly, to take this information on board).

Generally, bridge models appear to be better suited to forecast some components of aggregate supply (industrial output, construction) than to forecast components of aggregate demand or GDP directly (Baffigi *et al.*, 2004). This implies that it is necessary to build a framework for the forecast that can incorporate the benchmarked estimates for each separate component so as to derive a forecast for GDP. While this may be more time consuming, it can also help build up the economic story associated with the forecast.

The European Commission, for example, every month publishes GDP growth forecasts for the two quarters following the last quarter for which official data have been published (Grasmann and Keereman, 2001). The set of variables used also includes survey data and financial variables. In this case, car registrations in the euro area and business sentiment indicators in the retail and construction sectors do enter the equation, as well as the US ISM index, which reflects the importance of international linkages. Separate equations are run for each of the two quarters. The forecasts are presented as ranges for quarter-on-quarter real GDP growth rates.

Four times a year, the OECD publishes near-term GDP forecasts for six of the G7 countries (Canada being the exception) plus the euro area as a whole, based on a like minded but more elaborate approach (Sédillot and Pain, 2003). Again, both soft indicators, such as business surveys, and hard ones, such as industrial production and retail sales, are fed into the equations (Table 3.3). Consumer confidence is not included, as it is not found to add sufficient information. These high-frequency indicators are recast into quarterly GDP figures using bridge models. A key element is that, for each country, there are several indicator models depending on the available data. The model chosen will thus vary over time according to the information at hand. For the current quarter, models with only hard indicators, or combining these with survey data, tend to outperform models relying solely on survey data; in particular, 'pure' hard indicator models appear the most suitable for the United States and the euro area. For the one-quarter-ahead forecasts, in contrast, inclusion of hard indicator data adds little to the information provided by surveys, especially in France and Italy. Notwithstanding its high degree of sophistication, this approach cannot forecast the quarterly rate of GDP growth very precisely. Even when a complete set of monthly indicators are available for a quarter, the 70 per cent confidence band (corresponding to about one standard error) for GDP growth in that quarter ranges from 0.4 to 0.9 percentage point, depending on the country or region. *A fortiori*, it is wider still for the following quarter. That said, the GDP series itself are subject to sizeable revisions and the volatility of quarter-on-quarter rates is substantial (see Section 2.3).

*Table 3.3*   **Variables used by the OECD in near-term forecasting**

|  | *Indicator(s) selected* | *Sources* |
|---|---|---|
| **Surveys** | | |
| United States | ISM for manufacturing | ISM |
| Euro area | Level of order books, level of inventories | European Commission |
| Germany | IFO business climate index | IFO |
| France | Production tendency, future production tendency | INSEE |
| Italy | Production tendency, future production tendency, IFO business climate index | ISAE, IFO |
| United Kingdom | Future production tendency | CBI |
| Japan | Sales diffusion index | Japan Finance Corporation for Small Businesses |
| **Hard indicators** | | |
| United States | Industrial production, consumption in volume, new construction put in place, monthly export volumes, total monthly level of stocks | Federal Reserve, BEA, Census Bureau |
| Euro area | Industrial output, construction output, retail sales volumes | Eurostat, OECD calculations |
| Germany | Industrial production, construction output, retail sales volumes | Bundesbank, Statistische Bundesamt |
| France | Industrial production, consumption of manufactured goods | INSEE |
| Italy | Industrial production | ISTAT |

**Continued**

**Table 3.3**   **Continued**

|  | *Indicator(s) selected* | *Sources* |
|---|---|---|
| United Kingdom | Industrial production, retail sales volumes | ONS |
| Japan | Real living expenditure, tertiary industry activity, job-offers-to-applicants ratio, inventory-shipments ratio in industry | Japan Statistics Bureau, METI, Ministry of Labour |

*Sources*: Sédillot and Pain (2003); OECD.

An alternative approach is to go for synthetic indicators that directly serve as forecasts of output in the coming quarter(s), and which mix in both benchmarked variables and leading indicators. The idea is to combine the information provided by benchmarking components of overall activity and that embodied in the leading indicators, which on their own are only indicative of trends or possible turning points.

Such synthetic indicators have been developed in Europe in the form of Euroframe's euro area growth indicator for the current quarter and the next one, compiled for the *Financial Times* by the Observatoire Français des Conjonctures Économiques (OFCE), in cooperation with eight research institutes throughout Europe (Charpin, 2002).[9] The first step is to provide a quarterly coincident indicator for GDP growth in the current quarter. Then, one- and two-quarter ahead forecast equations are estimated, depending on the incoming monthly information that is available. The variables considered incorporate an industry survey factor, obtained as the first factor in a principal component analysis of the series of the monthly survey of industry in the euro area, information provided by surveys in other sectors, as well as rapidly available variables such as the relative term spread in the euro area compared with the United States, the euro's real exchange rate *vis-à-vis* the dollar and the price of oil in euros.

## 3.6   Final health warning

In sum, business cycle analysts can use very different empirical approaches, which end up with a blend of rather heterogeneous hard and soft variables and are not underpinned by any single economic model. Moreover, the available statistical information might change rapidly over time, in sharp contrast with longer-run forecasting exercises, which are more squarely based on a 'fixed' set of

---

[9] WIFO in Austria, ESRI in Ireland, ETLA in Finland, IfW and DIW Berlin in Germany, Prometeia in Italy, CPB in the Netherlands and NIESR in the United Kingdom. See Chapter 14 for more information on some of these institutes. The indicator is available on www.euroframe.org/indicator/index.php.

economic data. Finally, short-term economic analysis has to deal with a lack of sufficient statistical information in several sectors and, when data are available, high volatility.

This has several implications. First, short-term macro monitoring requires following disparate but complementary approaches; the use of an overly specialised forecasting technique would prevent seeing the wood for the trees. Second, one has to make the most of all the incoming information, not least because of large carry-over effects. Third, some prudence is in order when deciding whether a new piece of information is altering the outlook, say by foreshadowing a new trend, or whether it has to be disregarded, at least for the time being. The best way to address these challenges is to build a structured framework, derived for example from the quarterly national accounts, in order to integrate all this information in a consistent way and to try to make sense of seemingly contradictory signals.

# 4
# Time Series Methods

This chapter discusses how times series methods can be used for forecasting purposes. As mentioned in Chapter 1, their main distinguishing feature is that they take a statistical view which leaves limited room for economic analysis. Their appeal stems from the ease with which they allow generation of numerical forecasts for a host of variables. The flipside is that these forecasts do not lend themselves to much if any economic interpretation, which is a major handicap when it comes to disseminating and explaining them. Therefore, times series methods usually play an ancillary role, as an auxiliary tool or a benchmark. They can be useful to produce forecasts that are needed but for which the available resources are limited, such as *ad hoc* extrapolations in the context of business cycle analysis or forecasts of exogenous variables in a macroeconomic model. They can also serve as a check on forecasts obtained through other methods.

In principle, time series methods can be used at all forecasting horizons. In practice, they mostly assist with short-run forecasting, as an extension of the analysis of the current situation. Indeed, time series methods can quite effectively capture short-run dynamics but lack the economic spine needed when thinking about medium- and long-run developments.

Times series methods are either univariate (one variable is forecasted based on its past realisations) or multivariate (when several variables are). The latter have the advantage of taking into account the observed correlations between variables, albeit at the cost of greater complexity. The methods further differ by the degree of specificity of the model, the attention paid to the statistical validity of the estimations, and the scope to put an economic interpretation on the numbers. In all cases, the idea is, loosely speaking, to replicate past patterns over the forecast period. This chapter first covers the univariate methods, from straight extrapolation (Section 4.1) to ARIMA models (Section 4.2) and trend-cycle decompositions (Section 4.3). It then presents VAR analysis, as the main multivariate approach (Section 4.4).

## 4.1  Empirical extrapolation

Extrapolation is straightforward and for forecasting purposes it may in fact be sufficient in some cases, even in its simplest form, and especially when resources are scarce. The underlying idea is to extend a range of numbers in a rigorous way, in line with past observations.

### 4.1.1   Naïve methods

The simplest assumption to forecast a variable $X$ is that it remains unchanged at its latest observed level, so that for $t$ periods ahead:

$$P(X_{T+t}) = X_T$$

where $P$ stands for the forecast and $T$ is the time of the latest observation (with $t > 0$). This method is in fact optimal when $X$ follows a random walk, with $X_{t+1} = X_t + \varepsilon_t$, where $\varepsilon_t$ is a zero mean, white noise process ($E(\varepsilon_t) = 0$, $V(\varepsilon_t) = \sigma^2$ and $Cov(\varepsilon_t, \varepsilon_{t'}) = 0$ for any $t \neq t'$). The random walk assumption is not necessarily that far-fetched: in a famous article, Meese and Rogoff (1983) show that the best forecast for the exchange rate is precisely its latest observed value.

A variant is to replace the last observation by the historical mean of the data, or an average of recent observations, say:

$$P(X_{T+t}) = \tfrac{1}{4}(X_T + X_{T-1} + X_{T-2} + X_{T-3})$$

Another elementary method assumes that the latest observed change will persist:

$$P(X_{T+t}) = X_T + t(X_T - X_{T-1})$$

or, in a slightly more sophisticated rendition, that a weighted average of the changes observed over the last three periods can be applied recurrently as follows:[1]

$$P(X_{T+t}) = P(X_{T+t-1})(\tfrac{1}{2}X_T/X_{T-1} + \tfrac{1}{3}X_{T-1}/X_{T-2} + \tfrac{1}{6}X_{T-2}/X_{T-3})$$

Such methods are said to be naïve because they correspond to what a myopic agent, looking only at very recent information, might forecast. They fail to predict some very simple dynamic processes, such as geometrical declines. In fact, they mainly serve as a benchmark, to measure what is gained by using more subtle approaches.

### 4.1.2   Exponential smoothing

Exponential smoothing derives the forecast as a weighted average of past observations, with the weights declining geometrically:

$$P(X_{T+1}) = \alpha(X_T + \beta X_{T-1} + \beta^2 X_{T-2} + \cdots + \beta^J X_{T-J})$$

where $0 < \beta < 1$. It is then necessary to impose a condition so that the declining weights sum to one: $\alpha (1 + \beta + \beta^2 + \cdots + \beta^J) = 1$. Usually, the number of

---

[1] If one wishes to control for seasonality, with $s$ being the frequency at which seasonal patterns recur, one can use a formula such as $X_{T+t} = X_{T+t-s}(\tfrac{1}{2}X_T/X_{T-s} + \tfrac{1}{3}X_{T-1}/X_{T-s-1} + \tfrac{1}{6}X_{T-2}/X_{T-s-2})$.

observations $J$ is sufficiently large to treat the above as an infinite sum:

$$P(X_{T+1}) = \alpha(X_T + \beta X_{T-1} + \beta^2 X_{T-2} + \cdots + \beta^j X_{T-j} + \cdots)$$

so that the condition boils down to $\alpha = 1 - \beta$.

Turning to the forecast two periods ahead:

$$
\begin{aligned}
P(X_{T+2}) &= \alpha(P(X_{T+1}) + \beta X_T + \beta^2 X_{T-1} + \cdots + \beta^{j+1} X_{T-j} + \cdots) \\
&= \alpha P(X_{T+1}) + \beta\alpha(X_T + \beta X_{T-1} + \beta^2 X_{T-2} + \cdots + \beta^j X_{T-j} + \cdots) \\
&= \alpha P(X_{T+1}) + \beta P(X_{T+1}) \\
&= P(X_{T+1}), \text{ since } \alpha = 1 - \beta.
\end{aligned}
$$

The forecast made at time $T$ is therefore the same whatever the horizon. But once the realisation at $T + 1$ is known, the forecast for $X_{T+2}$ can be updated to become:

$$P_{T+1}(X_{T+2}) = \alpha X_{T+1} + (1 - \alpha) P_T(X_{T+1})$$

where $P_{T+1}$ denotes the forecast made at time $T + 1$ and $P_T$ the forecast made at time $T$. Updating the forecast then amounts to taking a weighted average of the past forecast (with a weight of $1 - \alpha$) and of the realisation (with a weight of $\alpha$).

The simplicity of this approach is one of the main advantages of exponential smoothing. It is a useful method when one has little insight into the factors driving variable $X$ and when the series' trend appears to change rapidly. The weighting scheme puts more emphasis on recent observations, reflecting an intuition that they are the most informative ones.

A drawback, however, is that the choice of the smoothing parameter $\alpha$ is somewhat arbitrary. To lessen this arbitrariness, one can test various values of $\alpha$ to select the one that seems to be most robust in explaining past observations.

## 4.2 ARIMA models

ARIMA (auto-regressive integrated moving average) models were popularised by Box and Jenkins (1976), in connection with the rapid development of econometric software. They were explicitly designed to produce forecasts. They combine a more rigorous statistical approach than the above extrapolation methods (although they still require the exercise of some judgement) and a great flexibility, allowing them to be used in many different contexts. At the same time, they rest on fairly banal functional forms, namely auto-regressive and moving average processes. The standard procedure, which is described below, involves three steps: identification, estimation and verification.

## 4.2.1   Definitions

Recall that a stochastic process $X_t$ is said to be auto-regressive of order $p$ – AR($p$) – when it can be written as:

$$X_t = a_1 X_{t-1} + a_2 X_{t-2} + \cdots + a_p X_{t-p} + \varepsilon_t$$

where $\varepsilon_t$ is white noise. It is said to be a moving average of order $q$ – MA($q$) – when:

$$X_t = \varepsilon_t + b_1 \varepsilon_{t-1} + b_2 \varepsilon_{t-2} + \cdots + b_q \varepsilon_{t-q}$$

$X_t$ is said to follow an ARMA ($p,q$) process when the two preceding specifications are combined, namely when:

$$X_t - a_1 X_{t-1} - a_2 X_{t-2} - \cdots - a_p X_{t-p} = \varepsilon_t + b_1 \varepsilon_{t-1} + b_2 \varepsilon_{t-2} + \cdots + b_q \varepsilon_{t-q}$$

This process is stationary: its probability distribution is constant over time. In practice, few variables are stationary, if only because they tend to grow over time, or are affected by seasonality, and ARMA models cannot be used directly. However, they can be used on modified series, namely series that have been transformed to obtain stationary series. This is at the core of ARIMA ($p$, $d$, $q$) models, which when differenced $d$ times morph into ARMA ($p$, $q$) processes. An ARIMA ($p$, $d$, $q$) process can be written as:

$$(1 - L)^d A(L) X_t = B(L) \varepsilon_t$$

where $L$ is the lag operator and $(1 - L)$ the first difference operator (often denoted $\Delta$), while $A(L)$ and $B(L)$ are distributed lag polynomials of order $p$ and $q$ respectively, and $\varepsilon_t$ is white noise.

## 4.2.2   Identification

Identification consists of deciding on the values of $p$, $d$ and $q$. First, one has to identify $d$, the number of times $X$ should be differenced to achieve stationarity (in some cases, $d$ is zero). This is an art as much as a science, as there are many ways to go about it, which do not all deliver the same result. Contemporary methods rest on stationarity tests such as the Dickey-Fuller and Schmidt-Phillips tests (for details, see for instance Hamilton, 1994).

Note that a non-stationary series is not necessarily integrated. Consider $X_t = 1.5 X_{t-1}$: no integer number of differencing operations can turn $X_t$ into a stationary series. But taking logarithms can: $Y_t = \log X_t$ is integrated of order 1 (since $Y_t = Y_{t-1} + \log 1.5$). This shows why it is often useful to work with the logarithm of macroeconomic variables that appear to grow at constant rates in the long run.

Once a stationary series is obtained, one must decide how many auto-regressive ($p$) and moving average ($q$) parameters are needed to yield an effective but parsimonious model of the process (parsimonious meaning that it has the fewest

*Table 4.1* **Properties of ARMA processes**

|  | Auto-correlations* | Partial auto-correlations** |
|---|---|---|
| AR($p$) | Exponential decay beyond $p$ | Nil beyond $p$ |
| MA($q$) | Nil beyond $q$ | Decline beyond $q$ |
| ARMA($p,q$) | Exponential decay beyond $p$ | Decline beyond $q$ |

Notes:
* The auto-correlation of order $s$ of series $X_t$ is $\rho_s = \text{Cov}(X_t, X_{t-s})/V(X_t)$.
** The partial auto-correlation of order $r$ is $\varphi_r$ in the regression: $X_t = \varphi_1 X_{t-1} + \varphi_2 X_{t-2} + \cdots + \varphi_r X_{t-r} + \varepsilon_t$.

parameters and greatest number of degrees of freedom among all models that fit the data). To this end, the correlation properties of auto-regressive and moving average processes are used (Table 4.1). Examination of the sample correlogram (which plots the auto-correlation coefficient at lag $s$ as a function of lag $s$) and partial correlogram (likewise for the partial auto-correlation coefficient) helps decide on $p$ and $q$, taking into account that:

- If the auto-correlation coefficient abruptly converges towards zero beyond lag $q$, the presumption is that the process is MA($q$).
- If the partial auto-correlation coefficient abruptly converges towards zero beyond lag $p$, the presumption is that the process is AR($p$).
- If neither of these is the case, the presumption is that the process is ARMA($p,q$), with $p > 0$ and $q > 0$. In practice, $p$ or $q$ are rarely taken to exceed 2, so that the number of possibilities that need to be tried out is limited. The shape of the two correlograms can help pin down $p$ and $q$. Alternatively, various statistical tests can be used for this purpose, especially in order to take the properties of the lags into account (Beveridge and Oickle, 1994). More than one candidate representation may emerge, however, at this stage.

### 4.2.3 Estimation

The next step is the estimation of the parameters. Different methods are available, which depending on the process are more or less convenient, but they all tend to produce similar estimates. Generally, an algorithm is used that maximises the likelihood (or probability) of the observed series, given the parameter values (by minimising the implied sum of squared residuals). Standard software packages include such algorithms, which are discussed at greater length by Hamilton (1994).

### 4.2.4 Verification

The last step prior to using the model in forecasting mode is to check that it is good enough for that purpose. This is also the point at which a choice is made between different possible representations, when more than one is plausible.

Two criteria come into play: the statistical properties of the estimated model on the one hand, and its simplicity and parsimony on the other. The first criterion encompasses the following questions: are the residuals white noise? are the parameters statistically significant? how good is the fit on past data? The answer to the last question is *a priori* that the larger $p$ and $q$, the better the fit. But this goes against the need for parsimony: while it is easy to enhance the model's fit on past data by adding explanatory variables that happen to be correlated with the explained variable (here, by increasing $p$ and $q$), this presents a risk of breaking down once the model is used in forecasting mode. With a more limited number of parameters, the chances are higher that the estimated relationship will be robust going forward. Some formal criteria can be used to decide what is best, given this trade-off (for example the Akaike information criterion or the Schwarz Bayesian criterion).

ARIMA models are relatively easy to implement and therefore widely used, not least in business cycle analysis to extrapolate series over the short run, for example to add a few points to a series for which one wants to construct a centred moving average.[2] Indeed, just repeating the last observation might introduce bias in that case, and an ARIMA forecast may avoid that problem.

The ARIMA approach, however, shares the usual drawback of statistical models, namely the absence of a straightforward economic interpretation of the model (what is the economic rationale for the chosen $p$ and $q$?) and of the forecasts it produces. It is also sometimes alleged that the relatively good performance of ARIMA models largely reflects their ability to replicate seasonal movements, in which case it would make more sense to tackle directly the issue of seasonality *per se*.

## 4.3　Decomposition into trend and cycle

As noted, one of the key issues in forecasting, when looking at how a variable evolves over time, is to properly distinguish between what corresponds to a durable trend and what reflects transient movements around that trend. A great variety of alternative techniques have been proposed for this purpose. A selection of statistical approaches is presented here (a more 'economic' approach to the trend–cycle decomposition is laid out in Section 7.1).

In virtually all cases, the decomposition between trend and cycle is either additive or multiplicative:

$$X_t = T_t + C_t + u_t \qquad \text{(additive form)}$$
$$X_t = T_t C_t u_t \qquad \text{(multiplicative form)}$$

where $X_t$ is the variable under consideration, $T_t$ the trend, $C_t$ the cyclical component and $u_t$ an unexplained residual. A fourth, seasonal component, could be introduced (as discussed in Section 3.4), but is abstracted from here. Once these components have been estimated over the past, they can be projected forward to forecast $X$, generally on the basis of some fairly simple assumptions. The various techniques differ in how $T$ and $C$ (and hence $u$) are identified. None of them is intrinsically superior to all the others, as each hinges on a number of explicit or

---

[2] As noted in Section 3.4, seasonal adjustment techniques often rely on ARIMA models in order to treat the latest points of the time series.

implicit assumptions, which depending on the circumstances are more or less satisfactory. But in practice, the relatively simpler approaches – deterministic trends and *ad hoc* smoothing – tend to be used most frequently.

In this context, an important point of controversy is what constitutes a cycle. For one thing, this depends on the chosen horizon, which may be rather short (especially in the financial area) or quite far off (several decades). In practice, the cycle often referred to in forecasting is the one followed by GDP, which typically spans several years. Also, cycles can be defined in level or first difference terms. In the first case, peaks and troughs in the level of activity or proxies thereof serve to identify the cycle. That is the approach pioneered by Burns and Mitchell (1946) in the United States, at the National Bureau of Economic Research (NBER). To this day, the NBER's Business Cycle Dating Committee continues to use this definition, even though it leaves some room for judgement. For instance, it defines a recession as 'a significant decline in economic activity spread across the economy, lasting more than a few months, and normally visible in real GDP, real income, employment, industrial production, and wholesale-retail sales'. An alternative approach, used in particular by the OECD when elaborating its leading economic indicators, is to focus on cycles in growth rates rather than in the level of activity.

Lastly, when thinking about trend and cycle, forecasters often refer to movements in real GDP, but the same concepts apply to other variables, and notably to the components of GDP, which contribute more or less to the cyclicity of GDP, depending on their weight in GDP and on their own cyclicity. For example, on the spending side of the national accounts, consumption typically represents about two-thirds of GDP but is not very volatile, as households tend to smooth spending over time, so it may not be the largest contributor to the cyclicity of GDP. Fixed investment instead is much more volatile and contributes substantially to fluctuations in GDP, even if its share in GDP is considerably smaller. The same holds for inventory investment. On the output side, manufacturing output contributes more than proportionately to the cyclicity of GDP, although this might be due in part to measurement issues and in particular to the way value added is measured in the non-manufacturing sectors. Finally, it is important to note the role played by international linkages in determining domestic cycles.

### 4.3.1  Deterministic trends

A simple way to identify an underlying trend in a series is to check whether it follows a deterministic trend. The latter can be linear or piecewise linear, when the trend displays one or several kinks because of one or several structural breaks. A typical example of such a break would be the one observed for real GDP in the early 1970s, when in many OECD countries a shift occurred from a relatively high to a lower rate of trend growth. Estimating the trend then respectively involves running the regression:

$$X_t = a + bt + \varepsilon_t \qquad \text{(linear trend)} \quad (4.1)$$
$$X_t = a + bt + c(t - t^*)D_t + \varepsilon_t \qquad \text{(piecewise linear trend with one break at time } t^*) \quad (4.2)$$

In the second case, $D_t$ is a dummy variable taking the value 0 for $t \le t^*$ and 1 for $t > t^*$. Up to time $t^*$, equation (4.2) boils down to equation (4.1). After $t^*$, the slope changes from $b$ to $(b+c)$, and the intercept from $a$ to $(a - ct^*)$. This can be generalised to several breaks.

Set against the general framework spelled out above, the residual in these two equations encompasses both the cyclical component $C_t$ and the unexplained $u_t$. Generally, some *ad hoc* functional form will be assumed for $C_t$, say, an AR(2) process. One can then characterise the theoretical distribution of $\varepsilon_t$ and infer the appropriate estimation method (taking into account any auto-correlation of the error term in particular).

This approach is conveniently simple, but the results are quite sensitive to the selection of the estimation period. It is important to cover an integer number of cycles, lest the estimate suffer from end-of-sample bias. Moreover, identifying changes in regime (that is, points such as $t^*$) is difficult, even if the choice of $t^*$ can in principle be checked by testing whether coefficient $c$ differs significantly from 0.

### 4.3.2   *Ad hoc* smoothing techniques

A different approach rests on *ad hoc* smoothing. The intuition is to try and extract the trend one would see when eyeballing a plot of the series under consideration. One method is to use moving average formulas of various orders, as for deseasonalisation purposes or for the calculation of summary indicators of the cycle (see Section 3.4). More complex smoothing techniques can also be applied, such as the Hodrick-Prescott (HP) filter, which is presented in detail in Section 7.1, but can be briefly described here as jointly minimising the distance between the trend and the actual observations and the variability of the trend, where the weight put on the second criterion is proportional to a 'smoothing parameter' called $\lambda$ and often set to a predetermined value in standard econometric packages.

All these techniques, however, have serious drawbacks. They are subject to end-of-sample biases insofar as they are not run on an integer number of cycles. Also, these techniques involve some degree of arbitrariness in the selection of the order of the moving average or of the smoothing parameter: depending on these choices, the derived trend may look extremely smooth or on the contrary rather irregular. Furthermore, they fail to separate the cyclical component $C_t$ and the residual $u_t$, which are in effect lumped together.

### 4.3.3   Spectral analysis

Spectral analysis instead does allow separation of trend, cycle and seasonality. It draws on the Fourier method of spectral decomposition used in physics. The idea is to split up a signal (here, a time series) into different frequency components, based on a search covering the whole range of possible frequencies. Then a subset of the latter is defined as the relevant frequency band and only the components falling within this band are retained. This band may include very low frequencies, extending far beyond the usual business cycle notion, and/or very high ones, for instance when looking at financial market data.

A popular type of spectral analysis is the so-called band-pass filter proposed by Baxter and King (1999). In the empirical application they present, they define the band based on Burns and Mitchell's definition that business cycles are cyclical components of no less than six quarters and their finding that they typically last fewer than 32 quarters in the United States. The filter then passes through components with periodic fluctuations ranging from 6 to 32 quarters, while removing high-frequency ('irregular', or 'noise') and low-frequency ('trend') components. The trend itself may thus fluctuate, but slowly. In theory, the optimal band-pass filter is a moving average of infinite order, so an approximation has to be used in practice. Baxter and King recommend a moving average spanning three years on both sides (both for quarterly and for annual data), but band-pass filters can be constructed in many different ways (see for example Christiano and Fitzgerald, 2003).

Band-pass filters have some drawbacks, however. When they are symmetric, using them in real time requires somehow prolonging the series of actual observations, in order to compute a moving average centred on the latest observation. As in the case of the HP filter, this can induce end-of-sample bias. In practice, it is advisable to test the sensitivity of the results to alternative choices of the order of the moving average used. Another problem is that the definition of the range of frequencies deemed to encompass the business cycle is rather arbitrary. Last but not least, it has been argued that under some circumstances, the band-pass filtered cyclical component can be spurious and may for example grossly misrepresent the output gap (Benati, 2001).

### 4.3.4   Stochastic trends

Another class of models emphasises the stochastic, as opposed to deterministic, nature of the trend. It posits that random shocks can have effects that are sufficiently persistent actually to influence the long-run trend. In this framework, the trend itself is decomposed into a deterministic component, $TD_t$, and a stochastic one, $TS_t$, and the series $X_t$ can be written as:

$$X_t = TD_t + TS_t + C_t + u_t$$

With a deterministic trend, the uncertainty associated with a long-run forecast is limited to the variation in the stationary deviation from that trend, $C_t$. With a stochastic trend instead, this uncertainty rises as the horizon is extended. Two methods are commonly used to implement this type of approach.

The first method, set out by Beveridge and Nelson (1981), applies to series that are integrated of order one. They showed that any ARIMA $(p,1,q)$ process can be decomposed into a random walk stochastic trend (possibly with drift) and a transitory, stationary, zero mean part with a cyclical interpretation.[3] This representation is derived as follows in the simple case of an ARIMA $(0,1,1)$ process. In this case, the first difference of $X_t$ is MA(1): $\Delta X_t = \varepsilon_t + b\,\varepsilon_{t-1}$, where $\varepsilon_t$ is independently

---

[3] From a statistical perspective, however, there is no guarantee for uniqueness and competing decompositions may be unidentifiable (Watson, 1986).

and identically distributed and $b$ is a constant. Let us normalise the series so that $X_0 = \varepsilon_0 = 0$. Then

$$
\begin{aligned}
X_t &= X_{t-1} + \varepsilon_t + b\varepsilon_{t-1} \\
&= X_{t-2} + (\varepsilon_{t-1} + b\varepsilon_{t-2}) + (\varepsilon_t + b\varepsilon_{t-1}) \\
&= (\varepsilon_1 + \varepsilon_2 + \cdots + \varepsilon_t) + b(\varepsilon_1 + \varepsilon_2 + \cdots + \varepsilon_{t-1}) \\
&= (1 + b)(\varepsilon_1 + \varepsilon_2 + \cdots + \varepsilon_t) - b\varepsilon_t \\
&= T_t + C_t \quad \text{(defining } T_t \equiv (1 + b)(\varepsilon_1 + \varepsilon_2 + \cdots + \varepsilon_t) \quad \text{and} \quad C_t \equiv -b\varepsilon_t)
\end{aligned}
$$

$T_t$, the stochastic trend, follows a random walk: $T = T_{t-1} + (1 + b)\varepsilon_t$. $C_t$, the cycle, is stationary.

For a more general ARIMA $(p,1,q)$ process, the decomposition becomes:

$$
X_t = T_t + C_t, \quad \text{with } T_t = T_{t-1} + g + h\varepsilon_t \quad \text{(random walk with drift } g) \\
\text{and } C_t = d(L)\varepsilon_t
$$

where $h$ is a constant which is a function of the coefficients in the lag polynomials of order $p$ and $q$ associated with the AR and MA components of the ARIMA process, and $d(L)$ a lag polynomial whose coefficients also depend on these coefficients. Note that in this decomposition, the trend and the cycle are perfectly correlated, since innovations in the two components are both proportional to $\varepsilon_t$.

In contrast, the second method – proposed by A. Harvey (1985) and Watson (1986) – assumes that innovations to the trend and to the cycle are orthogonal (perfectly uncorrelated). It is referred to as the unobserved component method and can be formulated as follows:

$$
X_t = T_t + C_t, \quad \text{with } T_t = T_{t-1} + g_t + \eta_t \\
\text{and } g_t = g_{t-1} + \zeta_t
$$

where the trend drift itself $g_t$ is allowed to evolve as a random walk and $C_t$ is a cycle with an ARIMA representation, say an AR(2) process of the form $C_t = aC_{t-1} + bC_{t-2} + \theta_t$. All errors terms ($\eta_t, \zeta_t, \theta_t$) are white noise. The permanent ($\eta_t$) and transitory ($\theta_t$) shocks are independent. Estimation is generally carried out using the Kalman filter procedure. It is often assumed that $\zeta_t = 0$, in which case the third equation is dropped (since $g_t = g$) and the second one simplifies to $T_t = T_{t-1} + g + \eta_t$, representing a random walk with drift. If in addition $\eta_t = \zeta_t = 0$, the trend is in fact deterministic.

In practice, the two methods yield very different results (Morley et al., 2003). When applied to US real GDP data, the first one suggests that much of the variation is that of the trend, and that the cyclical component is small and noisy. In contrast, the second one implies a very smooth trend accompanied by an ample and highly persistent cycle. The complexity of these methods makes them difficult to use in everyday business cycle analysis.

### 4.3.5  Non-linear approaches

All the decompositions described thus far implicitly assume that the cycle can be described in linear terms and that it is symmetric. However, it has long been

*Figure 4.1*　**Asymmetries**

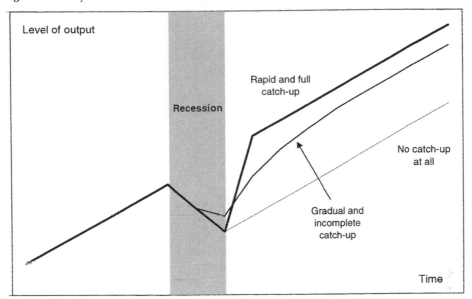

Note: The recession period is shaded.

recognised that this is not the case in practice. For example, Keynes (1936) wrote that 'the substitution of a downward for an upward tendency often takes place suddenly and violently, whereas there is, as a rule, no such sharp turning point when an upward is substituted for a downward tendency'. Asymmetry has a number of potentially relevant dimensions, including skewness (do expansions last longer than contractions?), steepness (are contractions steeper than expansions?), depth (are troughs deeper than peaks are tall?) and sharpness (are turning points more spiky at troughs or at peaks?). Empirical studies have explored some of these dimensions. Using a non-parametric procedure, Neftçi (1984) documents that increases in the US unemployment rate are shorter and sharper than declines. Razzak (2001), based on a different test and focusing on GDP, finds that the degree of symmetry of business cycles varies across countries, with clear evidence of asymmetry for Japan and Australia but much less in the United States, Germany and New Zealand.

A number of models have been built that capture the stylised features of steep and short recessions, but with different implications (Figure 4.1). This class of models includes the following univariate ones:

- Hamilton (1989) divides the business cycle into negative and positive trend growth regimes, with the economy switching back and forth between the two according to a latent state variable. During an expansion, output does not regain the ground lost in the downturn. Recessions thus permanently lower output, by an estimated 3 per cent in the United States.
- Kim and Nelson (1999) model recessions as regime switches affecting only the cyclical component of output, so that the effect of recessionary shocks is

constrained to be completely transitory: following a trough, output first bounces back to catch up with the earlier trend (high growth recovery phase) and then grows again along this trend (normal expansion).

- An intermediate model by Kim *et al.* (2005) augments Hamilton's model with a bounce-back term that generates faster growth in the quarters immediately following the output trough: output does catch up with its pre-recession trend, albeit not completely. The permanent effect of recessions is thus smaller than in Hamilton's model.[4]

In general, non-linear approaches are interesting in that they suggest that economies respond differently to shocks depending on circumstances. In a linear model, $X_t$ responds in the same way irrespective of the time at which the shock occurs, and the response will be proportional to the shock. In a non-linear setting instead, the response differs according to the economy's position in the cycle and depends in more complex ways on the direction and size of the shock. There has been a growing interest in recent years for these approaches, especially for the purpose of anticipating economic turning points (see Section 3.4). In practice, however, such calculations are relatively complex and hard to communicate to forecast users. Moreover, it is not clear whether allowing for non-linearities improves out-of-sample forecast performance, as documented by Stock and Watson (1999) in the particular case of smooth transition auto-regressive (STAR) models – where the economy is switching between two different linear states, depending on specific thresholds. One reason may be that the non-linear features that were prominent in the estimation sample fail to carry over to the forecast period. Another may be that the observed non-linearity is spurious in the sense that it reflects other features of the time series, such as heteroscedasticity or outliers (van Dijk *et al.*, 2002).

## 4.4   VAR models

Univariate methods provide simple and often fairly robust forecasting tools but they disregard the observed relationships observed empirically across variables, which can be very informative. The most common way to take them into account is to run a vector auto-regressive (VAR) model, which is simple to estimate and convenient for forecasting purposes. This approach was pioneered by Sims (1980), as an alternative to structural macroeconomic models (see Chapter 6). This section provides a brief overview of this class of models (which is presented in more detail in Hamilton, 1994).

### 4.4.1   Basic principles

Consider for example a forecast of the stock of money based on activity, prices and interest rates. One way to proceed would be to estimate the following

---

[4] This holds for US data. Kim *et al.* (2005) also look at Australia, Canada and the United Kingdom, and find that recessions have a greater permanent impact in the latter two countries.

money demand equation:

$$m_t - p_t = \beta_0 + \beta_1(m_{t-1} - p_{t-1}) + \beta_2 y_t + \beta_3 i_t + u_t$$

where $m_t$ is the money stock, $p_t$ the general price level, $y_t$ activity (all in logarithms), $i_t$ a representative interest rate and $u_t$ a shock. But $p_t$, $y_t$ and $i_t$ cannot be considered as exogenous variables, implying likely simultaneity bias. For example, $i_t$ might be determined as follows, reflecting central bank behaviour:

$$i_t = \delta_0 + \delta_1 p_t + \delta_2 y_t + \delta_3 m_t + v_t$$

In that case, $i_t$ is correlated with $u_t$ (even if $u_t$ and $v_t$ are uncorrelated) and the estimators of the parameters of the money demand equation would be biased.

The proper way to proceed is to start from the general structural form, which includes all the behavioural equations related to the system under consideration. For example:

$$\mathbf{B}_0 \mathbf{Y}_t = \mathbf{M} + \mathbf{B}_1 \mathbf{Y}_{t-1} + \mathbf{B}_2 \mathbf{Y}_{t-2} + \cdots + \mathbf{B}_k \mathbf{Y}_{t-k} + \boldsymbol{\omega}_t$$

where $\mathbf{Y}_t^T = (m_t, i_t, p_t, y_t)$,[5] $\mathbf{M}$ is a $4 \times 1$ vector of constants (intercepts), the $\mathbf{B}_i$ are $4 \times 4$ matrices, $\boldsymbol{\omega}_t$ is a $4 \times 1$ vector of structural disturbances, and the lag structure has been extended to $k$ lags (compared with the above money demand equation), so as not to unduly restrict it *a priori*.

This is a structural form because each equation now lends itself to an economic interpretation (money demand by private agents, interest rate setting by the central bank and so forth). However, this system of equations cannot be estimated directly. It has to be transformed into a reduced form for which parameters can be estimated, by multiplying the above equation by $\mathbf{B}_0^{-1}$, which gives:

$$\mathbf{Y}_t = \mathbf{A} + \mathbf{A}_1 \mathbf{Y}_{t-1} + \mathbf{A}_2 \mathbf{Y}_{t-2} + \cdots + \mathbf{A}_k \mathbf{Y}_{t-k} + e_t$$

where $\mathbf{A}_i = \mathbf{B}_0^{-1} \mathbf{B}_i$ and $e_t = \mathbf{B}_0^{-1} \boldsymbol{\omega}_t$. This is the general formula for a VAR model, as a simple auto-regressive form for a vector of variables. The above derivation of this formula shows that this representation of $Y$ is legitimate, since the VAR is simply a reduced form of the structural representation. The equations defining $Y$ involve reduced-form parameters (the $\mathbf{A}$ matrices and the variance-covariance matrix of $e_t$): these do not have an economic interpretation themselves but are a function of the structural parameters.

The reduced-form parameters can be estimated using straightforward ordinary least squares (OLS) regression equation by equation since the OLS estimators are consistent and equal to the maximum likelihood estimators. Forecasting then

---

[5] T is the transpose symbol, indicating that a line vector is turned into a column vector or vice versa.

simply requires to compute $Y_t$ as a function of its past values period after period. However, in practice, a number of problems arise.

### 4.4.2   Choosing the series

Indeed, VARs look deceptively simple. A decisive yet complex and difficult choice is the decision on which of the variables to include in the system. Generally, VAR models are intended to reflect some theoretical model, in line with the sequence presented above. In some cases, the theoretical model is in fact rather loose, and heuristic considerations are brought in to justify the shape of the VAR. In others – notably as concerns the so-called 'structural VARs' (see below) – the VAR is derived from an explicit and fully specified structural model, which dictates which variables should feature in the system. But in all cases, the choice of variables essentially reflects *a priori* ideas and modelling, subject to the practical constraint that the number of variables can only be very limited (usually two to five), lest the estimates become overly imprecise.

In principle, the variables can be selected on a purely statistical basis, using Granger-causality tests:[6] a variable that appears to be exogenous in a Granger sense can be excluded from the vector of endogenous variables of the VAR. However, applying this methodology to a large number of candidate variables, with a sufficient number of lags, requires that a great many observations be available, which is often not the case in macroeconomic analysis. Thus, the VAR approach is not really devoid of theory. On the contrary, the decision to include or leave out certain variables usually constitutes a strong *a priori* restriction with important implications as to what underlying model the VAR is consistent with.

Another delicate issue is whether and how to transform the selected time series before running the VAR: can they be kept as is, or should one take logs, or first differences? A key question in this respect is how to deal with non-stationarity. Take the above VAR, with $Y_t$ now generalised to a vector of $n$ variables:

$$Y_t = A + A_1Y_{t-1} + A_2Y_{t-2} + \cdots + A_kY_{t-k} + e_t$$

For OLS to be applicable, as indicated above, all the components of $Y_t$ should be stationary. In that case, the estimators are consistent and the usual asymptotic tests of the parameters can be applied. By contrast, if some of the variables are non-stationary (which is likely in the above example for money, prices and activity), they need to be transformed through differencing into stationary variables prior to running the VAR.[7]

---

[6] A variable $x$ is said to 'Granger-cause' variable $y$ if the forecast of the latter is improved by taking into account the information embodied in the former (in fact, this should be described in terms of correlation rather than causation; finding evidence of Granger causality can be an artefact of a spurious correlation, and lack of Granger causality can be misleading too if the true causal link is of non-linear form).

[7] The number of times $d$ a variable has to be differenced to become stationary is called its order of integration I($d$). Output and inflation often appear to be I(1) and prices I(2). See Box 5.1 for more details.

Considering I(1) variables only, two cases can arise. If the variables are not cointegrated,[8] the VAR can be estimated in first differences:

$$\Delta Y_t = A + A_1 \Delta Y_{t-1} + A_2 \Delta Y_{t-2} + \cdots + A_k \Delta Y_{t-k} + e_t$$

Alternatively, if there exist $r$ cointegration relations, an estimation of the VAR in first differences would fail to take account of the long-term relationships between the variables. The proper specification of the VAR is then a vector error-correction model (VECM):

$$\Delta Y_t = A + C Y_{t-1} + D_1 \Delta Y_{t-1} + D_2 \Delta Y_{t-2} + \cdots + D_{k-1} \Delta Y_{t-k+1} + e_t$$

where the $C$ is called the long-run impact matrix and the $D_i$ are the short-run impact matrices.

The transformation used to compute the VECM can be illustrated for the following simple VAR model:

$$Y_t = A + A_1 Y_{t-1} + A_2 Y_{t-2} + e_t$$

Subtracting $Y_{t-1}$ from both sides yields:

$$
\begin{aligned}
\Delta Y_t &= A - Y_{t-1} + A_1 Y_{t-1} + A_2 Y_{t-2} + e_t \\
&= A - Y_{t-1} + A_1 Y_{t-1} + A_2 Y_{t-2} + A_2 Y_{t-1} - A_2 Y_{t-1} + e_t \\
&= A + (A_1 + A_2 - I_n) Y_{t-1} - A_2 \Delta Y_{t-1} + e_t \qquad \text{(where } I_n \text{ is the } n \times n \\
&\qquad\qquad\qquad\qquad\qquad\qquad\qquad\qquad\qquad\qquad \text{identity matrix)} \\
&= A + C Y_{t-1} + D_1 \Delta Y_{t-1} + e_t
\end{aligned}
$$

where $C = A_1 + A_2 - I_n$ and $D_1 = -A_2$.

### 4.4.3 Estimation problems

Choosing the right number of lags is yet another difficulty when estimating a VAR model. In principle, this number can be determined in a fairly objective way. For example, in the case of quarterly series, it would be natural first to try out four and eight lags. Then a Fisher test can check whether lags five to eight can be dropped. If so, one can compare a three and four-lag specification using the same test, and so forth. If not, one might test a six-lag specification, and perhaps a seven-lag one. If eight lags appear to be a minimum, one could even test a 12-lag specification.

In practice, however, the number of lags and of variables cannot be that large. The higher they are, the more observations are needed if a reasonable degree

---

[8] A set of non-stationary variables are said to be cointegrated if some linear combination of these variables is stationary. If there exist $r$ independent stationary linear combinations, there are said to be $r$ cointegration relations.

of precision is to be preserved. For example, a VAR model with eight lags for three variables requires estimating 24 parameters for each of the three equations, and therefore 72 auto-regressive parameters, plus the six parameters of the covariance matrix. Given that quarterly time series often do not extend beyond two or three decades, the number of parameters could easily be of the same order of magnitude as the number of observations. Over-parameterisation tends to cause multicollinearity and loss of degrees of freedom, leading to large out-of-sample forecasting errors. Hence, VAR estimates obtained on relatively short data sets and/or with a rich structure in terms of variables or lags are not very robust.

### 4.4.4   VAR uses

On the whole, VAR models are a useful tool for business cycle analysis, generating forecasts that can be as good as those obtained through other means (Thomakos and Guerard, 2004). They also have the advantage of not requiring assumptions to be made about the exogenous variables. That said, in addition to their possible lack of robustness, VAR model results are difficult to explain in economic terms. While simulations may work well on historical data, the 'black box' nature of the exercise makes it difficult for VARs to serve as the anchor for the story that is part and parcel of a forecast.

Even so, VAR models contribute to shedding light on the short-run outlook in the following ways:

- They can help sort survey-based information. Chapter 3 showed that the relations between endogenous, quantitative variables and qualitative balance-of-opinion survey results cannot be viewed as proper behavioural equations. This can make it difficult to choose which information to use. VARs can then be of assistance to sort through such survey data (which are often stationary), without the need to worry about causality, simultaneity or links between them.
- They can help identify some causal relationships. VAR modelling can highlight how Granger causality runs and show which survey data are ahead of others.
- They can help interpret ongoing developments. By allowing to compare what would have resulted from the VAR with the actual developments, VAR modelling identifies 'innovations'. This prompts the analyst to reflect on how 'normal' the current situation is and if it does not appear to be so, to look for the special factors (say, weather conditions) that may explain deviations from what the VAR predicts.

### 4.4.5   Structural VARs

As shown above, a VAR can be seen as the reduced form of a structural model. This reduced form can be estimated, whereas in general, the parameters in a structural model cannot. The latter is said not to be identifiable.

However, when faced with a VAR estimation, it is natural to ask whether one can recover the structural model. This has led to the development of the so-called structural VARs. The idea is to posit that a number of restrictions apply to the parameters of the structural model, so as to be able to identify them based on the reduced-form parameters. Recall that:

$$B_0 Y_t = B_1 Y_{t-1} + B_2 Y_{t-2} + \cdots + B_k Y_{t-k} + \omega_t \qquad \text{(structural model)}$$
$$Y_t = A_1 Y_{t-1} + A_2 Y_{t-2} + \cdots + A_k Y_{t-k} + e_t \qquad \text{(VAR)}$$

where $A_i = B_0^{-1} B_i$ and $e_t = B_0^{-1} \omega_t$.

Identification requires to know matrix $B_0$, which is needed to compute the structural parameters $B_i$ based on the VAR estimates $A_i$, and the structural shocks $\omega_t$ based on the VAR innovations $e_t$. Economic considerations can help pin down $B_0$. Since $B_0$ is $n \times n$, it initially includes $n^2$ unknown parameters. The variance-covariance matrix estimated based on the VAR, which is equal to $B_0^{-1} (B_0^{-1})^{\mathsf{T}}$, allows identification of $n(n + 1)/2$ restrictions on these parameters.[9] Hence, $n(n - 1)/2$ identifying restrictions remain to be defined in order to arrive at the structural model.

A canonical example of this methodology is the bivariate system for unemployment and output growth considered by Blanchard and Quah (1989). They postulate that this system is driven by two orthogonal structural shocks ('supply' and 'demand'). The identifying restriction is that only supply shocks can permanently affect output (only one such restriction is needed here since for $n = 2$, $n(n - 1)/2 = 1$). Another classic example of an identifying restriction is that a monetary shock has no long-run impact on real variables.

The structural VAR approach sits half-way between pure VAR analysis and structural macroeconomic models. Once the VAR is identified, one can study its impulse response functions, which show how variables react over time to structural shocks. This can be useful when thinking about alternative scenarios. One can also retrace the sequence of past structural shocks and decompose the past values of the variables as a function of these shocks. For forecasting purposes, however, structural VARs may not add that much compared to simple VARs, and share the latter's lack of robustness. Also, it may be difficult to properly specify independent structural shocks over the short horizon of near-term analyses. Last but not least, the fact that VARs are run with a small number of variables implies that potentially important information is disregarded, which can lead to puzzling, if not outright misleading, results (Box 4.1).

---

[9] Without loss of generality, it is implicitly assumed here that the structural shocks are orthogonal and that their variance is unity.

---

*Box 4.1*   **How to use more information in VARs**

One of the problems with standard VAR analyses is that to conserve a sufficient number of degrees of freedom, they rarely include more than six to eight variables. In so doing, they discard information that economic agents do take into account when making decisions.

Sims (1992) has illustrated this in the case of a central bank. Suppose that the central bank systematically tightens policy when anticipating rising inflation down the road. If the signals of future inflationary pressures are not adequately captured by the variables included in the VAR, then what is interpreted in VAR analysis as a policy shock may in fact be the central bank's response to new information about inflation. But the policy response to the latter might only partly offset the inflationary pressure, so that the estimated impulse response function will show an interest rate hike to be followed by a rise in inflation, a counter-intuitive finding.

A recent strand of literature has proposed a way to condition VAR analyses on richer information sets without losing the statistical advantages associated with a small number of variables. Bernanke *et al.* (2004), for example, combine standard VAR and factor (principal component) analysis. They build on the finding that for forecasting purposes dynamic factor models summarising the information contained in large data sets outperform univariate auto-regressions, small VARs and leading indicator models (Stock and Watson, 2002).

---

# 5
# Modelling Behaviour

This chapter presents the specifications that are generally adopted to describe agents' economic behaviour. Section 5.1 deals with enterprise investment (fixed and stockbuilding), which plays a prominent role as a driver of economic fluctuations. Section 5.2 proceeds with household spending (consumption and residential investment). Section 5.3 discusses imports, exports, world demand and competitiveness. Section 5.4 covers employment and Section 5.5 wage–price dynamics. In the process, this chapter surveys the commonly used specifications, including their theoretical underpinnings and their typical results. The presentation draws heavily on error-correction equations, as they are intuitive, enlightening and frequently used by practitioners (see Box 5.1). Estimation methods *per se* are beyond the scope of this book but are presented in standard econometrics textbooks.

Some of the theoretical mechanisms will be shown to hold up well empirically. Examples include the effect of expected demand on investment, the effect of growth abroad on exports, or the influence of wages on prices and vice versa. Other purported mechanisms are more difficult to document in practice. For instance, the impact of a change in interest rates on investment and more generally on aggregate demand is hard to pin down, as is the impact of a wage hike on labour demand.

The equations presented in this chapter seek to reflect the main determinants of economic behaviour as they have been observed over the past. They constitute the backbone of the structural forecasting methods which combine economic reasoning and econometrics (see Section 1.3). When assembled, these equations lead to the macroeconometric models that can be used to produce overall forecasts (see Chapter 6).

## 5.1 Enterprise investment

This section deals with investment by private firms, as opposed to public sector investment and to residential investment by households. Fixed investment involves replacing or increasing firms' productive capital stock (structures and equipment). Stockbuilding instead is the change in the volume of inventories held by firms and has its own laws of motion.

---

*Box 5.1*  **Error-correction models: a primer**

Error-correction models (ECMs) enable analysts to account both for the links between economic variables over the long run and for the short- or medium-run dynamics around these equilibrium relationships. They are well suited to the statistical properties of macro-economic time series, in particular as regards their frequent non-stationarity.

First recall the following definitions:

- A stochastic process is said to be (weakly) stationary if its first and second moment (mean and covariances) are constant over time.
- A process is said to be integrated of order 1, and is denoted I(1), if it is non-stationary and if differenced once it becomes stationary, that is, I(0); likewise, it is I($d$) if it needs to be differenced $d$ times to become stationary.
- A set of I($d$) processes are said to be cointegrated if at least one linear combination of these processes is stationary.

The existence of such a cointegration relationship is the statistical counterpart of an economic equilibrium between the variables under consideration. For example, consumption and income are generally considered to be both I(1), but the ratio of consumption to income – the average propensity to consume – may be I(0): if so, while consumption and income grow indefinitely, and partly randomly, their ratio only temporarily deviates from its long-run average.

Economic theories suggest that *a priori* many such relationships may exist: between the capital stock and GDP, between prices, wages and productivity, between exports, world demand and the relative price of exports, and so on. The empirical relevance of these various equilibrium relationships has to be examined using cointegration tests.

When several variables are cointegrated, this relationship does not hold exactly at all times. That would only be the case in a fictional economy devoid of any disturbances and where each variable would expand at a constant rate. In practice, unanticipated shocks and variable adjustment lags entail deviations from these long-run paths. The difference between the cointegrating linear combination and its long-run mean then measures the distance from equilibrium. The idea underlying ECMs is that when there is such a gap, forces tend to pull back the relevant variables towards equilibrium.

Consider the example of consumption and suppose that the saving ratio (equal to one minus the average propensity to consume) is stationary. Then one cointegration relation can be $c = y$, where $c$ is consumption and $y$ income, both in logarithms. Let $U$ denote the unemployment rate; an ECM of consumption could then be written as:

$$\Delta c_t = \alpha + \beta \Delta y_t + \gamma \Delta U_t - \eta(c_{t-1} - y_{t-1})$$

The term $\eta(c_{t-1} - y_{t-1})$ is the error-correction term, where $\eta$ stands for the adjustment in each period back towards equilibrium. If there were no other term in the equation, one would simply have a partial adjustment model. In addition, the short-run dynamics of $\Delta c_t$ is captured by the term $\beta \Delta y_t$, which increases the speed of convergence towards the long-run equilibrium, and by the term $\gamma \Delta U_t$, which is added in to illustrate that variables that are not part of the long-run relationship may nonetheless have an impact over the short run.

The equation could also include other dynamic terms, such as lagged changes in consumption and income or other stationary variables. In fact, the selection of the appropriate specification is largely an empirical question. The practice is usually to include variables which seem sensible from an economic standpoint and which prove to be statistically robust, while ensuring that the equation residuals eventually be approximately white noise.

More generally, when a group of I(d) variables admits a single cointegration relation-ship, it can be shown that each of them has an error-correction representation akin to the example above (this is the so-called Engle and Granger representation theorem). When there are several cointegration relationships, each error-correction term may affect the evolution of all the other variables.

Note also that an equation in which only the level of variables would appear (here, regressing the level of consumption on the level of income) would allow to identify the cointegration relationship between these two variables, but would not accurately depict the short-run fluctuations in consumption. Conversely, an equation featuring only first differences of these variables might properly account for their short-run dynamics but would overlook their tendency to move towards the long-run equilibrium when they are away from it. The usefulness of ECMs may be limited for short-run forecasts, however, since gravitation towards the long-run equilibrium is often relatively slow. Hence, ECMs are in principle more relevant for longer forecast horizons.

## 5.1.1 Fixed investment

The dynamics of investment are often considered to be at the core of the economic cycle. In the traditional view, investment accelerates during a recovery, when capacity is deemed insufficient to meet future demand, and declines when the slowdown begins and the need for capital is more than met. Investment thus both reflects and drives the economic cycle: it depends on the fluctuations in demand and, at the same time, is a major contributor to these ups and downs. It is these underlying dynamics of investment that the econometric analysis seeks to cap-ture, discounting high-frequency movements which affect investment erratically (for example in the case of bunched aircraft deliveries).

A variety of theories may guide the econometric specification of investment demand (see Box 5.2). Most of them derive an expression for firms' optimal capital stock, which is generally considered as a long-run target. The determinants of the optimal capital stock vary according to the approach but the following are usually emphasised:

- Expected demand (for the goods or services that the capital under consideration will help produce), leading to the principle of the 'accelerator';
- The user cost of capital, defined as the cost of renting one unit of capital;
- Firms' financial situation, as revealed *inter alia* by the level of profits;
- Their 'profitability', defined as the difference between expected return and capital cost.

In practice, econometric tests almost always corroborate the notion that demand is one of investment's main determinants (Chirinko, 1993). In contrast, it is often more difficult to find a robust relationship with the other factors. One problem is that the time needed for capital to adjust to them is often considerable compared to the length of the available data set. Besides, investment may be dri-ven by a variety of other considerations, depending in particular on the type of capital considered (new technologies versus old ones for instance). As a result, the specifications used in practice in forecasting are fairly parsimonious, given the

---

*Box 5.2* **Investment and the capital stock: theories**

There are at least five different theoretical approaches to investment, understood as the outlays necessary to increase the stock of capital, over and above depreciation through wear and tear or obsolescence:

- The accelerator model: if the desired capital–output ratio is a constant $k$ (usually, $k > 1$) and if GDP is expected to rise by $x$ per cent, the required stock of capital will rise by $kx$ per cent of GDP; with investment averaging, say, one-fifth of GDP, the percentage point increase in investment ($5kx$) needed to raise the capital stock to its new desired level is much larger than the percentage point increase in GDP. This model captures the stylised fact that investment 'accelerates' in response to a variation in output and is therefore more volatile. It can be augmented to take into account the cost of capital and construction lags.
- The effective demand model: firms are assumed to minimise costs for a given level of production. The optimal capital stock then depends on the latter (proportionately in the case of constant returns to scale) and on the cost of capital relative to the cost of labour.
- The neo-classical model: under perfect competition, a firm maximises its profits by equalising the marginal product of capital and its cost. The corresponding equation could be seen as giving the optimal level of capital, the two determinants being the level of production and the real cost of capital. But the optimal level of output itself depends on the profit maximisation programme. To solve it, two cases need to be distinguished. Under decreasing returns to scale, the optimal level of capital ultimately depends on the (real) cost of labour and capital; empirically, however, such a specification without a demand term tends to perform poorly. Under constant returns to scale, the optimal level of capital remains undetermined, since profits are zero at any level of output; only the optimal capital–output ratio can be determined, which empirically is of no use to pin down the level of capital.
- Imperfect competition models: under imperfect competition and with a constant price-elasticity of the demand for goods, each firm maximises profit by jointly deciding on its prices, the quantity of factors used in production and its level of output, while considering aggregate demand as an exogenous variable. In this framework, aggregate demand and the real cost of capital are the ultimate determinants of aggregate investment.
- Models based on Tobin's $q$ theory: firms invest as a function of the difference between the expected return on the new investment and the cost of its financing (or the return on a financial asset, if the firm does not need to borrow to invest). This difference is defined as profitability. While in principle it is constant over the long run, it can vary in the short run, leading to investment cycles.

In addition, one generally considers that investment is sensitive to firms' financial situation, and specifically to their short-run liquidity position, as documented for example by Ashworth and Davis (2001) for the G7 countries. Indeed, firms may not have unrestricted access to external financing, owing to various credit and capital market imperfections. The current level of profits may therefore influence investment, insofar as profits allow an increase in the share of the project that can be financed by internal cash flow, and facilitate access to outside finance. This, however, pertains more to the feasibility than to the desirability of investment.

diversity of the theoretical explanations. They principally rest on the accelerator mechanism, although profits, the user cost or profitability are sometimes also taken into account.

A typical ECM equation for the stock of capital is:

$$\Delta k_t = \alpha + \sum_j \alpha_j \Delta k_{t-j} + \sum_j \beta_j \Delta y_{t-j} - \mu(k_{t-1} - \varepsilon_k y_{t-1}) + \gamma_k z_t^k \tag{5.1}$$

Similarly, for investment a typical ECM equation is:

$$\Delta i_t = \alpha + \sum_j \alpha_j \Delta i_{t-j} + \sum_j \beta_j \Delta y_{t-j} - \mu(i_{t-1} - \varepsilon_i y_{t-1}) + \gamma_i z_t^i \tag{5.2}$$

where $k$, $i$ and $y$ are the logarithms of the capital stock, investment and a variable standing for aggregate demand, while $z^k$ and $z^i$ are vectors of other explanatory variables (which may play a role in the short-run dynamic term of the equation as well as in the long-run one, but are subsumed in a single vector here, for the sake of simplicity).

In practice, the dependent variable can be either the stock of capital $K$ or the flow of investment $I$. The first option comes closest to the usual theories, based on the concept of an optimal capital stock. The second option has the advantage of not requiring a series for the stock of capital, which is important, given how difficult it is to measure capital properly and the poor quality of many capital stock series. It is also possible to adopt a specification in terms of the rate of accumulation of capital, $I/K$, since:

$$I_t = K_t - (1 - \delta_t)K_{t-1}$$

where $\delta_t$ is the rate of depreciation. The latter is usually treated as exogenous and projected by extrapolating past depreciation rates. This formulation is very close to one in $\Delta k$, since $\Delta k = \Delta \log K \approx \Delta K/K = I/K - \delta$, where the depreciation rate is assumed to be constant.

While the long-run relationship in equations (5.1) or (5.2) is generally associated with one of the above theories, their dynamic part can be interpreted in two ways. On the one hand, it reflects the existence of technical or organisational delays when installing new equipment, implying that it is not possible to jump immediately to the optimal level of capital: building a factory, for example, can take years. On the other hand, it is necessary to take into account the time it takes to reach the investment decision itself. The purchase of expensive machinery or the creation of a new plant are risky and largely irreversible decisions. To go ahead, entrepreneurs and those who finance them need to be confident enough that the investment will be profitable. In practice, these different types of lags cannot be distinguished lest the equations become excessively complicated. The dynamics are therefore estimated globally, letting the data determine the adjustment coefficients. One may expect, in particular, that some of the factors considered here, such as the cost of capital or profitability, have their full impact only if they are sustained for quite some time. Hence, one should not expect the coefficient $\mu$ to be high, especially for specifications in terms of capital stock or rate of accumulation.

It is worth discussing the various explanatory variables in greater detail, starting with the most consistently significant one, namely demand. Different measures of demand are used in practice, including gross output, value added and GDP. Since the left-hand-side variable is enterprise investment, it may be preferable, however, to focus on demand of the private sector, rather than overall demand. Econometric estimates usually confirm the accelerator mechanism described in Box 5.2, that is, that in the short run investment increases more than proportionately in response to rising demand. This pattern explains why investment tends to be so volatile and pro-cyclical. Typically (albeit far from universally), a sustained one per cent increase in demand would translate, after a lag of two to four quarters, into a 2 to 2.5 per cent increase in investment. The capital stock instead reacts much less rapidly, with an average adjustment lag of 5 to 10 years. Lastly, it is often considered that the capital–output ratio and the investment ratio should be stable over the long run, as predicted by constant returns-to-scale growth theories (see Section 7.2). This is indeed more or less the case in practice. It can be tested by testing the restriction $\varepsilon_k = 1$ or $\varepsilon_i = 1$ in the long-run term of the above equations.

The user (or rental) cost of capital is the second determinant of investment. In practice, it is sometimes proxied by an interest rate. But its usual definition – consistent with a set-up where the value of the firm is maximised – is:

$$C_t = (1 + R_t)P^i_{t-1} - (1 - \delta)P^i_t \approx P^i_t(R_t + \delta - \pi_t)$$

where $P^i$ is the investment deflator, $R_t$ the nominal interest rate and $\pi_t$ inflation. In words, the cost of one unit of capital in period t has three components: the unit of capital, which is bought in $t - 1$ at the price $P^i_{t-1}$; the interest rate $R_t$, which reflects the cost of borrowing funds (or by which the firm's own funds would otherwise have been remunerated); and the value of the capital stock that remains after depreciation $(1 - \delta)$ and that can be sold in $t$ at price $P^i_t$.

This formula can be augmented to take taxes into account. This can make a big difference, as suggested by Cummins *et al.* (1996), who document that in many OECD countries taxes do matter at the firm level. Even so, the impact of taxation is often ignored in practice because estimating the relevant effective tax rates, which often vary frequently over time, is very complicated.

The way this is taken into consideration when conducting empirical estimations reflects to some extend the theoretical views of the forecaster. As noted in Box 5.2 for the neo-classical model, the optimal capital stock depends on the real cost of capital. The latter may be measured as the ratio of the nominal user cost divided by the price of the produced goods. In Keynesian models stressing the role of demand, the optimal capital stock rather depends on the cost of capital relative to that of labour. Numerous empirical studies have attempted to find evidence supporting one or the other approach, and to quantify the elasticity of substitution between capital and labour. The results are mixed because of several practical complications over and above the difficulty of estimating the incidence of taxation.

Which interest rate should one use? Should it include a risk premium, and if so, how large? Is the price of investment, notably that of computers, adequately measured? If the cost of labour enters the picture, what is a good assumption for the evolution of labour productivity? In addition, adjustment lags imply that changes in factor costs only very gradually affect the production–input mix. It is easier to document substitution between capital and labour at the microeconomic level, but then the results cannot be readily extended to the macroeconomic level.

Profits also influence investment, because current profits may be seen as foreshadowing future profits, rendering investment more attractive, or because profits improve firms' cash flow and allow them to finance a significant share of investment using retained earnings, which makes a difference when firms lack unfettered access to outside funding. Models where investment depends both on demand and profits are referred to as accelerator-profit investment models. The most commonly used empirical measure of profits is the profit rate, defined as the gross operating surplus divided by the capital stock valued at replacement cost. Another option is to use real profits (the gross operating surplus divided by the value added deflator). Profits can also be measured in net terms, meaning deducting consumption of fixed capital. They can also be calculated after taxes, meaning after subtracting corporate income taxes. The significance of the chosen profit indicator can be tested in the short-run as well as in the long-run term of the investment equation.

Accelerator-profit investment equations can work well for forecasting purposes, and are therefore popular. Yet, they have some drawbacks. First, the cost of capital, or even simply the interest rate, is ignored. Given that investment is generally thought to be sensitive to changes in interest rates, this is a problem, notably when analysing the short-run effects of monetary policy. Second, it is difficult to disentangle the impact of demand and that of profits, given that the two are highly correlated. Last but not least, profits themselves are hard to predict with accuracy, particularly if after-tax profits are considered, which fluctuate a lot and are affected by firms' efforts to minimise the tax burden and smooth it over time.

Profitability, as the difference between the expected return on new investment and its cost, overcomes the first of these problems. The most frequently used indicator of profitability is Tobin's $q$, which is the ratio of the stock market valuation of a firm (or group of firms) to the replacement value of their capital stock. Firms invest until, at the margin, $q$ equals one.[1] An alternative indicator, proposed by Malinvaud (1983), is the difference between the after-tax profit rate net of depreciation and the long-term interest rate. These two indicators are in fact equivalent when stock prices correctly price in future profits (then the profit rate equals the interest rates times Tobin's $q$). Malinvaud's indicator is not sensitive to stock

---

[1] The intuition underlying $q$ theory was articulated by Keynes (1936): 'daily revaluations of the Stock Exchange ... inevitably exert a decisive influence on the rate of current investment. For there is no sense in building up a new enterprise at a cost greater than that at which a similar existing enterprise can be purchased; whilst there is an inducement to spend on a new project what may seem an extravagant sum, if it can be floated off on the Stock Exchange at an immediate profit.'

market over- or under-valuations, but whether this is an advantage in this context is a moot point, since investment cycles are precisely influenced by stock market bearishness or bullishness.

In principle, profitability should sum up all the determinants of investment: if a project is profitable, it should be undertaken. But empirically, investment equations solely containing profitability on the right-hand side perform rather poorly. One reason may be that the above indicators capture average rather than marginal profitability, whereas investment is driven by the latter. But marginal profitability cannot be directly observed at the macroeconomic level. A more pragmatic approach is then to test the significance of (average) profitability alongside the traditional accelerator effect.

### 5.1.2   Stockbuilding

Inventories can comprise raw materials, energy, semi-finished products and finished products that have yet to be sold. Although the level of inventories is small relative to GDP, arithmetically, they contribute significantly to the high-frequency cyclical ups and downs. Blinder (1990) even goes as far as to write that 'business cycles are, to a surprisingly large degree, inventory cycles'. Yet, stockbuilding is a very noisy series, which is hard to analyse and forecast.

Recall first that it is not the level of the stocks $S$ but stockbuilding $\Delta S$ that is added to the components of final demand $FD$ (consumption, fixed investment and net exports) to form GDP, noted $Y$:

$$Y = \Delta S + FD$$

Information on inventories is relatively poor, which complicates their analysis. Indeed, in many countries, the national accounts, especially at the quarterly frequency, partly estimate stockbuilding as a residual, namely as the difference between GDP estimated from the supply side and GDP estimated as the sum of the components of final demand.

Therefore, in addition to its intrinsic volatility, inventories contribute significantly to cyclical fluctuations, as illustrated in Figure 5.1 in the case of the United States. The decline in stockbuilding during the latest downturn in 2001 for example was larger than the contraction in GDP. In general and over longer periods than shown here, stockbuilding tends to be pro-cyclical, although at times it may clearly exert a counter-cyclical influence. Formally, its contribution to output growth can be computed by differencing the above equation. Dividing by GDP, this yields:

$$\Delta Y/Y = \Delta^2 S/Y + \Delta FD/Y$$

While stockbuilding tends to be pro-cyclical, this does not necessarily imply that it magnifies output fluctuations. That depends on whether stockbuilding tends to amplify the movements in GDP in response to variations in final demand, or to dampen them. In the former case, output should be more volatile than

**Figure 5.1** Stockbuilding: contribution to US GDP growth
(quarter-on-quarter, seasonality adjusted annualised rates of change)

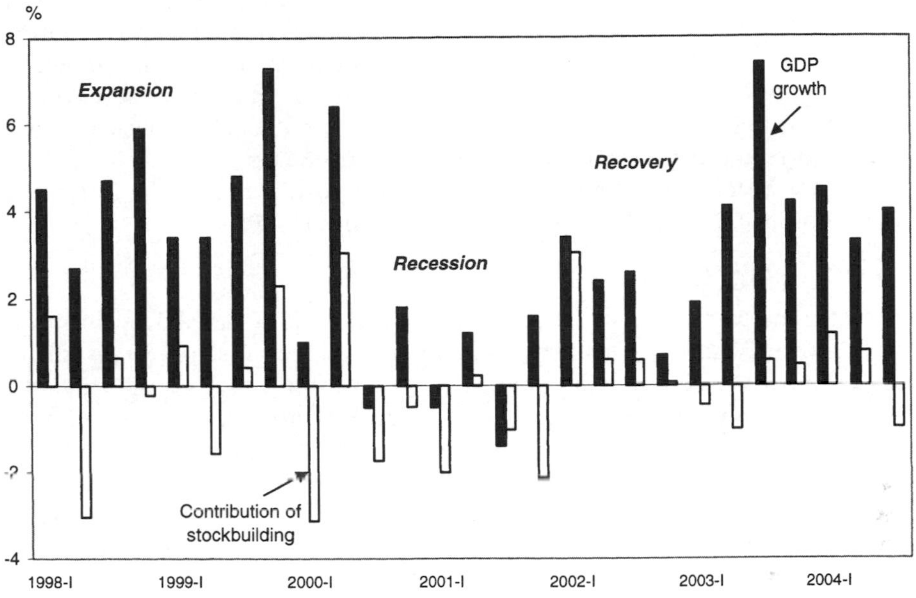

*Source*: US Bureau of Economic Analysis.

sales – Var (*Y*) > Var (*FD*) – and stockbuilding should be positively correlated with final demand – Cov (Δ*S*, *FD*) > 0. In the latter case, the opposite should hold. Empirical tests tend to favour the amplification hypothesis, but results vary over time and across countries, and are not clear-cut.

Theory itself is ambivalent, with two competing views of stockbuilding:

- One is that the accumulation or decumulation of inventories is a voluntary response on the part of firms to expected fluctuations in demand. If a firm anticipates rising demand, it will increase its inventories *ex ante*, with a view to be able to meet the extra demand whilst keeping the inventories to demand ratio roughly constant *ex post*. In the case of adaptive expectations, an increase in demand causes an increase in expected demand, and therefore in inventories. This notion of an 'inventory accelerator' is consistent with the first of the above empirical hypotheses.
- Alternatively, inventories are seen as a buffer. Faced with changes in demand, firms can draw down or build up inventories so as to smooth the level of production over time. This helps maximise profits insofar as production is subject to a fixed schedule of increasing marginal costs (though the costs of holding stocks should also be considered, as discussed below). Inventories would then decline in response to an unanticipated demand surge, and vice versa. At first glance, this seems to be consistent with the second of the above hypotheses.

In reality, the two views can be reconciled to some extent, by distinguishing anticipated and unanticipated changes in demand. An unanticipated rise in demand may first lead to a decline in inventories, if it is too expensive for the firm to step up production rapidly. But if the higher level of demand has been antici- pated to last, some restocking may be undertaken and the inventories-to-output ratio will rise (especially if *ex post* the upturn in demand proves to be more ephemeral than foreseen). In the end, it is thus mainly the gap between actual and expected demand that (negatively) influences stockbuilding.

Empirically, one way to exhibit these effects is to run the following type of equation, where the *i* denote the statistically significant lags:

$$\Delta S_t = \sum_i \alpha_i \Delta S_{t-i} + \sum_i \beta_i \Delta FD_{t-i}$$

Generally, the coefficients are then interpreted in light of the above considera- tions. In particular, $\beta_0$ measures the contemporaneous correlation between stock- building and the change in sales. *A priori*, a negative sign for $\beta_0$ is consistent with the production-smoothing/buffer-stock view, and a positive sign with the amplifi- cation view. In the latter case, however, it may be that short-run buffer effects are actually at work but that the frequency of the series used is insufficient to show it, especially if the series is an annual one. When the equation is run on quarterly data, one often obtains a buffer effect over the very short run ($\beta_0 < 0$) and an accelerator effect over more distant horizons (for $i \geq 1$, $\beta_i > 0$ and $\sum_i \beta_i > -\beta_0$).

Other possible explanatory factors can be brought in, notably speculative behaviour: firms may wish to build up inventories if they expect that their value will rise more than enough to offset the cost of financing them, the latter being directly related to the level of interest rates. This warrants testing a real interest rate variable in the equation, calculated as the nominal interest rate minus the anticipated increase in the output price (often proxied by the recently observed increase). The sign of the associated coefficient is expected to be negative: the more costly it is to carry inventories, the lower they will be. If that fails, one can try to quantify the influence of the nominal interest rate and the inflation rate separately, the expectation being that the coefficient for the former will be negative and the coefficient for the latter positive.

On the whole, this type of equation does not perform that well, however, not least because of the crude and purely backward-looking way in which expectations of demand are introduced. One alternative is to relate the evolution of inventories to business survey results, for example to businesses' sentiment on future demand. This helps forecast them over the very short run, but not beyond, as it would be hazardous to forecast business sentiment itself. Another solution would be to define a long-run target for the inventories/sales ratio, for instance by extrapola- ting its recent trend.

## 5.2   Household spending

Household spending is by far the largest component of aggregate demand, and there- fore plays a central role in forecasting the cycle. It includes current consumption, purchases of durables (cars in particular) and spending on new housing. The latter is usually treated as a category on its own, labelled residential investment. Purchases of durables are sometimes also analysed separately, as they do not behave like the rest of household consumption (see for example Palumbo *et al.*, 2002).

### 5.2.1 Household consumption

As explained in Chapter 2, there are two measures of household consumption: final consumption expenditure, which encompasses all purchases of goods and services, and a broader one which also includes final consumption expenditure of the non-profit institutions serving households and that of the general government that can be attributed to households individually. The focus here is on the former, which is more closely linked to household income. Generally, it represents well over half of GDP. When durables are treated separately, consumption in the equation below is restricted to expenditure on non-durable goods and services.

The Keynesian approach has emphasised the link between consumption and current income and the associated multiplier: an increase in activity, driven for example by rising investment, boosts income and therefore consumption, which in turn amplifies the initial increase in activity. In this framework, current household income is a key determinant of consumption. Subsequent theories, however, have highlighted other factors. Specifically, according to the permanent income hypothesis (Friedman, 1957) and the life-cycle hypothesis (Ando and Modigliani, 1963), households' consumption decisions are governed by the present value of their wealth, which alongside current income takes into account expected future income streams as well as existing assets holdings. Households are thus described as smoothing consumption over time, saving when their income is relatively high (in mid-career for instance) and borrowing, or dissaving, when it is low (youth and retirement).

This analysis can be enriched by bringing in liquidity constraints, unequal access to credit, bequest motives, risk aversion and uncertainty (notably about life expectancy), but the basic intuition can be tested by running an equation of the following type:

$$\Delta c_t = \alpha + \sum_i \alpha_i \Delta c_{t-i} + \sum_i \beta_i \Delta y_{t-i} - \mu(c_{t-1} - \eta y_{t-1}) + \gamma z_t \tag{5.3}$$

where $c$ is the volume of consumption and $y$ real income, both in logarithms, and $z$ is a vector of other explanatory variables which may be relevant over the short or longer run, including real wealth, inflation, real interest rates and unemployment. Consider each of these in turn.

Income is usually defined as household disposable income, that is, the income left after taxes and social contributions have been deducted. Hence, the equation indicates how households divide their income between consumption and saving. Income itself is sometimes split up in wages, current income from assets (including dividends and interest, but not capital gains) and transfer income (social benefits), as the propensity to consume may vary across these different components. In particular, it is usually deemed to be lower in the short run for asset-related income.

If the equation does not contain any wealth term, it is natural to test whether the long-run elasticity of consumption to income ($\eta$) equals 1. If this is the case, the long-run component of the equation implicitly defines a target for the saving rate, which can be constant or depend on the long-run component of $z$. The short-run coefficients ($\alpha_i$, $\beta_i$) indicate how fast consumers react to changes in income, thus providing an empirical characterisation of consumption-smoothing behaviour. The mean lag for the adjustment of consumption to income is typically on the order of one year.

While income clearly influences consumption, using equation (5.3) for forecasting purposes is not straightforward, since income itself then needs to be forecasted with sufficient accuracy. But income depends on activity, which in turn depends on consumption. Proper forecasting thus requires looking jointly at consumption, activity and income. This can be done using a full macroeconomic model (see Chapter 6) or iterations between the various elements of the forecast, until it has converged.

Furthermore, some components of income are difficult to assess, notably stock options. Also, households' perception of their income may matter more than actual income. Consider realised capital gains. In the national accounts, they are not considered as income, but as a change in the composition of wealth. However, the taxes levied on these capital gains are deducted from income. This treatment, while it has its logic, probably does not reflect households' perception of their income.

Alongside income, wealth plays a role in determining consumption, referred to as the 'wealth effect'. For instance, the positive wealth effect witnessed in the late 1990s, as stock and housing market valuations rose, helped explain the decline in the saving ratio in the United States at the time. Wealth effects have also been documented in the United Kingdom and in Continental Europe, even if they seem to be somewhat less strong in the latter case. There is also evidence that the potency of wealth effects has tended to rise over time, not least because financial liberalisation, by easing liquidity constraints, has facilitated inter-temporal consumption smoothing (Boone *et al.*, 2001).

The wealth variable used should in principle represent households' net wealth (assets minus liabilities), in real terms. But as timely data are at best incomplete, proxies are often used: for instance, financial wealth would be proxied by the capitalisation of the stock market (which does not include bonds nor unlisted securities), or simply by stock price indices. A key distinction is between financial and housing wealth. Empirical studies carried out on large samples of OECD countries suggest that these two types of wealth may have different effects on consumption. Indeed, a rather general view is that consumption could be more sensitive to changes in housing wealth than in stock wealth, as showed by Case *et al.* (2003) as well as Pichette and Tremblay (2004). But several uncertainties surround both these estimates and their underlying theoretical assumptions, as pointed out by Ludwig and Sløk (2004). In addition, Byrne and Davis (2003) find that illiquid components of net financial wealth (securities and pension savings on the asset side, mortgage debt on the liability side) tend to be more important long-run determinants of consumption than the liquid ones.

The inclusion of a wealth variable in equations such as (5.3) tends to weaken the sensitivity of consumption to current income, although often not by that much, suggesting that, all told, the strength of wealth effects is limited. It is also possible to test whether the sum of the long-run elasticities of consumption to income and wealth equals 1, and to impose this as a constraint if the data corroborate this assumption. This would mean, quite logically, that a one per cent increase in income and in wealth will push consumption up by one per cent over the long run.

In sum, the presence of a wealth term is satisfying from a theoretical standpoint but may not help much with forecasting consumption. Measurement errors may be very substantial and forecasting wealth (in particular asset prices) is perilous, not to mention that there is much disagreement on the exact potency of wealth effects. And while it makes sense to believe that rising wealth should ultimately boost consumption, the timing of the impact is quite uncertain (Poterba, 2000).

Turning to inflation, it has an obvious impact on consumption, since households' purchasing power and wealth is eroded by increases in the general level of prices. But, even though consumption and wealth are therefore expressed in real terms in equation (5.3), inflation may need to be included on the right-hand side, owing to two possible additional effects. One is that expected inflation could encourage households to frontload purchases. The other goes in the opposite direction and is called the 'Pigou effect': inflation eats into households' real balances (since liquid assets are not indexed one-for-one to inflation), which will be restored by higher saving. Empirically, the second effect of inflation dominates. In fact, the early Keynesian consumption functions that simply related $c$ to $y$ failed to capture the increase in the saving rate in the main advanced countries in the 1970s, which retrospectively was interpreted as a consequence of the Pigou effect in a context of rising inflation (Davidson *et al.*, 1978).

On this account, rising inflation depresses consumption both through a reduction in real income (if nominal income is not fully indexed) and via the real balance effect. Since the mid-1980s, however, the macroeconomic environment in OECD countries has changed: central banks have gained more independence and inflation, as well as inflation expectations, have declined to low levels and have remained there. In addition, the Pigou effect is somewhat analogous to a negative wealth effect (with real wealth losses stemming from higher inflation in this particular case) and may therefore already be captured by the inclusion of a wealth variable in the consumption equation. Therefore, econometric estimates sometimes fail to document any real balance effect.

Real interest rates are another important variable to consider in equation (5.3). They may affect household consumption in several ways, through a substitution, an income and a wealth effect. First, a rise in the real interest rate means that the present value of future consumption declines compared to that of current consumption: this substitution effect causes saving to increase. But at the same time, an income effect is also at work: the interest rate hike boosts the return on households' saving, thus easing their budget constraint and allowing for higher consumption both in the present and in the future. The key reason is that households' financial assets on aggregate exceed their liabilities. As net creditors, their interest income increases following a rise in interest rates, exceeding the adverse impact of higher debt service. Finally, higher interest rates may affect consumption via a third channel, by reducing the value of the assets – stocks, bonds but also housing – held by households. The ensuing negative wealth effect can be expected to depress consumption.

Which of the effects dominates is an empirical question. In practice, econometric estimation tends to be carried out using real long-term interest rates – though measuring real long-term rates is difficult since ideally one needs to consider long-term inflation expectations. In addition, a short-term rate is also occasionally introduced. Indeed, in some countries – notably the United Kingdom and Australia – short-term interest rates play a more prominent role, given that bank lending to households is largely at variable rates.

A number of other variables may impact consumption. Unemployment $U$, in addition to influencing current income (which is already captured in $y$), reduces expected future income, and therefore current consumption, according to the permanent income hypothesis. Unemployment also adds uncertainty, prompting risk-averse households to increase their precautionary savings. Hence, it is sensible to test for the significance of $\Delta U$ in the short-run component of the equation, and of $U$ in the long-run component.

Lastly, dummy variables may improve the quality of the econometric estimates by explicitly taking into account policy measures or exceptional events ignored in traditional consumption equations. One example are the time-bound incentives introduced by several OECD countries during the 1990s to stimulate purchases of new and less polluting automobiles, which temporarily boosted the acquisition of durables. Another example is weather conditions: an unusually cold winter for instance would drive up energy consumption (which represents a sizeable share of overall household consumption). Once again, this has to be tested empirically, since the impact of these sectoral effects on total consumption may also depend on cross-sector elasticities (higher car purchases could be compensated by lower consumption of other items).

### 5.2.2   Residential investment

Residential investment includes households' purchases of new housing as well as their spending on major improvement of existing dwellings. It represents a large chunk of household investment (which *inter alia* also includes unincorporated business capital formation if the self-employed are included in the household sector, as recommended by international national accounts guidelines). As illustrated in Figure 5.2, residential investment is far more volatile than GDP or household consumption. Looking at a longer time span, it tends to move pro-cyclically in many countries, although this was somewhat less the case in the latest downturn because of historically low interest rates.

From a theoretical standpoint, residential investment can be thought of in life-cycle terms, like consumption. The relevant determinants *a priori* include households' real gross disposable income $y$, real wealth and the real interest rate $r$.

*Figure 5.2* US GDP, household consumption and residential investment
(quarter-on-quarter, seasonally adjusted annualised rates of change)

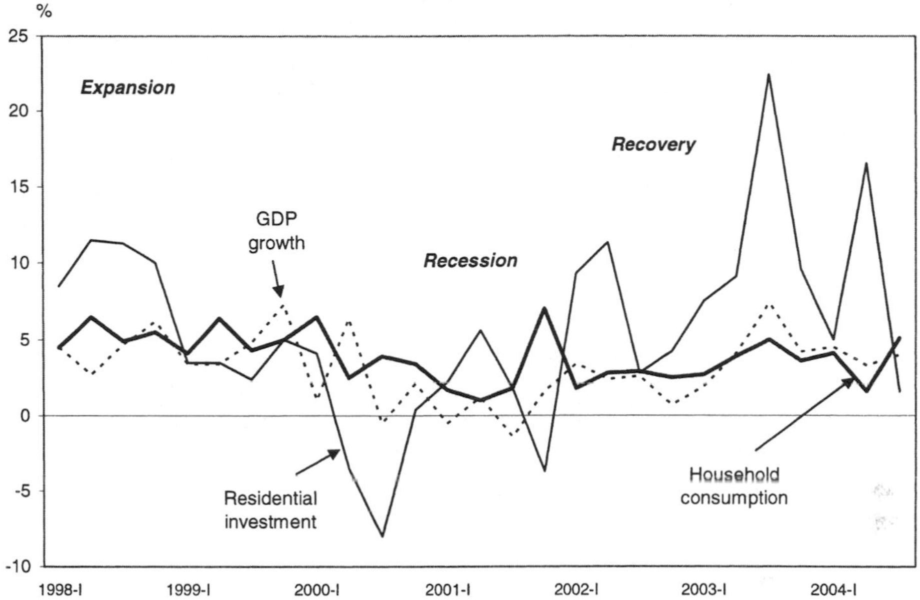

*Source*: US Bureau of Economic Analysis.

Generally, an equation of the following sort is estimated:

$$\Delta k_t = \alpha + \sum_i \alpha_i \Delta k_{t-i} + \sum_i \beta_i \Delta y_{t-i} - \mu(k_{t-1} - \eta y_{t-1} + \theta r_{t-1}) + \gamma z_t \qquad (5.4)$$

where $y$ and the (real) stock of housing $k$ are in logarithms and the vector $z$ includes other explanatory variables, such as the relative price of housing (which influences households' arbitrage between housing and consumer goods or services).

Note that equation (5.4) models the stock of housing rather than investment in housing. However, it is possible to model the accumulation rate instead, or the investment flow since, as for business fixed investment, $I_t = K_t - (1 - \delta_t)K_{t-1}$. In addition, it is often not convenient to rely on balance sheet information, which comes out with long lags. An alternative is to construct an *ad hoc* series for the stock of housing, using the permanent inventory method, which starting from the stock in a base year ($K_0$) adds up the subsequent net investment flows to get $K_t$.

The deflator used in this context is ideally the residential investment deflator though it can also in practice be some index of house prices. A rise in the real interest rate is expected to have a negative impact: it increases the cost of purchasing housing for households who borrow to finance the acquisition, whilst for owners renting out property it reduces the relative return on housing. The real interest rate is included here in the long-run component of the equation but can also or alternatively feature in the short-run component. It is typically a long-term interest rate, except in countries where mortgages are predominantly at variable rates, such as the United Kingdom (see Miles, 2003).

A major problem with equations like (5.4) is that residential investment is much more volatile than any of its putative determinants: some of the brutal swings in residential investment cannot be fully explained by the relatively smoother evolution of real incomes and even of interest rates. The only way to do so would be to have highly variable short-run elasticities. But this would be technically difficult and in any event hard to justify theoretically: why would decisions to purchase a new house, which are eminently long-run decisions, be so sensitive to the short-run ups and downs in income? Part of the explanation may have to do with the occasional presence of real estate market bubbles. How banks lend to households, as opposed to firms, may also play a role.

The basic model has been augmented in several ways. Demographics have been incorporated, to reflect the observation that younger working-age cohorts invest more than retirees (Lindh and Malmberg, 2002). Attempts have been made to factor in the numerous tax and other incentives that in most countries influence the housing market (tax breaks, subsidies, low interest rate loans). However, it is very difficult to properly quantify them in the context of a regression, and they may affect house and land prices more than the volume of housing consumption or home-ownership rates (Hendershott and White, 2000). Another and partly related avenue for improving equation (5.4) has been to model the psychological factors impinging upon investment decisions. Income or interest rate developments may affect households' mood and inclination to take the risk involved in the purchase of housing. One way to incorporate this dimension is to include unemployment ($U$ or $\Delta U$) on the right-hand side, like for consumption. Lastly, the impact of mortgage financing arrangements has been explicitly factored in. In the US case, their liberalisation and integration into the broader financial markets appear to have contributed to reducing the volatility of residential investment (McCarthy and Peach, 2002).

To conclude, it should be noted that over short horizons (a year or less), the econometric approach is generally less helpful for forecasting purposes than extrapolation based on variables that are known to foreshadow residential construction (such as building permits), taking into account the usual gestation lags in this sector (see Chapter 3 and Section 10.1).

## 5.3   Imports and exports

The theoretical background for foreign trade equations is relatively uncontroversial. On the import side, the standard underlying model features a representative consumer facing the choice between a foreign and a domestic good, which are imperfect substitutes, and deciding how much to spend on each. Utility maximisation subject to the budget constraint allows derivation of the demand for imports as a function of real income and the relative price of imports. Export behaviour is analysed symmetrically, as the imports from the rest of the world.

Exports therefore are a function of world income and their relative price. Hence, two variables take centre stage in empirical foreign trade equations: a demand variable and a variable measuring the competitiveness of domestic production.

The specifications used sometimes split up goods and services. Within the goods category, they often concentrate on manufactures. Indeed, data are available more rapidly for goods, and the econometric fit is often better. As to manufactures, they tend to reflect the economic cycle more closely, given that services and non-manufacturing goods encompass items that are less cyclically sensitive (such as energy, financial services and tourism).

The typical equations for real imports ($m$) and exports ($x$), both in logarithms, are:

$$\Delta m_t = \alpha^m + \sum_i \alpha_i^m \Delta m_{t-i} + \sum_i \beta_i^m \Delta y_{t-i} + \sum_i \xi_i^m \Delta c_{t-i}^m$$
$$- \mu^m(m_{t-1} - \eta^m y_{t-1} + \theta^m c_{t-1}^m) + \lambda^m t + \gamma^m z_t^m \tag{5.5}$$

$$\Delta x_t = \alpha^x + \sum_i \alpha_i^x \Delta x_{t-i} + \sum_i \beta_i^x \Delta y_{t-i}^* + \sum_i \xi_i^x \Delta c_{t-i}^x$$
$$- \mu^x(x_{t-1} - \eta^x y_{t-1}^* + \theta^x c_{t-1}^x) + \lambda^x t + \gamma^x z_t^x \tag{5.6}$$

where $y$ is now domestic demand, $y^*$ foreign demand, $c^m$ import competitiveness, $c^x$ export competitiveness (all in logarithms), $t$ a time trend and $z^m$ and $z^x$ vectors including other relevant variables, such as the domestic capacity utilisation rate. Consider each of these in turn.

Starting with demand and the import equation, $y$ is often defined empirically as total aggregate demand, including exports, rather than GDP or domestic demand. This enables taking into account the import content of exports, which in small open economies is large (and even very large in countries such as the Netherlands or Belgium). It is often useful to distinguish the different components of demand (consumption, investment and exports) since the associated propensities to import differ: in particular, the import content of investment is roughly twice that of consumption in a number of OECD countries, and the import content of exports is higher than that of consumption (Claus and Li, 2003).

The estimated coefficients $\eta^m$ and $\beta_i^m$ show how aggregate demand is distributed between imports and domestic production. This is important in practice: high $\beta_i^m$ coefficients imply that demand shocks (say, a fiscal boost) will largely leak out to trading partners, and that the stimulative impact on domestic activity will be limited.

On the export side, there are no readily available indicators of demand, so they need to be constructed. A shortcut is to proxy world demand addressed to the country under consideration by world GDP. But it is better to take into account the country's foreign trade structure, and to estimate how rapidly exports would grow if market shares remained unchanged (see Box 5.3). This provides a number for export market growth facing the national economy under consideration. The evolution of market shares is then captured in equation (5.6) by the competitiveness term.

A time trend is often included in the import equation in order to take into account the growing openness of economies (that is, the tendency for the ratio of imports to GDP to rise). This reflects the gradual dismantling of tariffs, the

---

**Box 5.3   World demand**

World demand in period $t$, $WD_t$, is defined as the weighted sum of the imports ($M_t^i$) of trading partners $i$, the weights being the country's market share ($MS^i$) in each of these trading partners:

$$WD_t = \sum_i MS^i \, M_t^i$$

where $MS^i = X_0^i / M_0^i$ is the ratio, in the base year, of the exports of the country to partner $i$ over total imports of partner $i$. In the base year, this world demand equals the country's exports. Its subsequent growth is not that of total world trade but rather, that of world trade seen from the perspective of the country, so to speak.

Building this type of indicator is not straightforward. In practice, disentangling prices and volumes is not easy, as different concepts are used across countries. The data are not only surrounded by significant uncertainty but also come out with substantial lags and are subject to large revisions. By the time world demand is properly estimated, the cycle will have moved on.

From an analytical standpoint, it is tempting to restrict the analysis to manufactures, which enables leaving aside the (often different) dynamics of services and special factors such as those related to the energy markets. Yet, in practice, up-to-date data are often limited to customs flows of overall goods, in US dollars, for a selection of countries (OECD plus some emerging market countries). Conversion into volumes requires to make difficult assumptions on the changes in deflators. In addition, a reliable decomposition between manufactures and other goods may not be at hand and data on traded services may be incomplete. It is certainly simpler to only look at national accounts data for goods and services but this may be too much of a shortcut, as it implies long lags and may be an overly aggregate approach.

How can world demand be forecasted? One useful option in the very short run is to use the survey data collected from businesses. Their assessment of export prospects and order books are usually a good predictor of export market growth in the coming quarters. A second option is to build an overall growth scenario allowing estimation of the future imports from the various trading partners. This runs into two problems, however. One is that the accounting framework tends to give a significant weight to countries that are not key players in world trade, but rather 'followers'. France for example trades a lot with Switzerland and relatively little with the United States. But the evolution of US imports is more informative on world demand, given the spillover effects to France's other trading partners. The other problem is circularity, because of trade interactions between countries. This can be particularly damaging in highly integrated trade zones, such as the euro area. A third, lighter and possibly more robust option, is to run a regression of world demand on domestic demand in a few key trading partners, and use the estimated equation to forecast world demand.

---

mounting importance of multinational firms and increasing specialisation. These factors are difficult to quantify but a time trend can serve as a proxy. The associated coefficient is of course expected to be positive. The time trend is usually introduced linearly, but can also be represented in a more general function, to reflect that the scope for and pace of further opening could decrease as openness rises. The inclusion of such a trend tends to reduce the apparent elasticities of imports to domestic demand, especially over the long run. In the absence of a trend, estimates often point to long-run elasticities as high as 2 or 3, while, with a trend, the assumption of unitary elasticity ($\eta^m = 1$) is often accepted. The estimated short-run elasticities, and therefore the leaks following positive demand shocks, also tend to be lower in the presence of a trend term.

A time trend is also sometimes added in the export equation, but for somewhat different reasons. Indeed, world demand being constructed based on the imports of the trading partners, it already incorporates the openness trend effect. The role of a time trend in the export equation is rather to capture any long-running changes in market shares linked to changes in non-price competitiveness. The time trend then proxies for product quality *lato sensu*, which is difficult to measure. The expected sign of the associated coefficient can be positive or negative, depending on the circumstances. As for imports, the inclusion of a time trend may help to accept the hypothesis of unitary long-run elasticity ($\eta^x = 1$), which may seem natural. In a forecasting context, however, extrapolating this time trend may not be warranted, or at least, involves a strong judgement call.

Price or cost competitiveness can be measured in various ways, by comparing domestic conditions with some average of conditions abroad (Box 5.4). Changes in competitiveness can amplify or offset changes in demand. Forecasters, however, often assume that nominal or real exchange rates will remain unchanged going forward, which implies that forecasted changes in competitiveness are limited. Then, competitiveness mainly affects forecasted trade flows via the lagged impact of its past changes, which themselves largely reflect past nominal exchange rate movements.

While competitiveness clearly influences foreign trade, there is no consensus on the empirical estimates of the respective elasticities and lags, nor on the stability of elasticities over time. Econometric estimation usually generates surprisingly low elasticities, given that the law of one price (premised on perfect substitutability, however) would imply infinitely elastic flows. This is the case for long-run elasticities and even more so for short-run elasticities, as shown for example by Hooper *et al.* (2000). More generally, such findings may be due to the fact that equations (5.5) and (5.6) assume that imports and exports depend on demand but not on supply (which could be the case if for instance imports arise because of domestic producers' inability to produce exactly the type of goods asked by consumers).

Domestic capacity utilisation is therefore sometimes included among the determinants of manufacturing imports and exports, as a measure of supply constraints. If it is high, one would expect more imports than otherwise, implying a positive coefficient in (5.5). One might also expect lower exports, and therefore a negative coefficient in (5.6), if indeed domestic producers tend to serve domestic clients first when they cannot fully satisfy demand. Whether this is actually the case has to be tested empirically.

## 5.4 Employment

Employment generally follows activity with a lag. On average, however, employment grows more slowly than value added, due to the trend productivity gains

---

*Box 5.4*    **Competitiveness indicators**

In a short- to medium-run perspective, competitiveness is traditionally measured by the real exchange rate, which can be calculated in a variety of ways, involving prices or unit costs expressed in the same currency:

- Indices of relative consumer prices are easy to construct and to update, since the data are readily available for virtually any countries and are published rapidly. A drawback, however, is that the associated basket of goods and services includes a large share of non-traded items (though it might also be argued that part of the competitiveness of a country's exporters is influenced by domestic costs in its non-tradeable sectors).
- Relative export price indices overcome this problem since by definition they only cover tradeables. Export price competitiveness is usually computed by comparing the average of foreign countries' export prices with national export prices. Import price competitiveness is obtained by comparing the price of national imports with the price of domestic production. These measures, however, ignore the trade flows which are not observed partly because of a lack of competitiveness.
- Relative cost indices are sometimes preferred because they avoid both of the afore-mentioned problems. The most frequently used indicator is the ratio of unit labour costs (possibly restricted to manufacturing). This indicator, however, may mismeasure short-run competitiveness developments as it ignores changes in profit margins. For example, exporters may prefer to absorb a rise in domestic costs by accepting lower margins, thereby keeping export price competitiveness constant. The same holds, *mutatis mutandis*, for importers. These effects can be substantial in large economies, especially in the United States, where importers are more inclined to be price-takers than price-makers. But over the longer run, margins cannot expand or shrink indefi-nitely, so that cost and price competitiveness tend to move in tandem.

These various indicators can be computed using weights reflecting bilateral competition, or preferably using a double-weighting scheme that also takes into account competition in third-country markets (Lafrance and St-Amant, 1999). Indeed, firms in country X may not export much to country Y but may compete fiercely with firms from country Y in country Z, which is ignored if only bilateral competition is taken into account. The OECD among others uses this methodology: for a given country, the procedure calculates the relative importance of each of its competitors in its domestic and foreign markets (which is deter-mined by the pattern of supply on these markets), and then weighs it according to the re-lative share of the different markets in the total demand directed at this country.

---

stemming from technical progress. Other factors, notably the cost of labour, may also affect employment.

From a theoretical standpoint, employment is usually thought of as firms' demand for labour, in a framework similar to the one discussed above for the opti-mal stock of capital. The determinants of employment are activity and the real cost of labour when targeted employment is derived from the profit maximisation behaviour of firms; or activity and the cost of labour relative to that of capital when demand is limited and firms minimise costs for a given level of activity. Technical progress enhancing productivity per head is often simply represented as a time trend. Employment is assumed to adjust gradually to its targeted level, but the adjustment process is in principle faster than for the capital stock, labour being a more flexible input.

Alternatively, the production function can be inverted to yield an employment equation. In this case, no maximisation behaviour needs to be assumed. The targeted level of employment is then a function of output, the other available factor inputs and technical progress. The cost of labour does not enter this 'technical' relation.

Implicitly, these two approaches assume that labour demand determines employment (irrespective of labour supply developments) and can be modelled along the following lines:

$$\Delta l_t = \alpha + \sum_i \alpha_i \Delta l_{t-i} + \sum_i \beta_i \Delta y_{t-i} + \sum_i \xi_i \Delta w_{t-i}$$
$$- \mu (l_{t-1} - \eta y_{t-1} + \theta w_{t-1} + \lambda t) + \gamma z_t \tag{5.7}$$

where $l$ is employment, $y$ output and $w$ the real cost of labour (all in logarithms), while $t$ is still a time trend and $z$ a vector of other explanatory variables.

This type of equation usually has private-sector employment on the left-hand side (or employment in a specific private industry), since public-sector employment has different determinants. Employment is usually also restricted to wage earners: the number of self-employed tends to evolve more smoothly, so that in forecasting it can often simply be extrapolated.

A more delicate choice has next to be made for $l$ between number of employees and number of hours worked. Forecasting the former is simpler, insofar as it is the variable that is focused on most in the end. But modelling the number of hours rather than the number of persons seems more sensible from the standpoint of firms' demand for labour. The problem in this case is that average working times need to be estimated and forecasted in order to derive a forecast for employment. This is usually done using some more or less robust accelerator-type relationship between activity and average working hours.

Turning to $y$, it is usually defined as gross output or value added (restricted to the business sector if only private employment is modelled). The dynamic component of equation (5.7) indicates the speed at which employment adjusts to changes in $y$. During a cyclical upturn, employment tends to increase with a lag, and when it does it rises less than $y$, so that productivity is pro-cyclical: this is the so-called 'productivity cycle'. Note, however, that in many countries the take-off of more flexible forms of employment (such as fixed-term contracts and temporary work) likely renders employment more sensitive to cyclical fluctuations and hence reduces the length of the productivity cycle. As for investment, the long-run restriction $\eta = 1$, which corresponds to constant returns to scale, is usually tested.

Equation (5.7) features the real cost of labour on the right-hand side, computed as the nominal cost deflated by producer prices. Alternatively, the relative cost of labour (compared to the cost of other production inputs) can be used. The choice between these two options depends on which of the above two analytical frameworks applies. Empirically, however, it is often difficult to decide which of the two is most suitable. The cost of labour should normally include the social contributions paid by employers and employees. The elasticity $\theta$ measures the sensitivity of the demand for labour to its cost over the long run, for a constant level of production. In the particular case of perfect competition with only two factors of production (labour and capital), $\theta$ could also be interpreted as the elasticity of substitution between capital and labour. This kind of identification with structural parameters is risky, though. In principle, one should go for a consistent model of the main decisions of the firm (capital and labour demand, price setting), estimate them simultaneously and jointly identify the structural parameters, provided of course that this can be done and that the data support the selected theoretical set-up.

As noted, technical progress, which increases trend productivity, can be captured by a time trend. But even in this simple framework, caution is called for: the interpretation of the coefficient attached to the technical progress term depends on the exact specification of the equation, and in particular on the presence or not of the cost of labour among the explanatory variables, as illustrated in Box 5.5.

---

**Box 5.5  Technical progress: three long-run employment relationships**

Consider the following three alternative formulations for the long-run employment target, where $e = bt$ is trend technical progress and $b > 0$ measures the pace of growth in productivity per capita:

$$l = y - e$$
$$l = y - e - \theta(w - e)$$
$$l = y - w$$

The first one does not feature the cost of labour. It assumes constant returns to scale. Employment simply depends on output, with a unitary elasticity, and on trend technical progress. This equation would be consistent with an assumption of full complementarity of the factor inputs or with the inverted production function approach coupled with the hypothesis that the stock of capital per head is constant.

The second equation is consistent with the maximisation of profits in a perfectly or imperfectly competitive market, under the assumption of a constant elasticity of substitution between capital and labour $\theta$. In this context, when the real wage rises in line with productivity ($w = e$), $l = y - e$ (which is the first formulation). The second equation can be rewritten as $l = y - (1 - \theta)bt - \theta w$. Hence, the coefficient associated with the time trend is not the pace of per capita productivity growth $b$, like in the first equation, but $(1 - \theta)b$. The inclusion of the cost of labour thus alters the interpretation of the technical progress coefficient.

The third equation is a special case of the second one, where it is assumed that $\theta = 1$, as when the production function is a Cobb-Douglas one. Then, the technical progress term vanishes altogether and the equation boils down to stating that the share of wages in value added is a constant.

These equations assume 'disembodied' technical progress. One could think instead that technical progress can only bear fruit when embodied in new capital. Then productivity growth depends on the speed at which the stock of capital is renewed. A simple way to take this possibility into account is to test the significance in equation (5.7) of a variable representing the average age of the capital stock.

## 5.5   Prices and wages

Forecasting focuses on a variety of inflation measures, including those associated with consumer prices, producer prices (possibly disaggregated by sectors), prices of capital goods, housing prices, import and export prices, and wages (the price of labour services). There are also different theories of inflation. In a perfectly competitive world, prices adjust to instantly equilibrate all markets at all times. But in the real world, inflation displays inertia. Theoretical models offer several possible explanations for price stickiness, including the infrequency of contracting, menu costs and strategic pricing behaviour in imperfectly competitive markets. Hence, prices only gradually react to real sector imbalances, even if they do indeed help redress them over the longer run. In the short run, there can thus be some disconnect between real and nominal variables. It should also be stressed that some prices are much more volatile than others, notably oil and raw material prices as well as some food prices. This can significantly affect short-run movements in 'headline' inflation. Measures of core inflation, which one way or another control for the high-frequency volatility of some components of the overall price index, are more stable.

Prices and wages are usually considered jointly, given their high degree of interdependence. Wages are negotiated with an eye on past and expected inflation. At the same time, prices are influenced by costs – particularly labour costs, which on average are the single largest component of total costs. More generally, various prices interact with wages (Figure 5.3). On the supply side feature deflators associated with aggregates such as value added, gross output and imports. On the demand side appear deflators pertaining to final consumption, intermediate consumption, investment and exports. The underlying intuition is that on the supply side, prices are essentially set in light of costs, with firms deciding on the mark-up they apply – depending on the conditions prevailing in their product markets. On the demand side, prices depend on what is charged by producers, on the relative weight of the various components of demand and on mark-up behaviour in the distribution sector. Figure 5.3 ignores international trade: in an open economy, one would have to add the influence of foreign prices on import prices (and therefore, indirectly, on the other demand prices) and on export prices (insofar as national producers are price-takers on their export markets).

Wage-price dynamics can be explored in more or less detail. A fairly elaborate representation can be obtained in a macroeconomic model such as the ones

*Figure 5.3*   **Wage-price dynamics in a closed economy**

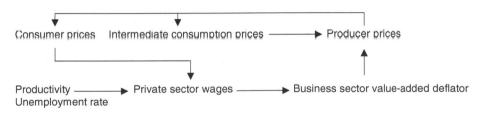

*Figure 5.4*   **Reduced forms of the wage–price dynamics**

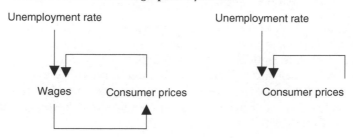

discussed in Chapter 6, with a distinction between the various sectors and several, interrelated feedback loops. But in many cases a more parsimonious approach may do, of the kind illustrated in Figure 5.4. The remainder of this section presents commonly used models of supply prices, demand prices and wages. None of them fully accounts for observed inflation, giving practitioners some latitude to pick and choose the framework that best fits their needs.

### 5.5.1   Price equations

*Supply prices*

Starting with supply, a choice has to be made between the value-added deflator and the producer price index (since the price of intermediate consumption is set on the demand side, knowledge of one of the two ensures knowledge of the other). The main difference between these two approaches has to do with the coefficient associated with intermediate consumption in the price equation. If producer prices are modelled, this coefficient can be expected to be positive. If the focus is on value added instead, the coefficient is likely to be zero, or even negative (if firms react to an increase in the cost of intermediates by reducing mark-ups). For illustrative purposes, only producer prices are considered below.

The usual assumption is that the equilibrium price is obtained by applying a given mark-up ratio to the production cost per unit of output. This is consistent with profit maximisation by producers in a perfectly competitive market (the mark-up is then nil) or in an environment of monopolistic competition *à la* Dixit/Stiglitz (the mark-up then depends negatively on the elasticity of demand). While the mark-up rate may be constant over the long run, it can fluctuate over the shorter run with the cycle, and more generally with macroeconomic conditions. A typical equation is:

$$\Delta p_t^s = \alpha + \sum_{i \geq 1} \alpha_i \Delta p_{t-i}^s + \sum_{i \geq 0} \beta_i \Delta uc_{t-i} + \sum_{i \geq 0} \xi_i c_{t+i}$$
$$- \mu(p_{t-1}^s - uc_{t-1}) + \gamma z_t \tag{5.8}$$

where $p^s$ is the price of output and $uc$ the unit cost of production, both in logarithms, while $c$ is an indicator of cyclical conditions and $z$ a vector of other explanatory variables.

In practice, $uc$ is taken to include at least labour costs, but also the cost of the intermediates (since in this example $p^s$ is the price of gross output) and possibly the cost of the physical capital used (see above). The unit labour cost for instance is a deflator defined as the wage bill (including employer-paid social contributions) divided by the volume of output. The various components of costs can be lumped together, as in equation (5.8), or identified separately, if there are reasons to think that they are not all passed through into producer prices with the same mark-up. Econometric tests can help settle this question empirically.

In the long-run term of equation (5.8), prices are indexed with a unitary elasticity on costs. This is the so-called static homogeneity property. In other words, a lasting increase in unit costs is ultimately fully passed on, in line with the theoretical assumption of constant mark-up rates in the long run.

The short-run coefficients $\alpha_i$ and $\beta_i$ reflect the speed at which prices adjust to changes in costs. The lower and more spread-out they are, the slower the reaction of prices. These coefficients are usually estimated freely, without trying to impose any *a priori* theoretical structure on them.

That said, the dynamic homogeneity constraint $(1 - \Sigma_{i\geq1}\alpha_i = \Sigma_{i\geq0}\beta_i)$ is sometimes tested. This means that prices and costs are fully indexed over the periods covered by the lags featuring in the equation. Given that producers tend to determine their prices with respect to past but also expected cost developments, this constraint can be interpreted as a sign of economic agents' ability to form inflation expectations consistently. Moreover, if the number of lags is limited, the indexation is fairly rapid. Whether this is so has to be tested empirically.

The variable $c$ features in equation (5.8) because of the presumption that the state of demand (relative to potential supply) does influence the price mark-up. Accordingly the coefficients $\xi_i$ are generally expected to be positive, and larger the greater the responsiveness of prices to tensions in the product market. The upward pressures on mark-up ratios from strong demand may nevertheless be mitigated on the supply side. A higher intensity of competition in particular may act as a drag on mark-ups when the economy is accelerating, as documented by Oliveira Martins and Scarpetta (2002). The choice of the right indicator is generally guided by the data, depending on what seems plausible and holds up well econometrically. The following specifications are typically tried out:

- Indicators of the cyclical position in level terms. The rate of capacity utilisation as captured in business surveys is often tested, as it is available rapidly. It is also possible to use the output gap (see Section 7.1), although the latter is not observable and can only be estimated.
- Similar indicators but in first-difference rather than level terms: the intuition is that shifts in activity or movements in demand, rather than their level, influence the mark-up.
- It is even possible to introduce these variables in second-difference, or acceleration form, if the econometric results are more robust.

*Demand prices*

On the demand side, prices can be thought of as set by the distribution sector, as a function of domestic producer and import prices, according to an equation of the following sort:

$$\Delta p_t^d = \alpha + \sum_{i \geq 1} \alpha_i \Delta p_{t-i}^d + \sum_{i \geq 0} \beta_i \Delta p_{t-i}^s + \sum_{i \geq 0} \xi_i \Delta p_{t-i}^m$$
$$- \mu(p_{t-1}^d - \eta p_{t-1}^s - \theta p_{t-1}^m) + \gamma z_t \tag{5.9}$$

where $p^d$ is the retail price, $p^s$ still the producer price and $p^m$ the import price expressed in domestic currency, while $z$ again stands for a vector of control variables. The static homogeneity condition is $\eta + \theta = 1$, which ensures that a lasting one per cent increase in producer and import prices translates into a one per cent increase in the retail price. In principle, $\eta$ and $\theta$ should reflect the shares of demand met respectively by domestic and foreign suppliers, and it is useful to check whether the estimated coefficients indeed broadly match these market shares.

### 5.5.2   Wage equations

Turning to the modelling of wages, the first problem facing the forecaster is to choose between wage per hour and wage per capita. *A priori*, the former might seem preferable. Indeed, if hours worked change one would expect the wage per capita to move in the same direction. In practice, the choice between the two options depends largely on how trustworthy the data are. Like in the case of employment, discussed above, both options can be problematic. Modelling wages per capita without having working time in the equation may be misleading when hours worked change significantly, as was the case in France around the turn of the millennium. But focusing on hourly wages requires to have a reliable measure of hours, since one generally needs some forecast of wages per capita as well. However, data on working time are typically unreliable and come out with long lags. Hence, some analysts prefer to use wages per capita and to ignore developments in average worked hours. It should also be borne in mind that a given change in working time may have different effects on productivity and wages depending on its cause (trend decline, legislated reduction in hours worked, expansion of part-time work and so on).

A second choice pertains to sectoral coverage and disaggregation. One option is to take the average wage in the business sector (public sector wages should be modelled separately, given that they usually behave somewhat differently). Alternatively, the wage can be modelled sector by sector, so as to show how wage formation processes differ across sectors. An intermediate approach is to focus on one robust overall equation (for the business sector or for manufacturing, say) and to derive sectoral equations as variants, for example by introducing sector-specific intercepts or trends. This makes sense when sectoral differences are significant but stable over time (because, for example, of long-run discrepancies in productivity levels or gains across sectors).

Lastly, it is customary to model gross wages, including the employee-paid social contributions but excluding those paid by employers, on the grounds that this corresponds to what wage earners bargain for. But it is sometimes preferable to reason on total labour cost, or on the contrary, on the wage net of any social contributions.

*Phillips curves*

In a famous article, Phillips (1958) exhibited a negative relationship, over the long run, between unemployment and nominal wage growth in the United Kingdom. Various types of 'Phillips curves' have been used in the literature since. A typical one is as follows:

$$\Delta w_t = c + \sum_{i \geq 1} \alpha_i \Delta w_{t-i} + \sum_{i \geq 0} \beta_i \Delta p_{t-i} - \lambda U_{t-1} + \gamma \Delta z_t \qquad (5.10)$$

where $w$ is the gross nominal wage and $p$ the consumer price index (both in logarithms), $U$ the rate of unemployment and $z$ a vector of other explanatory variables, typically including import price inflation (somewhat artificially, the notation $\Delta z$ instead of $z$ is used here because the explanatory variables are expected to affect the changes in wages, not their levels – see below). This specification does not incorporate any long-run equilibrium wage level.

Normally, $\lambda > 0$: low unemployment translates into high wage inflation, and vice versa. The value of $\lambda$ indicates how sensitive wage demands are to labour market tensions. The latter can be captured, alternatively, by a transformation of $U$ (for instance, log $U$) or by other indicators, such as the ratio of the number of unemployed to the number of job vacancies.

Wage earners aim for a certain level of purchasing power, hence their demands incorporate inflation expectations. In equation (5.10), these expectations are assumed to depend on the inflation rates observed in the recent past ($\Delta p_{t-i}$). This term did not feature in the original Phillips curve and its inclusion is reflected in the 'augmented Phillips curve' label used for equation (5.10) and the like.

When agents do not suffer from any money illusion, a change in the pace of inflation does not alter their real wage demands. In this case, one would expect that $1 - \sum_{i \geq 1} \alpha_i = \sum_{i \geq 0} \beta_i$, in other words that wages be fully indexed on prices, albeit with some lag. This condition means that there is no long-run trade-off between inflation and unemployment, an intuition dear to many economists. It has to be met if a NAIRU is to be computed (see Box 5.6). In practice, however, empirical estimates do not always support this condition, and the forecaster faces a trade-off between obtaining a better statistical fit and imposing more consistency with economic theory.

Equation (5.10) can be enriched by adding a number of other determinants on the right-hand side. In some cases, inserting $\Delta U$ in lieu or in addition to $U$ is warranted. This increases the estimated sensitivity of wages to ups and downs in activity and may significantly enhance the equation's fit, in particular when the labour market is of the insider–outsider type (in which case the wage claims of the insiders – whose jobs are relatively protected – are not heavily influenced by the level of unemployment affecting the outsiders but more by changes in the level of unemployment, which reflect the probability of job loss) A number of more specific effects can also be taken into account explicitly. One would typically test for the influence of changes in minimum wages, wages in the public sector, and tax and social contributions rates. It is also common practice to include dummies for particular episodes (such as important wage agreements) so as to avoid outliers for which there is a good explanation biasing the estimation of the structural coefficients. But even with such additions, wage equations are often not that robust, and should be used with caution when forecasting.

### The wage curve

Phillips curves have been criticised on theoretical grounds. They are most readily interpreted as showing the adjustment of wages when the labour market is out of equilibrium: for instance, when labour is in excess supply, competition for jobs amongst the unemployed will drive down, or at least slow, nominal wages. But this walrasian supply-versus-demand logic fails to acknowledge that unemployment tends to moderate wage claims in more indirect ways, notably by affecting the probability of job loss for the incumbent workers, which they take into account when formulating their wage claims. Most modern labour market theories (including those based on efficiency wages or on bargaining) rather point to a 'wage curve' relating the level – instead of the growth rate – of wages to its determinants (Blanchard and Katz, 1999). This leads to the following type of equation:

$$w_t = p_t + \alpha\pi_t + \eta\omega_t - \varphi U_t \tag{5.11}$$

where $\pi$ stands for the productivity of labour. Equation (5.11) is usually described as a wage-setting (WS) equation. The average wage and the unemployment rate are negatively related provided $\varphi > 0$, which one would normally expect. Wage claims take workers' productivity into account, with $\alpha > 0$. If $\alpha = 1$, changes in productivity are fully reflected in wage claims, both on the way up and on the way down. The other relevant variables, featuring in vector $\omega$, may be very diverse, potentially including the unionisation rate (as a proxy for unions' bargaining strength), the level of unemployment benefits or more generally of replacement incomes, the mismatch between demand and supply of skills, the tax and social contribution wedge (as the difference between the total cost of labour for the employer and the income after social contributions and taxes received by the wage earner), and the terms of trade.

Assuming that equation (5.11) properly describes the long-run determinants of wages, one can insert it into (5.10) and obtain the following dynamic wage equation:

$$\Delta w_t = c + \sum_{i\geq 1}\alpha_i\Delta w_{t-i} + \sum_{i\geq 0}\beta_i\Delta p_{t-i} + \gamma\Delta z_t$$
$$- \mu(w_{t-1} - p_{t-1} - \alpha\pi_{t-1} - \eta\omega_{t-1} + \varphi U_{t-1}) \tag{5.12}$$

This form is more general than the augmented Phillips curves and more consistent with modern labour market theories.

Combined with a price-setting (PS) equation, a WS equation implies an equilibrium unemployment rate that differs from the NAIRU obtained from a Phillips curve (Box 5.6). The merit of the WS/PS approach is that it allows for a richer model (see Cotis *et al.*, 1998). However, the empirical robustness of equation (5.12) is far from guaranteed: is $\mu$ significantly positive, as one would want, and is it stable over time? The great diversity of explanatory variables potentially included in $\omega$ and influencing the targeted wage may also complicate estimation considerably (L'Horty and Rault, 2003). In practice, it is often difficult to evaluate which of several specifications is best.

---

**Box 5.6   The NAIRU and the equilibrium unemployment rate**

The NAIRU (non-accelerating inflation rate of unemployment) is the rate of unemployment compatible with stable inflation. It can be derived from a wage–price loop combining a mark-up producer price equation and a Phillips curve. For example, keeping the same variable names as above:

$$p_t^s = w_t - \pi_t + z_t + \alpha \qquad \text{(producer price equation)}$$
$$\Delta w_t = \Delta p_{t-1} - \lambda U_{t-1} + \Delta z_t' + \beta \qquad \text{(Phillips curve)}$$

where $z$ and $z'$ are variables exerting inflationary pressures (there could be more than one in each equation), while $\alpha$ and $\beta$ are constants. For the sake of simplicity, the producer price $p^s$ is assumed to reflect instantly any change in unit wage cost, whereas the wage $w$ follows consumer prices $p$ with a one-period lag.

Differencing the producer price equation yields: $\Delta p_t^s = \Delta w_t - \Delta \pi_t + \Delta z_t$. Define the wedge between consumer and producer prices, which reflects the influence of import prices and of indirect taxes, as $\psi$. Hence $\Delta p_t = \Delta p_t^s + \Delta \psi_t$. Then the producer price equation in first difference can be rewritten as $\Delta p_t = \Delta w_t - \Delta \pi_t + \Delta \psi_t + \Delta z_t$. Inserting the latter into the Phillips curve leads to:

$$\Delta p_t - \Delta p_{t-1} = - \lambda(U_{t-1} - U^*)$$

where $U^* \equiv (\beta - \Delta \pi_t + \Delta z_t + \Delta z_t' + \Delta \psi_t)/\lambda$ is the NAIRU

When $U_{t-1} = U^*$, consumer price inflation is stable. The NAIRU is inversely proportional to $\lambda$, the sensitivity of wages to unemployment. It increases with the difference between average wage award demands ($\beta$) and productivity gains. The NAIRU also depends on the other variables that exert inflationary pressures, such as changes in import prices or in taxation. Therefore, $U^*$ may vary over the short run.

The concept of the NAIRU has significant implications for policy debates. In principle, when unemployment exceeds the NAIRU, there can be some scope for macroeconomic policy to stimulate demand without stoking inflationary pressures on the labour market. In contrast, if unemployment is at or below the NAIRU, expansionary demand policies would translate into higher inflation, and the ensuing losses in competitiveness and/or wealth would have a contractionary effect which offsets the stimulus.

$U^*$ as defined above is rather volatile, since transient inflation shocks (changes in $\Delta z_t$, $\Delta z_t'$ or $\Delta \psi_t$) move it around. It is often preferable to abstract from such disturbances, and to assume that $\Delta z_t = \Delta z_t' = \Delta \psi_t = 0$. This yields a long-run NAIRU $U^{**}$ which varies only with productivity:

$$U^{**} = (\beta - \Delta \psi_t)/\lambda$$

Moreover, if $\Delta \pi$ is added into the above Phillips curve as in the case of a WS formulation, and if it has a unitary long-run elasticity, then it cancels out in the NAIRU, which then becomes a constant ($\beta/\lambda$).

Turning to the concept of equilibrium unemployment, which is derived by combining a producer price level equation with a WS curve, one can start for example from the following long-run relationships:

$$p_t^s = w_t - \pi_t + z_t$$
$$p_t = p_t^s + \psi_t$$
$$w_t = p_t + \pi_t + z_t' - \varphi U_t$$

Through substitution this leads to:

$$U^{eq} = (z + z' + \psi)/\varphi$$

In contrast to the NAIRU, the explanatory variables enter the price and wage equations in level terms, rather that as changes. A permanent shock on oil prices, taxation or any other variable contained in $z$ or $z'$ will therefore have a lasting impact on unemployment, instead of a temporary one. The determinants of unemployment are more diverse than in the Phillips curve framework.

An obvious question is whether the equilibrium rate of unemployment can be considered as a (long-run) NAIRU as well, in the sense of being the rate compatible with stable inflation. In a number of studies, the two concepts are in fact implicitly treated as if they were equivalent. In the ECMs such as those presented in this Chapter, however, equivalence only obtains when dynamic homogeneity holds in all price and wage equations.

# 6
# Macroeconomic Models

A macroeconomic (or macroeconometric) model is a quantitative representation of an economy, or of several interdependent countries. It assembles a number of equations and allows study of the behaviour of the economy(ies) when all the various relationships between variables are operative simultaneously. In addition, a model synthesises data and knowledge with a view to explain economic history better and to forecast future developments.

Macroeconomic models are mainly created and maintained by governmental agencies, central banks and private forecasting institutions (see Chapter 14). They may be used for forecasting purposes, either over the short run (one to two years ahead), or over longer horizons. The central forecast is then called the baseline. The models also serve to experiment with different assumptions regarding the international or domestic environment, as well as regarding policies. These alternative scenarios depart more or less from the baseline.

While macroeconomic models are precious tools for forecasters, they are sophisticated instruments, to be manipulated with great care. A 'push-button' approach – feed the model with the latest data and let it do the work – would be uninformative at best, and outright misleading at worst. Understanding the model's inner properties and limitations is therefore essential if it is to be used successfully. This chapter reviews the main characteristics of macroeconomic models (Section 6.1), their practical uses in forecasting (Section 6.2), the construction of variants and alternative scenarios (Section 6.3) and models' limitations (Section 6.4).

## 6.1  What is a macroeconomic model?

### 6.1.1  Technical features

From a technical standpoint, a model is a juxtaposition of equations linking economic variables. The latter are of two sorts.

- Endogenous variables, which are explained by the model. They are jointly determined by the system of equations. There are thus as many endogenous variables as there are equations.

- Exogenous variables, which are considered as given, as opposed to derived by the model. They typically include assumptions about technology, the international environment and economic policy.

The number of equations varies from just a handful to several hundreds – or even thousands for the most disaggregated models – which delve deep into sectoral details, or which include a considerable number of countries (in the case of international models). Generally, these equations fall into one of three categories:

- Behavioural equations: as explained in Chapter 5, they describe how agents behave as concerns consumption, investment, price setting and so on. The specification is normally guided by economic theory, at least to some extent. Most frequently, their parameters are estimated so as to ensure that the equation fits the historical data as closely as possible. But even when they fit well, there always remains some difference between actual observations and the values predicted by the model. This random error term or 'residual' can be added onto the estimated equation so that the historical data be traced exactly by the model (see below).
- Accounting identities: they stem from the national accounts definitions. For example, a deflator for a given macroeconomic aggregate should equal its nominal value divided by its volume, or the budget balance should be equal to fiscal revenues minus expenditures. Unlike the behavioural equations, the accounting identities are always exactly met. This holds even when there are statistical discrepancies: in that case, they are identified as such and treated like variables.
- Technical relationships: some relations between variables are neither behavioural nor an accounting constraint. Usually, these are equations defining non-observable but important variables, such as production functions, for instance, which relate outputs to inputs.

The behavioural equations are at the heart of each macroeconomic model, but the latter's most important value added lies in its macroeconomic logic: how the equations are shown to interact and what this suggests about past and future economic developments.

### 6.1.2   Macroeconomic logic

A natural question is whether the behaviour described or predicted by empirical models matches what theory would suggest. One way to address this question is to impart some basic shocks to the model (such as a change in external demand, a tax cut, an interest rate shift or a wage hike). The model's response will then show whether the consequences of this shock are consistent with this or that theory. Usually, models are deliberately embodying some important theoretical properties, so one would expect them to deliver results that are in line with the theoretical priors of the models' builders. This is not always self-evident, however, especially with large macroeconomic models combining a great variety of mechanisms, whose interaction may at times lead to surprising results.

Most macroeconomic models used in forecasting and for economic policy purposes are inspired by what is often referred to as the 'neo-Keynesian synthesis', namely a blend of Keynesian and neo-classical ideas. The mix varies, though, and some models clearly depart from the mainstream, for instance the Liverpool model of the UK economy, which was developed in the early 1980s in the 'new classical' vein (see Whitley, 1994).

Indeed, the neo-Keynesian approach is sufficiently flexible to adequately capture many features of observed economic behaviour and to introduce the requisite nuances, where appropriate. Its key elements include the following:

- The starting point is the assumption that in the short run, output is determined by demand, in a context where prices exhibit some degree of stickiness. Traditional mechanisms such as the investment accelerator and the income multiplier significantly influence the short-run equilibrium. Hence, at a one-to-two-year horizon, effective fiscal and monetary policy action can significantly influence demand.
- The short-run equilibrium often involves over- or under-utilisation of labour and capital, but these imbalances are worked off over longer horizons. Trend growth is determined by structural factors such as technical progress, labour market participation and demographics. Typically, Keynesian short-run properties are combined with classical long-run ones.
- A crucial element of medium-run adjustment is the wage-price dynamics. Tensions or slack on labour or product markets influence wages and prices; in particular, real wages are generally sensitive to unemployment in these models. In this context, if for instance excess demand pushes inflation up, it will in turn crowd out real spending, via a negative impact on agents' wealth, and adversely affect net exports, by reducing price competitiveness: the excess demand pressures are thereby gradually offset. Hence, the interaction of real and nominal variables tends to ensure that when shocks knock it sideways, the economy will move back, over time, to its long-run growth path.
- Another equilibrating mechanism relates to monetary and financial conditions, notably insofar as they are influenced by monetary policy. If the latter is endogenised into the model in the form of some reaction function – say, a Taylor rule (see Box 8.2) – monetary policy will dampen the cycle. Changes in interest rates will affect real variables directly (for instance, consumption and investment) or indirectly (via their impact on exchange rates or asset prices). In this case, it is the interaction between the real and the financial blocks of the model that contributes to macroeconomic stabilisation.

### 6.1.3   Building blocks

Against this backdrop, macroeconomic models usually include the following interconnected building blocks:

- A real-side block: it tends to be centred around the Keynesian feedback loop, and describes household spending, firms' factor demand and foreign trade.

Public spending is typically treated as exogenous. Generally, the various components of demand are negatively affected by an increase in prices or interest rates.

- A price block: typically, it revolves around a couple of equations describing wage formation and price setting, which show wages and prices to be sensitive to labour and product market conditions.
- A financial and monetary block: it includes some monetary policy rule plus arbitrage conditions determining the constellation of interest rates, exchange rates and asset prices.
- An income block: its function is mainly to link agents' incomes to the macroeconomic aggregates, in the form of elementary or accounting relationships. This block includes the description of the public finances, particularly on the revenue side.

### 6.1.4   Diversity

While many models share important common features, they do not produce the same quantitative or even qualitative results. Table 6.1 shows some of the differences across a selection of prominent international or national macroeconomic models.

An obvious difference pertains to size, which ranges from just a handful of key equations (in the Canadian M1-VECM model) to several thousands of equations (in the international NiGEM and MSG2 models). To some extent, however, size should not affect the main properties of the model. Rather, models are often expanded to better render details, for example by disaggregating overall quantity

*Table 6.1*   Selected macroeconomic models

| Model | Institution | Approach | Described in |
|---|---|---|---|
| **International models** | | | |
| MULTIMOD (Mark III) | IMF | Flexible expectations structure, non-linear Phillips curves | Laxon *et al.* (1998) |
| GEM | IMF | Stochastic dynamic general equilibrium model | IMF (2004) |
| INTERLINK | OECD | Short-run neo-Keynesian, long-run neo-classical | Dalsgaard *et al.* (2001) |
| Small global model | OECD | Demand-side model for the US, euro area and Japan | Rae and Turner (2001) |
| QUEST | European Commission | Short-run neo-Keynesian, long-run neo-classical | Roeger and in't Veld (1997) |
| Euro-area-wide model | ECB | Treats the 12 euro area countries as one economy | Fagan *et al.* (2001) |
| NiGEM | NIESR | Model-consistent expectations | Barrell *et al.* (2001) |
| World model | OEF | Short-run neo-Keynesian, long-run neo-classical | OEF (2000) |
| MSG2 | Academia | Dynamic general equilibrium model | McKibbin and Sachs (1989) |
| **Country-specific models** | | | |
| US | FRB/US | Central bank | Forward-looking new-Keynesian structural model | Reifschneider *et al.* (1999) |
| Japan | CAO model | ESRI | Demand-oriented, Keynesian model | Murata and Saitou (2004) |
| UK | COMPACT | Academia | Rational expectations, intertemporal | Darby *et al.* (1999) |
| UK | BEQM | Central bank | Short-run neo-Keynesian, long-run neo-classical | Harrison *et al.* (2005) |
| Germany | Buba's | Central bank | Neo-Keynesian-neo-classical | Deutsche Bundesbank (1994) |
| France | MÉSANGE | Ministry of Finance | Short-run neo-Keynesian, long-run neo-classical | Allard-Prigent *et al.* (2002) |
| Italy | Banca d'Italia's | Central bank | Short-run neo-Keynesian, long-run neo-classical | Banca d'Italia (1986) |
| Canada | M1-VECM | Central bank | Vector error correction model, money matters | Côté *et al.* (2003) |
| Australia | Murphy II | Econtech | Integrated macro and industry model | Powell and Murphy (1997) |
| Belgium | MODTRIM II | Federal Planning Bureau | Short-run neo-Keynesian, long-run neo-classical | Hertveldt and Lebrun (2003) |
| Netherlands | JADE | CPB | Medium- and long-run model, estimated in error-correction form | CPB (2003) |
| New Zealand | FPS | Central Bank | Calibrated model with endogenous interest rates | RBNZ (2003) |
| Norway | RIMINI | Central Bank | Reduced form, vector error-correction model | Svensson *et al.* (2002) |
| Sweden | Rixmod | Central Bank | Calibrated single-good model | Nilsson (2002) |
| Switzerland | SNB's | Central Bank | Short-run neo-Keynesian, long-run neo-classical | Stalder (2001) |

and price variables to show sectoral developments. But a heavier model is not necessarily a more accurate one: adding equations adds information but also extra problems. Indeed, model builders are often reluctant to disaggregate too much, fearing that a very detailed machinery may become a black box, generating results that are difficult to comprehend. In practice, there is thus a trade-off between the need to describe the evolution of a large number of variables and the need to have a tractable and transparent tool. The new models that have emerged over the past two decades therefore tend to be relatively compact.

More fundamentally, models may differ by some of their main assumptions. Examples include:

- The choice of a production function allowing for substitution between inputs versus one in which factors are complements.
- Endogenisation versus an exogenous assumption for the exchange rate.
- Making consumption a function of current income only, or also of expected income and wealth.

Since economic theory leaves room for disagreement on such assumptions, model diversity serves as a reminder that they can and do yield disparate results. In fact, this has led some institutions – notably the Bank of England (1999) and the OECD (Sédillot and Pain, 2003) – to rely more on what a suite of models suggests than on what any single model predicts.

In other cases, the difference may seem minor at first, but can produce widely divergent outcomes. Seemingly benign differences in numerical values for a key parameter can be responsible for opposite results. For example, the sensitivity of imports to activity has a big influence on the demand multiplier, that is the additional activity entailed *ex post* by an *ex ante* demand shock (say, an increase in foreign demand or in public spending). The multiplier will be relatively small if imports are very elastic, since in that case the extra demand will be met largely by a rise in imports rather than by domestic producers. Conversely, the multiplier will be large if imports are rather inelastic. Hence, the policy implications differ significantly depending on the value of this parameter. One might object that the value of such important parameters is not set arbitrarily, but derived from econometric estimation. Hence, different modellers should work with similar estimates, all the more so as they constantly compare their estimates with those of their peers and as any outlier is closely scrutinised. In practice, however, this is rarely the case: significant uncertainty attaches to many important parameter estimates, which come with large standard errors and may vary depending on the sample period and on the exact specification used.

Furthermore, it should be borne in mind that models do not all evolve at the same speed. Innovations are introduced in some of them but not, or only much later, in others. Models evolve not just to work in new fancy techniques but also because economic structures change over time, leading modellers to realise that their instrument fails to take into account some phenomena. This is what happened for the traditional Keynesian models developed in the 1960s and 1970s: they were not suited, it turned out *ex post*, to handle the real and monetary shocks that hit OECD economies in the 1970s. Subsequent models therefore incorporated a richer supply-side block.

For all these reasons, the response to a given shock differs across models, illustrating that policy prescriptions can be model-dependent. Consider for example, in the case of France and Germany, the short-run impact on output and inflation of a standardised, unanticipated and temporary fiscal or monetary shock in three prominent international models (Table 6.2). A cut in government spending reduces real GDP more according to the IMF's MULTIMOD Mark III model than according to the NIESR's NiGEM model or to the European Commission's QUEST II model. Likewise, its immediate impact on inflation is stronger if MULTIMOD rather than NiGEM or QUEST is to be believed. A monetary shock also tends to have a stronger short-run impact on activity and inflation in MULTIMOD than in NiGEM – but it affects activity more in QUEST (while having about the same impact on inflation as in MULTIMOD).

Likewise, the response to a given oil shock differs across models (Table 6.3), although in this case some of the divergences also reflect differences in the precise calibration of the shock and in the ancillary assumptions used in the simulations (for instance, as regards the central bank's reaction function). In particular, the two

*Table 6.2*  **Responses across models to fiscal and monetary shocks**
(temporary and unanticipated shocks, per cent deviation from baseline)

| Model / Year | Fiscal shock* | | | | Monetary shock** | | | |
|---|---|---|---|---|---|---|---|---|
| | Impact on real GDP | | Impact on inflation*** | | Impact on real GDP | | Impact on inflation*** | |
| | France | Germany | France | Germany | France | Germany | France | Germany |
| **MULTIMOD III** | | | | | | | | |
| 1 | -1.26 | -1.33 | -0.28 | -0.22 | -0.17 | -0.22 | -0.20 | -0.17 |
| 2 | 0.25 | 0.25 | -0.18 | -0.16 | -0.13 | -0.12 | -0.23 | -0.20 |
| 3 | 0.29 | 0.27 | -0.02 | -0.05 | -0.03 | -0.02 | -0.21 | -0.18 |
| 5 | 0.19 | 0.16 | 0.12 | 0.05 | -0.02 | -0.05 | -0.10 | -0.12 |
| 10 | -0.05 | -0.03 | -0.04 | -0.02 | 0.03 | 0.02 | 0.02 | 0.00 |
| **NiGEM** | | | | | | | | |
| 1 | -0.78 | -0.99 | -0.09 | -0.09 | -0.12 | -0.20 | -0.04 | -0.02 |
| 2 | -0.15 | 0.08 | -0.03 | -0.26 | -0.22 | -0.25 | 0.00 | -0.07 |
| 3 | 0.02 | 0.08 | -0.04 | -0.04 | -0.13 | -0.10 | -0.03 | -0.10 |
| 5 | 0.02 | 0.02 | 0.00 | 0.06 | -0.05 | -0.04 | -0.03 | -0.01 |
| 10 | 0.01 | 0.02 | 0.02 | 0.01 | 0.00 | 0.00 | 0.00 | 0.01 |
| **QUEST II** | | | | | | | | |
| 1 | -0.87 | -0.86 | -0.19 | -0.15 | -0.52 | -0.59 | -0.18 | -0.17 |
| 2 | 0.25 | 0.14 | -0.09 | -0.05 | -0.11 | -0.13 | -0.11 | -0.10 |
| 3 | 0.21 | 0.11 | 0.07 | 0.04 | -0.03 | -0.04 | 0.01 | 0.00 |
| 5 | 0.06 | 0.04 | 0.03 | 0.01 | -0.02 | -0.02 | 0.00 | 0.00 |
| 10 | 0.03 | 0.01 | 0.00 | 0.00 | -0.01 | -0.02 | 0.00 | 0.00 |

*Notes*:
  \* One per cent of GDP cut in government spending.
  \*\* One percentage point increase in nominal short-term interest rates.
\*\*\* GDP deflator for MULTIMOD and QUEST, consumer expenditure deflator for NiGEM.
*Source*: Wallis (2004).

*Table 6.3*  **Impact of an oil shock**
($5 a barrel increase)*

| Model / Year | Impact on real GDP | | | Impact on CPI inflation | | |
|---|---|---|---|---|---|---|
| | US | Euro area | Japan | US | Euro area | Japan |
| **MULTIMOD III** | | | | | | |
| 1 | -0.3 | -0.2 | -0.1 | 0.8 | 0.7 | 0.3 |
| 2 | -0.4 | -0.4 | -0.2 | 0.5 | 0.5 | 0.2 |
| 3 | -0.4 | -0.4 | -0.3 | 0.3 | 0.4 | 0.1 |
| **GEM** | | | | | | |
| 1 | -0.4 | -0.4 | -0.2 | 0.1 | 0.1 | 0.1 |
| **INTERLINK** | | | | | | |
| 1 | -0.1 | -0.2 | -0.2 | 0.1 | 0.2 | 0.2 |
| 2 | -0.1 | -0.1 | -0.1 | 0.1 | 0.2 | 0.1 |
| **MSG2**\*\* | | | | | | |
| 1 | -0.2 | -0.0 | -0.1 | 0.3 | 0.3 | 0.3 |
| 2 | -0.3 | -0.2 | -0.1 | 0.2 | 0.2 | 0.0 |
| 3 | -0.3 | -0.2 | -0.1 | 0.1 | 0.1 | 0.1 |

*Notes:*
* Starting from a baseline oil price of around $20 per barrel. Permanent shock, except in INTERLINK.
** McKibbin-Sachs Global 2 model.

*Source*: IMF (2000, 2004).

IMF models (MULTIMOD and GEM) generate different results, especially for inflation.

### 6.1.5   Further complications

While the above differences matter, there are further complications, in particular those related to the modelling of supply, the degree of theoretical structure imposed on the model, the importance given to the financial sector and the treatment of expectations.

The distinction between supply and demand behaviour is not watertight. Investment, for example, has to do with demand insofar as it is one of the components of expenditure-based GDP, but also with supply since it determines the evolution of productive capacity. In fact, the custom is to include on the supply side the variables related to the behaviour of firms (which supply goods) and of workers (who supply work). Thus, the demand equations for the production factors, the production function itself and the wage–price equations are at the core of what is referred to as supply.

Various supply-side shocks have hit the advanced economies over the past few decades, highlighting the importance of the modelling of supply: several oil shocks, the general slowdown of productivity in the 1970s, its acceleration in the late 1990s in the United States, and others. In order to understand such shocks better, modellers have introduced new equations describing the impact of profitability on investment or that of the cost of labour on labour demand. More fundamentally, they have started to pay more attention to models' long-run properties. A frequent question is whether the model includes an equilibrium unemployment rate, and if so, what its determinants are. As underlined in Section 5.5, an important distinction is between models with a Phillips curve (where the wage enters in rates of change) and those where the wage enters in level terms. In the latter case, the equilibrium unemployment rate depends on a greater variety of structural factors. In this context, one often checks whether equilibrium unemployment is independent from the inflation rate, by looking at the homogeneity of price and wage equations. Indeed, imposing such constraints on the data may significantly affect parameter estimates.

Choosing between alternative representations reflecting different theoretical priors is difficult, however, because econometric testing on macroeconomic data frequently fails to deliver clear-cut verdicts. Testing for the substitutability of factor inputs, for example, tends to yield mixed results at the aggregate level. Moreover, theory generally suggests that, rather than isolated equations, one should test systems of equations, which embody the constraints imposed on parameters that play a role in more than one equation. But estimating equations jointly is technically heavier and does not always provide informative answers, so that in practice behavioural equations are often estimated individually. This also means that the assumptions used by modellers have a normative element. Faced with a supply shock, for example, models support the reasoning that 'if reality is as assumed in the model, then the impact of the shock will be ...', but can offer no certainty as to the shock's actual effects.

In any model, there is a tension between theoretical purity and goodness-of-fit. The first generation of macroeconomic models essentially aimed at capturing the mechanisms that were empirically most robust. This remains of concern in today's models but alongside another objective, which is the consistency with theoretical priors. The latter usually can be assessed by checking the implied long-run constraints on the parameters, on the grounds that if theory is to hold, it is more in the long run rather than at high frequencies. When looking at single equations, an example of such constraints is the unitary elasticity of consumption to revenue (see Section 5.2). In the case of a set of equations, it could be the parameters determining factor input demand. Hence, models with few imposed constraints tend to be used for short-run analysis and forecasting, in a spirit akin to that underlying VAR models. Model consistency and stability is more important for medium- or long-run scenario analysis. Hence, the models used for those purposes tend to be more 'structured' and to embody more constraints. But there is always a risk that by imposing too much structure, one would oversimplify and incorrectly assess reality. Modellers are generally well aware of this risk, but policymakers or the broader public may not be.

The degree of interdependence between the real and the financial sector also varies across models. Most contemporaneous models feature tangible effects of interest rates on domestic demand, in line with the traditional Keynesian IS curve. But the determination of the interest rates itself differs from one model to the next. It may stem from a money demand equation, a monetary policy rule or the interest rate may simply be set exogenously. Likewise, the degree of endogeneity of the exchange rate, which influences the speed of adjustment to shocks, is far from uniform across models. Whether or not a model incorporates wealth effects also makes a big difference. For example, in the case of an inflationary demand shock, its expansionary impact will be mitigated by the erosion of real wealth. However, simulated consumption, when wealth effects are incorporated and assets prices bounce around, may be overly volatile. It should also be borne in mind that to include wealth effects, the model needs to have a sufficiently fleshed-out financial and monetary block, and that asset prices themselves are hard to predict.

Last but not least, agents' expectations are modelled in a variety of ways, with major implications for predicted behaviour. Indeed, the principal source of simulation differences across the models shown in Table 6.2 is the different degree of forward-lookingness embedded in agents' consumption and investment decisions as well as in price and wage setting. This affects not only the dynamics of the economic responses to any policy impulse but also their magnitude.

The simplest approach is to assume that agents form expectations by extrapolating the past and the present: these are the naïve and adaptive expectations approaches. Alternatively, it can be assumed that agents are more forward-looking and that they take into account what the model predicts: these are the rational expectations, or more precisely 'model-consistent', approaches. The latter, however, involve an element of circularity, since they postulate that agents' decisions hinge on expected variables whose realisation depends on these very decisions.

Empirical models nowadays often combine adaptive and rational expectations. Some, such as NiGEM, can even be run in either mode. Others rest squarely on rational expectations, notably MULTIMOD. Rational expectations are particularly useful to describe financial markets and the arbitrage between alternative assets (entering the model, for instance, as a condition stipulating that expected returns be equalised). But for forecasting *per se*, rational expectations are not used that often, in part because of the greater technical difficulties they involve. In particular, they imply that forward-looking variables such as exchange rates jump following unanticipated shocks, a pattern which is preferably avoided in short-run forecasting. Hence, MULTIMOD is not used to generate the IMF's baseline forecast but rather to explore alternative scenarios (Isard, 2000).

## 6.2   Forecasting with a model

Forecasting with the help of a model is by no means a 'push-button' exercise, which would only require updating the series entering the model and then letting the model run freely over the forecast period so as to collect the results. First of all, assumptions about the evolution of the exogenous variables are needed, since their path is not determined by the model. In addition, one has to take into account the specificities of the ongoing cycle, both to integrate the conclusions drawn from the short-term diagnosis and to assess the relevance of the relationships embedded in the model in the context of the forecast. And in the end, it is essential to ensure that the forecast is consistent and convincing. Far from being a purely mechanical exercise, model-based forecasting is thus a delicate art, involving the following steps, which are discussed in this section: reading recent developments through the lens of the model; forecasting the exogenous variables; formulating assumptions about the residuals; and refining the baseline scenario through iterations and amendments. In addition, the forecast should be monitored on an ongoing basis, as new information comes in, which may call for adjustments.

### 6.2.1  Interpreting recent developments by using a model

The first step of the forecasting process is to check whether the model properly accounts for recent developments. Indeed, its equations have been estimated over some earlier period, and one should start by examining whether these estimated relationships continue to hold over the recent past. Most crucial are the very latest observations, since they serve as the jump-off point for the forecast. This work is usually done equation by equation, although model blocks or even the whole model are sometimes simulated to measure their performance over recent periods. For each individual equation, for instance, one can evaluate its stability over time by using a Chow test. A more common procedure, however, is to look at the sequence of residuals. Consider the following example:

$$\varphi(L)y_t = \boldsymbol{\theta}(L)\boldsymbol{x}_t + u_t \tag{6.1}$$

where $y$ is the explained variable, $\boldsymbol{x}$ the vector of explanatory variables, $L$ the lag operator, $\varphi(L)$ and $\boldsymbol{\theta}(L)$ lag polynomials and $u$ the residual. This can be rewritten as:

$$u_t = \varphi(L)y_t - \boldsymbol{\theta}(L)\boldsymbol{x}_t \tag{6.2}$$

The sequence of $u_t$ can then serve to balance the equation over the period for which observations of $\boldsymbol{x}$ and $y$ are available. For the model as a whole, this operation is generally automatised: the endogenous $y$ are treated as exogenous, the exogenous $u$ as endogenous, and the software 'solves' the model over the said period.

Examination of the residuals provides a quick diagnosis on how well the equations perform over the recent past. Usually, one expects the residuals to have a zero mean and to be uncorrelated over time. If not, several cases may arise: a positive or negative bias may come to light for the recent observations; the residuals continuously increase or shrink from a certain date onwards; or there are large changes in the residuals for the latest observation(s). However, before concluding that the equation has broken down, the recent fluctuations in $u$ need to be compared with its behaviour over a longer period, to check whether indeed recent movements are outside the historical range.

If that is the case, four main types of reasons may explain the deterioration of the model's performance:

- Measurement problems. Some of the recent data are provisional and subject to significant subsequent revisions. If the model is right but the data wrong, incorrect measurement of any variable will be reflected in the residual. In fact, one of the oft-overlooked merits of good models is their ability to highlight potential data problems. This can be very helpful to establish a proper near-term diagnosis.

- Incorrect parameter estimation. Even if the specification is all right, some of the parameter estimates may be off base. Parameters may be unstable or may have moved since the last estimation period.
- Erroneous specification. The specifications used in the model reflect the theoretical knowledge and the data available at the time it was constructed and estimated, and are intended to represent the mechanisms that were most prominently at work in the past. When shocks or structural breaks occur, the specification may become obsolete. A frequent problem is the omission of explanatory variables which were unimportant in the past but have recently become influential. For example, traditional consumption equations with only income and inflation on the right-hand side failed to explain the increase in household saving observed in France in the late 1980s and early 1990s. New specifications adding in unemployment or interest rate variables, however, did yield more satisfactory results.
- Exceptional factors. A host of special factors may come into play which are difficult to model, including targeted economic policy measures (such as subsidies to the automobile sector or to housing), adverse weather conditions (storms or droughts), political or social events (such as major terrorist attacks or strikes), bunched orders to specific sectors of the economy (say orders of a batch of aircraft), epidemiological surprises (mad cow disease or severe acute respiratory syndrome (SARS)), and so on. Unforeseen developments abroad may spill over, as was the case with the Asian crisis in 1997–98: capital moved back from the emerging markets to the advanced economies, causing a decline in long-term interest rates that could not otherwise be explained by the evolution of the fundamentals in the advanced economies.

During a forecasting round, one or several of these problems almost invariably arise with some of the equations. It is then important to understand the underlying reasons, and whether the divergence between observed and predicted values is temporary or durable, so that the equation can be used as it should in forecasting. If incorrect parameter estimation and/or erroneous specification are uncovered, one might in principle wish to respecify and re-estimate these equations. But, in practice, there is rarely time to do so and resource constraints often preclude it, all the more so as, once an equation has been altered, the properties of the model as a whole may change, which calls for further and more ambitious work. Very often therefore, forecasters prefer to retain the original equations but with some *ad hoc* assumptions as regards the behaviour of the residuals over the forecast period (see below).

The interpretation of recent developments requires integrating what the model says and what incoming information suggests. The latter usually encompasses the data released for the variables included in the model but also other 'hard' or 'soft' data, such as survey data, qualitative or sectoral information, and so on. These allow formation of an estimate of the 'present' for which national accounts data are not yet available (see Chapter 3). Using this type of information can greatly enhance the quality of the model-based forecast by helping to choose the right assumptions for the behaviour of the residuals.

There are several ways to combine the model and other tools for this type of near-term analysis. One is to use all the available information to build a benchmark forecast for the very short run, which is meant to be a stylised version of the more detailed quarterly national accounts data to be published later. The model-based forecast then starts a couple of quarters down the road, using this benchmark as a base.

Lastly, the model itself can help refine the diagnosis of the current situation: if the latter is inconsistent with what the relationships in the model imply, a reconsideration of the diagnosis may be warranted.

### 6.2.2   Forecasting exogenous variables

In order for the model to predict the endogenous variables, the exogenous ones need to be forecasted. They belong to one of three groups: the international environment (such as growth in partner countries, foreign prices, price of oil and other raw materials, exchange rates or foreign interest rates), macroeconomic policy (such as taxes, public spending or the monetary stance) and miscellaneous others (such as demography or technical progress).

In the case of an international model, the international environment is of course endogenous, even though certain variables such as the oil price or exchange rates may still be treated as exogenous. In the case of a national model, growth in the partner countries enters as an indicator of world demand, which can be thought of as a weighted average of the imports from these countries, with the weights being the share of each in exports of the national economy (see Box 5.3). Similarly, foreign prices enter as a national competitiveness indicator, with partner country weights reflecting both trade with these countries and competition on third markets (see Box 5.4). All this assumes that prior forecasts have been produced for the rest of the world, or at least for the country's main trading partners. This may not be feasible in-house. One way to proceed is then to use the forecasts published by international organisations such as the OECD, the IMF or the European Commission, or to use consensus forecasts.

The macroeconomic policy assumptions can be introduced as a conventional set of hypotheses or as the most likely scenario. Alternatively, reaction functions or rules can be used. In the first case, announced fiscal policy measures which are deemed likely to be implemented are taken into account. For the rest of the time horizon, however, projected budget developments are typically assumed to be in line with past trends, unless there are specific reasons to think otherwise. As regards monetary policy, the convention used in official forecasts is often to keep policy-controlled interest rates unchanged at their current level. Alternatively, a constant real interest rate assumption is sometimes used, or the interest rate path expected by the market. Likewise, the exchange rate is often assumed to remain frozen at its latest level, which is justified if it follows a random walk (see Section 8.4). Such assumptions are not necessarily realistic but they do have the advantage of simplicity. For official forecasts, another advantage is their relative neutrality. For instance, central banks may not wish to reveal possible future moves (although they may wish to prepare markets) and governments do not want to be seen as dictating monetary policy. A forecast based on such assumptions is informative, but only provided its conditional nature is well understood: it shows how things are likely to unfold if, for better or for worse, current policies do not change course.

In the second case, the most plausible – unconditional – economic policy scenario is used, even if it departs from what has been officially announced or if it involves measures that have not yet been unveiled. This approach tends to be favoured by private sector forecasters and clients, who are more interested in what is likely to happen than in what would happen under some more-or-less contrived policy assumptions. It is also pursued alongside the first one by public-sector forecasting teams when they advise policymakers, although the results then often remain confidential.

*De facto*, this second approach endogenises economic policy variables, since it usually considers that the latter depend on the near-term outlook. For example, if a slowdown in demand is forecasted, the conventional assumption of an unchanged interest rate may be highly implausible and will be replaced by a cut. In a similar vein, one might want to assume some exchange rate appreciation if its current level is widely considered to be significantly undervalued.

Yet another approach is to endogenise the behaviour of policymakers by introducing policy rules. For example, interest rates may be set according to a rule which combines an inflation target, a full-employment objective and some aversion *vis-à-vis* interest rate instability (see Chapter 8). Tax rates can be derived as ensuring the sustainability of public finances (for instance, a forecasted increase in the deficit or in the public debt ratio would automatically entail an assumed tax hike) or the respect of some rule to which the authorities have committed themselves (see Chapter 9).

None of these approaches is intrinsically superior to the other two. Rather, they correspond to different needs.

### 6.2.3   Dealing with residuals: add-on factors

The next challenge is to decide how to deal with the residuals $u_t$ over the forecast period. *A priori*, one might presume that $u_t$ should be set at zero over the forecast period, since by construction it should have a zero mean and not display any auto-correlation over time. In practice, however, this may not be appropriate, owing to measurement, estimation or specification errors, or to special factors causing the residuals not to behave in that fashion. Indeed, in many cases, setting the residuals for all variables to zero throughout the projection period would produce an awkward forecast. Instead, part or even the entirety of the recent residuals will be added onto what the equation itself predicts. These additions are sometimes referred to as 'add-on factors' or simply 'add factors'.

Tracing out the residuals over the forecast period is done equation by equation and reflects the views of the forecaster on the magnitude and persistence of factors that are not adequately captured by the model. In particular, future developments in the residuals (the $u_t$ provided by the original estimation of the model) will be extrapolated depending on the interpretation of their past values and on the near-term diagnosis.

In order to illustrate this procedure, equation (6.1) can be rewritten as follows, after inversion of $\varphi$ and differencing:

$$\Delta y_t = \varphi(L)^{-1}\theta(L)\Delta x_t + v_t \tag{6.3}$$

where $v_t = \varphi(L)^{-1}\Delta u_t$. The right-hand side of equation (6.3) is the sum of two contributions to the growth rate of the endogenous variable: the first term is the contribution from the changes in the explanatory variables, and the second the contribution of the 'add-on factors' that are not captured by the explanatory variables.

When this equation is used in forecasting, a variety of assumptions can be made regarding the profile of the add-on factor going forward:

- The simplest is to set $u_t = 0$ for all of the forecast period. This is consistent with the model and is indeed warranted if $u_t$ has behaved as white noise over the estimation period and if no disturbances other than those transiting via the $x_t$ are foreseen.
- The second option is to freeze $u_t$ at its most recently observed level, or at its average over the recent past, if one believes that the recent residuals correspond to a permanent shock.
- The third possibility, which is often the preferred one in practice, is to assume that $v_t = 0$ over the forecast period. In a sense, it is a 'neutral' assumption, since it means that only the factors explicitly captured in the model's explanatory variables influence the evolution of $y_t$.[1]
- Yet another option is to postulate a gradual convergence of $u_t$ or $v_t$ to zero, if one feels that the factors that caused the endogenous variable not to move in line with the model's prediction are likely to wane over time. The speed at which this is posited to happen should in principle be given some justification.

The variables for which this type of exercise is usually conducted are those that are hardest to pin down in a macroeconomic model, due to their great volatility or because they have too many different determinants. Examples include stockbuilding (which is notoriously volatile at quarterly frequencies) and exports of manufactured goods (when lumpy orders make for abrupt shifts in the series). Some economic policy measures (one-off investment incentives, for instance) are also reflected in the residuals, insofar as they are not integrated in the exogenous variables.

The seemingly *ad hoc* nature of these adjustments is sometimes criticised, but they do have a statistical rationale. In an econometric model, the residual reflects the influence of the factors that the exogenous variables leave out. When relevant information is available that cannot be adequately incorporated into the explanatory variables, it thus does make sense to adjust the residuals to take it on board. Ideally, however, such adjustments should be based on some rigorous quantification outside the model.

---

[1] Note that the second and third option are clearly different: a constant $u_t$ going forward does not imply that $v_t = 0$, since past values of $u$ also enter $v$.

Furthermore, when a particular econometric equation in the model is open to serious doubts, it may be even preferable to set it aside and use an alternative forecasting method – and in turn explicitly estimate the future path of the 'add-on factors'. For instance, residential investment is often poorly explained econometrically, as it is highly volatile and may react strongly to special fiscal incentives or other temporary elements. Given the considerable gestation lags associated with housing construction, it is frequently preferable to use housing starts as a leading indicator of residential investment in the context of short-term forecasting. But even then, the equation remains of interest: the behaviour of the residual over the forecast period says something about the imbalances that may have built up in the past or about how 'normal' the forecasted path is.

In sum, playing around with the residuals give forecasters some leeway to nuance what the model would mechanically ordain. Therefore, two teams of forecasters using the same model and the same data may still come up with palpably different forecasts.

### 6.2.4   Refining the baseline scenario

Once the exogenous variables and the add-on factors have been set, the model is run to generate the values for the endogenous variables over the forecast period. The fact that by construction the model has to be consistent with the national accounts identities imparts some coherence to this initial set of forecasts. But this is not enough, as it does not guarantee that they make economic sense. Indeed, the first run usually has a number of flaws, be it as regards the overall story or some of the components. The next step is thus to identify and fix these shortcomings, in order to rerun the model differently.

Some elements of the forecast may sound implausible to sectoral specialists. There may also be inconsistencies between the different blocks or as concerns the exogenous assumptions. A typical checklist would include such questions as:

- Is the rate of GDP growth consistent with what is assumed for partner countries?
- Are the forecasted increases in prices, wages and productivity consistent with the phase of the cycle?
- Is the evolution of the saving rate consistent with household confidence indicators?
- Is the exchange rate assumption sensible given the forecast for activity, interest rates and the external accounts?
- Might the forecasted developments prompt an economic policy reaction?

A forecast that fails on some of the above criteria should be reconsidered and the model should be run again, for instance with a different set of assumptions for the exogenous variables or new add-on factors. In principle, this process is iterated until a consistent and plausible forecast emerges.

A common way to help bring out the logic of the forecast is to decompose the latter into different blocks, and to try to tell a credible story for each of the main behavioural aspects, and then a robust overall story that weaves all the elements together. The treatment of the 'add-on factors' will play an important role when communicating these stories.

### 6.2.5   Monitoring the forecast

A forecasting round is thus a heavy undertaking, especially with large models. Very often, it takes place quarterly at best. However, in between two forecasting rounds, the world moves on and the forecast needs to be adjusted.

Monitoring first involves checking whether what is observed is in line with the model's forecast. Where the two diverge, the deviation must be analysed, so that the proper adjustments can be effected for the remainder of the forecast period. Broadly speaking, three sorts of discrepancies can arise:

- National accounts data revisions for the recent past, which had previously served as the launchpad for the forecast.
- An inaccurate forecast for an exogenous variable: for instance, oil prices may have risen much more than anticipated. In some cases, the implications may be assessed by constructing an alternative scenario, as described below.
- An incorrect choice of add-on factors, which may be redressed by altering their profile for the rest of the forecast period.

## 6.3   Building alternative scenarios

Once a forecast is produced, the risks surrounding it also have to be considered, for instance by estimating the consequences of a given shock or even by building complete alternative scenarios.

### 6.3.1   Variants and alternative scenarios

The numerous assumptions underpinning a forecast consist of bets on the stability of behavioural relationships, the evolution of exogenous variables, the forthcoming economic policy initiatives and so on. The implied uncertainty and the relevance of the forecast can be better understood by constructing variants or alternative scenarios around the central forecast (also called the reference or baseline scenario). This helps fathom the risks and their transmission channels.

A variant can be defined as an alternative scenario resting on a slightly different set of hypotheses, and designed to evaluate their impact. For that reason, the results are often presented as deviations from baseline. Simple variants involve changing only one assumption, regarding for example the price of oil, interest rates, the propensity to consume or investment. Complex variants combine several changes, and tend to become alternative scenarios, telling altogether different stories. This exercise is often conducted by contrasting an optimistic scenario, where several key variables evolve favourably, with a pessimistic one, which has them all move in the opposite direction. While a bit extreme, this can be a useful pedagogical device.

Macroeconomic models are well suited for this type of analysis. Indeed, many of their exogenous variables – be they command variables (related to monetary and fiscal policy) or variables describing the environment (such as world demand or oil prices) – are precisely those for which one would like to try out alternative assumptions. Moreover, models highlight the mechanisms through which risks can affect the forecast, which suggests the likelihood of alternative scenarios: the first-round effects of changes in assumptions will be quantified, but also their ultimate impact, once all the feedback mechanisms have worked their way through. This is a valuable contribution, which other approaches, such as VARs and indicator-based methods, do not offer. That said, too much should not be expected either: not all the underlying hypotheses can be tested, nor can all the risks be pinned down *ex ante* (as the unexpectedness of the 11 September 2001 terrorist attacks painfully illustrated). The best way to proceed, therefore, is to focus on some of the shakiest assumptions which are known to strongly influence the shape of the forecast.

### 6.3.2   Techniques and limitations

A simple variant is typically obtained by altering the level or growth rate of the exogenous variables or the add-on factors. This experimental 'shock' can be confined to the short run or extended indefinitely. Four types of shocks can therefore be envisaged, depending on whether they affect levels or growth rates, and on whether they are temporary or permanent (Figure 6.1). Suppose, for example, that policymakers are to decide that an extra €1 billion will be spent as public

**Figure 6.1   Four types of shocks**

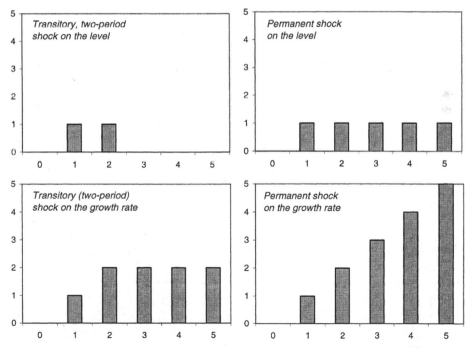

*Note*: X-axis: time; Y-axis: change in the level of a fictitious variable in the wake of various shocks.

investment over the forecast period: this would be considered as a permanent level shock. Or suppose that the minimum wage would be raised: this would be treated as a temporary shock on the growth rate of wages.

This type of analysis may run into a number of difficulties, however:

- It may be hard to calibrate the shock, in particular when the type of shock one is interested in forecasting cannot be described as a mere shift in the exogenous variables. Consider a tax cut granted to a specific sector that is not treated separately in the model: a proxy then has to be constructed, for instance a change in the economy-wide tax rate scaled down according to the size of the sector in question. It is also possible to draw on other sources of information to establish the first-round effect of the tax cut and then to use the model merely to compute the feedback effects.
- The model may not adequately capture the mechanisms that one would expect to matter most for the shock at hand. For instance, in the case of a change in interest rates, it may be that the model does not have a sufficiently rich financial and monetary sector, so that some crucial aspects of the transmission of the shock are missed. It may also be that some behavioural relationships have mutated since the model was last estimated, calling at a minimum for a reconsideration of the obsolete equations.
- Economic policymakers may not react as assumed. Many variants are run on the basis of the conventional hypothesis of unchanged policies, or assuming that policymakers will follow some rule (such as the Taylor rule). This may be unrealistic for some of the less standard shocks. Then, some *ad hoc* policy reaction has to be built in.

While understanding simple variants can be relatively straightforward, more complex combinations do not lend themselves as readily to interpretation. However, if the model is linear, one can treat such combinations as sums of simple variants. This holds more generally, even in models involving a degree of non-linearity, provided the shocks under consideration are small and one is ready to ignore second-order effects. Also, in many cases, and in particular for output or prices, deviations from the baseline are presented in level terms. Users have to bear this in mind when comparing growth rates (GDP growth or inflation) across scenarios and over the years.

### 6.3.3   An example: the impact of the Asian crisis in 1997–98

A telling example is the Asian crisis that broke out in 1997, which caused massive shifts in trade and capital flows and had worldwide repercussions. Looking at its impact on the US and European economies, it can be analysed as four overlapping and interrelated shocks:

- An adverse trade shock stemming from currency depreciation and decline in demand in the crisis countries (mainly Thailand, South Korea, Indonesia, the Philippines and Malaysia).

- A second and partly related adverse trade shock due to yen depreciation and demand contraction in Japan.
- A stimulatory financial shock, with central banks in advanced OECD countries lowering interest rates and downward pressure on bond yields due to the repatriation of capital from emerging market economies.
- A commodity price shock, as the price of oil and other raw materials declined.

Using NiGEM, the French Ministry of Finance in its budget documentation estimated around mid-1998 that:

- Together, the two trade shocks would reduce the level of US and EU GDP by some $1\frac{1}{2}$ per cent by 1999.
- The central banks' policy reaction coupled with the reflux of capital to US and EU markets and the decline in commodity prices would partially but significantly offset the impact of the trade shocks on activity.
- The net impact of the Asian crisis on the level of GDP, taking into account short-run feedback effects, would thus be on the order of $\frac{1}{2}$ per cent in 1998 and $\frac{3}{4}$ per cent in 1999 (implying an impact on annual output growth of respectively $\frac{1}{2}$ and $\frac{1}{4}$ per cent).
- Inflation would be pushed down substantially, as all four shocks were working in the same direction.

## 6.4  How far can models go?

Models can do a lot. Even so, they have been criticised for lacking consistency or theoretical foundations, for using overly restrictive empirical specifications, for insufficient robustness to changes in regime and for mediocre forecast accuracy. This section discusses these allegations and concludes that despite their limitations, models are clearly useful.

### 6.4.1  Reasons for disenchantment

The first type of critique applies less to models *per se* than to the very activity of modelling, which is deemed to lack rigour. The indictment runs as follows:

- Even when the specifications are in line with theoretical models of behaviour, the latter hinge on a number of simplifying assumptions, such as that of a representative agent. How appropriate they are is rarely questioned, and they may in fact not constitute valid approximations.
- In addition, empirical models take liberties with the theories that inspire them. In particular, behaviour is often studied in a partial equilibrium framework, ignoring many of the agents' concomitant constraints and decisions. A concrete example is the analysis of household consumption abstracting from their residential and financial asset investment decisions, or from their labour supply decisions. Intertemporal budget constraints are often ignored as well.

The estimated equations therefore frequently fail to be fully consistent with optimisation behaviour.
- Lack or poor quality of data entails departures from the theoretical model in the empirical equations. In addition, the choice of the functional form for dynamic equations is rarely based on a theoretical rationale but rather on what seems to fit best.

These are admittedly genuine limitations. However, they do not suggest that modellers should stop forecasting but instead that they should strive to ensure that their instruments be internally consistent, subject to what the data seem to impose. Progress is indeed being made in this respect. Several leading macroeconomic models have been reconfigured since the early 1990s or so to integrate the different blocks better and to strengthen the connection between microeconomic optimisation behaviour and the macroeconomic relationships embodied in these models.

A second and more fundamental line of criticism was promoted by Sims (1980), who deplored that empirical model specifications were unduly restrictive, even when the econometric estimations are conducted properly. He pointed to the following reasons:

- The specifications used in practice are often imposed equation by equation, on a partial equilibrium basis. Economic theory instead implies more complex, cross-equation restrictions. Moreover, the formation of expectations has to be considered.
- In practice, the distinction between exogenous and endogenous variables is largely arbitrary and is not formally tested for.
- Moreover, the dynamic structure of the specification is typically *ad hoc* (an argument which overlaps with the first set of criticisms).

Sims argued that it was impossible to overcome all these problems in the context of traditional macroeconomic models, and advocated the use of pure time series techniques, such as VARs, which *a priori* seem less restrictive (see Section 4.4). Other researchers have taken this cue to investigate computable general equilibrium (CGE) models (see Section 9.4 for an application to public finances).

Subsequent developments in macroeconometric modelling, plus the emerging limitations of times series techniques and CGE models, have certainly weakened the Sims critique (Hall, 1995). In particular, the spreading of cointegration techniques and of error-correction models has allowed the combination of theoretically reasonable long-run properties and data-driven short-term dynamics. In addition, increased use is being made of multivariate systems in which theory sets the identifying constraints, while the technology available to estimate them has improved.

The third objection to models is the so-called Lucas critique, which states that models are vulnerable to regime shifts (Lucas, 1976): macroeconomic models cannot serve to predict the impact of future shocks or policy initiatives because their estimated parameters reflect average behaviour in the past. If the environment or policies are now different, these parameters might have changed as well. The reason is that they are reduced-form parameters that reflect the combination of truly deep structural parameters (like tastes and technology), which are the only ones that will not change, and regime-dependent characteristics. Hence the only way out is to write and estimate an authentically structural model, devoid of any reduced-form parameters.

While much ink has been spilled on the Lucas critique, its practical importance is open to doubt. First, the forward-looking models based on optimising firms and consumers that have been developed since Lucas and Sims aired their reservations can be unstable across policy regimes, if only because they too may incorrectly specify agents' constraints, objectives or expectation formation. Estrella and Fuhrer (2003) even argue that such models may be less robust in the face of regime shifts than their backward-looking, reduced-form counterparts. In any event, it seems vain to believe that a purely structural, policy-invariant, model can be constructed (Altissimo *et al.*, 2002).

Lastly, macroeconomic models are frequently criticised for poor forecasting performance. As discussed at length in Chapter 11, their forecasting accuracy indeed leaves much to be desired. Moreover, the uncertainty relates not only to the baseline scenario, but also to the alternative ones. The assessment of the risks depends on the calibration of the corresponding assumptions, which is difficult not only *ex ante* but even *ex post*. Take the above example of the Asian crisis: even with the benefit of hindsight, the magnitude of the interest rate decline that can be specifically ascribed to this shock remains unclear; also, the size of the negative foreign trade impact stemming from lower import demand in the crisis countries was revised up several times in the course of 1997–98, as the extent of the crisis became apparent (see Richardson *et al.*, 1999).

Furthermore, model-based evaluation of economic policy measures is equally delicate. It requires to bring in assumptions that are not unambiguously supported empirically and for which economic theory does not provide clear-cut answers. For example, will tax cuts stimulate consumption by boosting households' disposable income, or will they encourage precautionary saving because households factor in the tax increases needed in the future to finance today's largesse?

### 6.4.2   A still useful toolkit

That said, macroeconomic models tend to do better than purely statistical ones, at least at horizons exceeding one year. In addition, while their forecasting performance is especially disappointing around turning points, this weakness is shared by the other forecasting methods. And macroeconomic models provide an explicit economic story when communicating the forecasts, especially compared with more 'press button' or 'black box' approaches.

Moreover, though the various criticisms described above are well taken, the profession has tried to address them. Technological progress in forecasting has helped to develop new tools. At the same time, models are used more wisely, with more systematic recourse to variants and a more thorough documentation of the underlying assumptions and mechanisms. Notwithstanding their enduring weaknesses, models remain widely used and continue to play a key role in forecasting as well as in policy analysis.

On the forecasting side, they enable a wealth of data to be assembled and processed in a coherent framework, and provide structure for an internally consistent forecasting story. Granted, the modelled relationships describe average behaviour in the past, but this is an incontrovertible benchmark when evaluating possible future developments. Furthermore, model variants shed light on the risks surrounding the forecast. More prosaically, but no less importantly, models allow the coordination of the work of different specialised teams.[2]

In policy analysis too, models are powerful instruments, allowing us to answer 'what if ...' questions. As discussed at greater length in Chapter 12, models can test practitioners' or policymakers' views by working out their implications before any real-life experimentation.

---

[2] At the US Federal Reserve, one senior economist has the title of 'GDP coordinator', indicating that she or he has to ensure that all the components of GDP, which are estimated by different staffers, fit together in the framework of the overall model.

# 7
# Medium- and Long-Run Projections

Interest in medium- and long-run projections is on the rise, not least due to concerns about the economic implications of population ageing, but also against the background of the ongoing rebalancing of the global economy towards some large emerging economies, especially in Asia. Medium- and long-run projections differ from the short-run forecasts discussed in previous chapters. Beyond the next few quarters, it is indeed pointless to try and forecast the business cycle. However, it is possible and instructive to look at the underlying trends further out. To differentiate the two types of exercises, the term 'projection' tends to replace that of 'forecasts' for longer-run horizons. Even so, projections are and should be quantified rather than purely qualitative. In this context, the numbers are not meant to convey what would be an illusory sense of precision. Rather, they serve to illustrate broad trends and to highlight constraints, notably through recourse to alternative scenarios.

Roughly speaking, the medium run can be thought of as extending over the next three, five or even ten years. The horizon here is the time it takes for any existing cyclical disequilibria (excess supply, misaligned asset prices and the like) to unwind. Indeed, at the one-to-two-year horizon contemplated in short-run forecasts, these imbalances are typically not expected to be resolved and often they persist at the end of short-run forecasting periods. In contrast, a natural assumption over the medium run is that they are worked off.

The long run (ten years or more) can only be thought of in terms of very broad trends. Growth theory is the obvious framework to do so, putting emphasis on supply-side factors such as demography and technical progress, and abstracting from cyclical fluctuations.

This chapter first explains how medium-run projections are produced (Section 7.1). Macroeconometric models similar to those used for short-run forecasts are often also used, thereby allowing fairly detailed depictions. But it is also common to go for a more streamlined approach, related to growth models, and to focus on concepts such as potential growth and output gaps, which can be seen as summary indicators of the trend and the cycle. Potential growth is also at the heart of the longer-run projections (Section 7.2).[1]

## 7.1   The medium run

Usually, the medium-run forecast is added onto a short-run one rather than built from scratch. This is a good way to connect what is projected for the outer years with what is known about the recent past. In particular, it is helpful in thinking about the unwinding (or not) of the imbalances that are observed at present or foreseen in the short run. However, the model used for the medium run may contain variables that are not forecasted in the short-run model. Hence, there may be a need to start with augmenting the existing short-run forecast so that the path for these variables is mapped out. Once that is done, the outer years can be projected following procedures similar to those described in Chapter 6 for short-run forecasts. Among other things, that involves making assumptions about the exogenous variables (external environment and policies), deciding on how to deal with the residuals, and checking the projection for internal consistency and for plausibility. This exercise, however, need not be conducted with the same attention to detail as for short-run forecasts. Usually, the focus is restricted to a few key concepts, notably potential GDP and the output gap.

### 7.1.1   The concept of potential GDP

Potential GDP is key when looking at long-term economic developments since it is aimed at measuring the country's productive capacity. When the economy is overheating, actual GDP exceeds potential GDP, and vice versa when there is slack. Productive capacity should not be understood as a technical ceiling but as the maximum sustainable level given available technology and agents' preferences. Though it cannot be directly observed, economic theory suggests that a gap between actual and potential GDP leads to price movements that will tend to restore equilibrium. From this perspective, potential GDP can be defined as the level of GDP consistent with stable inflation.

Potential growth is then defined as the growth of potential GDP and the output gap as the difference between actual and potential GDP (meaning that the output gap is or becomes negative during economic downswings). The output gap summarises the position of the economy in the cycle. It is also an indicator of inflationary pressures: a positive output gap denotes tensions on the labour and product markets which may push up inflation; conversely, a negative output gap tends to foreshadow disinflation (Figure 7.1).[2] The link between output gaps and

---

[1] This distinction is somewhat arbitrary since growth models can be viewed as stripped down and supply-side focused versions of large macroeconomic models. Conversely, the latter can in principle be used as well to generate long-run projections, provided they exhibit reasonable long-run properties, namely that they converge on some sustainable growth path.

[2] While potential GDP is mostly derived from the supply side, it also reflects demand that can be sustained over the longer run. Hence, the output gap can also be interpreted as an indication of temporary excessive or lacking demand, prompting the use of the expression 'demand-driven inflation/disinflation'.

*Figure 7.1* Output gap and inflationary pressures in the United States

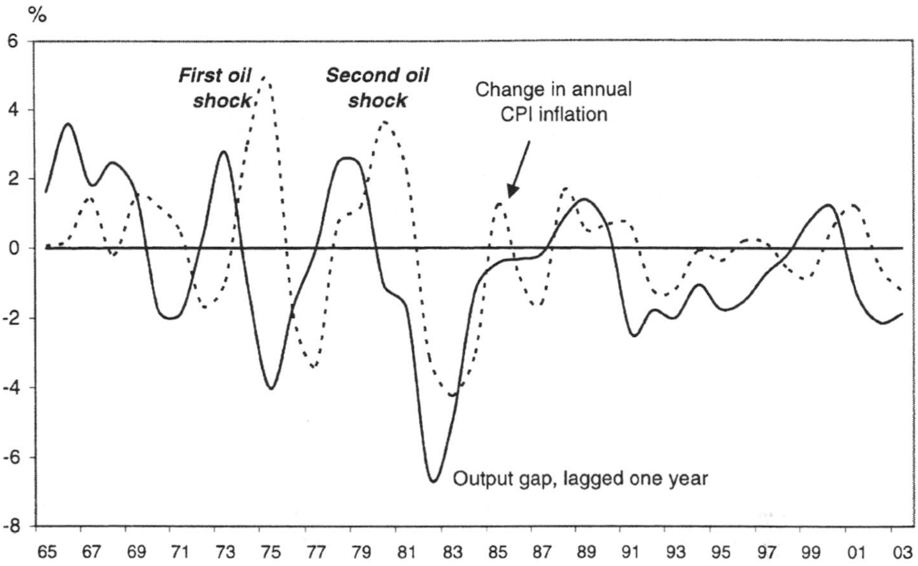

*Source*: OECD.

the change in inflation is not that stable, however: the lag between the opening up of a gap and the (demand-driven) reaction of prices varies; and other factors influence inflation, such as changes in prices on world markets, exchange rate movements or expectations – say following shifts in the perception of the central bank's reaction function.

The concept of potential GDP is crucial in a medium- or long-run perspective, as it provides a baseline for what growth can expected to be, on average, over such horizons. The assumption is that in the long run the path of potential and actual GDP coincide, on the same trend. Hence, sooner or later, GDP should revert to potential (see Figure 7.2).[3] Let $T_0$ be the start of the projection period. In the example depicted here, output and growth were below potential prior to $T_0$, implying a widening negative output gap. The projection here assumes a progressive catch-up: with growth above potential between $T_0$ and $T_1$, the output gap gradually closes. Beyond $T_1$ and until the end of the projection period $T_2$, it is assumed that growth settles at its potential rate, so that the output gap remains nil.

While such a simple scenario is not necessarily implausible, complications can arise. One is that the imbalances witnessed prior to $T_0$ may increase for some time after $T_0$ before they start to unwind, so that the output gap closes later. Another is that it may seem naïve – albeit convenient – to posit that beyond $T_1$, the cycle vanishes; indeed, it might be natural to expect that years of negative output gaps

---

[3] However, it is possible to assume that the output gap does not close over the projection period. Indeed, economies can experience protracted periods of below (or above) potential growth, as some observers have argued was the case of France in the 1980s and 1990s.

*Figure 7.2*   GDP, potential GDP and the output gap

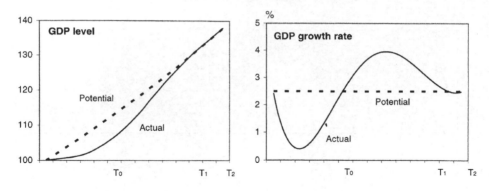

will be followed by years of positive output gaps, and vice versa. The reason why the back-to-trend scenario is nonetheless often the best possible assumption is that it is very difficult, if not altogether vain, to try and foresee whether beyond $T_1$ growth will continue above potential or slow. Rather than attempting to fine-tune the projection in this way, it is sensible to opt for a neutral, if artificial, assumption, which gives equal weight to upside and downside risks. Some forecasters nevertheless prefer to extrapolate past cyclical patterns, on the grounds that this produces a more plausible picture.

### 7.1.2   Estimating potential GDP

Potential GDP is a theoretical construct, not a directly observable variable. Hence, it has to be estimated. A variety of methods can be used, which sometimes produce significantly different results. The main two sets of approaches are the 'statistical' ones, based on observations of GDP, and the 'economic' ones, relying on a production function. Other types of approaches include 'semi-structural' ones, which focus on the link between the output gap and inflation, and decompositions based on structural VARs (*à la* Blanchard and Quah, 1989). In practice, the various methods are used in parallel, and each of them can be implemented in several different ways.[4]

*Statistical approaches*

The statistical approaches draw one or several lines through the actual GDP series, thereby producing a stylised representation of the GDP trend(s), which is taken to

---

[4] Output gap estimates are routinely published by national and international institutions. The approaches followed by the Congressional Budget Office (CBO) in the United States and by the OECD and the IMF are described respectively in CBO (2004a), Giorno *et al.* (1995) and De Masi (1997). For most purposes, the European Commission has switched from the first, 'statistical' approach (see McMorrow and Röger, 2001) to the second, 'economic' approach (see Denis *et al.*, 2002). For a comparison of the various methods, see Cotis *et al.* (2005).

be potential GDP. Two methods are most commonly used to that effect:[5]

- One interpolates the rate of actual GDP growth between comparable points in the cycle. Thus, in the United Kingdom, HM Treasury (2002) calculates average growth between points where the economy is judged to have been 'on trend', that is at around average levels for the economic cycle, drawing on evidence from business surveys and labour market indicators. Potential GDP is projected forward from 'on trend' points. While there is room for judgement in deciding what constitutes an 'on trend' point, this approach has the merit of considering a wider range of cyclical indicators than a purely statistical approach looking exclusively at trends in output.
- The other method is to use the HP filter proposed by Hodrick and Prescott (1980), which is run through the GDP series so as to satisfy:

$$Min\sum_{y_t^*}(y_t - y_t^*)^2 + \lambda\sum(\Delta y_t^* - \Delta y_{t-1}^*)^2$$

where $y$ is the logarithm of GDP and $y^*$ the logarithm of trend, or potential, GDP. The filter thus takes into account both closeness to actual GDP (the first term of the minimisation) and the variability of the trend (second term). The relative weight of these two criteria, and hence the trade-off involved in the smoothing operation, is set by the choice of the parameter $\lambda$. In practice, $\lambda$ is typically set at 1600 for quarterly data and 100 for annual data. Intuitively, the choice of 1600 reflects an assumption that the standard deviation of the cycle is 40 times as large as that of the acceleration in the trend. This would be consistent, for instance, with an average absolute output gap of 4 per cent and an average absolute change in trend growth of 0.1 per cent (for quarterly data).

There are, however, two main difficulties. First, the results obtained with the HP filter are quite sensitive to the choice of $\lambda$:

- Changing $\lambda$ alters the amplitude of the cycles: the higher $\lambda$, the smoother the trend and the more pronounced the cycles. However, the choice of $\lambda$ generally has little impact on the dates at which actual and trend GDP coincide, so does not affect the length of the cycles much.
- Running the HP filter through annual data usually leads to longer cycles (say, 10 to 12 years) than if it is run through quarterly data (which generates cycles of, say, 4 to 6 years). Thus, the choice of the frequency matters for the length of the cycles.

Second, the HP-filter estimated $y^*$ tends to be overly influenced by the latest observations of $y$. This is the 'end-of-sample bias': as the filter is symmetric, it forces the output gaps to sum to zero over the period being covered, even though the latter only exceptionally corresponds to an exact number of cycles.

---

[5] There are other ways to separate trend and cycle, as explained in Chapter 4, but they are less frequently used in a medium-term forecasting context.

While these statistical methods are fairly easy to implement or replicate and do not depend on any particular economic theory, they are of limited use when conducting medium- and even more long-term projections. One reason is that they rest on somewhat arbitrary assumptions, be it regarding the determination of 'on trend' points or the choice of λ. More importantly, they do poorly in estimating the current trend, which is a major handicap in a forecasting context. Indeed, for either method to work properly, one needs to be at the end of a cycle rather than somewhere in the middle. The usual patch involves somehow extrapolating the GDP series forward before extracting the trend. But this introduces a circularity when the aim is precisely to get a handle on potential GDP for forecasting purposes. Finally, the economic rationale for explaining the projected path of output growth is almost absent. Therefore, and also because they enable decomposition of growth into various components, production-function based approaches are often preferred in forecasting, even if they have their own pitfalls.

### Production-function based approaches

The first choice to be made is that of the production function itself, which should capture the relationship between output and factors of production. Almost always a constant return to scale function is used, with two substitutable production factors, capital and labour. Usually, a Cobb-Douglas form – which is particularly easy to manipulate[6] – is selected, or more generally speaking a constant elasticity of substitution (CES) form.

The production function can be written as $Y = F(K, L, A)$, where $Y$, $K$, $L$ and $A$ respectively stand for output, the capital stock, labour input, and a residual. $Y$ and $K$ are both expressed in real terms. $L$ is usually measured in hours of work rather than in number of bodies, so as to take into account trend changes in hours worked. $A$ is called total factor productivity (TFP) and captures the contribution of all the factors not incorporated in the measures of capital and labour, such as technical and organisational progress, effort, and so on. As $Y$, $K$ and $L$ are observed, $A$ can be calculated as a residual. Potential output is then $Y^* = F(K^*, L^*, A^*)$, where the asterisks denote trend, or potential.

$K^*$ is usually set equal to $K$, since the capital stock that is in place represents its potential contribution to output. Via $K$, potential growth thus depends on investment so far (assuming no sudden shift in the rate of capital depreciation). So if investment slows down, say, because of rising interest rates, potential growth declines. Since

---

[6] *A priori*, using a production function highlighting the contribution of capital to potential growth makes sense for the medium run but less so for the longer run. Indeed, over the long run, it is often assumed that the evolution of the capital stock is determined by that of labour resources and technology (see below). This would argue for having only labour as an input in a long-run production function. However, it is also possible to keep capital as a factor alongside labour, provided that it is projected consistently with the projected labour force and productivity. More fundamentally perhaps, the capital/output ratio may change over the long run, in response to changes in relative prices (witness the ongoing fall in information technology prices), and taking this into account does require retaining a production function with the two factors.

investment is positively correlated with the cycle, estimated potential growth will tend to be pro-cyclical.

$A^*$ is generally derived by smoothing observed TFP. The latter moves with the cycle,[7] owing to the lags with which labour and even more so capital adjust to changes in output. One of two methods is usually employed to smooth TFP:

- Regressing $A$ on a time trend. For instance: $\log A = aT + b + u$, where $T$ is time, $a$ and $b$ are parameters and $u$ is the residual. $A^*$ is then obtained as $\log A^* = a^*T + b^*$, where $a^*$ and $b^*$ are the estimated parameters. This regression can be improved by adding a variable capturing the cycle on the right-hand side, say, the ratio of capacity utilisation in manufacturing. Note, however, that the period of estimation may affect the results, and that the estimated trend can display some breaks over time.
- Running some smoothing algorithm through $A$, such as the HP filter. The smoothed series may then retain some pro-cyclicality. This might, however, be justified insofar as technical progress or work effort are pro-cyclical.

Calculating $L^*$ is tricky. $L^* = POP^*PR^*(1-U^*)H^*$, where $POP^*$ stands for the trend working age population, $PR^*$ for the trend participation rate, $U^*$ for structural unemployment and $H^*$ for trend hours worked per job. Estimating each of these requires exercising judgement:

- $POP^*$ is usually set equal to $POP$ (often the population aged 15 to 65, although different age brackets may be used).
- $PR^*$ is generally obtained through statistical smoothing of $PR$, so as to control for the pro-cyclicality of participation rates.
- The same holds for $H^*$, as $H$ is also pro-cyclical (overtime most conspicuously so).[8]
- $U^*$ is probably the most difficult component, as there are many ways to estimate structural unemployment.

A simple way to define $U^*$ is as that component of $U$ that is unrelated to the cycle. Part of $U^*$ corresponds to 'frictional' unemployment, due to the normal time it takes to find a new job. But $U^*$ may also reflect inadequate skills, minimum wages, the tax wedge, weak job-search incentives, insufficient competition in the goods markets, and so forth. The impact of these factors is hard to quantify. An apparently easy way around this problem is to derive $U^*$ through statistical smoothing of $U$. This can be appropriate if the cyclical component of unemployment is not too persistent, which may be the case in flexible labour markets such as in the United States but was less so in Continental Europe during the 1980s and 1990s.

---

[7] Productivity gains are not strictly speaking pro-cyclical since they tend to be the highest during periods when output is accelerating – that is, when the change in the output gap is the largest, not when the economy is peaking.

[8] When there is a structural shift, this can be problematic, as straight smoothing would not distinguish cyclical effects from other sources of variation (notably in the case of France in the late 1990s, following the introduction of the 35-hour working week).

In any event, the $U^*$ obtained by statistical smoothing is often fairly close to $U$, so that $Y^*$ does not differ much from $Y$.[9]

One more economic but also complex approach is to compute the NAIRU, understood as the unemployment rate consistent with stable inflation (see Section 5.5).[10] Several approaches are possible in this respect. The first is to estimate an augmented Phillips curve, enabling the estimation of a short-run NAIRU which moves around in response to temporary shocks, and a long-run NAIRU, which is determined by productivity trends. It is also possible to estimate the NAIRU using a 'semi-structural' approach (see Box 7.1). Yet another approach is to use a notion of

---

**Box 7.1   Semi-structural estimation of the NAIRU**

The NAIRU can be estimated using an unobservable component model including a Phillips curve. It is based on the assumption that the unemployment rate $U$ can be decomposed into a trend component, identified as the NAIRU, $U^*$, and a cyclical one, $C$, which is not observed but is assumed to affect inflation, $\pi$:

$$U_t = U_t^* + C_t + e_t$$

$$\Delta\pi_t = \sum\alpha_i\Delta\pi_{t-i} + \gamma C_t + \delta z_t + u_t$$

where lagged inflation is introduced to take inflation inertia into account and $z$ is a vector of variables further explaining inflation (supply shocks for instance), while $e$ and $u$ are error terms. The unobserved component $C$ enters both equations and $\gamma$ indicates how strongly it affects inflation.

Estimation of the model (parameters $\alpha_i$, $\gamma$ and $\delta$ as well as $U^*$, $C$ and $e$) requires to make assumptions about the statistical properties of trend and cyclical unemployment and about correlations. A simple but representative example would be as follows:

- The trend follows a random walk with drift: $U_t^* = U_t^* + \beta + \eta_t$ (this assumption would be consistent with the likely non-stationarity of the NAIRU – witness its tendency to rise in Continental Europe through the mid-1990s, a case of positive drift).
- The cycle is an ARMA stationary process, that is an AR(2) process of the form $B(L)C_t = v_t$, with $B(L)$ a second-order polynomial distributed lag and $v_t$ white noise.
- The error term is nil: $e_t = 0$.
- Trend and cycle are uncorrelated: $E(v_t, \eta_{t'}) = 0$ for any $(t, t')$.

Based on such a set of assumptions, the model is written in space-state form which allows Kalman-filter estimation (see Chapter 4). Unlike the univariate trend-cycle decompositions (such as the two statistical approaches presented above), this allows use of the information contained in the Phillips curve and thereby comes closer to the theoretical NAIRU concept. At the same time, and in contrast with traditional Phillips curve analysis, allowance is made here for the fact that the NAIRU may change over time, even if nothing is said about why. This time-varying NAIRU approach is therefore often dubbed 'semi-structural'.

In practice, however, the hypotheses underpinning this type of approach are somewhat arbitrary, notably as regards the statistical properties of the cycle (in particular, more symmetry than one might like can be retained). More generally, such methods are delicate to implement properly and difficult to communicate to outsiders, so that transparency is limited.

---

[9] The advantage of a production-function-based approach is then somewhat limited, as compared to directly filtering GDP. To a degree, this caveat extends to the other methods used to estimate $U^*$.

[10] A detailed discussion of the NAIRU is provided in Turner *et al.* (2001) and Ball and Mankiw (2002).

equilibrium unemployment defined as the rate that stabilises the share of labour in national income, in the context of a model of wage and price setting *à la* Layard *et al.* (1991). But whatever the method used, the estimates of $U^*$ are fragile, especially in euro area countries, where the cyclical and structural components of unemployment appear to be particularly difficult to disentangle empirically.

### 7.1.3   Growth accounting

Projecting potential GDP requires to make some reasonable assumptions about the evolution of the various 'trend' components:

- TFP trend growth is usually posited to be in line with historical averages.
- Working-age population projections are usually available from demographic studies.
- It is more difficult to foresee the evolution of trend-participation rates, to which the results are quite sensitive, as illustrated by Burniaux *et al.* (2003). The same holds for working hours. In practice, judgement will be key in determining whether their historical trends are maintained over the projection period, or whether some stabilisation might be preferred.
- It may be prudent to keep $U^*$ at its latest estimated level. But depending on the circumstances, it can be useful to explore variants, for example when it is expected that past or ongoing labour market reforms will gradually reduce structural unemployment.
- Capital accumulation cannot be assumed exogenously, as it depends on the evolution of output over the projection period. One caveat is that potential and actual growth projections are thus interdependent; hence, one frequent option is to assume that the capital–output ratio will remain constant, consistent with a long-run approach of economic development (see below).

In a nutshell, the production-function-based methods are not only dependent on the statistical uncertainties surrounding their determinants but also on the choice of the economic assumptions that have to be retained for forecasting purposes. Hopefully, their formulation highlights the sources of growth in a transparent way, allowing examination of how sensitive the projection of trend output is to the underlying economic assumptions. Indeed, for any production function:

$$\frac{\dot{Y}}{Y} = \frac{K}{Y}\frac{\partial Y}{\partial K}\frac{\dot{K}}{K} + \frac{L}{Y}\frac{\partial Y}{\partial L}\frac{\dot{L}}{L} + \frac{A}{Y}\frac{\partial Y}{\partial A}\frac{\dot{A}}{A}$$

where dots denote time differentiation. If in addition production factors are remunerated at their marginal productivity:

$$\frac{\dot{Y}}{Y} = \alpha\frac{\dot{K}}{K} + (1 - \alpha)\frac{\dot{L}}{L} + \zeta$$

where $\alpha$ is the share of capital in value added, $(1 - \alpha)$ the share of labour and $\zeta = (A/Y) (\partial Y/\partial A) (\dot{A}/A)$ stands for TFP gains.[11] Thus, the contributions to the medium-term evolution of GDP of the stock of capital, the labour force and technical progress can be readily disentangled. Moreover, the likely range of medium-term growth can thereby be identified and communicated, with an explanation on how it depends on a transparent set of alternative economic scenarios.

### 7.1.4 Dealing with uncertainty

This is not to say that uncertainty has disappeared, on the contrary. Indeed, some of the judgement calls needed to anchor the projection are just very difficult, as illustrated by the questions surrounding the foreseeable evolution of labour productivity in the United States (Box 7.2). As already mentioned, significant uncertainty attaches to the choice of one versus the other method in estimating a medium-term path for potential growth. Moreover, the assessment of the current state of the economy is itself crucial; for instance, an error of 2 per cent in estimating the present size of the output gap can lead to an error of around 0.5 point in annual GDP growth over several years – if for instance the output gap is assumed to be closed over the next four to five years of the horizon. Moreover, real world factors can obviously easily throw off any medium-run forecast. This has been the case worldwide with exogenous shocks such as the oil shocks of the mid and late 1970s, or in certain regions, such as in Asia in 1997–98. Finally, policy choices also matter for the evolution of both potential and actual GDP – not least because they may be instrumental in shaping the development of supply-side factors on the medium-term horizon.

Chapter 13 discusses in detail how such uncertainties can best be dealt with. In a nutshell, it is advisable to use fairly simple and conventional assumptions rather than to try and second-guess future changes in trends. Scenarios can help illustrate the range of possible outcomes (including the more prudent ones) and should sketch out the likely implications of the alternative policy options that may be under consideration.

### 7.1.5 A case in point: medium-run fiscal programmes in Europe

Medium-run projections are used in particular in the stability or convergence programmes that European countries are required to submit towards the end of each year to the European Commission, in the context of the Stability and Growth Pact (see Chapter 14). These programmes are focused on budget forecasts but obviously involve a set of underlying macroeconomic projections. Comparing successive vintages of the programmes illustrates how large the uncertainty can be, even when the medium run barely extends beyond the short run (Figure 7.4). Indeed, the programmes submitted around end-2000 reflected the euphoria prevailing at a time when real GDP growth in the euro area exceeded $3\frac{1}{2}$ per cent.

---

[11] This formula always holds in the simple case of a Cobb-Douglas production function.

*Box 7.2* **What is trend labour productivity in the United States?**

One of the surprising and distinguishing features of the downturn at the start of the 2000s in the United States was the behaviour of labour productivity. The latter is typically highly pro-cyclical, so that analysts widely expected it to slow down significantly, all the more so as productivity gains had been high in the late 1990s, when the new economy bubble inflated. Instead, labour productivity growth remained strong and measured as output per hour in the non-farm business sector it averaged close to $4\frac{1}{2}$ per cent in 2002–03, compared to an historical average of around $2\frac{1}{4}$ per cent (Figure 7.3).

Against this intriguing backdrop, what would an appropriate medium-run productivity projection be? The consensus view has tended to move up as productivity outcomes exceeded expectations. The general view appears to be that the underlying growth in productivity over the next few years would likely soften a bit but would remain well above the weak performance of the 1970s and 1980s. One difficult judgement call in this respect pertains to the efficiency enhancements associated with information technology. One view is that the massive investments in high-tech equipment made in the late 1990s are paying off with some delay, partly because businesses discover unexploited areas of cost reduction that had accumulated during the boom years. But how large any further gains in the pipeline may be is far from obvious.

It is hard to overstate the importance of these trends. Higher US trend productivity growth would have major implications for US potential growth, increases in living standards and fiscal margins in the years to come.

*Figure 7.3* **US labour productivity growth***

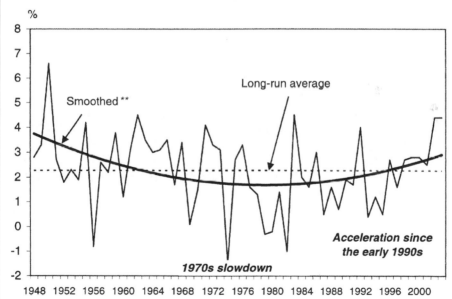

*Notes*:
* Annual percentage rate of change of labour productivity in the non-farm business sector.
** Second-order polynomial trend line.

*Source*: US Bureau of Labour Statistics.

*Figure 7.4*   **Diminishing growth expectations in the euro area**
(real GDP growth euro-area-wide, as projected in successive vintages of the stability
programmes)

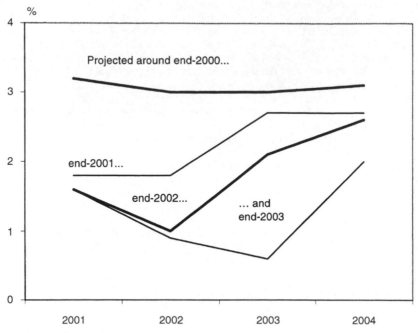

*Source*: European Commission.

GDP growth was estimated at close to 3 per cent over the following years and this
did not seem wildly optimistic. But in the event, the short-run forecasts on which
the medium-run ones rested turned out to be a full $1\frac{1}{2}$ percentage point above the
mark. Not only were the forecasts for actual growth revised downwards time and
again during the next three years, but the projection for GDP growth for the next
years was pulled down by some $\frac{3}{4}$ percentage point – in part because of a less optimistic assessment of potential growth. In level terms, these revisions imply that by
end-2003, the level of GDP projected for 2004 was 5 percentage points lower than
expected three years earlier. Based on an elasticity of around $\frac{1}{2}$ for fiscal balances
with respect to GDP, this shortfall implies a deterioration of the euro-area-wide fiscal
deficit by $2\frac{1}{2}$ percentage points of GDP – compared with an actual deficit not far
from the 3 per cent threshold in 2004.

## 7.2   The long run

Long-run projections are usually produced using streamlined models: attempting to
describe economic developments a decade or more down the road in any detail would
be futile, as attested by the considerable uncertainty already hanging over short- and
medium-run forecasts. The purpose of these models is to depict how selected key
variables may interact over the long run, keeping in mind that certain regularities can

be expected to hold, such as the six 'stylised facts' identified by Kaldor (1961):

1. Output and per capita output grow over time, with no tendency to decline.
2. Capital per worker grows over time.
3. The rate of return to capital is broadly constant, at least in advanced economies.
4. Capital–output ratios are steady over long periods (no rise or fall in the long term).
5. The shares of labour and physical capital in national income are broadly constant in periods when the share of investment in output is constant.
6. The growth rate of output and output per worker differs substantially across countries.

Notwithstanding the considerable margins of error surrounding long-run projections, they can enable some important qualitative conclusions to be drawn: for instance, they make it clear that in the absence of major reforms, pension systems in many OECD countries will not be able to cope with the pressure of population ageing (as discussed in more detail further below).

These long-run projections should not be confused with futures research, which tries to discern the trends and innovations that are likely to reshape the world over the coming decades (see Section 14.1). Long-run projections, in contrast, essentially extrapolate past trends taking into account only those changes that can be fairly confidently expected.

### 7.2.1 Solow's model and the golden rule

Growth theory is the natural springboard for long-run economic projections. While it has evolved substantially over the past two decades, the starting point remains the model introduced by Solow (1956). It has the advantage of being both simple and consistent with the first five of Kaldor's six stylised facts. In its basic rendition, the model rests on the following assumptions:

- The production function includes two substitutable inputs, labour and capital, with constant returns to scale. It can be written as $Y = F(K,EL)$, where $Y$, $K$ and $L$ respectively are output, the capital stock and the quantity of labour, while $E$ is labour efficiency, which is assumed to grow at the constant rate $\mu$.[12]
- $L$ expands at a constant, exogenous rate, $n$, consistent with a long-run perspective wherein demographic factors dominate.
- The investment rate is also constant and equal to the saving rate (as the economy is assumed to be closed). It is therefore called $s$. Given that capital depreciates at a rate $\delta$, $dK/dt = sY - \delta K$.

---

[12] $E$ represents the contribution of factors other than capital and labour and plays the role TFP did above in Section 7.1. It is in fact necessary to assume that $E$ enters multiplicatively with labour for the model to have a balanced-growth-path solution. Technical progress in this case is said to be labour-augmenting, or 'Harrod-neutral'.

Let $k = K/EL$ and $y = Y/EL$ be the stock of capital and output per unit of 'effective labour', and define $f(k) = F(k,1) = y$. Then:

$$dk/dt = sf(k) - (n + \mu + \delta)k$$

This equation summarises the model's dynamics. It says that, per unit of effective labour, the increase in the capital stock equals the saving (or investment) minus the investment needed to keep the stock of capital constant given population growth, technical progress and depreciation.

Figure 7.5 illustrates this.[13] The stock of capital per unit of effective labour converges to $k^*$, which is such that:

$$sf(k^*) = (n + \mu + \delta)k^*$$

Hence, output per unit of effective labour converges to $y^* = f(k^*)$. Once there, the economy remains on a balanced, or steady-state, growth path. Along this long-run path, output per worker and the stock of capital per worker grow at the constant rate $\mu$, while output and the stock of capital grow at the constant rate $(\mu + n)$.

The model thus suggests a simple way to carry out long-term macroeconomic projections: the only variables for which assumptions are indispensable are the growth of the labour force and that of labour efficiency. Assuming the economy is

*Figure 7.5*  **Solow's growth model**

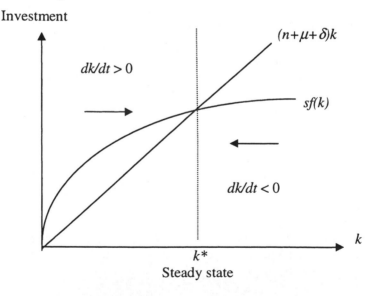

----

[13] The underlying and very standard assumption is that $f$ satisfies the so-called Inada conditions: it should be strictly increasing ($f' > 0$) and concave ($f'' < 0$), with $f(0) = 0$, $f(\infty) = \infty$, $f'(0) = \infty$ and $f'(\infty) = 0$.

on its steady-state growth path, and assuming that production factors are remunerated at their marginal productivity (which will be the case under perfect competition), the following holds:

- The profit rate $r$ (equal in this context to the real interest rate) is constant, at $r^* = f'(k^*) - \delta$, which is the constant marginal product of capital per unit of effective labour net of the depreciation rate.
- The share of income going to capital is constant and equals $r^*K/Y$, with the capital–output ratio $K/Y$ constant, since both $K$ and $Y$ grow at the same pace $(\mu + n)$.
- The share of income going to labour is also constant and equals $wL/Y$, where $w$ is the real wage per capita, which rises at the same rate $\mu$ as productivity per worker.

In sum, along the steady-state growth path, income shares are constant, the profit rate is constant and wage earners reap all the productivity gains in the form of rising wages. Note, however, that the real interest rate depends on $k^*$, and hence on the saving rate $s$ (via the above condition $sf(k^*) = (n + \mu + \delta)k^*$). Thus, to project the real interest rate using the result $r^* = f'(k^*) - \delta$, one needs an assumption about $s$, as well as about the shape of the production function.

One way to go about this is to ask which steady-state path would maximise consumption (production less saving) per capita $c$. Since $c^* = f(k^*) - sk^* = f(k^*) - (n + \mu + \delta)k^*$, it will be maximised for the value of $k^*$ for which the first-order condition holds, namely $f'(k^*) = n + \mu + \delta$. This in turn gives the optimal saving rate (plugging the optimal value of $k^*$ into $sf(k^*) = (n + \mu + \delta)k^*$). Using the fact that $r^* = f'(k^*) - \delta$, the real interest rate is:

$$r^* = n + \mu$$

The real interest rate thus equals the economy's real growth rate: this is growth theory's so-called golden rule.

But why would agents spontaneously wish to save at this rate? The golden rule does not allow for any inclination to discount the future, as opposed to the present, and for any risk aversion. One way to bring these elements in is to endogenise saving behaviour in an intertemporal utility maximisation model as first proposed by Ramsey (1928). Let $\theta$ denote the rate of time preference (or subjective discount rate) and $\sigma$ risk aversion (which corresponds to the degree of concavity of the utility function). Then, one can show that the economy will converge on a growth path such that $r^* = f'(k^*) - \delta = n + \mu/\sigma + \theta$. A common simplifying assumption is then that the utility function is logarithmic, so that $\sigma = 1$. Then, the relationship boils down to:

$$r^* = n + \mu + \theta$$

This is the 'modified golden rule': the real interest rate is higher than in the golden rule to the extent that agents discount the future.

### 7.2.2   More recent approaches

*Shortcomings of the Solow model*

While simple and operational, the Solow model suffers from two major shortcomings. First, it predicts that two economies with the same saving rate and having access to the same technology will end up on the same long-run growth path. If one starts out with a lower capital stock per head than the other, it will initially grow faster, because the marginal productivity of capital will be higher. But over time it will catch up, and eventually both economies will enjoy the same level and growth rate of GDP per capita. This type of 'absolute convergence' jars with observed cross-country trends. Some countries, notably in East Asia, have indeed caught up to a large extent with the advanced economies, but others, especially in Africa, have blatantly failed to do so.[14] In addition, a reasonable calibration of the Solow model implies that convergence to the long-run growth path should be fairly rapid (with half of the gap closed after some 15 years), which is also inconsistent with actual trends.

The second problem is that the most fundamental driver of growth, namely labour efficiency, is treated here as an exogenous variable, rising at a constant rate. The underlying assumption is that technical progress is costless and that firms and countries can all equally benefit from it, free of charge. The real world is of course rather different – not least because of the role played by profit incentives in driving technical progress.

*The 'augmented Solow model'*

One avenue followed to deal with these problems has been to broaden the concept of capital beyond that of physical capital. Capital accumulation is correlated with technical progress, since innovations are to a large extent incorporated in new physical assets. At the same time, it is important to focus on the quality of human capital, which depends, among other things, on education, training and the ability to use new technologies. Mankiw *et al.* (1992) have augmented the Solow model to include human capital $H$ alongside physical capital and the sheer volume of labour in the production function. Using a Cobb-Douglas production function, this leads to:

$$Y = K^{\alpha} H^{\beta} (EL)^{1-\alpha-\beta},$$

where $(\alpha + \beta) < 1$ (decreasing returns to total capital – physical and human – but constant returns to scale in production).

Assume that a fraction $s_k$ of income is saved to accumulate physical capital and a fraction $s_h$ to accumulate human capital. For simplicity, also assume that both

---

[14] While evidence of absolute convergence is weak, there is some of conditional convergence, meaning, broadly speaking, that homogeneous groups of countries tend to converge towards a common steady-state level of GDP per capita. For a detailed discussion, see Islam (2003).

types of capital depreciate at the same rate $\delta$. Keeping the same notations as above and defining $h \equiv H/EL$ and $f(k,h) \equiv Y/EL = F(k,h,1) = k^\alpha h^\beta$, the model's dynamics can be summarised as follows:

$$dk/dt = s_k f(k,h) - (n + \mu + \delta)k$$
$$dh/dt = s_h f(k,h) - (n + \mu + \delta)h$$

As indicated by the arrows in Figure 7.6, the dynamics are stable: the economy converges to a steady-state growth path where both physical and human capital per unit of effective labour are constant, with:

$$k^* = \{s_k^{1-\beta} s_h^\beta / (n + \mu + \delta)\}^{1/(1-\alpha-\beta)} \quad \text{and} \quad h^* = \{s_h^{1-\alpha} s_k^\alpha / (n + \mu + \delta)\}^{1/(1-\alpha-\beta)}$$

*Figure 7.6* **Convergence to a steady-state growth path with physical and human capital**

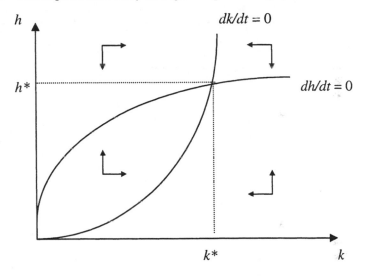

Empirically, this model shows convergence towards the steady-state growth path to be twice as slow, which is more realistic. Another feature is that the income share of each of the three factors is roughly similar, at around one-third, implying that human capital would contribute about as much as physical capital. However, the way the model is tested against the data has its own problems. Human capital is very hard to measure properly, and the enrolment ratios used by Mankiw *et al.* as well as by others may be poor proxies (Wößmann, 2003). Also, the results are highly sensitive to a few outlier observations (Temple, 1998). Moreover, the underlying assumption, shared with the Solow model, that steady-state rates of technical progress are identical across countries is rather unrealistic.

*Endogenous growth theory*

The other avenue explored to overcome the Solow model's limitations is to try and describe the forces driving growth in economic terms: this is what endogenous growth theory does.[15] This class of models attempts to reduce the contribution made by the residual in growth accounting, for example by treating research and development (R&D) as a separate factor input. Much of the focus in this context has been on the economics of innovation, highlighting the role played by R&D and the temporary monopoly rents associated with patents. An important aspect here is that unlike physical capital, technical knowledge is non-rival in consumption (it can be used in several places at the same time), opening up the possibility of increasing returns to scale.[16]

This approach takes into consideration the factors driving the pace of technical progress – the policies pertaining to R&D, education and training, market regulations, public infrastructures, entrepreneurship, openness and so forth. Taking these factors into account is in principle much better than somehow extrapolating past TFP trends. In practice, however, numerous endogenous growth models have been put forward – many of them quite abstract – and it is far from clear which ones are most robust to capture actual trends. Hence, these elements will at best be used qualitatively, and this approach is of limited direct value for forecasting purposes.

### 7.2.3   The economic consequences of ageing

A prominent example of the relevance of long-term projections are the economic consequences of ageing, as baby-boom cohorts retire. Many countries, and especially the OECD ones, face massive population ageing during the first half of the twenty-first century. The proportion of the elderly in the total population is set to rise dramatically, reflecting past fertility declines and continuously increasing life expectancy. As a result, old-age dependency ratios will soar, as illustrated in Figure 7.7 for the United States and in Table 7.1 for the main OECD countries. Indeed, the ratio of those aged 65 and above over the working-age population is projected to more than double in the typical OECD country between 2000 and 2050. This demographic transition has a number of serious macroeconomic implications, notably on real GDP growth, public finances and current accounts.

Past fertility declines translate into slower growth of the labour force. This will significantly reduce potential growth in the typical OECD country, even if it were to be mitigated somewhat by higher immigration and fertility rates than embodied in central projections. On one estimate, the per annum effect may amount to $\frac{1}{4}$ per cent in the United States and approach $\frac{1}{2}$ per cent in the EU-15 and Japan over this half-century (McMorrow and Röger, 2004). Real GDP and real GDP per capita (and hence overall living standards) would continue to grow, but over time, their level would be significantly affected. By 2050, GDP per capita would be

---

[15] For an authoritative introduction to a burgeoning literature, see Romer (2001).

[16] A simple example illustrates this. Consider a firm producing $Y$ in a plant with $L$ workers and a given stock of knowledge. If it opens a second, similar plant, it can produce $2Y$ with $2L$ workers but without needing any additional knowledge, thereby doubling output without having to double all inputs. However, technical knowledge is also partly non-excludable, implying that its owner cannot completely prevent others from using it, especially in the longer run.

*Figure 7.7* US old-age dependency ratio*

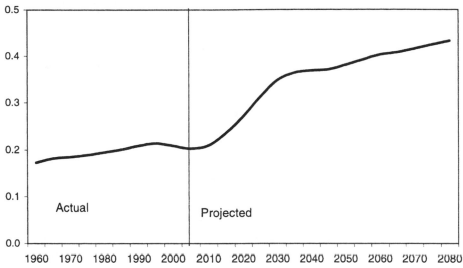

Note:
* Population aged 65 and up, divided by population aged 20–64.

Source: *Annual Report of the Board of Trustees of the Federal Old-Age and Survivors Insurance and Disability Insurance Trust Funds*, 2003.

*Table 7.1* Ageing-related public spending pressures

| | Old-age dependency ratio* | | Old-age pension outlays in % of GDP | | Health and long-term care spending in % of GDP | |
|---|---|---|---|---|---|---|
| | **2000** | **2050** | **2000** | **2050** | **2000** | **2050** |
| Canada | 20.4 | 45.9 | 5.1 | 10.9 | 6.3 | 10.5 |
| France | 27.2 | 50.8 | 12.1 | 16.0 | 6.9 | 9.4 |
| Germany | 26.6 | 53.2 | 11.8 | 16.8 | 5.7 | 8.8 |
| Italy | 28.8 | 66.8 | 14.2 | 13.9 | 5.5 | 7.6 |
| Japan | 27.7 | 64.6 | 7.9 | 8.5 | 5.8 | 8.2 |
| United Kingdom | 26.6 | 45.3 | 4.3 | 3.6 | 5.6 | 7.3 |
| United States | 21.7 | 37.9 | 4.4 | 6.2 | 2.6 | 7.0 |
| OECD at large** | 23.8 | 49.9 | 7.4 | 10.8 | 5.9 | 9.0 |

Notes:
 * Persons aged 65 and up, divided by persons aged 20–64.
** OECD average excludes countries for which the information was unavailable.

Source: Casey *et al.* (2003).

one-eighth lower in the United States and around one-fifth lower in Europe and Japan than it would have been absent ageing.

Slowing real GDP growth coupled with rising age-related public spending will squeeze public budgets. A very large portion of general government spending is indeed sensitive to the population's age structure, notably publicly financed old-age pensions, early retirement programmes, health and long-term care, child or family benefits and education. Ageing will add $6\frac{1}{2}$ per cent of GDP to public outlays in the typical OECD country (Casey *et al.*, 2003) and will only very partially be offset by a projected 1 per cent of GDP decrease in spending on child benefits and education. On average, the ratio of public debt to GDP would increase by over 200 percentage points between 2000 and 2050.

Actions taken in recent years have aimed at reducing average benefits, tightening eligibility requirements and complementing public commitments with private savings. But much more needs to be done to ensure long-run fiscal sustainability. Importantly, the room for reducing *ex ante* public transfers to future pensioners is limited, given that an overly wide gap between the incomes of active and inactive persons would raise severe redistribution issues, with unattended fiscal consequences. As to promoting private saving schemes, a risk is that future pensioners would face an unexpected meltdown in asset prices as they would all start at the same time consuming their savings.

The key challenge is in fact to increase the pool of resources (that is, national income) from which future social benefits will be drawn so as to limit the tax burden on future generations – assuming that retirees' demands themselves would not grow as much as national income. Boosting productivity gains would help but might not suffice to offset the demographic drag. Another solution is to boost labour supply and its utilisation, not least via higher participation rates for women and older workers. For example, if the female participation rate were 5 percentage points higher and if participation rates of older workers were to increase half as much as they fell since 1970, total age-related public spending as a share of GDP would be reduced by $\frac{3}{4}$ percentage point. Raising the retirement age would help alleviate future tensions even more, as it would both reduce outlays on pensions and boost GDP and general government revenue. Measures to curtail structural unemployment would also help: in Europe, every percentage point reduction in the unemployment rate boosts potential output and improves the fiscal balance by around $\frac{1}{3}$ percentage point of GDP, through lower transfer spending and increased tax receipts. Even so, and barring large-scale immigration, all these measures may not be enough to fill the gap, implying hikes in social contributions or tax rates, which in turn are likely to be inimical to potential growth.

As populations do not all grow old at the same time or at the same speed across countries, ageing also has international implications. Current account positions within the OECD area and between the latter and the rest of the world may be in for large swings. In theory, developing countries, with their younger populations, are likely to invest more than they save, and the ensuing current account deficits will be financed by more rapidly ageing OECD countries. In practice, however, this is less certain: witness the large US external deficit since the mid-1990s and the parallel improvement in emerging countries' current account balances, especially in Asia.

### 7.2.4 World growth over the coming decades

Indeed, looking far ahead, major shifts in economic gravity can be expected, partly as a result of demographic differences, but also reflecting catch-up phenomena.

*Figure 7.8*  **GDP rankings today and in 2050**
(in billions of 2004 US dollars)

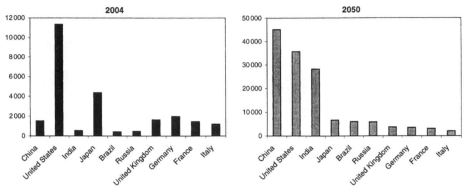

*Source*: Wilson and Purushothaman (2003).

Specifically, some Asian economies, and possibly also Brazil and Russia, could overtake many of the current G7 countries, provided they durably stick to growth-enhancing policies.

A set of projections through 2050, undertaken by Wilson and Purushothaman (2003), can serve to illustrate this prognosis (Figure 7.8). They assume Solow type Cobb-Douglas production functions everywhere. Technical progress is more rapid the poorer the country so that the speed of convergence depends on how far behind it lags. Real exchange rates are supposed to be driven only by productivity differentials and other basic assumptions are retained to project the labour force and population, the rate of depreciation, the share of income going to capital, alongside a steady-state labour productivity growth of 2 per cent in the United States. With these assumptions, China's GDP overtakes US GDP by 2041. Income per capita, however, would remain low, even by 2050. In China – where living standards would be almost twice as high as in India – dollar GDP per capita would still be only 37 per cent of the US level. Hence, compared with the rest of the world, the large OECD economies would remain way ahead in terms of income per capita, but their relative importance would fall dramatically, whilst some large emerging economies would join the club of dominant players. Moreover, the importance of the latter economies would be even more significant using PPP exchange rates instead of US dollars.

# 8
# Financial and Commodity Markets

Financial and commodity prices are not forecasted in the same way as national accounts aggregates. These prices are volatile and very much driven by market participants' expectations. A great variety of tools are used to analyse and forecast them, ranging from traditional models of interest rate determination to 'heterodox' methods such as chartism, to country-risk analysis.

The chapter opens with a discussion of what distinguishes these variables and the methods used to forecast them (Section 8.1). It proceeds with the modelling and forecasting of short- and long-term interest rates (Section 8.2). Bond, stock and house prices are covered next (Section 8.3), followed by exchange rates (Section 8.4). Commodity prices, with a special focus on oil prices, are dealt with in Section 8.5. The chapter ends with country-risk analysis (Section 8.6).

## 8.1 Dealing with volatility

Financial and commodity prices exert a strong and sometimes even decisive influence on the real sector variables that are at the heart of macroeconomic forecasting. But financial and commodity prices are volatile and at times seem only remotely connected to macroeconomic fundamentals. Hence, their evolution is difficult to predict. In addition, public-sector forecasters often refrain from publishing any forecasts for these prices, in order not to interfere with the operation of the markets. Indeed, an official exchange rate forecast, for instance, could be interpreted as a policy objective which the authorities will defend rather than as a purely technical hypothesis. For all these reasons, conventional working assumptions of one type or another are often used for financial and commodity prices.

Broadly speaking, six different approaches are followed to project these variables:

- The first one is to freeze them at some recently reached level, or at the average level observed over a given period of time. As noted in Section 4.1, this is good practice when the variable under consideration follows a random walk. This method is frequently used for exchange rates. It is also occasionally adopted for stock prices and commodity prices. Some central banks like it for interest rates because it allows them not to tie their hands as regards their future moves. For some variables, forecasters can select the period that serves to set the assumption so that in practice they retain some leeway to decide which value suits their forecast best.

- Expert judgement calls are the second way to go. For instance, oil market experts may consider that the balance of power with the Organisation of the Petroleum Exporting Countries (OPEC) is such that prices will be in line with the cartel's target. Economic forecasters can then simply use the latter. This approach is used in particular when building alternative scenarios.
- Market expectations, as reflected in futures prices, can serve as an anchor and are indeed explicitly used by the Bank of England when preparing the forecasts presented in its quarterly *Inflation Report*. The price of futures contracts, however, may not be a good predictor of the spot prices that will prevail down the road (see Box 8.1). Moreover, it incorporates a risk premium, implying that it does not coincide with the price actually expected by agents. The price of options (which give the buyer a right to sell or to buy a security or a barrel of oil at a certain price) also contains information about agents' expectations, especially as regards perceived risks. In practice, however, derivatives markets may not be deep enough for price quotes to be very informative, especially at longer horizons. Furthermore, market expectations may be at odds with the baseline scenario contemplated by the forecaster.
- Financial and commodity price forecasts can be derived in the context of a full macroeconomic model. This is done at times for interest rates or, to a lesser extent, for other variables.
- Alternatively, they can be forecasted outside the model, by trying to relate them to their key determinants. This provides equilibrium, or target values to which the variable under consideration will be assumed to converge over time.
- Lastly, the time series techniques described in Chapter 4 can be used.

In practice, the distinction between these different approaches is not that clear-cut, and some combination of them is commonly put to work.

## 8.2   Interest rates

The spectrum of interest rates is very broad, depending on the quality of the security or loan and on the horizon. The focus here will be on short-term money-market rates, which are very much influenced by monetary policy, and on long-term low-risk rates, say 10-year government bond yields.

### 8.2.1   Short-term interest rates

Short-term money-market interest rates are highly sensitive to central bank decisions or announcements, with the policy-controlled rates (often referred to as the central bank's repo rates) playing a key role. In practice, however, the measure used for short-term interest rates is typically the three-month interbank rate (depicted in

178

---

*Box 8.1*  **Bubbles, noise and herds**

Financial and commodity markets are notoriously prone to excesses, manias and crashes. Bubbles recurrently arise, in the sense of a widening divergence between economic fundamentals and the quoted price, with the latter far exceeding what even an optimistic assessment of the fundamentals – which are themselves uncertain – would warrant. Paradoxically, bubbles are not synonymous with irrationality on the part of traders, who can make a fortune as long as they get out before the market turns around. Bullish expectations become a self-fulfilling prophecy once a sufficient number of agents share them, so that a bubble can continue to inflate for a surprisingly long time after irrational exuberance has been diagnosed, with each trader knowing that the asset is overvalued but believing that he will be able to sell to one who has not yet realised it. At some point, however, a triggering event occurs, causing the bubble to burst. Awkwardly enough, this event may well be a 'sunspot', unrelated to any fundamentals but highly visible and serving as a coordination device to trigger the collapse.* The specificities of these markets, surveyed by Brunnermeier (2001), include:

- Herd behaviour, which can be rationalised as resulting from traders trying to make short-run profits by following the others and thereby amplifying market swings. In fact, traders are disinclined to depart from the average views: if they sell too early in a rising market, they will be blamed for under-performing their competitors, while if they record losses in the context of a general market collapse, they will not be singled out. As Keynes (1936) put it: 'it is better for the reputation to fail conventionally than to succeed unconventionally.'
- The fact that access to information is key. Two types of market participants can be distinguished, with asymmetric information: on the one hand, informed or professional traders, who are in a position to exploit arbitrage opportunities; and on the other hand, 'noise traders' or amateurs, who are less well informed. If the latter are numerous, even efficient behaviour on the part of the informed traders will not be sufficient to prevent prices from deviating from what the fundamentals would warrant. Moreover, even sophisticated traders may engage in herd behaviour if they are risk-averse and have short horizons, thus contributing to the formation of bubbles.

An example of self-fulfilling prophecy is the United Kingdom's exit from the European exchange rate mechanism in 1992: the British pound was not wildly overvalued, compared to the levels it subsequently reached in the late 1990s; however, speculative attacks on the currency led market operators to believe that defending the pound by raising interest rates would be untenable in a context where activity was already weak, which only reinforced speculators' pressure, so that ultimately the authorities abandoned the exchange rate peg.

Globalisation and financial innovation have complicated relationships between variables and made them more uncertain. For instance, a rise in oil prices will affect the financial holdings of oil-exporting countries and therefore the demand for dollars. Another example pertains to portfolio management. Investors tend to have risk diversification objectives, aiming at keeping the weights of the different asset classes in their portfolio at some desired level. When the risk of some component of their portfolio increases, they may reduce their holdings of some other risky assets even though the latter's risk/return profile has not changed. At times, one has thus observed a link between the price of certain domestic US assets (such as high tech shares) and capital flows to and from emerging markets.

Since financial and commodity prices are so unpredictable in the short run, many forecasters prefer to work with a simple technical assumption freezing them at some level rather than trying to forecast them.

* Likewise, the event that sparked the onset of the bubble may also be unrelated to fundamentals.

Figure 8.1), which moves in a less discontinuous fashion than the central bank's rate(s) and is less volatile than the overnight rates in the money market, which occasionally spike or plummet depending on liquidity conditions.

In forecasting, short-term interest rates are treated in a variety of ways. Many central banks, notably the ECB, use an unchanged interest rate assumption, which does not reveal their thinking about possible future policy moves. The OECD as well as many private-sector forecasters map out a trajectory for short-term interest rates over the forecast period, based on what is perceived as the policy stance consistent with central banks' objectives. Alternatively, the term structure and quotes for derivatives are used to infer market expectations, even though the latter cannot be perfectly pinned down in this way, owing to the existence of unobservable and time-varying risk premia.

***Figure 8.1***   **Short-term interest rates**
(nominal three-month money market rates)

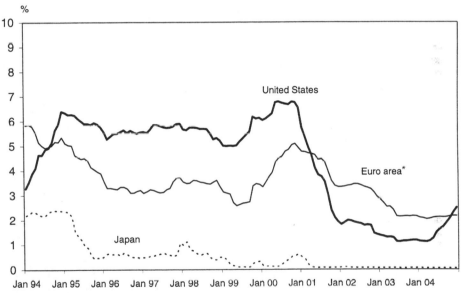

*Note*:
* Germany until end-1998, euro area since.

*Sources*: ECB and Bundesbank.

### Monetary reaction functions

Yet another approach is to endogenise the interest rate by estimating the central bank's reaction function, which relates it to the fundamentals that the central bank takes into account, either explicitly or implicitly – for instance when it says it targets some variable but acts on a different basis in practice. A prominent example is the Deutsche Bundesbank before the advent of the euro; it had an explicit objective for the growth rate of broad money M3 but *de facto* set interest rates more as a function of inflation, unemployment and exchange rate considerations (in such a case, the explicit objective may be excluded from the estimated reaction function). A typical ECM reaction function equation (see Box 5.1) would be as follows:

$$\Delta i_t = \alpha + \sum_j \beta_j \Delta i_{t-j} + \sum_j \gamma_j \Delta FC_{t-j} + \sum_j \delta_j F_{t-j} - \mu(i_{t-1} - \eta_i FC_{t-1}) \tag{8.1}$$

where $i$ is the short-term interest rate, $F$ the vector of relevant fundamentals and $FC$ the vector of the fundamentals that are cointegrated with the short-term interest rate, possibly with some lag structure (not shown here, for the sake of simplicity).

The fundamentals that are natural candidates to enter equation (8.1) include real sector variables (such as output growth, the output gap, capacity utilisation or unemployment), cost and price variables (such as import prices, producer prices or unit labour costs), the fiscal stance (although this is *a priori* more relevant for long-term interest rates) and variables depicting the international environment. The fundamentals may of course also include deviations from the central bank's explicit policy objectives.

External environment variables are particularly important for open economies with capital mobility, where domestic interest rates depend heavily on interest rates abroad. As is apparent in Figure 8.1, short-term interest rates often tend to fluctuate in synchrony across the main countries. This was particularly striking in the 1980s and 1990s amongst the countries that ended up adopting the euro in 1999, but is also noticeable when looking at cross-Atlantic interest rate relationships, with econometric tests often showing US interest rates to influence European ones. Therefore, key foreign interest rates are often included in equation (8.1), possibly alongside other external sector variables such as the exchange rate, foreign exchange reserves or the current account balance.

The form of the long-run cointegrating relationship depends on the nature and statistical properties of the series under consideration, as well as on the time period. Nominal variables such as inflation or nominal interest rates are often not stationary but I(1), so that it is sensible to estimate a long-run relationship between the domestic interest rate, inflation and possibly some foreign interest rate.

Furthermore, when searching for the best specification of equation (8.1), it is important to bear in mind some of the defining features of monetary policy. Central bank interest rate moves impact macroeconomic aggregates with a lag and gradually. In addition, central banks often tend to smooth their interest rate adjustments, opting for a gradual rather than a hyperactive approach, so as to have time to gauge the effect of their decisions and so as not to surprise agents too much. From this perspective, interest rates are 'path-dependent', as they depend on their own past developments and not just on fundamentals.

*Monetary rules*

At first sight, an alternative to estimating a reaction function is simply to posit that the central bank follows some kind of rule. When monetarism was in vogue, the normative rule was to keep the stock of narrow or broad money growing at a certain rate, leaving little room for discretionary action on the part of the central bank, at least in principle. But inferring the interest rate for forecasting purposes was not so simple, since in practice central banks continued to use discretion, *inter alia* because the relationship between money and output or inflation was insufficiently stable or even very weak.

Gradually, however, the focus shifted towards less normative and more descriptive types of rules, intended to capture rather than to prescribe central banks' behaviour.[1] Most prominent in this genre is the 'Taylor rule' (see Box 8.2). If indeed policy-controlled interest rates do seem to move in accordance with such a rule, the latter may look like a useful forecasting device, even if the central bank denies following any rule. In principle, however, it is preferable for forecasting purposes to estimate reaction functions rather than to assume that a given rule – the specification and parameters of which are somewhat arbitrary – will universally apply. That said, a rule can be useful:

- In contrast to reaction functions, it is formulated in a simple and easily understandable way – a great advantage in terms of communication.
- It allows assessment of the stance of monetary policy: the difference between the observed interest rate and the one the rule would imply signals how tight or loose policy is, or how much discretion is being exercised by the central bank, as compared to a 'neutral' stance merely reflecting fluctuations in the variables entering the rule. In 2002–03 for instance, short-term interest rates in the United States were significantly below what most formulations of a Taylor rule would have predicted, as the Federal Reserve tried to guard against the risk of deflation through aggressive cutting followed by a long spell of record low rates.
- A rule also serves as a guidepost in an uncertain environment or a new regime, in which previously estimated reaction functions become obsolete. Since the 1970s, the environment surrounding central banks has changed enormously, and so have their own independence and credibility. In Europe, the advent of a new currency area has completely altered the landscape, making it impossible to estimate the new central bank's reaction function over some past period (insofar as ECB actions depart from the simple aggregation of the decisions of 12 different central banks). A rule can then be quite helpful.

*Monetary conditions indices*

Another way to look at monetary policy is to use a monetary conditions index (MCI), which aims at summarising the factors that matter for the central bank when it sets its interest rate. In its simplest form, a MCI encompasses only $r$, the real short-term interest rate, and $q$, the log of the real effective exchange rate (where a rise represents an appreciation):

$$MCI_t = \theta_r(r_t - r_0) + \theta_q(q_t - q_0)$$

---

[1] In this sense, the term 'rule' may be confusing, as it refers to what is traditionally observed and not to optimality.

---

**Box 8.2   The Taylor rule**

Taylor (1993) described the Federal Reserve's behaviour between 1987 and 1992 in terms of a rule, as if it was setting monetary policy directly and solely as a function of inflation and output deviations from target:

$$r = r^* + 0.5(\pi - \pi^*) + 0.5(y - y^*)/y^*$$

where $r$ is the real short-term interest rate, $r^*$ its 'neutral' level (consistent with full employment), $\pi$ annual inflation, $\pi^*$ targeted inflation, $y$ GDP and $y^*$ potential GDP. The rule states that the interest rate is above its neutral level if inflation exceeds the target and/or output is above potential, and conversely. At times, the inflation and output goals are in conflict, for example when inflation is above target whilst the economy is below full employment. Then, the rule shows how these competing considerations are balanced in setting the interest rate. The Taylor rule can be recast in nominal terms, either in a backward or in a more forward-looking fashion as regards inflation (with $\pi^e$ standing for expected inflation):

$$i = r^* + \pi + 0.5(\pi - \pi^*) + 0.5(y - y^*)/y^* \qquad \text{(backward-looking)}$$
$$i = r^* + \pi^e + 0.5(\pi^e - \pi^*) + 0.5(y - y^*)/y^* \qquad \text{(forward-looking)}$$

Noting that $(y - y^*)/y^*$ is the output gap, the rule can be rewritten more simply in terms of changes:

$$\Delta i = 1.5\Delta\pi + 0.5\Delta gap \qquad \text{(backward-looking)}$$
$$\Delta i = 1.5\Delta\pi^e + 0.5\Delta gap \qquad \text{(forward-looking)}$$

Suppose that inflation picks up from 1 to 2 per cent (or is expected to), and that growth is running at 3 per cent while potential growth is only 2 per cent. Then the rule would predict that the central bank will raise rates by 2 percentage points.

While appealing, the Taylor rule is not devoid of problems as regards its contribution to forecasting:

- The neutral rate is often computed as some historical average, or as trend output growth, but whether this is the best assumption is not obvious.
- The inflation target may not be spelled out by the central bank. The US Federal Reserve in particular does not have a well-defined numerical inflation target.
- Output gap estimates are surrounded by considerable uncertainty (see Chapter 7), as is expected inflation. Moreover, the central bank's estimates of these magnitudes may not be public information.
- Inflation may not be that straightforward to measure. In many cases, there is scope for interpretation as to what the most pertinent index is (headline versus core inflation in particular).
- Other variables entering the central bank's decision are left aside, notably unemployment and exchange rates.
- The weights are not universal but simply those Taylor set as a rough approximation. In addition, central banks do not all share the same targets; for instance, the Federal Reserve has an explicit mandate to focus on inflation and activity, whereas the ECB is first and foremost focusing on price stability.

One way around some of these problems is to generalise the Taylor rule so as to explicitly take into account a broader set of variables of concern to the central bank. For example:

$$i = c + \alpha\pi + \beta p + \gamma(y - y^*)/y^* + \delta\Delta y$$

where $c$ is a constant, $p$ the log of the price level ($\Delta p = \pi$), and $\Delta y$ is real GDP growth. Depending on the value of the coefficients, the following rules obtain:

- $\beta = \delta = 0$: Taylor-type rule, with a target for inflation and for the level of activity (with the latter sometimes interpreted as an advance indicator of inflation).
- $\beta = \gamma = 0$: Taylor-type rule, but with a target for growth rather than for activity.
- $\alpha = \delta = 0$ and $\beta = \gamma$: nominal GDP or money stock target (depending on the assumptions made regarding the income velocity of money).
- $\delta = 0$ and $\beta = \gamma$: inflation and nominal GDP or money stock target.
- $\beta = \gamma = \delta = 0$: inflation target.

Going one step further, one could econometrically estimate, rather than impose, the coefficients. But then, in essence, one is estimating a reaction function.

where $r_0$ and $q_0$ are reference values, corresponding to a base period or some historical average. The weights $\theta_r$ and $\theta_q$ reflect the importance of the two variables from the point of view of monetary policy: for example, if the central bank wants to stabilise activity (and hence inflation), the coefficients could be proportional to the impact on aggregate demand of changes in $r$ and in $q$ respectively.

A few small open economy central banks have actively used MCIs (Canada, Sweden and New Zealand), and many central banks monitor MCIs, even if they do not publish them. Private-sector analysts also frequently compile them. In the Bank of Canada's headline MCI – which in contrast with the formulation above is expressed in nominal terms – the interest rate (measured as the 90-day commercial paper rate) receives a weight of 1, and the effective exchange rate (measured against Canada's six main trading partners) a weight of $\frac{1}{3}$: a one percentage point change in the short-term interest rate is estimated to have about the same effect on the policy goal as a 3 per cent change in the effective exchange rate.

The MCI concept has been broadened to incorporate other financial variables, in particular long-term interest rates and stock price indices, as done for Canada by Gauthier *et al.* (2004). The MCI is then typically referred to as a MFCI (monetary and financial conditions index) or more briefly FCI.

From a forecaster's standpoint, the MCI (or MFCI) sums up information in a convenient way. It can be computed almost instantaneously and is not subject to significant revisions down the road. Given the lags between changes in interest rates and exchange rates and their impact on activity, the current value of the index can help predict developments over the next few quarters. Also, one can assess what a reversion of the index to its long-run historical average would imply for financial variables. Notwithstanding these advantages, such indices have weaknesses, including the fact that the choice of the included variables and of the associated weights is model-dependent and therefore somewhat arbitrary (Batini and Turnbull, 2002). Moreover, defining where 'neutrality' lies for the index is tricky. For policy purposes, a movement in the MCI or MFCI has very different implications depending on which component of the index has shifted, and why. Indeed, the index averages a rate of return and an asset price, which may affect inflation at different speeds. Hence, the policy implications that can be inferred from the index's behaviour are limited. This is why the Sveriges Riksbank and the Reserve Bank of New Zealand no longer base their decisions and communication on a MCI, and why the Bank of Canada has de-emphasised it.

### 8.2.2   Long-term interest rates

Long-term interest rates can be approached from the angle of financial markets, as averages of current and expected future short-term rates, or from the macroeconomic angle, as the price that equilibrates saving and investment. In practice, forecasters tend to combine the two approaches.

The link between expected short-term interest rates and current long-term interest rates stems from the fact that agents arbitrage between the expected return from rolling over short-term deposits or bills and the known yield on long-term fixed-rate bonds. The proliferation of financial innovations and rising substitutability between financial assets has probably strengthened this connection. Arithmetically:

$$1 + i_t^\ell = [\Pi_j (1 + E_t i_{t+j}^s)]^{1/(T-t)} + \varphi_t^T$$

where $i_t^\ell$ is the long-term nominal interest rate at time $t$ and for time horizon $T$, $E_t i_{t+j}^s$ the expectation as of time $t$ of the one-period interest rate that will prevail at time $t + j$, and $\varphi_t^T$ the $(T - t)$-period ahead risk premium (all interest rates being expressed at annualised rates). The risk premium varies over time and is very difficult to pin down. It reflects agents' preference for liquidity and their degree of risk aversion but also a host of other factors including inflation expectations and cyclical conditions.

From a macroeconomic perspective, expected short-term interest rates and the risk premium can be viewed as depending on:

- International interest rates: insofar as investors arbitrage between domestic and foreign financial assets, domestic interest rates will be influenced by those prevailing abroad and/or by exchange rate expectations. Econometrically, and as transpires in Figure 8.2, long-term US interest rates are indeed found to be a significant determinant of the interest rates observed in most OECD countries (more so than for short-term interest rates).
- Fiscal policy: a fiscal expansion may foreshadow rising inflation in the future and therefore push up expectations of future short-term rates; it also increases the supply of long-term bonds so that a rise in long-term rates is required to balance saving and investment. In cases where fiscal sustainability looks threatened, the risk of ultimate default adds to the risk premium. The effect of fiscal policy is difficult to capture empirically, especially if past or current deficits or debt rather than the expected fiscal position are used on the right-hand side of the regression. For the United States, Laubach (2003) has estimated that, other things being equal, a 10 percentage point increase in the projected ratio of public debt to GDP will push long-term interest rates up by 40 basis points, a result broadly confirmed by Engen and Hubbard (2004). This is perhaps not that much, however, for the purpose of forecasting, given the volatility of long-term interest rates.

- Monetary policy: if for instance interest rates are below what a rule or an esti- mated reaction function suggests, they may be expected to rise. Interest rate expectations may also be influenced by the degree of credibility of the central bank: the more credible it is, the less it needs to raise rates to reach its objectives.

These influences can be quantified jointly through econometric estimation in a way similar to what was described above for short-term interest rates.

**Figure 8.2**   **Long-term interest rates**
(nominal 10-year government bond yields)

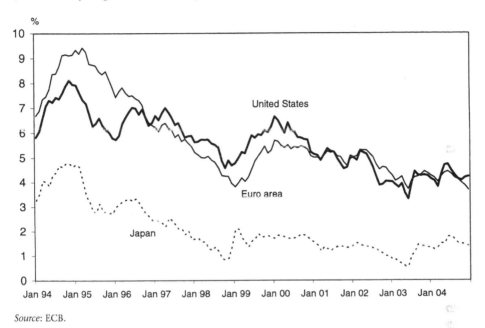

*Source*: ECB.

A less ambitious approach is to start from a forecast for the short-term interest rate and to model the spread *s* between the latter and the long-term rate. In its crudest form:

$$s_t = \alpha i_t + \beta$$

where $i_t$ is again the short-term nominal interest rate. *A priori*, $\alpha < 0$: all else equal, a higher short-term interest rate means the central bank is serious in the pursuit of its price stability objective, so that the component of the risk premium corresponding to inflation risk, and hence the spread, is lower. This can be extended to include other determinants of the spread on the right-hand side, such as the aforemen- tioned variables (expected inflation, foreign interest rates or the fiscal position).

This type of equation can be improved upon, depending on the statistical properties of the series under consideration. Nominal interest rates and inflation are often cointegrated, so that the spread and the real short-term interest rate *r* are stationary, which suggests to use the real rather than the nominal rate in the equation above:

$$s_t = ar_t + b$$

Again, this could be augmented to include a richer menu of explanatory variables. The full equation, including the short-run dynamic component, then becomes:

$$\Delta s_t = \sum_i \alpha_i \Delta s_{t-i} + \sum_i \beta_i \Delta r_{t-i} + \gamma Z - \mu(s_{t-1} - ar_{t-1} - b)$$

where $Z$ is a vector with the other variables entering the short-run dynamics.

## 8.3   Bond, stock and real estate prices

As stressed in Chapter 5, asset prices can exert significant effects on consumption and investment behaviour. A large share of household wealth is held in the form of bonds, stocks and housing. Their price is influenced *inter alia* by interest rates, taxation, demography and international factors (such as the portfolio strategies of global fund managers). As noted in Box 8.1, these asset prices can exhibit great volatility and at times fads or other forces push them far above or below what is warranted by the fundamentals.

### 8.3.1   Bond prices

Forecasting bond prices is essentially equivalent to forecasting long-term interest rates, as they are directly related. While long-term interest rates can be highly volatile over the very short run, they tend to move relatively smoothly over longer periods. Hence, foreseeable changes in bond wealth are usually not particularly abrupt, so that forecasters often pay little attention to bond holdings, extrapolating their value in accordance with some simple algorithm.

When long-term interest rates undergo lasting and large shifts, however, the associated wealth effect is sizeable. This was the case with the long-lasting decline in bond rates recorded during the 1990s in Japan (against the background of prolonged economic anaemia) and in Italy (in the context of the run-up to monetary union, when Italian bond rates converged towards German ones). In both countries, households who had large holdings of bonds enjoyed a temporary positive wealth effect.

Bond markets can experience bubbles, in the sense that yields can fall significantly below what the fundamentals may suggest is sustainable. A recent example may be the market for Japanese government bonds, where yields are several percentage points below those in the United States and Europe, despite a very rapidly rising public debt, which in per cent of GDP is about twice as high as in the OECD area at large. While the Bank of Japan's policy of keeping short-term interest rates at the zero bound in order to fight enduring deflation means that expected short-term rates are extremely low, there is a risk that bond prices would collapse at some point, as yields back up. Given the size of the outstanding bond portfolio, this would have serious adverse repercussions, in particular on bank balance sheets.

### 8.3.2   Stock prices

Stock prices are also prone to fluctuations over and beyond what the associated fundamentals would warrant, as witnessed in most OECD countries in the late 1990s, in a climate of 'new economy' euphoria (Figure 8.3). One way to analyse stock prices is to start from the return expected by their owner. The rate of return on a stock priced $P$ is the sum of the dividend $D$ plus the capital gain $\Delta P$ over the considered holding period, divided by $P$: $(D + \Delta P)/P$. The expected rate of return on stock prices should exceed government bond yields, which are normally considered as the risk-free benchmark asset. Assuming a constant dividend $D$, the equilibrium value for $P$ ($\Delta P = 0$) equals $D/(i^\ell + \varphi)$, where $i^\ell$ is the nominal risk-free long-term interest rate and $\varphi$ the risk premium. But this is of limited help in practice, since interest rates, risk premia and dividends all vary over time and are uncertain.

*Figure 8.3*   Stock prices

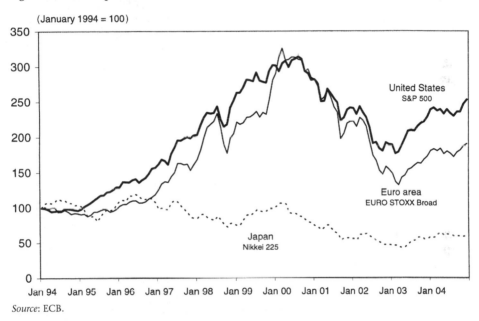

*Source*: ECB.

One way to proceed from here is, as financial analysts do, to carefully examine the firms that issued the stock and to evaluate how well they and their stock price are likely to perform. From the standpoint of the macroeconomic forecaster, however, it is not clear how to aggregate the profit forecasts published by financial analysts, both because the information is often very idiosyncratic and because the concepts used differ from those embedded in the national accounts. In addition, analysts' forecasts are more or less reliable, as cruelly illustrated in the emblematic case of Enron in 2001: until just a few days before the US firm's collapse, a number of analysts were still advising investors to buy or to continue to hold its stock, touting Enron's wonderful prospects. Financial analysts are in fact often viewed by macroeconomists as too close to the traders and therefore likely to get carried away by market fads.

An alternative approach uses the Gordon–Shapiro formula for the equilibrium stock price. Let dividends now be assumed to grow at a constant rate $d$. Then:

$$P = D/(i^\ell + \varphi - d)$$

where $D$ is now today's dividend. If the ratio $c$ of dividends to profits $\Pi$ is a constant, then the price–earnings ratio (PER), $P/\Pi$, equals $c/(i^\ell + \varphi - d)$ and one can look for a cointegration relationship between $\log P$, $\log \Pi$ and $i^\ell$. In principle, this relationship can then be used to forecast stock prices as a function of forecasted profits and interest rates.

In practice, however, this may not work well, since $c$ and $\varphi$ are not constant, and stock prices may soar or sink far beyond the level consistent with fundamentals. In addition, domestic equity prices are heavily influenced by developments in foreign markets. Therefore, a common assumption in forecasting is instead that stock prices are unchanged, either in nominal or in real terms, or that going forward they are indexed on nominal GDP or profits. Recourse to more sophisticated but more precarious assumptions tends to be confined to alternative scenarios as opposed to the baseline forecast.

### 8.3.3   Real estate prices

Like stock prices, real estate prices go through momentous swings. While some of their determinants are identical, they do not necessarily move in synchrony: witness the remarkable resilience or even buoyancy of house prices following the stock market collapse that started around 2000 (Figure 8.4).[2] Moreover, real estate prices are less fickle, given that some of their determinants are very slow-moving, or even fixed (in the case of land, if one abstracts from polderisation). But when property markets do go bust, as they did in Japan in the early 1990s, then, on average, the pain lasts twice as long and the impact on output is twice as large according to some estimates (Helbling and Terrones, 2003).

House prices are normally a function of the present value of expected rents. Over the short run, supply of real estate is quite inelastic, owing to construction lags and a limited availability of land, so that rents are largely demand-driven, reflecting developments in real income and real interest rates. Other factors affecting house prices include the efficiency of mortgage markets, taxation of real estate transactions and capital gains, mortgage interest rate deductibility, zoning and building code restrictions, tenancy and lease laws, demography and so on. But they are harder to quantify and therefore to include in empirical specifications.

---

[2] It should be borne in mind that in many countries, house price indices make insufficient allowance for changes in quality, so that measured house price inflation is upward biased compared to CPI inflation. This bias varies across countries, distorting straight cross-country comparisons.

***Figure 8.4*** **Real house prices**
(deflated by the overall consumer price index)

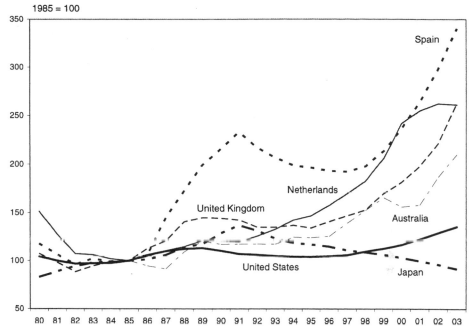

*Sources*: Australian Commonwealth Bank Housing Industry Association; Bank of Spain; Japan Real Estate Institute; Statistics Netherlands; UK Office of the Deputy Prime Minister; US Office of Federal Housing Enterprise Oversight; OECD Main Economic Indicators.

Some of the features of property markets increase the risk of boom and bust (Herring and Wachter, 2003):

- Imperfect information, in a context of supply rigidities, allows prolonged period of euphoria or depression before enough agents reach the conclusion that a market reversal is in order.
- Moral hazard arising from explicit or implicit deposit guarantees and weaknesses in financial regulation or oversight leads banks (especially when they are 'too big to fail') to lend too much, fuelling booms.
- Adverse selection works in the same direction, with the riskiest investors most actively seeking loans.
- The real estate cycle is amplified by banks' behaviour: rising house prices increase the value of banks' capital (insofar as they hold real estate) and of real estate lending collateral, leading banks to lend more, which in turn pushes house prices up further. These feedback effects go into reverse when the market turns, and may be aggravated when regulators or supervisors react by tightening real estate loan classification and provisioning rules, or when interest rates go up.

Against this backdrop, forecasters often try to play it safe by adopting a technical assumption similar to the one used for stock prices (constant nominal or real prices, or indexation to wages), and shy away from attempting to judge where prices are headed based on fundamentals. A more refined approach is to bring in an indicator analogous to the price–earnings ratio, namely the price-to-rent ratio, and to assume for instance that over a certain period it will converge to some long-run average. But again, this is usually left for alternative scenario purposes rather than built into the baseline forecast.

## 8.4   Exchange rates

The exchange rate is one of the key variables in any open economy model and fore-cast. Since the end of the Bretton Woods system in the early 1970s, it is also one of the most volatile variables, not least because of the huge amount of transactions observed in foreign exchange markets (dwarfing the magnitude of transactions in goods and services). Hence, exchange rates present modellers and forecasters with a major chal-lenge. For example, the euro's rollercoaster ride since its launch at the start of 1999 (Figure 8.5) is difficult to capture in an econometric equation, and its very short-run jitters may be even harder to explain in a rigorous fashion (although casual stories

*Figure 8.5*   **Real effective exchange rates**
(January 1999 = 100)

*Note*:
* Synthetic euro prior to January 1999.

*Sources*: Federal Reserve Board and ECB.

abound). This section reviews the main exchange-rate determination theories, high-lighting their practical limitations, and discusses the options facing the forecaster.

*Exchange rate theories*

The simplest relationship between the exchange rate and the fundamentals is the purchasing power parity (PPP) one, which in its modern form dates back to the 1920s. In its absolute version, it states that when converted in a common currency a given good should have the same price everywhere, as any difference would be arbitraged away. If this holds for all goods, and with $P$ standing for the domestic price level, $P^*$ the foreign price level and $E$ the value in the foreign currency of one unit of the domestic currency:

$$P^* = PE$$

or, in log form:

$$p^* = p + e$$

Due to trade barriers, imperfect competition, transportation and distribution costs, and different consumer preferences across countries, absolute PPP does not hold in practice. An infamous test of PPP is the regular cross-country comparison of the price of a Big Mac sandwich by the magazine *The Economist*: even for such a homogeneous product, the price differs substantially from what PPP would imply, partly because a substantial portion of the cost of a Big Mac corresponds to non-tradeable services, but also for a host of other reasons. Lastly, indirect evidence against PPP is provided by the low price elasticities typically obtained in export and import equations (see Section 5.3).

As a result, less demanding versions of PPP have emerged, although they are not fully convincing either. The first is relative PPP, which states that exchange rate movements reflect changes in relative prices, implying that the real exchange rate is a constant:

$$\Delta e = \Delta p - \Delta p^*$$

Another version is PPP restricted to the tradeable sector. Most researchers, however, prefer an even looser version of PPP, which simply states that over the long run, real exchange rates are mean-reverting. The problem is that even if indeed that is the case, it takes quite some time for relative prices to move back to equilibrium, so that PPP offers little guidance to forecasters. In addition, for many countries and periods, the real exchange rate is not stationary, not least owing to the so-called 'Balassa-Samuelson' effect, which posits that productivity catch-up in the less advanced countries' tradeable sectors causes faster overall wage and price increases, translating into trend real appreciation of their currencies.

Other avenues have therefore been explored, based on explicitly modelling the real equilibrium exchange rate as a function of economic fundamentals, which allows it to vary over time. J. Williamson (1985) proposed a macroeconomic balance approach, estimating a fundamental equilibrium exchange rate (FEER), defined as the one ensuring internal as well as external equilibrium over the medium term. The former obtains when the level of activity is consistent with full employment and low inflation. The latter means that the underlying, or 'structural', current account balance should match desired, or 'sustainable', capital flows – derived from several factors, such as the state of development or demography. For this to be the case, the exchange rate should bring about the requisite levels of imports and exports, which is where trade elasticities come in – first to estimate the current account position that would occur should the output gap be closed, and second to estimate the exchange rate movements that would be needed to obtain the required external balance. FEERs thus abstract from Keynesian cyclical effects and other transient shocks.

Empirically, FEERs can be calculated in a number of ways, but the most widely used approach is based on a partial equilibrium analysis, which plugs exogenous estimates of trend output and structural capital flows into a trade model. Wren-Lewis (2003) for example used this approach to calculate an equilibrium rate for the British pound *vis-à-vis* the euro, in the context of an assessment of the United Kingdom's readiness to join the euro area: assuming that the sustainable current account level was zero in the United Kingdom, he concluded that the FEER was 1.37 €/£, implying that the pound was significantly overvalued at the time. A variant of FEERs are DEERs, where D stands for desired and which are in essence FEERs incorporating an optimal fiscal policy trajectory (Artis and Taylor, 1995).

The great advantage of FEERs is that they are operational in the context of model-based forecasting, given that estimates of output gaps and trade elasticities are usually available. However, treating trend output and the structural current account as exogenous may be an extreme assumption. Moreover, estimating structural capital flows involves very substantial judgement, even if there is a wide consensus on the general notion that older and more advanced economies should have a structural current account surplus, and finance the investments that younger emerging market economies cannot fund out of their own saving and for which the return on capital should be higher. Another complication is that the structural external balance of a given country interacts with those of other countries, since current account positions should sum to zero at the global level.

Trying to extend the analysis, Stein (1994) put forward a natural real exchange rate (NATREX) model, which endogenises the interaction between the flows considered in the macroeconomic balance approach and the capital and foreign debt stocks. The NATREX models the exchange rate as moving from a medium-run FEER-type equilibrium (where flows are balanced) to a long-run equilibrium (where net foreign debt is constant at its steady-state level). In the process, it highlights the determinants of the medium-run capital flows, notably:

- The propensity to consume: higher consumption increases interest rates and hence capital inflows, causing exchange rate appreciation.

- Technical progress: accelerating productivity raises investment and therefore also pushes up capital inflows and the exchange rate.

However, the increase in external indebtedness caused by rising consumption cannot be sustained indefinitely, so that over the long run the exchange rate depreciates, allowing for an increase in net exports which serves to pay the extra interest due. The long-run impact of technical progress is more ambiguous: external debt service also increases, but higher potential growth generates higher national saving.

The NATREX is usually tested in reduced form, which again means that the feedback effects are not rigorously accounted for. One example is the structural estimation of the euro's equilibrium exchange rate by Detken *et al.* (2002), who found that at its end-2000 trough, and measured against the euro area's four largest trading partners, the euro was some 25 per cent weaker than its medium-run equilibrium level, and some 28 per cent weaker than its long-run equilibrium level. Such precise estimates, however, should be taken with a pinch of salt, since they are quite sensitive to small changes in the behavioural equations.

Both the FEER and the NATREX approach may impose too much theoretical structure, and focus on horizons extending far beyond standard forecasting periods. A popular alternative are behavioural equilibrium exchange rate (BEER) models, which can be applied with shorter time horizons. They amount to reduced-form modelling and test for the significance of a vast array of variables, such as productivity differentials, interest rate differentials, relative fiscal stance, the price of oil and the current account balance. Maeso-Fernandez *et al.* (2002) apply this to the euro. Since most of these variables are non-stationary, they estimate VECMs. Their study confirms that the euro was greatly undervalued in late 2000. In this context, it is possible to distinguish:

- The predicted value of the exchange rate based on the actual values of the explanatory variables, which can be thought of as the current and cyclical equilibrium exchange rate. This is the most relevant one for forecasting purposes.
- Its value based on the 'permanent' component of the explanatory variables, namely the so-called permanent equilibrium exchange rate (PEER), which is smoother, since it is purged of transitory effects.

In addition to the recurrent exogeneity conundrum plaguing most empirical exchange rate models, there are serious measurement problems. Some of the key fundamentals are not measured in the same way across countries, notably productivity or the capital stock (see Schnatz *et al.*, 2004). Others are measured with error, notably current accounts, since they fail to add up to zero internationally. Others still are simply unobservable, for instance risk premia. Moreover, several crucial indicators are subject to large revisions down the road. Ironically, however, models based on real-time statistics (that is, on those available at the time the spot exchange rate was observed) tend to fit better than those estimated using final and more accurate data, possibly because market participants' behaviour is shaped by the information they have rather than by what will ultimately end up as the definitive series.[3] But real-time data sets are rare and most models are estimated on subsequent data vintages.

### Practical approaches

All these difficulties lead many forecasters to rely on an implausible but simple and transparent constant nominal (or real) exchange rate assumption, and others to base their forecast on the forward rates quoted on the foreign exchange market. As noted, these can be good practices when the variable under consideration is very volatile.

An alternative option is to take a pure financial market view and not to refer to any real sector equilibria. This is what the Bank of England for instance has long done in its core macroeconomic model (Bank of England, 1999), where the exchange rate is determined by a risk-adjusted uncovered interest parity (UIP) condition. Let $e$ now denote the effective nominal exchange rate (in log), $e^a$ its anticipated value, $i$ the domestic one-period interest rate and $\varphi$ a risk premium. Then:

$$e^a_{t+1} = e_t + i^*_t - i_t + \varphi_t$$

UIP posits that an investor has to be indifferent between holding the domestic currency, earning $i_t$ and benefiting from its expected appreciation $(e^a_{t+1} - e_t)$, or holding the foreign currency and earning $i^*_t$. But the investor may believe that the domestic currency will appreciate by more than the interest rate differential, in which case he or she will only be ready to hold the foreign currency if he or she also receives a positive risk premium $\varphi$. The latter can be defined as a function of the current account balance, inflation and other variables, or for simplicity it can be assumed to equal zero, as done by the Bank of England in its exchange rate equation (although its *Inflation Report* assumes that the nominal exchange rate will evolve along a path halfway between an unchanged rate and the path implied by the UIP condition).

A last option, which economic modellers tend to shy away from or even disparage, but which is embraced by many traders, is 'technical analysis'. Its premise is that the inspection of past exchange rate movements may reveal patterns that enable prediction of where the exchange rate is headed over the coming hours, days, weeks or even months (Box 8.3).

## 8.5   Commodity prices

Commodity prices are an important exogenous variable in many macroeconomic forecasts, given that they significantly affect core variables such as output and

---

[3] See Faust *et al.* (2003), who document this starting from the following, widely used, ECM: $\Delta e_t = \alpha + \beta[(m_t - m_t^*) - (y_t - y_t^*) - e_t] + \varepsilon_t$ (where all variables are in logs, $m$ stands for the money stock, $y$ for output and an asterisk denotes foreign), and then extending it to include the short-term interest rate, inflation and the accumulated current account balance (as a measure of the net external investment position).

*Box 8.3* **Technical analysis**

Technical analysis – otherwise known as chartism – is widely used by traders in the foreign exchange markets, as documented by Cheung and Chinn (2001). It has also long been popular in other financial markets and in commodity markets. While macroeconomic forecasters focus on the fundamentals driving these markets and on hypothetical equilibrium values, traders try to 'beat the market', or at least not to be beaten by it, and typically have much shorter horizons. Technical analysis, rather than macroeconomic modelling, often tends to be their favourite tool. Some traders, however, use technical analysis in conjunction with fundamental analysis, doubling their positions when both sets of indicators point in the same direction. There are several varieties of technical analysis, presented in detail by Edwards and Magee (2001):

- Charting. This involves graphing the history of prices over some period, selected by the practitioner, to predict their evolution over some horizon, on the assumption that past patterns are informative. Chartists spot troughs (local minima) and peaks (local maxima), declare them to be support or resistance levels, and identify downtrends and uptrends (stringing together series of troughs or peaks) as well as formations portending market reversals (head-and-shoulders, double tops and bottoms, triple tops and bottoms, V patterns and so on). They also claim that certain round numbers are psychological barriers (say, the 100 ¥/$ level), or that markets react to past developments (say, with investors willing to consolidate their positions once their earlier losses are offset by new gains). Furthermore, chartists pay close attention to traded volumes, which reveal underlying momentum. Chartists argue that when properly interpreted this type of evidence helps predict behaviour. There may be an element of self-fulfilling prophecy here, insofar as a sufficient number of traders see the same patterns at the same time, and react in accordance with chartists' expectations.
- Mechanical rules. A well-known type of rule is the filter rule or trading-range break rule, which counsels to buy an asset when it rises $x$ per cent above its previous local minimum (or conversely for a local maximum), with $x$ typically chosen somewhere between 0.5 and 3 per cent. Another class of rules rests on moving averages, and will advise buying when a short moving average (calculated, say, over five days) crosses a longer moving average (say, 20 days) from below, in other words, when the asset price is rising rapidly (and vice versa). Yet another variety are the rules using so-called Bollinger bands (usually plotted two standard deviations above and below some moving average). While mechanical rules are advertised as a way to avoid the subjectivity inherent in charting, their definition and use are in fact also very subjective.
- Waves. Some chartists proceed on the assumption that prices follows laws and go through certain phases. One such approach rests on Elliott's wave theory, dating back to the 1930s, which states that market prices (and many other phenomena) follow a repetitive rhythm of five-wave advances followed by three-wave declines, with nine different degrees of trend ranging from a 'grand supercycle' spanning two hundred years to a 'subminuette' degree covering only a few hours.

Economists have traditionally dismissed the claims of technical analysts on the grounds that they violate the efficient market hypothesis (which in its weak form says that historical data cannot help forecast future market developments, since this information should already be embodied in current prices). Indeed, these approaches rely on fairly subjective assumptions and in particular the implicit view that markets' movements have an inherent logic, whereas they could simply reflect random walk movements. Nevertheless, there is abundant empirical evidence against the efficient market hypothesis and some technical trading rules have indeed been profitable. Compared with traditional macroeconomic models, some of the chartist approaches have the merit of taking into account real-life factors such as market conditions (the volume of order flows and very short-run volatility), information asymmetries (the whole idea, pioneered over a century ago by Charles Dow, being that those who know more get in and out before the others) and market psychology (thresholds and herding in particular). That said, the apparent success of some chartists over some past period offers no guarantee whatsoever that their tools will deliver excess returns going forward. And last but not least, these techniques fail to provide forecasters with any economic story.

inflation. Indeed, total trade in commodities accounts for a large share of overall world trade. Commodities encompass such diverse items as unprocessed agricultural products, energy, metals, textiles and, in broader definitions, computer chips. Forecasters often focus on the oil price, as oil alone accounts for about one-tenth of world trade and because of the prominent role oil price shocks have played since the 1970s. Hamilton (2003) documents this, showing also that the effect of oil prices on activity is non-linear, with oil price increases depressing output more than similarly sized oil price declines boost it, and that increases have significantly less predictive content if they simply correct earlier decreases.

### 8.5.1   Oil prices

Historically, the price of oil was very low until 1973–74, when OPEC implemented production cuts, largely for political reasons. The price of a barrel of crude oil jumped from $3 to $12. In 1979–80, it soared to $37 against the backdrop of the revolution in Iran and the Iran–Iraq war. The mid-1980s witnessed a reverse price shock, as OPEC eased the restrictions on output. In the early 1990s, with the first Gulf War, the price jumped again (see Figure 8.6), but it rapidly fell back to low levels. In the late 1990s, as OPEC cut production, it rose anew, although it was soon brought down by the global downturn. As geopolitical tensions mounted during the run-up to the second Gulf War and as strikes in Venezuela weighed down on supply, the oil price rose to close to $35. It subsequently dropped by over $10, before rising again, confounding expectations that following the war it would remain below the $25 mark. In fact, in the course of 2004 and into 2005, the oil price soared, reaching some $55 by March 2005. Against this turbulent background, how can oil prices be forecasted?

In principle, the price of a rare and non-renewable resource such as oil (or more precisely the price associated with its sale minus its marginal extraction cost) should rise at a rate equal to the interest rate.[4] This is the so-called Hotelling rule. Indeed, if the price were seen as set to rise faster, producers would at the margin want to keep oil in the ground and let it appreciate, instead of extracting it straight away and investing the proceeds in financial assets. Lower production in turn would push up the spot price, reducing the expected pace of oil price increases. Conversely, if the price were expected to rise by less than the interest

---

[4] Assuming a competitive market. However, insofar as the oil market is dominated by a few large players, it is the producer's marginal revenue net of extraction costs that has to be considered.

*Figure 8.6*   **Oil prices**
(Year-average spot price, fob, in US$ per barrel)*

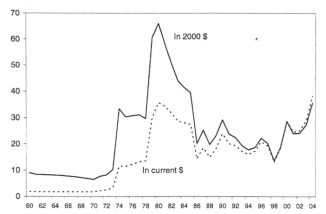

*Note*:
* Until 1985, Arabian Light posted at Ras Tanura; thereafter, Brent.
Sources: US Energy Information Administration and OECD.

rate, it would be profitable to extract and sell more oil, and to earn a higher financial
return on the proceeds. This would push the spot price down, making for faster
expected price increases. In practice, however, this theoretical principle is of limited help, given that the future levels of reserves and interest rates are uncertain,
that rates of time preference may not accord with theory and that producers may
be liquidity constrained. Hence, analysts have tried to assess the fundamentals of
the oil market, namely physical supply and demand over various horizons.

Over the next few decades, oil reserves would seem to be relatively abundant, in
the sense that new discoveries (fields or extraction methods) continually push out
the prospect of exhaustion, although at what price is not entirely clear. Hence, it
might be sensible to focus on trend consumption growth, as a function of potential GDP growth, of its energy intensity and of the share of oil in total energy use.
Other factors may, however, come into play, including the fact that owing to
its larger reserves OPEC will control an increasing share of the market, giving it
more monopoly power, and the fact that energy is likely to be taxed more and
more heavily, due to the need to stem greenhouse gas emissions. The International
Energy Agency (IEA)'s long-run model incorporates most of these elements,
with demand a function of GDP growth, prices (including an allowance for the
taxation of carbon dioxide emissions), technological progress, and other factors,
and supply a function of ultimate recoverable resources (which themselves depend
on the price of oil and on improvements in drilling, exploration and production
technologies). Taking into account only existing government policies, the IEA was
projecting, in the third quarter of 2004, that international oil prices would fall
back to around $22 (in constant 2000 US dollars) by 2006 and stay there during
the remainder of the decade. They would rise linearly thereafter, to $29 by 2030,
with the share of cheap production from giant oil fields shrinking and that of
smaller fields bearing higher production costs per barrel on the rise (IEA, 2004).

Over the medium run, production capacity is partly endogenous, as is demand. When production is falling behind demand, the price rises, encouraging higher-cost producers to expand capacity. With a lag (due to the time needed to build new wells) output rises and prices decline, which in turn reduces investment in the oil sector and thus supply, and so on. At the same time, demand reacts to oil prices over the medium run, given their impact on growth and on the energy intensity of production. However, in practice, it is very difficult to forecast oil prices over the next few years, given that many players are less than forthright about their true reserves, stocks and costs, and that the major oil producers engage in strategic games. In addition, there are many different qualities of oil, which are traded on different markets. It is therefore not surprising that medium-run oil price forecasts are often widely off the mark. Until 2003, an anchor for these forecasts was the $22 to $28 band within which OPEC officially wished to contain price fluctuations. This led some forecasters to assume that the price would average $25. But in the event, the price has been significantly higher much of the time, and as noted surged in 2004.

In the short run, supply varies depending on OPEC cohesion, on the tactics of non-OPEC producers and on Saudi Arabia's behaviour as 'swing producer'. Its level can be forecasted drawing on market expertise. Demand is rather price-inelastic over the short run, depending essentially on activity, and can be modelled in ECM form as follows:

$$\Delta D_t = \alpha + \sum_i \beta_i \Delta D_{t-i} + \sum_i \gamma_i \Delta FC_{t-i} + \sum_j \delta_j F_{jt} - \mu(D_{t-1} - \eta FC_{t-1})$$

where $D$ is the log of demand, $F$ are the fundamentals and $FC$ those fundamentals that are cointegrated with demand. At the global level, this type of equation tends to point to a trend decline in energy intensity of around $1\frac{1}{4}$ per cent per annum, to a unitary elasticity of oil demand to activity, and to a negligible price elasticity. Proper deseasonalisation is key, given the strong seasonal patterns of oil demand (up in winter in particular due to heating needs).

Given that quantities do not respond much to prices in the short run, much of the adjustment between supply and demand takes the form of changes in stocks, which then indirectly influence prices. This can be modelled to forecast a price path. But in practice, information on stocks is incomplete, even for the advanced economies. Moreover, the development of financial derivatives based on oil contracts has reduced the role of stocks as a buffer. It has also led to lower stock levels, making for more precarious equilibria on the spot market. The fact that large volumes of transactions no longer pertain to physical flows on the spot market also facilitates self-fulfilling speculative behaviour before the fundamentals have time to play their equilibrating role. Thus, when forward prices exceed spot prices – a situation described as 'contango' – stocking is encouraged, which is interpreted as a sign of oversupply and pushes spot prices down even further, creating room for self-fulfilling expectations. Specifically, when the contango is wide enough to cover the costs of holding stocks, a company can lock in a profit by selling oil in the futures market while simultaneously putting the same volume of oil into storage. When spot prices exceed forward prices, the market is said to be 'backwardated', and the mechanism works in the opposite direction.

### 8.5.2   Non-oil commodity prices

Similar price formation mechanisms are observed for the other non-renewable resources. The fact that they are exhaustible would suggest that their price should increase over the long run. But as in the case of oil, a number of factors stand in the way of Hotelling's rule, including the existence of producing countries cartels, fluctuations in the evaluation of available world reserves, and changes in demand behaviour. Consider gold: in some developing countries, with untrustworthy banks, it has long served as the principal saving instrument; but if such countries take off and their financial systems become more reliable, demand for gold as a store of value will decline.

As regards renewable resources and the commodities whose value has less to do with rarity, it is often claimed that their price is on a trend decline relative to the price of industrial goods, for several reasons and in particular the low income elasticity of demand for commodities. This is referred to as the Prebisch-Singer hypothesis. It is consistent with the fact that since the 1860s, real non-energy commodity prices have been declining on average by about one per cent per year (Cashin and McDermott, 2002).

Price volatility around this trend, however, is enormous. It has even increased since the end of the Bretton Woods fixed exchange rate regime in the early 1970s, since most commodity prices are quoted in dollars, implying that the prices in other national currencies started to fluctuate with their exchange rate *vis-à-vis* the dollar. In addition, various price regulation mechanisms which were put in place after the Second World War (agreements between producer and consumer countries, stabilisation funds and the like) gradually lost whatever effectiveness they may have had. The secular downward trend is therefore of little practical relevance for forecasters, the associated change in price being dwarfed by large and long-lasting booms and slumps. Microeconomic expertise on specific markets – based on intimate knowledge of weather conditions (for agricultural products), stocks and demand – can be more useful in this context than blanket assumptions about a return to trend. A key element in this respect is estimating supply capacity in light of past investments in the sector under consideration. The mechanism at play is that strong prices initially stimulate investment, pushing supply up and, in turn and with a lag, prices down.

For forecasting purposes, three frequencies are distinguished in the modelling of commodity price fluctuations:

* In the (very) short run, stock movements, speculative behaviour and information constraints play a major role. Information from commodity futures markets might also be useful, as argued by Bowman and Husain (2004).
* Over the medium run, stocks matter less. Demand depends positively on the position in the cycle of consumer countries, on the price of the goods using the commodities as inputs and on the price of their substitutes, and negatively on commodities' dollar price and on the strength of the dollar *vis-à-vis* consumer countries' currencies. Supply depends positively on commodities' dollar price, on the strength of the dollar *vis-à-vis* producer countries' currencies and

on expected demand, and negatively on production costs. These relationships are usually more stable for commodities such as metals than for agricultural products, given the strong impact of weather conditions on the latter.

- Long-run fluctuations are more clearly driven by structural trends, such as changes in consumption patterns, productivity trends and the evolution of producers' capacity (which is shaped, with a lag, by prices). Structural models are usually built to capture these forces, including CGE models which simultaneously take into account the different commodities and regions and their interactions.

## 8.6   Country-risk analysis

Country-risk analysis originally focused on sovereign default risk, but its scope has widened since. Two approaches can be distinguished. The first one is the assessment of a country's fundamentals, which is useful for international investors seeking to diversify their portfolio as well as for forecasters trying to map out economies' prospects, especially over the medium and long run. The second one is the *ex ante* evaluation of the likelihood of a structural break, be it a favourable one (such as a shift to a stable political and economic growth path), or a crisis (such as a collapse of the banking system and/or of the exchange rate).

### 8.6.1   A broadening scope

Macroeconomic models are typically linear: a given exogenous increase in income, say, will boost consumption, and twice as large an increase in income will boost consumption twice as much. Implicitly, this assumes that agents behave in the same way irrespective of the circumstances. By contrast, country-risk analysis tries to anticipate changes in economic regime, or at least to quantify their probability. Such breaks are likely to alter behavioural relationships.

The first of the two country-risk approaches broadens the analysis of the traditional assessment of sovereign default risk to encompass the overall political, economic and financial situation of a country, including its growth prospects, the sustainability of its public finances and so on. The aim becomes less to quantify sovereign default risk *per se* – which historically has been relatively low – than to get a handle on the factors that will influence the risk/return profile of investments in the country under consideration. The focus is then very much on getting an accurate picture of the fundamentals. The second perspective on country-risk centres on the possible occurrence of crises, which can be very sudden or instead drawn out. It involves monitoring indicators that may signal crises ahead of time, so as to prevent them or as to minimise their costs.

In practice, the two approaches are obviously linked. The first one could be described as that followed by international rating agencies, to inform investors. This activity has taken off as countries opened up and cross-border capital flows grew. Official international institutions, which are mandated to safeguard global financial stability, combine the first and the second approach in a macroprudential perspective. The succession of international financial crises (South America in the 1980s, Mexico in 1994–95, East Asia in 1997–98, Russia in 1998, Brazil in 1999, Argentina and Turkey in 2000–01) has stimulated research on the prediction and prevention of crises in the face of the great volatility of capital flows.

Country-risk analysis first and foremost concerns emerging and developing economies, where evolutions are more hectic and harder to forecast. But country risk is relevant for advanced economies as well, since they also experience crises (recall the European Monetary System shake-up in 1992–93 or witness Japan's prolonged crisis in the 1990s).

### 8.6.2 Rating

Rating agencies (Standard & Poor's, Moody's Investors Service, Fitch Ratings and the like) actively monitor countries issuing securities. The rating takes place at several levels:

- The sovereign dollar rating measures country risk *stricto sensu* and focuses on the ability of the government to service its external debt.
- The sovereign local currency rating measures the country's ability to service its local currency-denominated debt. *A priori*, it is easier to reimburse domestic debt since the question of the availability of foreign exchange reserves does not arise, but at the same time it may be easier for a government to renege on domestic than on external debt.
- Rating the country's other issuers takes into account their individual situation. This is connected in some ways to sovereign risk, however, since experience shows that the failure of some large debtors (local governments, firms or banks) can turn into a systemic crisis: a banking sector crisis for instance will have dire fiscal implications insofar as the government will have to finance the clean-up (or will at the very least see tax receipts decline as activity slumps).
- Rating ranges from the short to the long run, that is from liquidity to solvency analysis. Indeed, investors have different horizons: for example, in 1998–99, Brazil experienced outflows of short-term capital, owing to a heightened perception of exchange rate risk, but at the same time direct investment inflows continued, driven by privatisation operations and attractive long-run opportunities.

In practice, and broadly speaking, rating involves analysing a country's fundamentals by looking at different risks and variables (see Table 8.1):

- Political risk: might there be a political upheaval leading to debt repudiation?
- Fiscal risk: are the public finances sound and is there room for manoeuvre if a shock hits?
- Economic risk: is growth broadly based and sustainable?
- Exchange rate risk: is the exchange rate overvalued and are foreign exchange reserves sufficient?
- Financial risk: is the financial system solid and properly supervised?
- External repayment risk: will the country be able to service its external debt?

*Table 8.1*  Rating criteria

| Risk type | Main criteria | Economic indicators |
| --- | --- | --- |
| Political | • Conflicts with neighbours or internally<br>• Stability of the regime<br>• Political and social tensions, inequalities | • Demographic data<br>• Literacy rate<br>• Gini income distribution index |
| Fiscal | • Fiscal balance, taking the economic and debt situation into account<br>• Evolution of public debt, given public sector assets, external and implicit liabilities<br>• Debt service burden<br>• Size and composition of revenue and expenditure<br>• Room for manoeuvre | • Overall, structural and primary balance<br>• Public debt (gross, net, external)<br>• Debt service (fixed rate, variable rate, exchange rate indexed component), in per cent of GDP or of tax receipts<br>• Tax pressure (overall, import duties)<br>• Share of public consumption and in particular of public sector wage bill<br>• Share of investment spending |
| Economic | • Overall situation: resources, income level<br>• Position in the cycle<br>• Structural trends<br>• Vulnerability to various types of shocks<br>• Likelihood of catastrophic events (such as earthquakes) | • GDP per capita in current and PPP dollars<br>• GDP growth, inflation, unemployment<br>• Saving and investment rates<br>• Degree of diversification of production and exports |
| Exchange rate | • Credibility/sustainability of forex policy<br>• Forex reserves given imports and potential capital outflows<br>• Competitiveness (price, quality, investment climate) | • Forex reserves in months of imports and as a share of short-run external liabilities<br>• Effective exchange rate, productivity, surveys of international investors |
| Financial | • Central bank credibility<br>• Monetary policy stance<br>• Soundness of the financial system<br>• Fragility of domestic borrowers | • Interest rates, monetary aggregates<br>• Credit to government, to private sector<br>• Banks' capital ratios<br>• Share of non-performing loans |
| Ability to repay external debt | • Liquid forex assets<br>• External financing needs<br>• Prospective evolution<br>• External liabilities: level, composition, likely evolution | • Export and import growth<br>• Terms of trade<br>• Current account balance<br>• Composition of external financing (share of FDI in particular)<br>• Gross external debt, public and private<br>• Net external liabilities<br>• Debt service schedule |

Each of these risks is rated, on the basis of quantitative indicators but also using a fair amount of qualitative judgement. The ratings are then aggregated into an overall rating, which allows ranking of countries or issuers. While rating is partly subjective, the grades given by different agencies are usually very similar. Table 8.2 displays the scales used by the three leading agencies. The higher the rating, the lower the interest rate the issuer can obtain. Ratings are assigned when paper is first issued, and reviewed on a regular basis: if an issuer's creditworthiness is deemed to have improved, its paper may be upgraded. Conversely, it may be downgraded. Paper that is 'investment grade' is considered to be of good quality and has a rating of Baa or higher from Moody's, a rating of BBB or higher from Standard & Poor's, or both. Paper with lower ratings – or no ratings at all – is termed 'non-investment' or 'speculative' grade. Many institutional investors have policies that require them to limit their investments to investment-grade issues.

*Table 8.2*  Rating scales

|  | *Moody's* | *Standard & Poor's* | *Fitch* |
|---|---|---|---|
|  | *Long-term ratings* | | |
| **Investment grade** | | | |
| Superior/Highest quality | Aaa | AAA | AAA |
| Excellent/Very high quality | Aa1, Aa2, Aa3 | AA+, AA, AA− | AA+, AA, AA− |
| Good/High quality | A1, A2, A3 | A+, A, A− | A+, A, A− |
| Adequate/Good quality | Baa1, Baa2, Baa3 | BBB+, BBB, BBB− | BBB+, BBB, BBB− |
| **Non-investment grade** | | | |
| Maybe adequate/Speculative | Ba1, Ba2, Ba3 | BB+, BB, BB− | BB+, BB, BB− |
| Vulnerable/Highly speculative | B1, B2, B3 | B+, B, B− | B+, B, B |
| Extremely vulnerable/High default risk | Caa, Ca, C | CCC+, CCC, CCC− | CCC, CC, C |
| Default | D | D | DDD, DD, D |
|  | *Short-term ratings* | | |
|  | Superior: P-1 | Strong: A-1 | High: F1 |
|  | Strong: P-2 | Satisfactory: A-2 | Good: F2 |
|  | Acceptable: P-3 | Adequate: A-3 | Fair: F3 |
|  |  | Speculative: B | Speculative: B |
|  |  | Doubtful: C | High default risk: C |
|  |  | Default: D | Default: D |

### 8.6.3  Anticipating crises

Although related to traditional country-risk analysis, the second approach is less about characterising the fundamentals than about identifying specific vulnerabilities so as to quantify the probability of a crisis (the likelihood of a favourable regime change tends to get less attention). This is a delicate exercise, as the nature and mechanisms of crises vary a lot across countries and time, as do the channels of cross-border crisis contagion.

There are at least four different types of crisis:

• Traditional sovereign default crises, when a government fails to repay according to schedule. This has been avoided in a number of cases through preventive rescheduling in the Paris Club (for public-sector creditors) or in the London Club (for bank claims).

- Foreign exchange crises, often following the recognition that a country will be unable to service its external debt or to withstand capital outflows. Such crises can break out very suddenly, although they may result from imbalances that have been building up for years.
- Collapses of domestic financial institutions causing systemic, economy-wide crises. Such crises may then last for several years.
- Bond market crises, taking the form of soaring spreads (the latter being defined as the difference in yield compared with US Treasury paper).

The mechanisms producing a crisis are also varied. There are three generations of explanations:

- Balance of payments and thus foreign exchange crises *à la* Krugman (1979): they stem from accumulated imbalances or ill-conceived policies, for instance, a fiscal stance that ultimately turns out to be too loose for the exchange rate peg to hold. A number of such crises took place in Latin America in the 1980s.
- Second-generation crises, as described by Obstfeld (1994), can erupt because agents' expectations interact with policymakers' behaviour to become self-fulfilling even when the fundamentals are not intrinsically that weak. Multiple equilibria arise: even in the absence of imbalances *ex ante*, the exchange rate may be attacked if market participants believe that to defend it the authorities will raise interest rates so much that the fundamentals will deteriorate, leading policymakers to abandon the peg; or market participants may simply expect that the authorities will not want to resist attacks in the first place, knowing that in the end they will be defeated, so that the authorities give in immediately. This framework has been used to analyse the speculative attacks on the European Monetary System in the early 1990s.
- Third-generation crises, as characterised by Corsetti *et al.* (1999), stem from moral hazard problems: imbalances build up in the form of financial or real estate market bubbles because agents believe, rightly or wrongly, that they will be bailed out by the public sector if things go amiss. The implicit guarantees actually or seemingly offered by national governments or international financial institutions allow reckless overinvestment and are therefore at the root of the crisis. This model has been used to explain the 1997–98 Asian crises, which were not preceded by large fiscal deficits or poor growth but had to do with 'crony capitalism', namely the intermingling of interests among financial institutions, political leaders and corporate elites witnessed in the region. Krugman (1999), however, has proposed a different interpretation: in his model, a loss of confidence forces the authorities to turn a heretofore 'legitimate', investment driven, current account deficit into a surplus, through massive depreciation; the latter worsens domestic firms' balance sheets, validating the loss of confidence.

As the emerging market upheavals of the late 1990s have illustrated, crises can also be triggered by cross-border contagion rather than by the revelation of domestic weaknesses (Claessens and Forbes, 2001). Innocent or at least distant bystanders can thus be hit by what is happening in another part of the world, as Brazil was by the Russian crisis. Crisis spillovers occur through a variety of partly interrelated channels:

- Real sector channels: when two countries trade amongst themselves or compete in the same third markets, an exchange rate crisis cum depreciation in one country deteriorates the other's competitiveness, and both may end up with depreciated currencies. Other types of real links, notably foreign direct investment, may also play a role in contagion.
- Financial market channels: a crisis in one country may heighten risk aversion in financial markets at large and push up bond spreads, hurting all other borrowers and especially those with large exposures or that were already deemed vulnerable beforehand (rightly or wrongly).
- Psychological channels: a crisis in one country may cause investors to panic and to leave neighbouring countries, in the belief – especially when information on fundamentals is scarce – that they may suffer from the same problem or because historically crises in countries in that region have been correlated.
- Portfolio management channels: open-end mutual funds foreseeing redemptions after a shock in one country need to raise cash and may sell assets in other countries.

Trying to foretell crises thus requires to identify potential weaknesses in the fundamentals but also factors that make the economy vulnerable to contagion. A large set of indicators thus needs to be monitored, including most of those listed in Table 8.1. They can serve to underpin a qualitative diagnosis, not unlike in traditional country-risk analysis, or a more quantitative approach, by finding coincident or advance crisis indicators, or even by constructing a probabilistic crisis signal.

In the latter case, consider a binary set-up: let $Y = 0$ if there is no crisis and $Y = 1$ in the event of a crisis, and suppose that the vulnerability indicators $X$ are distributed normally (probit model) or logistically (logit model). The associated probabilities can be derived based on a panel of countries that have experienced crises. In the logit case:

$$P \equiv P\,(Y = 1) = 1/[1 + e^{-(\alpha + \beta X)}]$$

This can be estimated under the following form:

$$\log P/(1 - P) = \alpha + \beta X$$

One challenge here is to empirically define the crisis state. Some studies for instance consider that an exchange rate movement exceeding 25 per cent qualifies. But any such definition is somewhat arbitrary. Moreover, some types of crises, notably banking crises, are difficult to date. In fact, given the relatively limited number of crisis episodes in the historical data, specification searches through the large number of potential right-hand side variables may well be spuriously effective to predict past crises (Berg and Patillo, 1999). The key test, therefore, is not the ability to fit a set of observations after the fact, but the prediction of future crises. In other words, models need to be judged on their out-of-sample performance. In this regard, while they can help indicate vulnerability to crisis, the predictive power of even the best models remains limited. In part, this may be due to endogeneity of policy to the risk of crisis, insofar as a country's authorities or creditors react to advance crisis signals: an initially successful early warning system might thus cease to work following publication. But to a large extent, the reason lies in the inherent volatility of capital flows and in the unpredictability of political U turns.

# 9
# Budget Forecasts

Budget forecasts try to anticipate the evolution of the fiscal accounts based on an economic scenario. They are therefore one specific aspect of overall economic forecasting. They range from the rather global to the very detailed, depending on the purpose of the exercise (Section 9.1). Over the short and medium run, budget forecasting mainly involves assessing the sensitivity of receipts and spending to changes in macroeconomic conditions and estimating the impact of new measures (Section 9.2). Over the long run, the focus is more on the evolution of public spending and on the underlying demographic trends (Section 9.3). Budget scenarios can be put together in several ways (Section 9.4), following a fairly general top-down approach or a more detailed bottom-up one (Section 9.5). In practice, these two approaches complement each other. Budget forecasts come with substantial error margins, which is a cause for concern given the large size of the public sector in the overall economy (Section 9.6). One way to analyse and prevent fiscal surprises is to look at the budget from a more analytical angle, bringing in the concepts of structural balance, debt sustainability and rules (Section 9.7).

## 9.1 A more or less detailed approach

In projecting future receipts and outlays based on an economic scenario, budget forecasting ensures that fiscal policy decisions take into account macroeconomic constraints. This is crucial because of the sheer size of the public sector in total GDP. The painful experience of many OECD countries with fiscal slippages shows how important it is to properly forecast budget developments.

The required degree of detail of budget forecasts varies. The government needs both general and very detailed information. It obviously wants to know what its overall room for manoeuvre is. At the same time, the government needs budget flows to be assessed at a quite disaggregated level, so that the costs and benefits of any measure under consideration can be quantified as precisely as possible. Such a 'bottom-up' approach is resource-intensive and is usually undertaken only by the fiscal authorities or some specialised institutions, which are normally also best placed to translate the detailed budgetary data into national account aggregates.

This approach is typically carried out in the context of the preparation of the budget bill, which also requires close monitoring of the fiscal accounts on a monthly or quarterly basis. This is tricky given the bumpy seasonal profile of many of the relevant series, and the noise introduced by working-day effects (see Section 3.4 on how to deal with such problems). A prerequisite for successful monitoring is good coordination between the various government departments or agencies involved, which in practice can be difficult to achieve.

Another perspective is the 'top-down' one. It is more concerned with the economic analysis of fiscal policy choices, and looks only at broad fiscal aggregates such as overall spending and receipts, the budget balance and public debt, asking for example what the fiscal stance is or what is driving its evolution. By reasoning only at the most aggregated level, the top-down approach in effect takes a number of shortcuts, relying on average elasticities and abstracting from some details. While the horizon here is also often the short or medium run, the top-down approach is the most relevant one for longer-run forecasts: as the horizon under consideration lengthens, details that may matter a lot for short-run analysis become less important.

The general government sector – which encompasses central government but also local governments and social security – on average spends over 40 per cent of GDP in OECD economies. Therefore, the budget forecast and the overall economic forecast are interdependent, implying that they should be carried out jointly, or that a sufficient number of iterations between the two need to take place. For example, an initial macroeconomic scenario is prepared, providing forecasts for GDP and its components, inflation, interest rates, asset prices, and so forth. Based on past relationships between these variables and fiscal variables, and on some assumptions about the foreseen changes in fiscal policy, a first set of fiscal accounts can be derived. These are then fed back into the macroeconomic model and will affect the shape of the macroeconomic forecast. Thus modified, the latter can then serve as the starting point for a second iteration.

## 9.2   Forecasting budget flows over the short and medium run

Over the short and medium run, it is useful to distinguish between the components of the budget that are directly affected by the economic cycle and the others, which are not. The latter include a sizeable share of spending, which corresponds to nominal appropriations that are voted into being by Parliament (or introduced by decree by the government). Also included in this category are the sales of public assets or transfers from public corporations to the government. For these discretionary elements, the forecast amounts to collecting the information from the relevant decision-makers, taking into account the lag between the decision and actual outlays or receipts. What is forecasted in the narrower sense of the word is the first component of the budget, which mainly corresponds to tax revenue, although it also includes some spending items, such as public debt service, which vary with interest rates, or transfers to the unemployed, which depend on their number.[1]

### 9.2.1   Tax receipts

One usually proceeds tax by tax. More attention is paid to those that bring in most revenue: direct taxes (personal income tax, corporate tax, ...), indirect taxes (notably the value-added tax (VAT) and import taxes) and social contributions. For each of them, the following decomposition holds:

$$R_t^i = \tau_t^i B_t^i \tag{9.1}$$

where $R_t^i$ stands for the receipts expected from tax $i$ in period $t$, $B_t^i$ is the base on which this tax is levied and $\tau_t^i$ its average rate.

The base and the rate obviously depend on the specifics of the tax, including statutory rates, rebates, exemptions and so on. Hence, the forecast has to start with an update of the tax system's parameters and the identification of any new measures. The challenge is then to relate this information to the evolution of the tax rate and tax base, and to relate the latter to projected activity.

Two types of assumptions are typically used in practice to compute the tax rate, which, disregarding any change in legislation, can vary over time due not only to the cycle but also to changes in tax-specific trends:

- The rate is assumed to be constant, so that tax receipts are strictly proportional to the tax base. The value for $\tau^i$ can then be its last observation, or some average of past observations. This is of course a very crude method.
- The elasticity of tax receipts to the base is constant. This is a generalisation of the previous assumption, which boiled down to a unitary elasticity. It can be written as $R_t^i = k(B_t^i)^\alpha$, where $\alpha$ is the elasticity and $k$ a constant; $\alpha$ can be estimated as the average growth rate of tax receipts divided by the average growth rate of the base, over some past period. In practice, this assumption is also rather crude: tax elasticities often appear unstable and somewhat pro-cyclical. Also, taking for instance the personal income tax, which often has a progressive structure, the elasticity is much higher if the base increases because of a rise in income per tax return than if it increases because of a greater number of individual returns (Cohen and Follette, forthcoming). This points to the need for a more sophisticated approach encapsulating cyclically-driven changes in elasticities.

The legally defined tax base rarely if ever coincides with a macroeconomic aggregate. A proxy for the tax base therefore has to be used, in the form of an economic

---

[1] This is a very standard distinction but it is somewhat simplistic. One could argue that no budget item is completely unrelated to the business cycle: in a cyclical upturn, receipts are abundant and control over spending tends to loosen even as the appetite of spending ministries or agencies sharpens; conversely, lean times lead to tighter spending controls and discretionary tax measures to offset the cyclical tax shortfall. Even within the horizon of the fiscal year, the provisions voted by Parliament may be overtaken by supplemental budgets.

base. The latter may depend on activity and its components, inflation (since tax bases are usually nominal), asset prices, and the like – both current values and past ones, given taxation lags. For example, a certain level of activity will be consistent with a certain level of household income, which will be the economic base from which to infer the personal income tax base and receipts.

The approximation of the tax base may not be that good. In addition to the lags between macroeconomic developments and actual tax payments, the often numerous past adjustments of the tax system are difficult to trace all the way through, so that computing average tax rates or elasticities is difficult. Moreover, tax bases and macroeconomic aggregates may diverge for a variety of reasons:[2] for instance, the base for the personal income tax or social security contributions depends on the evolution of employment and wages, but also on the share of the self-employed, which may or not vary with the cycle. In addition, the productivity cycle induces a lag between changes in output and changes in employment, and this lag may not be the same in upswings as in downswings.

From this perspective, the base of the corporate income tax is particularly hard to forecast. Indeed, taxable profits differ from profits as captured in the national accounts, owing to tax exemptions, the treatment of provisions and derogatory tax regimes. Moreover, past losses can often be carried forward and deducted from current profits. This can lead to over-projecting tax receipts when activity picks up. Another complication pertains to cross-tax elasticities. For example, the indirect tax receipts from the sales of drinks with a high alcohol content depend not only on the price of these beverages but also on the tax rates on close substitutes, such as wine.

A simple framework to deal with these difficulties is to use equation (9.1) in difference form:

$$R_t^i = R_{t-1}^i + \Delta B_t^i \alpha_t^i \tau_{t-1}^i + NM_t^i \qquad (9.2)$$

where

- $\Delta B_t^i$ is the change from one year to the next in the size of the base of tax $i$, to which the past tax rate is applied, with a possible correction $\alpha_t^i$ reflecting departures from the unitary elasticity assumption, for instance because of changes in the contours of the tax base;
- and $NM_t^i$ stands for the impact of any new revenue measures in period $t$.

In this case, the forecaster first needs to predict receipts on an unchanged legislative basis, and then to add on his best estimate of the impact of any new measures. The latter can only be done based on detailed knowledge which may not be available outside government. Often, the authorities publish some such estimates, with

---

[2] In addition, macroeconomic aggregates themselves may diverge: in some countries, GDP as computed from the supply side differs substantially from GDP computed from the expenditure or income side.

more or less in-depth explanations. In some countries, such as the United States, Germany or the Netherlands, these estimates are actually prepared and released by specialised institutions (see Section 14.3).

In some cases, a more disaggregated approach can be useful. For example, it may help to forecast profits and tax receipts for specific enterprises or sectors (say, the oil sector in the United Kingdom or in Norway). Likewise, different groups of households can be distinguished and separate forecasts can then be made for each group. Such an approach requires resources that only specialised government bodies may have.

Analysts outside the relevant government departments typically focus only on the main categories of tax receipts, using fairly streamlined rules of thumb, which can be as simple as:

- For VAT: receipts in year $t = \alpha C_t$, where $C_t$ is household consumption in value terms;
- For the corporate income tax: actual receipts in year $t = \beta \Pi_{t-1} + \beta(\Pi_{t-1} - \Pi_{t-2})$, where $\Pi$ stands for profits (possibly proxied by nominal GDP minus the wage bill), and the first payment made in year $t$ on profits in year $t$ is based on profits observed in year $t-1$, $\beta(\Pi_{t-1} - \Pi_{t-2})$ being the remainder of the tax due on account of year $t - 1$ (on which the initial payment, made in $t-1$, was related to $\Pi_{t-2}$, the profits in the year $t - 2$) and paid in year $t$.

A somewhat extreme top-down approach would be to compute total government revenue as:

$$R_t = F_t \, (GDP, \, Exo, \, T) \tag{9.3}$$

where $R_t$ stands for total government revenue, *Exo* for exogenous budget information (new measures for instance) and *T* for a trend. Some of the variables may then come in with distributed lags.

### 9.2.2   Debt service

As regards debt service, which in some cases represents a sizeable share of total public outlays, a bottom-up approach involves a detailed inventory of the existing stock of public debt, bond issue by bond issue. This information is available, at least to governments themselves. One can then compute the amount of debt service, though interest payments have to be calculated on an accruals basis if the forecast is couched in national accounts terms. How precise the forecast will be mainly depends on two elements. First, on the projection of the nominal interest rate that will affect new government borrowing – and also the existing stock of public debt, depending on the share of variable interest rate bonds. And secondly, on the forecast of the new borrowing itself, which equals the deficit (in national account terms) forecasted for the period under consideration, plus the renewal of the borrowing expiring during that period, plus any adjustments for the differences between national and budgetary accounts (for example, subtracting any net privatisation receipts when assessing new borrowing). In this regard, one should note that in national account terms, the repayment of principal and the related issuance of new debt are not treated as spending but as 'below-the-line' financial operations.

A simpler and less disaggregated approach is to compute $IP_t$ (interest payments in period $t$) as:

$$IP_t = \sum_e (\alpha_{e,t} \, IP_{e,t-1} + r_{e,t} \, B_{e,t}) \tag{9.4}$$

where:

- $e$ is the type of bond: it can be short- or longer-term, at a fixed or at a variable rate, in domestic or in foreign currency (in which case an exchange rate assumption needs to be made), and so on. Depending on the type of bond, the degree of inertia of interest payments, captured by the coefficient $\alpha_{e,t}$, will vary.
- $IP_t$ stands for the interest payments made on $e$ bonds during period $t$.
- $r_{e,t}$ is the expected interest rate on $e$ bonds for period $t$. The assumption used is often a simple one, such as to freeze interest rates at some recent level, although subtler approaches are possible (see Section 8.2). Future interest rates may of course be affected by the evolution of the fiscal position itself.
- $B_{e,t}$ is the borrowing requirement for period $t$ to be covered by issues of $e$ bonds. This borrowing requirement depends on the term structure of the public debt. It is also affected by privatisation operations for example, which are not reflected in the national accounts measure of the fiscal balance but which reduce the need for new borrowing.

This approach requires less detailed information on the structure of public debt, especially if some simplifying assumptions are introduced. For example, it may be assumed that $\alpha_{e,t} = \alpha_{e,t-1}$, with $\alpha_{e,t-1}$ computed using equation (9.4) and actual observations for period $t - 1$. It is also possible to aggregate bonds into a small number of categories, say short-term fixed rate bonds, long-term fixed-rate bonds and variable-rate bonds. Suppose for instance that public debt $D$ is exclusively financed by fixed rate 10-year bonds and has a homogeneous age structure (with one-tenth arriving at maturity every year), and that the budget is balanced. Then $IP_t = IP_{t-1} + 0.1 \ (r_{t,10} - r_{t-10,10})D_{t-1}$, where $r_{x,10}$ stands for the interest rate in period $x$ on 10-year fixed-rate bonds issued in that period.

Lastly, a fully streamlined approach is simply:

$$IP_t = \alpha_t \, IP_{t-1} + r_t \, B_t \tag{9.5}$$

where $\alpha_t$ measures debt service inertia for the whole stock and $r_t$ is the average interest rate on new borrowing.

### 9.2.3 Non-discretionary public spending

Some public spending items, referred to as non-discretionary (or mandatory), are quite sensitive to the cycle. The most prominent example is unemployment benefits. These items are forecasted in relation to the cycle as:

$$S_t = F_t \left( C_y, \, Exo, \, T \right) \tag{9.6}$$

where $S_t$ stands for spending on these items, $C_y$ is an indicator of the cycle (say, unemployment), and *Exo* and *T* are as above.

In practice, spending is decomposed by category and the effect of the cycle for each category is estimated separately, looking at their historical elasticity with respect to the cycle and at possible trends. This sort of calculation requires what is cyclical (such as unemployment benefits or spending explicitly indexed on infla-tion) to be clearly distinguished from what is politically decided (say, public works outlays), what depends on administrative constraints (say, rules forbidding some levels of government to borrow) and what relates to trends (say, the underlying drift in pension or health-care spending). To enhance the accuracy of the forecast, it will often be useful to take into account more detailed information on demo-graphics (age cohorts and mortality for instance) or social behaviour (for example, divorce rates) in the case of social transfer outlays.

As for tax receipts, it is possible to first estimate what the spontaneous change in spending may be, assuming no new measures, and then to add on an estimate for the impact of the latter. Over the longer run, the exercise becomes trickier. One might want to extrapolate recent trends, or to assume that the rules or objectives spelled out by governments will be adhered to (for instance that a government will indeed manage to contain spending growth at the announced rate), provided they are sufficiently credible. In the absence of such information, a crude method is to endogenise public spending using some very simple rules of thumb, such as a con-stant ratio of public expenditure to GDP, or based on an estimate of the demand for public goods and services as a function of income levels.

## 9.3   Forecasting long-run fiscal trends

The above methods are mainly used for short- and medium-run forecasts, although they are sometimes also applied over longer periods, for instance by the Congressional Budget Office (CBO) in the United States. But a different approach is usually followed for long-run projections. Less attention is then paid to the decomposition between various types of taxes. Rather, a broad-brush assumption is imposed, such as a one-to-one relationship between GDP and government re-venue, or a trend rate of increase in the ratio of government revenue to GDP is assumed (in the case of developing countries). In contrast, more attention is paid to spending trends and in particular to demographic influences thereon. In this context, spending tends to be decomposed into three categories:

- Debt service, which is influenced by the projected evolution of debt and interest rates.
- Spending that is not directly related to demographic determinants. This com-ponent is often assumed to be stable in real terms, or to rise at some constant

rate, or to remain constant as a share of GDP. Which assumption is most pertinent depends for example on what can plausibly be assumed about employment and wages in the public sector.

- Spending that is directly related to demographic developments, such as spending on child benefits, education, pensions, and the like. For each of these categories of spending, calculations are carried out separately, taking into account the number of people concerned (which depends on demographics *stricto sensu* but also on the generosity of benefits and on social trends, such as increasing female participation in the labour force or shifts in the effective retirement age), and spending per head (which changes as entitlements evolve, but is sometimes simply extrapolated from past trends).

The spirit here is not to aim for some illusory projection accuracy, but rather to highlight likely trends which call for preventive action now.

An important example pertains to public health expenditure, which absorbs a rising share of national income across OECD countries. In this case, assumptions are made about:

- The elasticity of health spending to GDP, which tends to exceed 1, but with a complicated lag structure owing to the fact that the relation between demand and supply is mediated by the government and insurance providers.
- The price elasticity of demand for health, where it is useful to distinguish between those items that are reimbursed to some extent and those that are paid for in full by patients; again, there are lags.
- The changes in the structure of the market for health care: the evolution of the share of publicly financed care in total care, the introduction of new management techniques, the substitution between inpatient hospital care and outpatient medical care, and so on.

Forecasting health spending over such long periods is of course hazardous. One plausibility check is to compare the results derived through this macroeconomic approach with the aggregation of more microeconomic projections of spending on various types of care by sectoral experts. Yet another benchmark might be some normative notion of the evolution of health spending per capita which society would be ready to pay for.

## 9.4   Putting together a budget scenario

In practice, the way a budget forecast is put together depends on the desired degree of detail. The simplest approach is to directly forecast the budget balance, based on fiscal trends, new measures, the position of the economy in the business cycle and recent high-frequency data on its own evolution (when they are available).

A slightly richer yet still simple approach is to plug the above equations (9.3), (9.5) and (9.6) into a macroeconomic model:

$$R_t = F_t\,(GDP,\,Exo,\,T\,)$$
$$IP_t = \alpha_t\,IP_{t-1} + r_t\,B_t$$
$$S_t = F_t\,(C_y,\,Exo,\,T\,)$$

where $S_t$ is now understood to cover all non-interest public spending. The closure of the macroeconomic model is thereby facilitated. This can be done at a more disaggregated level (with distinctions between the main types of taxes and categories of spending). But there are limits as to how much detail can be incorporated in these model equations, lest the model become intractable.

What is often done in practice in official institutions is to elaborate a separate, specialised model for each main tax or spending category. In the United States for example, the CBO uses many such models, based on tax return data, to produce simulations and forecasts. The projection for personal income tax receipts rests on a detailed analysis of receipts by group of households, where groups are defined crossing a number of criteria (income bracket, number of children, and so forth). The size of these groups changes over the forecast period as a function of foreseen demographic and income developments. On the spending side, households are often disaggregated in similar ways in order to forecast transfer outlays in particular. The idea here is to dig as deep as is needed to produce plausible results for each of the specialised models. Then, the independent results are aggregated and both their consistency and their impact on the macroeconomic picture are assessed. This generates a new forecast for the exogenous variables (*Exo*), which can be reinjected in the specialised models to produce a second round of fiscal forecasts. This iterative process should in principle continue until convergence is achieved. Practical resource constraints, however, limit the number of feasible iterations, implying that a discrepancy may subsist between the aggregation of the specialised models and the global economic scenario. For instance, in Germany, only the first-round effects of new fiscal measures on the macroeconomic outlook are normally estimated by the tax receipt working group (see Section 14.3), so that any feedback effects of the outlook on the fiscal accounts are ignored.

In this way, the need to delve into the details of the fiscal outlook can be reconciled to some extent with that of macroeconomic consistency. The feedback effects that are taken into account are mostly demand-side (Keynesian) ones, since supply-side effects are harder to pin down. For example, it can be relatively straightforward to estimate the *ex ante* cost of a measure to stimulate the supply of labour, but its effective *ex post* cost is harder to evaluate. It depends on how the measure affects activity and the structure of production, which is difficult to establish, not least because its impact may only materialise in the long run. This is clearly a major problem, since such measures often precisely aim at changing agents' behaviour.

An alternative approach is to turn to the class of computable general equilibrium (CGE) models (see Devarajan and Robinson, 2002). These are general in that they combine an economy-wide framework with strong assumptions about agents' microeconomic behaviour, representing households as utility maximisers and firms as profit maximisers (or cost minimisers), while often also including optimising specifications for governments, trade unions, importers and exporters. They are equilibrium models because they describe how the decisions made by these different economic actors determine the prices of goods and factors, ensuring that in each case demand equals supply. And they are computable models in the sense that they produce numerical results. The coefficients and parameters in CGE model equations are evaluated by reference to a numerical database, which usually includes a set of input–output accounts showing for a given year the flows of commodities and factors between agents, supplemented by numerical estimates of various elasticity parameters (such as substitution elasticities between inputs in production, price and income elasticities of household demand for different goods, and foreign elasticities of demand for exported products). An alternative name for CGE models is applied general equilibrium (AGE) models, underlining that they use data for actual countries or regions and produce numerical results relating to specific real-world situations.

This is an ambitious and intellectually appealing approach. It allows estimation of the impact of fiscal measures by comparing two equilibria: one without the measures in place, and the other including them and the endogenous responses of all agents. The focus is often on tax rather than on spending measures, not least because the latter may be better assessed using a different and simpler partial equilibrium framework, namely that of project appraisal (see Box 9.1). One example is a study on the United States showing the overwhelmingly favourable effects of unifying the corporate and personal income tax and of replacing capital taxation with consumption taxation (Jorgenson, 1997). CGE models are also frequently mobilised to examine energy and environmental taxation, which clearly have economy-wide ramifications. Indeed, CGE model results have informed energy policy in the United States as well as in Europe, for instance to calculate the level of carbon taxation required to meet the Kyoto protocols. Among the drawbacks of CGE models are their complexity, especially when they are dynamic rather than static, the uncertainty surrounding many of the expert judgements about behaviour and parameter values, and the underlying assumptions about equilibrium.

## 9.5   Top-down and bottom-up approaches

As discussed, budget forecasting can be done at a more or less disaggregated level, one extreme being an exhaustive, line-by-line forecast, and the other a summary approach involving only a few broad fiscal indicators, which fit in directly with the overall macroeconomic forecast. Ideally, these two approaches ought to be complements rather than substitutes.

The summary approach is often the only feasible one in the absence of detailed information about tax receipts, new measures or the structure of public

*Box 9.1* Project appraisal

One way to assess proposed public spending projects is to carry out a careful *ex ante* cost/benefit analysis, which then feeds into fiscal policy forecasts and decisions. This is often done for large projects, notably by the World Bank (Belli *et al.*, 1997). The starting point is to establish the counter-factual, that is, what would happen in the absence of the project. For example, in the case of transport infrastructure, how will traffic evolve given economic growth, demography and relative prices? Then the net present value (NPV) of the project is derived as the difference between its benefits (planned receipts, welfare gains, positive externalities) and costs (financial outlays, negative externalities), with the planned flows of benefits and costs expressed in present value terms. If $F_t$ is the difference between benefits ($B_t$) and costs ($C_t$) in period $t$, and if $d$ is the discount rate:

$$NPV = \sum_t F_t /(1 + d)^t$$

The project's internal rate of return (IRR) is then the value of $d$ equalising the projected costs and benefits:

$$\sum_t (C_t - B_t)/(1 + IRR)^t = 0$$

The project is thus assessed by comparing it to the counterfactual or by checking whether its internal rate of return exceeds the discount rate. In practice, however, numerous difficulties arise:

- Being a partial equilibrium approach, this method ignores sectoral or macroeconomic feedback effects, which can be important.
- The non-monetary elements of the projects are hard to measure, for example congestion costs or the value of human lives saved. Sometimes, competing projects can only be assessed with respect to their effectiveness in reaching non-monetary objectives, and the comparison is then in terms of cost/efficiency rather than cost/benefits.
- *Ex post* results may differ considerably from *ex ante* plans, owing to unexpected events and complications, which add to costs.
- Some of the consequences of the project are difficult to assess, even *ex post*, in particular opportunity costs (for instance when the project displaces other types of public spending) and the impact on agents' behaviour of the tax increase needed to finance the project. The counter-factual itself is often difficult to pin down. One relatively recent approach is to take project irreversibility explicitly into account through the use of options theory, which emphasises the value of waiting to go ahead in an environment where some of the costs or benefits of the project are uncertain.
- Most projects begin with negative net benefits that turn positive and remain positive until the end of the project. Then, there is only one IRR and the IRR and NPV criteria are equivalent. But multiple IRRs arise when net benefits change sign more than once during the life of the project. For example, a project with negative net benefits during the first two years, positive net benefits during the next two, negative net benefits in the fifth (say, because of new investments), and positive net benefits thereafter can have up to three IRRs. More generally, there can be as many IRRs as there are sign changes in the stream of net benefits. For this reason among others, the NPV criterion (using a predetermined value for the discount rate) is to be preferred.

In addition, there are two important conceptual problems. One pertains to the aggregation of preferences. The cost/benefit analysis reflects collective preferences, which may not coincide with microeconomic preferences (since the latter depend on individual circumstances, risk aversion, income, and so on). This is all the more troublesome as usually some stand to gain from the project, while others will be negatively affected. Consider a transport infrastructure project which would save human lives by improving safety. From a citizen's point of view, the value of a human life is the same whether that piece of infrastructure is a road, used by private vehicles, or a rail track, for public use. But the government sees things differently: it is fully responsible for train safety (in the case of public ownership) while car drivers can and should insure themselves to some extent (including by driving carefully). The government is thus entitled to put more weight on each human life saved with the rail transport than with the road transport project.

The other conceptual problem has to do with the discount rate. First, using discounting mechanically leads to putting less weight on more distant costs and benefits – much less in fact when the project has impacts far into the future. This may not be sensible, notably when the project has significant long-run environmental repercussions. Second, there is the issue of the choice of an appropriate discount rate. Opting for a market rate is not a simple solution, given the dispersion of market rates one then has to choose from. In fact, the discount rate used by private firms is often way above any bond rate, because it reflects high opportunity costs. In the public sector, it is usually lower, albeit still above bond rates, because of budget constraints. That said, the uncertainty about the right discount rate is more a problem when analysing the intrinsic costs and benefits of a given project than when comparing the costs and benefits of competing projects that pursue the same objective.

debt. But its very simplicity means that some important issues cannot be addressed properly, such as:

- The link between the economic cycle and tax receipts: for many taxes, receipts fluctuate with the cycle in activity; however, some taxes are based on wealth rather than income, and for those receipts depend on asset prices; other tax receipts are less dependent on output or asset price cycles (say, indirect taxes on tobacco); and others still do depend on the cycle in activity, but in complex ways (corporate income taxes in particular).
- The impact of growth composition on tax receipts: when growth is led by exports, which are typically lightly taxed, it generates less tax revenue than when it is led by household consumption, which is more heavily taxed.
- The evolution over time of tax elasticities, as a function of how progressive tax schedules are, of the evolution of the caps on social contributions, and so on.
- Changes in the behaviour of taxpayers: a summary approach may implicitly assume too much inertia on their part.
- The impact of shifts in the yield curve on debt service, which depends on the exact composition of the stock of debt.

In the short run, the link between budget and economic developments sometimes appears to be tenuous, underscoring the need to check, on an ongoing basis, whether adjustments in the forecast procedures are warranted. The line-by-line approach is the most effective one for this purpose, as it allows exploitation of the incoming intra-annual budget data (though the available information pertains mostly to the revenue side). It can help assess, for instance, why a forecast based on the summary approach went off track. So, in practice, it is useful to conduct both an estimation of tax receipts as a function of forecasted GDP and an estimation of the evolution of the main categories of tax receipts as a function of forecasted consumption (for indirect tax receipts), wages (for the personal income tax and social contributions), and so forth. Another enlightening exercise is to compare the general government budget forecast with the evolution of the budgets of the various government levels (central or state, local, social security).

Conversely, a line-by-line forecast is not always more accurate than a summary one, even in the short run, for two reasons. First, the forecast of the individual lines may not be that accurate. For instance, car sales (and the associated tax receipts) are not necessarily easier to predict than GDP. Moreover, problems can be more serious at the sectoral than at the macroeconomic level. Indeed, sectoral errors to some extent offset each other in the process of aggregation. Secondly, disaggregation introduces complications. A risk is that the aggregation of the individual lines produces an inconsistent forecast, due for example to inadequate treatment of cross-elasticities. In order to check the macroeconomic plausibility of the aggregation, one should examine the implied evolution of some summary fiscal indicators, to see in particular if it is consistent with what the cycle in activity would suggest. For instance, if GDP growth exceeds its potential rate, the fiscal balance, controlling for any new measures, would be expected to improve. Likewise, a line-by-line calculation adding up to a jump in the forecasted ratio of government revenue to GDP might look rather implausible, unless there is a substantial tax policy change.

In sum, both approaches need to be pursued in parallel, with a view to ensure consistency. In the United States for example, budget forecasting by the Office of Management and Budget (OMB) and the CBO (see Section 14.3) involves line-by-line as well as global forecasts. The same holds in most other countries.

## 9.6   Uncertainties

The difficulties described above translate into fairly large fiscal forecasts errors. In the United States, the federal fiscal balance has been vastly over- or under-forecasted in some years (Figure 9.1). The mean error for the one-year-ahead forecast over the 1982–2002 period amounted to 0.4 percentage point of GDP and the mean absolute error, which as discussed in Section 11.2 measures forecasting accuracy better, to 1.3 percentage points of GDP. This is broadly similar to what has been observed in the United Kingdom, where the mean absolute error averaged 1 percentage point of GDP in the second half of the 1990s (HM Treasury, 2001). Not surprisingly, the size of the forecast error increases substantially as the horizon extends further out. Note also that, in general, spending can be forecasted better than tax receipts, since it is less dependent on the business cycle.

Three sources of error are usually distinguished in this context: new measures, erroneous GDP forecasts, and a residual encompassing various sorts of 'technical' forecast errors. The recent US example is telling. Over three-quarters of the 3.8 percentage points of GDP total forecast error made in fiscal year (FY) 2002 for the

*Figure 9.1* Errors in forecasting the US federal budget balance

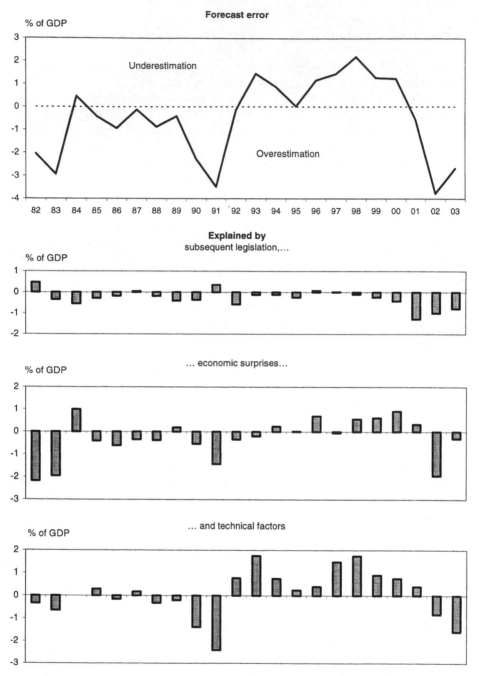

*Source*: OMB (2004) plus authors' calculations. The forecast incorporates the expected impact of the budget's policy proposals, thus implicitly assuming that they will be enacted.

federal budget balance can be explained by:

- A large forecasting error on nominal GDP, which was predicted to grow by 5.3 per cent but instead rose by only 3.1 per cent, coupled with a collapse in an important tax base, namely the stock market; altogether, economic surprises accounted for half of the forecast error.
- The policy decisions taken in the wake of the 11 September terrorist attacks – including Congressional appropriations for disaster recovery, homeland security and war efforts – which were obviously not envisioned in the President's original budget proposal (tabled in February 2001).

Figure 9.1 illustrates that the largest errors in budget forecasting tend to occur around cyclical turning points. This was particularly noticeable during the recessions of the early 1980s, early 1990s and early 2000s. Errors in the opposite direction can also be considerable, witness the 2.2 percentage points of GDP underestimation of the balance in FY 1998, which reflected stronger-than-expected economic growth and rising share prices coupled with a surge in personal income tax receipts (including on capital gains) beyond what available tax elasticity estimates would have predicted.

Improving forecasting accuracy is difficult, however, for a number of reasons:

- The contours of the general government, which is taken here as the relevant concept (so that subnational governments and social security administrations are factored in alongside the central government, while public enterprises are usually not included), are less clear in practice than in theory. The accounting rules applying to subnational governments for instance may differ from the ones used elsewhere. Substantial transfers between government levels occur, adding to opacity. Witness the case of Japan, where extra-budgetary funds play a major role.
- Budget and national accounts concepts are not identical. Privatisation receipts (or nationalisation outlays) and government loans are treated differently in the two sets of accounts. More generally, while the national accounts operate on an accruals basis, budget accounts are often established on a cash basis.
- It is hard to properly capture revenue and expenditure elasticities, not least because it is difficult to properly factor in earlier changes in the tax regime and to determine whether they were strictly discretionary or not (for instance regarding the indexation of rebates and abatements for inflation). In addition, assessing the feedback impact of fiscal policy measures on the macroeconomic environment is challenging.
- Some optical illusion may also be at play. First, the quality of budget forecasts is often gauged by looking only at a few summary indicators, notably the government balance. But the latter is the difference between two large masses which are both forecasted with error: even a small percentage point mistake on the forecast of revenue or expenditure can translate into a huge percentage

point error on the forecast of the balance. Second, so-called fiscal forecasts are not always pure forecasting exercises and may incorporate policy factors such as the government's attempt to shape agents' expectations. US law, for instance, stipulates that official forecasts must be based on assumptions, regarding for example the pace of growth in discretionary spending, which may at times look rather implausible.

- While close monitoring of budget execution during the fiscal year helps, the information available at quarterly or monthly frequencies tends to be incomplete, since it often concerns only the central government (which in Germany, for instance, accounts for only one-quarter of total public spending), is sometimes heterogeneous, and is frequently expressed in cash rather than in accruals terms. In addition, surprises often spring up in the course of the fiscal year, related to the geopolitical situation or weather conditions, for example.

Against this backdrop, it is useful to be clear upfront about how uncertain budget forecasts are. One way to do this is to couch the forecast in the form of ranges rather than simple point estimates (see Section 13.1). Alongside its central forecast, the CBO thus publishes a fan chart showing a wide spread of possible outcomes, based on a probability distribution reflecting its past forecast errors and on their cumulation over time. In addition to this statistical construct, the CBO presents a series of alternative scenarios. For example, in its January 2003 *Budget and Economic Outlook*, it explored two cyclical variants (a faster recovery and a double-dip recession), several scenarios involving the outbreak of war in Iraq (which actually materialised a couple of months later), and two additional scenarios underpinned by different assumptions regarding trend productivity growth, effective tax rates and medical costs.

## 9.7   An analytical view of the budget

Another way to cope with uncertainty is to rely more explicitly on an analytical view, in a longer-run perspective. The focus is then on a few summary indicators such as the underlying fiscal balance and the public debt ratio, to ask whether, given current fiscal rules and policies, the fiscal position may one day appear to be 'unsustainable', triggering policy adjustments.

### 9.7.1   The structural balance

In buoyant times, when GDP growth exceeds its potential rate, tax receipts tend to be stronger and some categories of public spending tend to slow, so that the 'headline' fiscal balance improves markedly. The converse holds during downturns, when tax receipts fall short and some spending rises. These changes in budgetary outcomes caused by the business cycle are viewed as 'automatic fiscal stabilisation', which helps smooth output even in the absence of any discretionary government action. Hence, it is sensible to decompose the fiscal balance into a cyclical and an underlying, or structural, component. Precisely for this reason, the interpretation of the European Stability and Growth Pact was amended in 2002–03, to shift the emphasis from the headline balance to the underlying position.

More specifically, the identification of a cyclical and a structural component requires to take into account the sensitivity of the fiscal flows to the cycle and the size of the government sector. This allows to compute the budget balance that would obtain on average over the cycle. To this end, the elasticities of receipts and spending *vis-à-vis* GDP are computed. In the OECD countries, they average $1\frac{1}{4}$ for the corporate income tax, 1 for the personal income tax and indirect taxes, $\frac{3}{4}$ for social contributions and $-\frac{1}{4}$ for public spending at large, which amounts to $\frac{1}{2}$ for the fiscal balance (Van den Noord, 2002). In other words, if GDP turns out to be 1 per cent above forecast, the fiscal balance will be $\frac{1}{2}$ per cent above forecast, and vice versa. However, these elasticities vary considerably across countries and even over time: in the United States for example, the elasticity for the federal fiscal balance since the mid-1980s is only 0.3, down from 0.4 in the 1960s and 1970s (Cohen and Follette, forthcoming).

Arithmetically, let $b$ denote the budget balance, $b^{struc}$ the structural budget balance and $b^c$ the cyclical component of the budget balance, all in per cent of GDP. The output gap as a share of potential GDP is $(Y - Y^*)/Y^*$, where $Y$ stands for GDP and the asterisk denotes potential. Let $R$ denotes receipts and $S$ spending. With $R^*/R = (Y^*/Y)^\rho$ and $S^*/S = (Y^*/Y)^\eta$, $\rho$ and $\eta$ are the elasticities of $R$ and $S$ with respect to GDP. Then:

$$b_t^{struc} = b_t - b_t^c$$
$$b_t^c = (\rho R_t/Y_t - \eta S_t/Y_t)(Y_t - Y_t^*)/Y_t^*$$

*R* and *S* can be defined as total receipts and spending or restricted to the part that is sensitive to the cycle. In the latter case, the excluded components of *R* and *S*, which are not cyclically sensitive, will be included in the structural balance.

More sophisticated formulations can be used, in particular to take into account the lags associated with tax receipts, which are partly based on income in the previous year. For example, one might write: $R^*/R = (Y^*/Y)^{(1-h)\rho}(Y^*/Y)_{-1}^{h\rho}$, where $h$ reflects the distribution of receipts over the current and past year (noted $-1$ here). In practice, the Dutch Bureau for Economic Policy Analysis for instance builds into its estimates a lag of three-quarters both for taxes and for unemployment benefits (Kranendonk, 2003). If the only type of government spending to be cyclically sensitive is unemployment benefits, and if the unemployment gap (namely, $(U - U^*)/U^*$) is proportional to the output gap, the cyclical component of government spending can be written directly as a function of the unemployment gap.

Based on the elasticities prevailing on average in OECD countries and quoted above, the cyclical component of the budget balance can be estimated as $(R/Y + \frac{1}{4} S/Y)$ times the output gap. With an average government size of around 40 per cent of GDP, this implies that as a rule of thumb $b^c$ equals about half of the output gap.

A number of caveats ought to be highlighted, related to estimation as well as conceptual issues. Estimation of the elasticities is often done by regressing budget flows on activity. However, this provides average elasticities as observed over past cycles, which may not be pertinent when the tax regime has been amended or when spending rules have changed, as is almost always the case in practice. The elasticities can also be estimated in a more refined way, by distinguishing the elasticity of the tax base from the elasticity of the tax receipts. Some analysts, in particular at the OECD, then carry out detailed calculations to take into account marginal tax rates, the distribution of households across income brackets and so on. But the resulting estimates are not very robust. The same holds for the link between unemployment outlays and the cycle, which depends on the share of the unemployment benefit recipients in total unemployment and on the effectiveness of labour market policies: for example, the cyclical component of unemployment spending may be underestimated if costly public employment programmes are put in place to stem the rise in unemployment. This is discussed in more detail by Bouthevillain *et al.* (2001), who also present an even more refined method used by the experts of the Eurosystem, which seeks to better capture the impact on the budget of changes in the composition of aggregate demand and in the distribution of income. A second problem is that these elasticities may well vary over the cycle, in contrast to the above assumption of constancy. One way out would be to allow for some short-run dynamics in the formulation of elasticities, but this is difficult in practice.

As a result, and given the uncertainty surrounding the output gap itself, measures of the level of the structural deficit are fragile. However, measures of the change in the structural deficit – which allow characterisation of the stance of fiscal policy – are usually considered to be more robust. Nonetheless, it is wise to try out several variants in practice, based on more or less rosy assumptions about potential output and elasticities. In this context, it should be noted that the occasional proclivity of the fiscal authorities to adopt unduly optimistic estimates of potential output makes the underlying fiscal situation look stronger than it really is. Furthermore, the very concept of structural balance is controversial. Some prefer to look at the primary structural balance, arguing that one should focus on current fiscal decisions, excluding what results from past deficits and monetary policy (the interest payments on the public debt).

The US administration has also developed the concept of standardised balance (CBO, 2004b), which not only removes the impact of the cycle, but also that of other short-lived factors which are not directly related to changes in fiscal policy and are unlikely to significantly affect private agents' real incomes in the short run, such as:

- Swings in the collection of capital gains tax receipts. These movements are traditionally not captured by cyclical adjustments, though they are partly linked to the state of the business cycle. In addition, they can be misleading. Consider an anticipated increase in the capital gains tax. It will encourage individuals to frontload the realisation of their potential capital gains, so that tax receipts will first rise above normal and then fall below. Yet, it would be wrong to interpret the resulting swing in the structural balance as signalling a loosening of fiscal policy.

- Temporary changes in the timing of tax payments or government outlays: legislation sometimes shifts them from the end of a fiscal year to the beginning of the next, which affects the annual pattern of the fiscal series but might not change private agents' perception of their real income or wealth – although this could be the case for those agents whose financial liquidity is constraining their actions.
- A substantial discrepancy between tax liabilities and tax payments. For instance, lags in fiscal procedures can lead to overpayments one year that will be compensated by higher refunds the following year. These swings might only marginally affect people's perceived incomes.
- Changes in the inflation component of the government's net interest payments: that component effectively adjusts the value of outstanding public debt for the impact of inflation and hence does not alter real private incomes.
- Government outlays for deposit insurance as well as government asset sales and the like. Deposit insurance payments are recorded in the fiscal accounts long after deposit compensation was activated (at the time the financial institutions in question failed), so that they do not impact current private incomes. Asset sales are a voluntary redistribution of existing assets but have little or no effect on real incomes or net worth. They are excluded from the US calculations of the standardised balance because cyclically adjusted balances estimated by the US administration are derived from budget accounts. In contrast, most other calculations of cyclically adjusted budget balances such as those produced by international financial organisations are derived from the national accounts, which do already exclude sales of financial assets (say, government-held shares in companies) from the government budget balance.

The standardised balance avoids these pitfalls.[3] While the structural and the standardised budget balance tend to move in synchrony, they do at times diverge (Figure 9.2).

Yet another approach has been experimented with, using a structural VAR model to capture the effects on fiscal balances of specific economic shocks in EU countries (Dalsgaard and de Serres, 2001). In this framework, no output gaps estimates are required. While this is an advantage, the results are not directly comparable to those obtained through the other approaches because the elasticities derived here include not only the impact of automatic stabilisers, but also that of discretionary fiscal policy insofar as it reacts in a systematic fashion to economic disturbances. A somewhat similar approach would be to measure the underlying fiscal position by explicitly considering the traditional fiscal policy response to the state of the business cycle, as observed over the past.

In sum, these various approaches suggest that any summary measure of the underlying fiscal position should be used with care. Moreover, several uncertainties also surround the actual impact of any change in the measured fiscal stance

---

[3] For EU countries, such a measure is generally unavailable, even though one-off factors affecting the fiscal balance are rife (Koen and Van den Noord, 2005).

*Figure 9.2*   **Two measures of the underlying US federal budget balance**

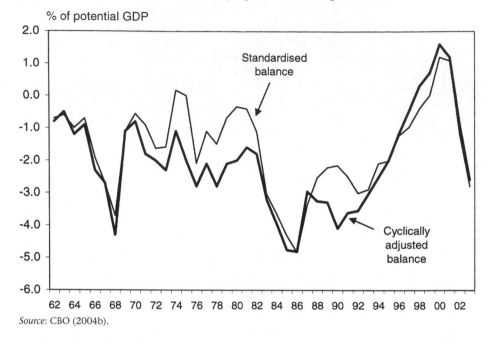

*Source*: CBO (2004b).

itself. Indeed, this impact depends on a host of factors, including the temporary or permanent nature of the change, the mix between adjustments on the revenue and on the spending side, private agents' confidence in the future or lack thereof, their foresightedness or myopia concerning future fiscal adjustments and the degree to which they are liquidity constrained, induced supply-side effects (incentives to work or save more, or less), the uses of public monies (extra spending on the public capital stock may enhance potential output, contrary to some other types of public spending), the economy's openness and so forth. Hence, as pointed out by Blanchard (1990), it is advisable to use a battery of indicators rather than a single one. Finally, assessing the consequences of any underlying fiscal position can mix several issues, which need to be clearly kept separate:

- What the impact on the budget of the economic environment is, as opposed to the impact of discretionary policy measures;
- How fiscal policy affects demand;
- To what extent it changes relative prices and hence the allocation of resources among agents;
- Whether current fiscal arrangements are sustainable over the long run or whether the government will have to increase taxes, cut spending or even monetise or repudiate its debt at some point.

### 9.7.2   Debt sustainability

Indeed, if sizeable deficits persist and debt rises more rapidly than GDP, a snowballing effect may get in motion whereby the deficit adds to the debt and debt service in turn aggravates the deficit. In order to stay clear of this trap, governments sometimes tend to define explicit deficit or debt ceilings. The Maastricht Treaty thus introduced thresholds at 3 per cent of GDP for the deficit and 60 per cent of GDP for gross debt. In the United Kingdom, the so-called sustainable investment rule requires the ratio of net public debt to GDP to be maintained below a 'prudent' level over the cycle, defined as 40 per cent of GDP.

The arithmetics run as follows. Let $b^0$ be the level of the budget balance, as a share of GDP, that stabilises the ratio of public debt $D$ to GDP, denoted $d$, as a function of real GDP growth $g$ and inflation $\pi$. Then the stable debt ratio is such that $d_t = d_{t-1}$.

Since $D_t = D_{t-1} - b_t Y_t$, this condition becomes $(D_{t-1} - b_t^0 Y_t)/Y_t = D_{t-1}/Y_{t-1}$.

Moreover, to a first approximation $Y_t = (1 + g)(1 + \pi)Y_{t-1} \approx (1 + g + \pi)Y_{t-1}$ (as $g\pi$ is small, it is dropped).

Hence, $b_t^0 = D_{t-1}/Y_t - D_{t-1}/Y_{t-1} = D_{t-1}/Y_{t-1}(Y_{t-1}/Y_t - 1) \approx d_{t-1}[(1/(1 + g + \pi)) - 1]$.

Therefore (knowing that for any small $x$, $1/(1 + x) \approx 1 - x$):

$$b^0 \approx -d(g + \pi)$$

This is one rationale for the Maastricht Treaty thresholds: a deficit of 3 per cent of GDP is compatible with a stable debt ratio of 60 per cent of GDP multiplied by a trend growth rate for nominal GDP of 5 per cent (assuming 3 per cent for potential growth plus 2 per cent for trend inflation – though these numbers are themselves debatable).

One can infer the associated primary and structural balances consistent with a stable debt ratio. Let $bp$ be the primary balance and $i$ the average interest rate on public debt.

Then $bp_t = b_t + i_t d_{t-1}/[(1 + g)(1 + \pi)] \approx b_t + i_t d_{t-1}$

Injecting this relation in $D_t = D_{t-1} - b_t Y_t$ yields $D_t \approx D_{t-1}(1 + i) - bp_t Y_t$.

Hence, $d_t \approx d_{t-1}(1 + i)/[(1 + g)(1 + \pi)] - bp_t$.

Therefore, the debt-stabilising primary balance is $bp^0 \approx d(i - g - \pi)/(1 + g + \pi)$. As long as $g$ and $\pi$ are small, this boils down to:

$$bp^0 \approx d(i - g - \pi)$$

Finally, noting that the real interest rate $r = i - \pi$, this condition becomes:

$$bp^0 \approx d(r - g)$$

This stability condition is widely used. It simply states that the primary balance should equal the debt ratio multiplied by the spread between the real interest rate and real GDP growth.

One can also derive the level of taxation as a share of GDP, $t^0$, needed to stabilise the debt ratio. The higher $t^0$, the more worrying the debt dynamics.

In sum, several sustainability indicators can be constructed. Three are widely known (Blanchard, 1990):

- The primary gap, defined as $bp_t - d_t (r - g)$.
- The medium-run tax gap, defined as the tax ratio that will keep the debt ratio constant for three years minus the current tax ratio.
- The long-run tax gap, similarly defined, but over a horizon of 50 years.

Other indicators in the same vein exist (Kopits, 2001). For instance, a benchmark might be to achieve a gradual reduction in the public debt ratio, which implies a certain target for the budget balance, or for the structural budget balance (if the automatic stabilisers are given a free rein). Another rule is to target the implied current budget balance, which is the balance excluding government investment, on the grounds that investment spending generates future returns and may boost economy-wide growth, so that it should not be treated on par with government consumption. The so-called 'golden rule', which stipulates that on average over the cycle the government should borrow only to invest (that is, the current budget should not be in deficit), is one particular case in point. This rule is a key element in the UK fiscal framework, alongside the aforementioned sustainable investment rule. However, it is not foolproof: it does not guarantee that the government will invest wisely, and it can invite opportunistic reclassifications of spending items or, worse, distort the composition of public spending at the expense of some worthy current expenditure. A logical complement of a golden rule is to provide a fairly comprehensive public sector balance sheet. This in principle is very valuable to assess sustainability since all public liabilities have to be taken into consideration, be they, say, future pensions for civil servants or the consumption of fixed capital induced by using existing equipment. However, so far only a few countries (of which one is New Zealand) have made good progress in producing such information.

The existence of rules helps the forecaster, since they provide useful benchmarks, be it on a year-on-year basis, over the cycle or over some longer horizon. Checking whether they are adhered to allows formation of a view about possible fiscal policy inflections and private-sector reactions.

# 10
## Sectoral Forecasting

This book mostly deals with forecasting developments at the macroeconomic level, even when discussing specific aspects such as financial markets (Chapter 8) or fiscal policy (Chapter 9). In contrast, sectoral forecasts follow a microeconomic approach. Here, the focus is on sectors, or even on one particular sector. This is a relevant perspective for a firm concerned with the outlook its sector faces, or for a local government wondering how much needs to be spent on infrastructure to ensure that firms in the area can grow without encountering local bottlenecks (such as road congestion).

Sectoral forecasts are useful in at least three ways. First, they offer a more concrete reading of economic developments. Macroeconomic analysis is often somewhat abstract: a given growth rate of GDP for instance can reflect a steady, broad-based expansion, with all sectors doing well; or it can mask considerable divergence across sectors, with some booming and others in recession. A sectoral approach thus sheds light on important differences across sectors, reflecting both exposure to dissimilar shocks and heterogeneous behavioural responses.

It also makes it possible to check on the internal consistency of economy-wide forecasts by explicitly factoring in the interdependence across sectors. Indeed, sectoral forecasting was used actively during eras where some form of central planning played a significant role. For example, in France, a concern in the 1950s and 1960s was that some sectors, such as steel, might not grow fast enough to meet the demands of other sectors. Input–output matrices were used to forecast steel demand by sector for a given pace of GDP growth, with a view to ensure sufficient supply of steel. This approach remains of interest today in some cases, albeit in a different spirit, for example when looking at the emergence of new sectors.

Lastly, short-run sectoral forecasts are crucial for those economic agents who are involved in the given sector. Managers and investors have to think ahead and prepare budgets or decide on inventory levels and working schedules. Likewise, investment and hiring decisions more durably locking in resources require careful longer-run sectoral forecasts.

This chapter reviews two approaches to sectoral forecasting: the microeconomic one, which zooms in on one particular sector, sub-sector or firm; and the cross-sectoral one, which jointly looks at the different sectors and their interrelationships, typically using input–output analysis. While the emphasis is on production, value added and intermediate consumption, similar techniques can be used to forecast consumption, investment, prices or employment by sector.

## 10.1   Microeconomic forecasts

The microeconomic approach focuses on production or value added in a given sector, in the sense of a set of activities as defined in the national accounts classification (see Chapter 2) or at a more disaggregated level. The sectoral forecast can then incorporate pointed microeconomic expertise and idiosyncratic information. This does not mean, however, that macroeconomic developments are necessarily ignored.

In fact, there are two ways to carry out this exercise. Let $Q$ be value added in the sector under consideration, $S$ a vector of relevant sector-specific variables (including for instance past values of $Q$, prices, inventories and so forth) and $Y$ a macroeconomic variable, say GDP. Then $Q$ can be forecasted, either in 'partial equilibrium' fashion, as $Q = f(S)$, or with due account for macroeconomic developments, as $Q = f(S,Y)$.[1]

The second approach generally ensures a better fit to past observations, as fluctuations in a given sector are often fairly strongly correlated with overall movements in activity. Even when the correlation is negative (the sector behaves counter-cyclically), taking it into account improves the fit. But this does not *ipso facto* imply that for forecasting purposes the second approach will deliver superior results. For that to be the case, the forecast of $Y$ itself should be sufficiently accurate. An illuminating parallel is the usefulness of taking into account world demand when forecasting national GDP, especially for small open economies. This can substantially improves the GDP forecast, but of course it can also worsen it if the international environment is assessed incorrectly. Similarly, here, a poor forecast of $Y$ can increase the forecast error on $Q$.

### 10.1.1   'Partial equilibrium' approaches

One way to forecast $Q$ for a given sector independently of the global outlook is to use one of the time series methods presented in Chapter 4, notably when no other detailed statistical information is available. This, however, does require purging the series from its seasonal component (when the frequency is higher than annual) and controlling for any identified exceptional factors. The adjusted series can then be subjected to simple extrapolation techniques or to modelling *à la* Box-Jenkins.

An alternative and more structural approach is to look for the factors that have accounted for the evolution of $Q$ in the past and at how they are set to evolve over the forecast period. A classic example is the use of data on housing starts to forecast

---

[1] In the first approach, one can of course sum up the sectoral $Q$s and infer GDP, thereby mimicking what national accountants do when they build up GDP from the supply side. The inferred GDP forecast can then be compared with one derived on aggregate data from the demand side (see Chapter 5).

activity in the construction sector, since there is a strong positive correlation between the former and construction several months later.

More generally, this type of sectoral forecast tends to exploit available survey information, such as enterprises' answers to questions regarding their investment plans, the evolution of capacity and their own production forecasts. Household surveys on their intended durable goods purchases for instance might be useful when forecasting sectors such as the automobile one. In this context, survey data foreshadow future behaviour and play the role that leading indicators play at the macroeconomic level (see Chapter 3). How successfully they can be used depends, however, on how robust the correlation is between the surveys and actual developments. And, in practice, the forecast of Q can be improved by adjusting for any extraneous news, say for the likely impact of announced tax measures in a given economic sector.

### 10.1.2 Taking the macroeconomic environment into account

A simple way to bring in the macroeconomic context is to write demand for the sector (or firm) under consideration as $Q = f(Y,P)$, where $Y$ is economy-wide income and $P$ the relative price of output in that sector. Suppose the sector produces a given set of consumer goods or services.[2] Then:

- $Q$ is usually taken to be output (in volume terms) rather than value added, as demand pertains to the product including the embodied intermediates; an ancillary assumption would thus be needed to go from output to value added (such as that of fixed technical coefficients).
- $Y$ would typically be real disposable household income (using the CPI as a deflator), or the volume of total household consumption (when the view is that households first split up income between saving and spending and then decide how to allocate their spending across goods and services).
- $P$ would normally be the price of $Q$ relative to the CPI. As microeconomic demand functions are typically homogeneous of degree one, a similar increase in all prices would not change the composition of real demand, so what matters here is the relative rather than the absolute price.

It is standard practice to estimate the demand function in logarithmic form, so as to directly obtain the underlying elasticities:

$$\log Q = \eta \log Y + \beta \log P + \varepsilon \tag{10.1}$$

where $\varepsilon$ is a residual, $\eta$ is income elasticity and $\beta$ price elasticity. For 'normal' goods or services, $\eta > 0$, while for 'inferior' ones $\eta < 0$. When $\eta > 1$, they are said to be 'luxury' goods or services. Besides, $\beta$ is generally expected to be negative.[3]

---

[2] A similar reasoning applies when Q is sold to firms, government agencies or foreigners.
[3] In this simplified framework, demand for a given good does not depend on that for other goods, so that no cross-elasticities come into play.

The above formulations are static in nature. As such, they represent long-run rather than short-run relationships. A standard way to add some short-run dynamics is to consider equation (10.1) as the long-run component in an error-correction equation:

$$\Delta q_t = \alpha + \sum \alpha_j \Delta q_{t-j} + \sum \beta_j \Delta y_{t-j} - \mu(q_{t-1} - \eta y_{t-1} - \beta p_{t-1}) + \varepsilon_t \tag{10.2}$$

where small letters are used to denote logarithms ($q = log\ Q$, and so on) and it is assumed for simplicity that the relative price does not affect the short-run dynamics.

Equation (10.2) is similar to the types of equations presented in Chapter 5, where macroeconomic behaviour was modelled. Such equations are frequently used, in isolation or within a model, to forecast output in a given sector as part of a more global scenario. Conversely, macroeconomic analysis can be usefully complemented by checking whether sectoral developments implied by the global outlook appear sensible and coherent.

## 10.2   Input–output analysis

In principle, the above techniques, including equation (10.2), can be applied across all sectors. The results can then be summed up, provided the adding-up constraint is met (that is, the aggregation does equal GDP). But there exists an alternative approach, based on input–output matrices. In addition to sectoral value added, it provides, for each sector, the detail of what goes in as intermediate consumption and the decomposition of what goes out between final demand and intermediate consumption of other sectors.

### 10.2.1   The method

The input–output matrix is identical to the input–output table introduced in Chapter 2. For each group of products (henceforth 'product'), it shows:[4]

- How much is supplied overall, through domestic production and imports;
- How much is used per sector, including the one producing it, as intermediate consumption;
- The final uses: consumption, fixed capital formation and exports.

For each product, the sum of the intermediate and final uses equals total supply.

The way to proceed with this analysis is as follows, bearing in mind that this is essentially an accounting method, and a static one, which can be applied to values as well as to volumes. The first step is to extract from the input–output table the matrix of technical coefficients, called $A$. If there are $n$ sectors, $A$ is a square, $n$-by-$n$, matrix. The coefficient $a_{ij}$, at the intersection of the $i^{th}$ line and $j^{th}$ column, is the

---

[4] For the sake of simplicity, sectors and products are assumed to overlap (the distribution sector is abstracted from) and indirect taxes net of subsidies are ignored.

ratio of the intermediate consumption of product $i$ by sector $j$ on the production of sector $j$.

Three n-dimensional column vectors are then introduced:[5] $Y = (Y_1, \ldots, Y_n)^T$, the outputs of products 1 to $n$, $M = (M_1, \ldots, M_n)^T$, the imports of products 1 to $n$, and $D = (D_1, \ldots, D_n)^T$, the final uses of products 1 to $n$.

Then $A \times Y$ is the n-dimensional column vector of intermediate consumption by product. It first term for example is $a_{11}Y_1 + a_{12}Y_2 + \cdots + a_{1n}Y_n$, which is equal to the total consumption across sectors of product 1.

The equality between supply and uses of each product can then be summed up as follows:

$$M + Y = A \times Y + D \tag{10.3}$$

where each term is an n-dimensional column vector. Equation (10.3) says that imports plus domestic production of each product equals its intermediate plus final consumption. This can also be written as:

$$Y = (Id - A)^{-1} \times (D - M) \tag{10.4}$$

where $Id$ is the $n$-by-$n$ identity matrix (with ones along the diagonal and zeros everywhere else).[6]

Equation (10.4) allows to derive the production by sector given final demand and imports. Then, having derived $Y$, the intermediate consumption of each product can be computed as $A \times Y$. Value added by sector is then the difference $Y - A \times Y = Y \times (Id - A)$.

However, in practice, forecasts for $M$ and $D$ are rarely available. Rather, what are available are forecasts for total imports, $m$, and the components of final demand: final consumption, $c$, fixed investment, $i$, and exports, $x$. In order to forecast $M$ and $D$, they need to be split up amongst products. This can be done using another matrix related to the input–output table, the matrix of final demand coefficients. Here, this matrix, named $B$, would have $n$ rows (one per product) and 4 columns (for imports, final consumption, fixed investment, and exports). Coefficient $b_{31}$ for instance would be the share of the imports of product 3 in total imports. Hence:

$$M = B \times (m, 0, 0, 0)^T \quad \text{and} \quad D = B \times (0, c, i, x)^T \tag{10.5}$$

It is thus possible to forecast $M$ and $D$ once imports and the main components of final demand have been forecasted, on the assumption that the final demand coefficients are unchanged. From there, sectoral output can be forecasted using equation (10.1).

---

[5] T is the transpose symbol, indicating that a line vector is turned into a column vector or vice versa.

[6] The matrix $(Id - A)$ is assumed to be invertible, which is indeed the case in practice.

## 10.2.2   Pros and cons

Input–output analysis was pioneered by Leontief (1941). It enables translation of the forecast of the components of final demand into a forecast of the intermediate and final demand addressed to each sector. In addition, it provides a forecast of the inputs that each sector will need from the others. The inbuilt consistency of this approach is appealing: by construction, the resulting sectoral forecasts add up to the macro picture.

This is particularly interesting for sectors that are important suppliers or heavy users of intermediates. For the former, the method makes it possible to estimate the traction they get from changes in final demand. For the latter, it provides estimates of the volume and costs of the inputs they will need. In the context of economy-wide planning, this enables forecasting of import requirements and identification of potential future bottlenecks which could stifle overall economic expansion.

As presented above, however, input–output analysis rests on the stringent assumption that both the technical coefficients and the final demand coefficients are fixed over the forecast horizon. In other words, it is assumed that the structure of production and demand does not evolve. This is unrealistic in at least two cases:

- When the forecast extends only a few quarters out: in the very short run, the technical and final demand coefficients are unstable, owing to lags between the production of intermediates and their incorporation into final products, and to inventory fluctuations.
- When the forecast spans many years: over time, technological progress and new investment alter production patterns, while consumption habits change, not least in response to shifts in relative prices (for instance in the case of information technology goods). It may then be necessary to use time-varying technical and final demand coefficients.

Therefore, the most relevant horizon for input–output analysis is the short to medium run. Over periods of a few years, firms are generally not going to overhaul their *modus operandi*: once a piece of equipment is installed, it will be used for quite some time before being replaced. Likewise, clients' behaviour will probably not change that much. On the whole, however, this type of tool is not routinely used in macroeconomic forecasting, even if it does offer useful insights into the workings of the economy, not unlike general equilibrium models.

# 11
# Accuracy

Though demand for economic forecasts is strong, their reliability is frequently questioned and scepticism is widespread among the general public regarding the accuracy of any forecast. Granted, forecasters often get it wrong, not least when it comes to foreseeing turning points or crises. But uncertainty is part and parcel of advanced economies. In addition, forecasters themselves consider that they tend to be unduly criticised. They argue that their track record is more respectable than is often alleged, noting that professional forecasts have been proved to be more reliant than the so-called 'naïve forecasts' produced by elementary methods. Moreover, accuracy is perhaps not the best criterion to judge the value of forecasts. Indeed, their usefulness may have more to do with the associated diagnoses and policy implications (see Chapter 12).

Yet, forecasting accuracy remains a key issue. First, it needs to be properly defined (Section 11.1). Next, it has to be measured (Section 11.2) and forecast errors must be analysed (Section 11.3). Looking at forecasters' performance over the past sheds light on what to expect going forward (Section 11.4). It is also worth scrutinising past forecasting errors to establish what caused them (Section 11.5). Lastly, avenues for improvement are explored (Section 11.6).

## 11.1 Conceptual issues

### 11.1.1 How to look at forecast accuracy

Many studies try to assess the accuracy of forecasts, taking this concept for granted. Defining accuracy is not straightforward, however. For starters, accuracy should not be confused with certainty. A high degree of accuracy does not mean that the forecast will be 'just right'. Rather, it means that the risk of error is limited, in a probabilistic perspective. Here lies a first source of misunderstanding between the public and forecasters, since a forecast, by its very nature, cannot offer the kind of certainty the broader public may be wishing for.

That said, how should one assess whether the risk of error is large or small? Obviously, the size of the 'tolerable' uncertainty depends on the quantitative properties of the variable under consideration. The latter include its intrinsic volatility as well as the precision with which this variable is measured. For example, a 1 per cent forecasting error on a variable that is only measured with a precision of ±2 per cent is clearly not a big mistake. A relevant measure of accuracy should take such caveats into account.

Another important point to bear in mind is that the degree of desirable accuracy depends on the purpose of the forecast. In particular, it may hinge on users' room for manoeuvre. For example, in the European Union, the Stability and Growth Pact sets a limit of 3 per cent of GDP on fiscal deficits. In that context, a forecasting error on growth that would add one percentage point of GDP to the deficit would be deemed serious. And if the country already approaches or breaches the 3 per cent deficit threshold, even a much smaller error, raising the deficit by only a few decimal points, might be seen as significant.

This has two implications for assessing accuracy. First, users of forecasts need to have a sense of the accuracy of a broad set of forecasted variables. In the example above, for instance, one may want to get a range of likely public finance outcomes. Second, the perception of the reliability of a forecast also depends on users' risk aversion, and may not be symmetric. An error leading to an understatement of GDP growth, for example, might be considered benign, insofar as the fiscal position will then look better than foreseen. But an error of the same size in the opposite direction would create unexpected problems and hence attract more criticism. Hence, one may want to put different weights on positive versus negative risks when gauging accuracy.

In sum, the interactions between perceived accuracy and use of the forecast are important: the accuracy of a forecast nobody uses would be irrelevant. Questions about forecast accuracy have therefore gained prominence as governments and central banks, but also private agents, started to rely more and more on economic forecasts.

### 11.1.2   What should a forecast be compared to?

In principle, the reliability of a forecast is assessed by looking at the size of the errors made. But what is the relevant benchmark? There are at least three main issues to consider.

First, it is not obvious to which string of data forecasts should ultimately be compared. The data themselves tend to change over time, as statistics are refined and revised. With which vintage should the forecast then be compared? The initial one, some firmer one, or the definitive one, which in principle best describes what actually occurred but may become available only several years down the road? In fact, the revised data often incorporate new information, including changes in methodology, that was not initially available. From this perspective, it makes sense to compare the forecast with the first vintage of the data, such as the advance, or 'flash', national account estimates published four to six weeks following the quarter in question. Unfortunately, things are not quite as clear-cut in practice. A forecast may look mediocre when compared to the initial data while turning out to do a much better job when set against the final data. In such cases, the forecast might in effect have anticipated subsequent statistical revisions. This can happen, for example, with those short-run GDP forecasts that incorporate qualitative survey information: they sometimes approximate the final data better than the flash estimate that is computed with incomplete hard data.

The second issue is whether one should look at the intrinsic accuracy of a forecast – that is, the size of the forecasting error, duly normalised – or rather at how it compares with other forecasts. While these two approaches may at first sound similar, the second one is more demanding since in practice different forecasts cannot be readily compared. They are not carried out at exactly the same time, hence some benefit from more recent information than others. They may also pertain to somewhat different time horizons and statistical concepts: for example, when forecasting inflation, a measure based on a CPI index may be forecasted in one case, as opposed to the private consumption deflator in another. In addition, the nature of the forecasts can differ: a projection based on a macroeconomic model provides a comprehensive and relatively detailed picture, whereas a time-series based forecast for instance is restricted to a few aggregates; hence, simply comparing the results of these two exercises would be too simplistic. Forecasts further differ depending on whether they are published (and therefore possibly normative) or for internal use. Some are conditioned on specific policy and other assumptions, others not: for example, the exchange rate may be frozen or may itself be forecasted. In practice, it is therefore difficult to meaningfully compare institutions' forecasting records.

Yet a third problem is time consistency. Straight comparisons across forecasts assume that each institution invariably and strictly follows certain well-defined procedures. In practice, this is not the case. For example, in the late 1970s, the US CBO's long-run economic projections were strongly normative, directly reflecting policy goals; nowadays, even if they are not always very plausible, they are more clearly meant to show what will happen if recent historical trends are extrapolated (CBO, 2003). Furthermore, forecasting teams and tools change over time, and the forecasts themselves are not generated mechanically but involve considerable discretion. When contrasting institutions' track records, it is thus advisable to focus on only a few key variables, such as growth and inflation, and on a relatively short horizon, say the current year and next.

## 11.2 Measuring accuracy in practice

Four types of methods are used to gauge the accuracy of a forecast: summary statistics describing past errors, benchmarking against simple or 'naïve' projections, testing whether errors tend to be one-sided or correlated, and directional tests showing whether turning points in activity are well anticipated.

### 11.2.1 Summary statistics

An intuitive way to assess accuracy is to characterise the size of past errors. Consider a sequence of $T$ forecasts carried out between time $t = 1$ and $t = T$, with $X_t$ being the forecasted variable and $P(X_t)$ the predicted value. Then the errors can be defined as $E_t = P(X_t) - X_t$.

The statistical properties of $E_t$ over the period under consideration can be described using various standard summary statistics, including:

- The mean error, equal to $(\Sigma_1^T E_t)/T$.
  This is the bias. It should be close to zero for a good forecast.
- The mean absolute error (MAE), equal to $(\Sigma_1^T |E_t|)/T$,
  where $|E_t|$ is the absolute value of $E_t$.
- The mean square error (MSE), equal to $(\Sigma_1^T E_t^2)/T$.
  Its square root is called the RMSE (root mean square error).

The mean error is a simple and commonly used measure of forecast bias. But as an arithmetic average, it says little about the variance of the errors. A small mean error could indicate that all the errors were small. However, it would also obtain if many of the errors were large but with the over- and underestimates offsetting each other.

The MAE and the RMSE do not suffer from this ambiguity. They are both measured in the same units as $X_t$, and should also be small for a good forecast. The RMSE tends to be preferred to the MAE, however, as the RMSE gives more weight to the largest errors, which are the ones forecasters worry most about. Whether the RMSE or the MAE is 'small' or not should be judged taking into account:

- The variability of $X_t$, as measured by its standard deviation.
- The precision of $X_t$ itself. If $X_t$ is measured imprecisely, the forecast cannot be that precise.
- Whether the errors diminish over time or not.
- The performance of competing forecasts.

If $T$ is relatively small, these summary statistics should be interpreted with extra care, since individual forecast errors can have an unduly large influence in small samples: the mean error, for example, can change sign when a single observation is added.

Generally speaking, a 'decent' forecast of growth or inflation at a one-year horizon would display an RMSE of about 1 to 2 per cent, which is deemed acceptable given the uncertainty surrounding the measurement of such variables.

### 11.2.2   Comparison with simple or 'naïve' projections

A drawback of the above summary statistics is that they are expressed in units that depend on the values taken by the variable under consideration. Hence, one cannot readily compare them across variables, say in order to find out whether it is growth or employment that is forecasted most accurately. One way to overcome this problem is to 'normalise' them, that is, to divide them by a statistic describing how large the values of the variable are. To this end, Theil has proposed the following inequality coefficient (called Theil's *U*):

$$U = \frac{\sqrt{\sum_1^T (X_t - P(X_t))^2}}{\sqrt{\sum_1^T X_t^2}}$$

where $U^2$ is the ratio of the MSE over the average of the squared values of $X_t$. $U = 0$ indicates that the forecast was perfect.

When $X_t$ is a growth rate, say of the CPI, $U$ can be interpreted in a special way. A naïve projection of the CPI would be that the price level remains unchanged, so that for all periods $P(X_t) = 0$. $U$ would in that case equal 1. So when $U$ is close to 1, the forecast of the growth rate in question does not perform much better than a naïve forecast.

Other similar indices can be computed, for instance by dividing the RMSE by the standard deviation of $X_t$ or dividing the MAE by the mean absolute deviation of $X_t$. In addition, several other approaches can be followed, depending on the type of naïve or simple projection used as a benchmark. For example, 'no change in the rate of change' as opposed to 'no change in the level' can be set as the benchmark. A somewhat more sophisticated approach is to compare the forecast with what purely 'statistical' techniques such as ARIMA and VAR processes would predict, based solely on the past behaviour of the variable.

### 11.2.3 Bias and efficiency

Forecast errors are said to be rational if they are unbiased (they average zero) and efficient. Efficiency here means that all the information available at the time the forecast was produced has been used optimally. Unbiasedness is in fact a necessary, though not sufficient, condition for efficiency. Another necessary condition in this regard is that the errors be random (white noise) and uncorrelated with past values of $X_t$ or of the errors themselves (auto-correlation). Indeed, if such correlations existed, they should have been exploited to reduce the errors and the forecast could have gained in efficiency.

Two types of tests are generally carried out:

- A regression of the forecast errors on their own lagged values: $E_t = \alpha + \beta E_{t-1} + \varepsilon_t$. The forecast will be efficient if $\alpha$ and $\beta$ equal zero. If $\beta$ differs from zero, past errors carry over into present ones. If $\alpha$ differs from zero, the forecast is biased.
- A regression of the observed on the predicted values: $X_t = \alpha + \beta P(X_t) + \varepsilon_t$. Efficiency requires that the constant $\alpha$ be zero (necessary condition for unbiasedness), that the slope $\beta$ be equal to 1 and that $\varepsilon_t$ be white noise. To test unbiasedness alone, it is sufficient to regress the forecast error on a constant: $E_t = \alpha + \varepsilon_t$. If $\alpha$ is significantly different from zero, the forecast is biased.[1]

---

[1] This type of test also requires checking for auto-correlation of the residuals.

## 11.2.4   Directional accuracy

Directional tests seek to establish whether the forecast points in the right direction. This is especially important when the concern is to make sure that turning points are not missed too frequently. A simple way to proceed is to group outcomes $X_t$ and predictions $P(X_t)$ in a contingency table as follows, where $N(P_+, O_+)$ for instance stands for the number of cases where both the prediction and the outcome have $X_t$ rising, and $N = T$ is the total number of observations (Table 11.1):

*Table 11.1*   **Directional tests**

|  |  | Predictions | | |
| --- | --- | --- | --- | --- |
|  |  | $\Delta P(X_t) > 0$ | $\Delta P(X_t) \leq 0$ | Sub-total |
| Outcomes | $\Delta X_t > 0$ | $N(P_+, O_+)$ | $N(P_-, O_+)$ | $N(O_+)$ |
|  | $\Delta X_t \leq 0$ | $N(P_+, O_-)$ | $N(P_-, O_-)$ | $N(O_-)$ |
|  | Sub-total | $N(P_+)$ | $N(P_-)$ | $N$ |

A good forecast should have the prediction and the outcome move in the same direction. In other words, $N(P_+, O_+) + N(P_-, O_-)$ should be large compared to $N$. A formal statistical test here is the chi-squared independence test. Let:

$$\chi^2 = \sum_i \sum_j \frac{(N_{ij} - N_{i.}N_{.j}/N)^2}{N_{i.}N_{.j}/N}$$

where $i$ and $j$ take the values $+$ and $-$, and where for example $N_{++}$ is shorthand for $N(P_+, O_+)$ and $N_{+.}$ for $N(P_+)$.

The null hypothesis is that predictions and outcomes are independent, in which case this statistic follows a chi-squared distribution with one degree of freedom. If the null is rejected, the forecast is deemed to be directionally accurate.[2]

## 11.3   Analysing errors

How can forecast errors be analysed in practice to improve the understanding of economic mechanisms and the quality of future forecasts? Several methods are commonly used: *ex ante* versus *ex post* forecast comparisons, *post-mortems* and time series decompositions.

---

[2] There are other directional tests. Greer (2003) for instance uses a battery of directional tests to examine the long-term interest rates forecasts of the *Wall Street Journal*'s panel of economic forecasters. He finds that, at the 5 per cent significance level, few of them predicted the direction of change in long-term interest rates better than they would have by tossing a coin. However, the forecast of the panel as a whole was directionally accurate.

### 11.3.1 *Ex ante* versus *ex post*

*Ex ante* versus *ex post* forecast comparisons decompose the error so as to separate what can be ascribed to the properties of the model used from what is due to the forecaster's other choices. For this purpose, one defines the *ex ante* forecast error as:

$$EA_t = X_t - P(X_t) = X_t - P(X_t(P(EX_t),R_t)),$$

where $EX_t$ is the set of exogenous variables and $R_t$ stands for the residuals of the behavioural equations plugged into the forecast. This can be further decomposed as follows:

$$EA_t = X_t - P(X_t(EX_t,0)) + P(X_t(EX_t,0)) - P(X_t(P(EX_t),0)) + P(X_t(P(EX_t),0)) - P(X_t(P(EX_t),R_t))$$

| *ex ante* error | *ex post* error | error on the exogenous variables | contribution of the residuals |
|---|---|---|---|

- The *ex post* forecast error is due to the model: it corresponds to the difference between the outcome and a forecast simply plugging the values of the exogenous variables observed *ex post* into the model, without any adjustment.
- The second error is the one made on the values of the exogenous variables (which are themselves either simply assumed or forecasted).
- The contribution of the residuals pertains to the forecaster's judgement calls on the residuals to be retained when going forward.

If it turns out that the *ex ante* error is mainly due to the model, the latter may misspecify some behavioural relationships. If instead the *ex ante* error principally stems from the exogenous variables, there is a case for trying to build up some more expertise, outside the model, on these exogenous variables. This decomposition is somewhat artificial, however, insofar as in practice the three elements are not independent. For example, the forecaster's choices as regards the residuals may be linked to the treatment of the exogenous variables: if exchange rates are frozen by assumption but the forecaster feels that, say, some depreciation is likely, he might adjust the residuals accordingly, at least to some extent. Likewise, the choices on residuals tend to take into account the shortcomings of the model, as a substitute for fully revamping it.

Though the situation differs across forecasts, a general feature is that the *ex ante* error is smaller than the *ex post* one, at least when forecasts are done properly. This may seem surprising at first, since one might expect the model to perform much better if the exogenous variables were known with certainty rather than assumed or forecasted. In fact, the error made on the exogenous variables is often offset by the forecaster through the educated choices made regarding the residuals.

### 11.3.2 *Post mortem* analysis

A related way to learn from past forecasting errors is to periodically undertake a *post mortem* analysis. The purpose here is first and foremost to examine the errors in order to better understand how the economy has recently been functioning.

The focus is on the nature and causes of the unforeseen exogenous shocks that have occurred, and on agents' reactions. This may in turn lead to changes in the behavioural equations of the model but this is not the primary purpose of this exercise.

The first step is the identification of the shocks that unexpectedly took place after the forecast was completed (oil price shock, recession in a partner country and the like). Their impact is then quantified through simulation exercises, such as variants around the central forecast. From a formal standpoint, this amounts to ascribing differences between prediction and outcome to two sources: changes in exogenous variables, and changes reflected in equation residuals.

From this perspective, this exercise has some similarities with the *ex post/ex ante* analysis described above. But the aim is different. It is less to disentangle the sources of errors than to infer a measure of agents' change in behaviour. A key element is the quality of the forecasting tool used, which has to be sufficient so that misspecification problems can be fairly confidently ruled out. The type of behavioural change can then be of two sorts:

- Either the average behavioural patterns, which are the ones embodied in the estimated model equations, are not questioned, but agents are seen as temporarily reacting somewhat differently because of a peculiar context (say, they show more reluctance to spend than normally because of transient geopolitical concerns);
- Or the average behavioural patterns are evolving, which is difficult to realise early on because it takes quite some time for the change to transpire in a statistically significant fashion. In that case, the model's parameters and even structure will be reconsidered. One example is the influence of interest rates on private spending in Europe, which changed following financial liberalisation in the mid-1980s but became statistically significant only with a lag.

In reality, the distinction between exogenous and endogenous variables is not that clear-cut, and sources of errors are not necessarily independent, calling for caution when interpreting individual equation residuals.

In principle, a *post mortem* requires a reliable macroeconomic model, and therefore cannot be carried out to analyse forecasts produced using other tools. In practice, however, more 'qualitative' *post mortems* are undertaken even then, along similar lines.

### 11.3.3   Using time-series methods

In the absence of a model, forecast errors can be analysed using VARs representing the key endogenous variables that are suspected of having played a role in the errors. For example, the contribution of each of the components of aggregate demand to a revision of the forecast of GDP can be generated. Such an approach is of course cruder and less detailed than using a full model, given that it focuses on only a few variables and ignores some of the feedback effects.

Specifically, a VAR representation allows identification of the innovations affecting variables compared with their usual dynamics (see Section 4.4). One can see how these innovations changed between the time of the forecast and the outcome, and quantify their contribution to the forecast error.

However, the innovations in a VAR may have a common component. In order to identify variable-specific innovations, a structural VAR can be run based on some simple hypotheses. For instance, it will be assumed that public consumption as one element of aggregate demand is completely exogenous (admittedly a simplification, but not an outrageous one). The other elements will be assumed to be linked through changes in GDP. Then, their 'structural' innovations will be obtained as the residuals of the regression of the innovations on the estimated innovation in GDP. They will be considered as specific disturbances to the various components of aggregate demand and their respective contribution to the forecast error will then be computed.

## 11.4   Forecasters' track record

Passing an overall judgement on the accuracy of forecasting is difficult. The diagnosis depends on the institution, the country, the period, the variables and the horizon. Generally speaking, however, forecast errors are substantial but forecasting is relatively efficient (in the aforementioned sense). One problem is that turning points are poorly anticipated.

### 11.4.1   Errors are substantial but forecasts are generally efficient

The RMSE for short-run GDP forecasts is typically on the order of 1 to 2 percentage points, as illustrated for the G7 countries in Table 11.2 (Italy and Japan stand out as more difficult to forecast, even controlling for the underlying volatility of growth). For inflation, the RMSE is of a similar magnitude, albeit with more cross-country dispersion. Errors on GDP are often negatively correlated with the cycle, with growth under-predicted when activity accelerates and over-predicted when it slows down. Also, accuracy improves as horizons shorten, since incoming high-frequency data, say quarterly GDP statistics for year $t$, allow to firm up the forecast for year $t + 1$ as time goes by – not too surprisingly given the important role played by carry-over effects (see Section 3.1).

Also noteworthy is that different forecasters tend to produce fairly similar predictions. Thus, they generally err simultaneously. This reflects that they use broadly similar models, fed with the same raw data, and face the same unexpected shocks. In addition, they influence each other, as discussed below. Some studies suggest, however, that international institutions such as the OECD perform relatively well (Pons, 2000). This can be ascribed to their explicitly taking into account international linkages, so that imports and exports across countries are consistent with the projections for each of them. In addition, they interact regularly with national authorities, both to exchange data and in the context of multilateral surveillance. But how much of an edge this gives the international institutions

*Table 11.2*   **Accuracy of the OECD's growth projections***
(real GDP growth projections published in the *Economic Outlook*)

|  | United States | Japan | Germany | France | Italy | United Kingdom | Canada |
|---|---|---|---|---|---|---|---|
| **Current year** | | | | | | | |
| RMSE | 0.82 | 1.30 | 0.93 | 0.89 | 1.11 | 0.82 | 1.03 |
| RMSE/$\sigma(X_t)$** | 0.34 | 0.44 | 0.47 | 0.48 | 0.54 | 0.41 | 0.43 |
| Directional accuracy*** | 81 | 81 | 81 | 81 | 85 | 93 | 93 |
| **Year ahead** | | | | | | | |
| RMSE | 1.34 | 2.42 | 1.69 | 1.30 | 1.99 | 1.53 | 1.80 |
| RMSE/$\sigma(X_t)$** | 0.55 | 0.81 | 0.86 | 0.74 | 0.95 | 0.75 | 0.76 |
| Directional accuracy*** | 92 | 88 | 73 | 85 | 76 | 69 | 81 |

*Notes:*

 * Over the period 1971–98. Current year denotes the projection for year *t* finalised in April of year *t*, and year ahead the projection for year *t* + 1 finalised in November of year *t*. Outcomes are the data published one year after the finalisation of the projection.

 ** RMSE divided by the standard deviation of the observed outcomes.

 *** Defined as the percentage of forecasts correctly predicting the sign of the change in annual GDP growth between the initial year and the forecasted year, compared to outcomes.

*Source*: Koutsogeorgopoulou (2000).

remains a moot point, and in practice, the conventional wisdom is that there are no major differences in forecasts amongst public and private institutions, as emphasised by Loungani (2001) in the case of growth forecasts.[3]

Furthermore, forecast accuracy varies considerably across variables. Relatively less volatile variables, such as GDP or consumption, are easier to pin down than more volatile ones, such as investment. Uncertainty is particularly acute in the case of external trade, as forecast errors for individual countries tend to be correlated, and because international feedback effects stemming from unexpected developments in certain countries are hard to properly factor in.

Even so, the above forecasts are generally fairly efficient: they are not systematically biased one way or the other;[4] and usually they do adequately incorporate the information that was available when they were prepared. Hence, errors would largely be due to the arrival of new information. At the same time, these forecasts do better than naïve predictions, although their superiority *vis-à-vis* certain time-series based forecasts, such as VAR-based short-run forecasts, is not always obvious. Whether forecasting accuracy has improved over time, as forecasters' learned from their mistakes and more sophisticated techniques were developed, is unclear. Some argue that it has, but this remains controversial, especially if one takes into account that growth appears to have become less volatile over the past few decades.

---

[3] Likewise, in the US case, the track record of the CBO, the administration and the Blue Chip consensus (an average of private sector forecasters) is very similar (CBO, 2003).

[4] One notable exception are the inflation projections presented by the IMF in the *World Economic Outlook* for countries that have an IMF programme, which are downward biased. However, these projections are typically programme targets rather than unconditional forecasts (Musso and Phillips, 2002).

### 11.4.2 A typical shortcoming: misgauging turning points

A fundamental and largely shared weakness of forecasting institutions is their poor track record as regards the anticipation of turning points in activity, be they turn-arounds in growth rates or structural breaks. In addition, forecasters have a strong propensity to miss these with disconcerting unanimity.

Looking at 60 recession episodes worldwide, Loungani (2001) found that they are predicted only one-third of the time in April of the very year in which the recession occurs: in other words, recessions tend to arrive before they are forecasted![5] And when recessions are anticipated, their severity is generally underpredicted. The same holds for the closely monitored US economy, where the recognition lag is also considerable, as noted long ago by Zarnowitz (1986) and again more recently by Fintzen and Stekler (1999). That said, recessions are relatively rare events. Hence, when judging the quality of a forecaster, one should also recognise his or her ability not to predict recessions that do not happen (recall the long-standing joke that 'economists are so sharp they have predicted eight of the last five recessions'). Recourse to directional tests allows this to be taken into account, and thus to soften the critique.

Furthermore, it turns out that recoveries are better anticipated than recessions (Loungani, 2002). Since recessions have typically lasted under a year, forecasting recovery in a recession has been a good bet. In a few cases recessions did drag on, however, and forecasters' ability to predict which ones would do so has been less impressive.

## 11.5 What causes the errors?

Forecast errors can have many causes, including mismeasurement problems, model mis-specification, the forecaster's psychological inclinations, and exceptional non-economic events. But they can be grouped in three categories: statistical complications; unforeseeable shocks, decisions or reactions; and biases related to forecasters' behaviour.

### 11.5.1 'Statistical' hurdles

Economic magnitudes are measured imprecisely and some of them are rather volatile. As discussed in Chapter 2, there are often significant differences between the first national account estimates published by the statistical office and the final one. In addition, certain aspects of economic activity are poorly captured by the statistical apparatus. Furthermore, forecasters may not have full access to the relevant data: for instance, existing information on tax returns may be out of reach. Some forecasters may also fail to appreciate fully how some of the official statistics are put together. And of course, forecasters may simply overlook less easily available but nonetheless important information: for example, they may focus too

---

[5] Recessions were defined here as any year in which real GDP declined. Another conventional definition of a recession is that of two consecutive quarters of negative real GDP growth.

exclusively on the real sector without paying sufficient attention to agents' balance sheets.

At the same time, forecasters need to make choices on how to treat the incoming data, knowing that they are at best a lagged image of reality. In particular, after how many unusual observations should they decide that a trend has changed? This question was answered in a variety of ways in the case of the evolution of US productivity since the mid-1990s for example, with some analysts declaring early on that trend productivity growth had increased, while others long preferred to remain doubtful. Another difficulty pertains to the construction of long time series needed for estimation or extrapolation: forecasters have to make some difficult choices, for example on how to handle breaks, such as German unification in the early 1990s (which has implications for long-run euro area series as well). Proper treatment requires in-depth knowledge of data construction procedures and peculiarities.

### 11.5.2   'Economic' sources of error

More obvious sources of error involve shocks that forecasters cannot be expected to anticipate. Natural disasters belong to this category, as do political and social surprises (such as wars or strikes). Other, more economic, factors are also hard to foresee. In particular, monetary and fiscal policy decisions cannot be predicted with certainty. In fact, uncertainty regarding these decisions is also a problem for official forecasters, since they are not necessarily fully informed about policymakers' intentions, and more fundamentally policymakers themselves do not always know the shape or size of future measures. Also complicating the picture is the fact that globalisation implies a growing exposure to developments beyond national borders, on which forecasters in any given country know relatively less. In addition, errors may be correlated across countries, due to the existence of common shocks and the systemic importance of the larger economies: if forecasters in Europe align their assumptions for the US economy on the consensus forecast across the Atlantic, and if the latter turns out to be wrong, both sets of forecasts will be off the mark.

Another source of error has to do with the nature of economic science. Experimentation is impossible, casting doubts on any theory, and the structure and functioning of economies mutate over time. New production techniques emerge (say, information technologies), aspirations change (say, as regards demand for leisure), institutional arrangements are altered (say, concerning retirement) and regulations evolve (say, deregulation of the network sectors). In many cases, the forecasting tools need to adapt.

Lastly, the central forecast is only an approximation of what may happen, on average, when looking at the whole range of possibilities, based on a linear description of economic relationships. In the real world, non-linear reactions are observed, notably in the case of extreme events, which are rare but can have disproportionate impacts. While the forecast should contain a discussion of risks, its accuracy will usually be assessed solely based on the central scenario.

### 11.5.3  Forecasters' behaviour

Keynes understood the herd instincts of his fellow economists: 'Worldly wisdom teaches us that it is better for the reputation to fail conventionally than to succeed unconventionally', he wrote at the depth of the Great Depression. Forecasters may prefer to cluster around a common prediction rather than issue outlier forecasts, as documented in the case of the United States, Japan and the United Kingdom by Gallo *et al.* (2002), who show that an individual forecaster's predictions are strongly influenced by the consensus forecast of the previous month. This mimetic behaviour sometimes leads the consensus to converge on a forecast that later turns out to be far off the mark.

To some extent, such herd behaviour may reflect the fact that preparing a full-blown forecast is very costly, so that some in the forecast business cut corners and rely on the average view of others. Another explanation is that one forecast, in particular the authorities', plays a leading role because it is widely believed that it relies on a superior information set, including inside knowledge about forthcoming policy decisions. Granger (1996) for example argues that in the United Kingdom, forecasters tend to cluster around the Treasury's forecast.

Another behavioural reason for forecasting errors has to do with the forecaster taking into account users' reactions. A government may be reluctant to predict some developments, even if they are very likely, for fear of political embarrassment or in the belief that such a prediction would become a self-fulfilling prophecy. Forecasters may also try to smooth forecast revisions on the grounds that users would not understand or like a succession of frequent and large up and down revisions. This translates into long recognition lags when the economy changes course.

Alternatively, some forecasters may crave publicity and try to distinguish themselves from their peers. Looking at the growth forecasts of the Blue Chip Economic Indicators panel in the United States, Laster *et al.* (1999) found that the forecasters working for banks and industrial corporations (firms that might be expected to make forecast accuracy a priority) tend to stay close to the consensus, whereas independent forecasters, who stand to gain most from publicity, tend to produce outlier forecasts. Yet other forecasters indulge in 'wishful expectations': in a study of foreign exchange forecasts in Japan, Ito (1990) documented that they are biased towards scenarios that would benefit the forecaster's employer, with forecasters working for exporters being more prone to expect yen depreciation and conversely for those employed by importers.

Naïve forecasters may also become unduly influenced by developments abroad. A well-known example is that of forecasters outside the United States considering that the US cycle must be an advance indicator of their own country's economic situation, without duly taking into account the possible reasons for divergence.

A last source of error pertains to humans' natural inclination to put more weight on current or recent developments than on what happened in the more distant past, so that the latest observations often have a disproportionate influence on the forecast. For example, if the oil price suddenly surges, forecasters will either carry the new high price forward or build in a gradual return to a lower price which would be deemed consistent with the fundamentals of the oil market. Rarely will they be so bold as to predict a prompt fall.

## 11.6   Can and should accuracy be improved?

The above diagnosis suggests a number of possible improvements. Combining a variety of forecasts can also seem useful, although there are a number of pitfalls. More fundamentally, however, forecasting accuracy is only one of the criteria that should be considered when assessing the quality of a forecast.

One way to improve forecasts is to enhance the quality of the data serving as inputs. In a number of countries, there is considerable scope to do so, witness the overestimation of CPI inflation in the United States, notwithstanding the efforts made to fix the problems identified in the mid-1990s by the Boskin Commission (Lebow and Rudd, 2003), the endemic problems of Japanese deflators (Ariga and Matsui, 2003), or the deficiencies of euro-area-wide statistics, owing to insufficient harmonisation across member countries (ECB, 2001a). More broadly, the progress in economic knowledge and in applied economics benefits the quality of forecasting. Finally, the more forecasters are involved in the decision-making process, the easier it is for them to serve users' needs, communicate about the limits of their forecasts, and thereby avoid misunderstandings.

An alternative and easier approach is to combine all the published forecasts, weighing them according to their track record or simply taking a straight average. The idea is that since forecasts draw on different information sets but do not systematically outperform each other, taking all of them into account will yield extra information. To the risk averse, an added attraction is that extreme predictions are thereby avoided.

While this may sound appealing, several caveats are in order. As noted, forecasts are often clustered around similar numbers. In practice, there may thus be little diversity to profit from. Moreover, combining different forecasts amounts to mixing genres and makes it difficult to interpret the numbers. And if the underlying models and information are relatively similar after all, averaging the forecasts again will not add that much. Ideally, an optimal forecast would use the best information set and the most accomplished model, rather than a mixture of heterogeneous ingredients.

Against this background, some have tried to find ways to select the most valuable forecasts and to eliminate the rest. One criterion for a superior forecast is of course that it be unbiased. But the list of forecasts to be retained also depends on the correlation of forecast errors: the forecasts that are combined should display uncorrelated errors. What weights should be assigned to the selected forecasts? One criterion is to simply take a straight average. Another is to minimise the RMSE of the combined forecast based on past performance, meaning that forecasts with high variances would count for less and vice versa. Another method would be to regress the forecasted variable on the various forecasts and retain the forecasts that have the largest influence. Yet another way to proceed would be to put most weight on those forecasts that recently performed well. A problem with all these methods, however, is that past success is no guarantee for the future. Determining an optimal set of weights may therefore be very tricky in practice, and taking a straight average for combining forecasts has at least the advantage of simplicity.

Empirical work on the subject leads to the following conclusions, not all of them uncontroversial though:

- *A priori*, accuracy can be improved by combining a model-based forecast with time-series based forecasts.
- The gains depend on the horizon, and are in principle larger over the longer run, insofar as short-run uncertainty is dominated by unanticipated shocks that neither approach captures.
- While in any one year some forecasters will probably outdo the consensus in terms of accuracy, these top performers vary from year to year and can hardly be identified in advance.
- Conversely, a combination might have outperformed individual forecasts over some past period but could fail to do so in subsequent years.

Theoretical work on the subject is somewhat less conclusive and of limited use for practitioners, not least because it is difficult to know beforehand whether a consensus forecast will be superior. However, conducting several theoretical experiments, Hendry and Clements (2002) find that combining forecasts adds value and can even dominate the best individual device. Nevertheless, some theoretical problems are insuperable. In particular, forecasting models are living creatures, and in principle their latest version incorporates the lessons from earlier mistakes, implying that past errors are not bound to recur. And even with a decent consensus forecast, accuracy diminishes as the horizon is extended, some variables remain more difficult to forecast than others, and so forth.

Nevertheless, forecasters can benefit from comparing their predictions with those of others. Since the late 1980s, the publication *Consensus Forecasts* (described further in Section 14.1) enables them to do that in a systematic fashion. The dispersion amongst individual forecasts is also informative: a high standard deviation of forecasts, as is observed in the case of Japan, signals a more difficult forecasting terrain (Juhn and Loungani, 2002). But, for the reasons spelled out above, forecasters should not rely too much on the consensus.

Finally, two points need to be borne in mind when dealing with accuracy. First, the assumptions incorporated upstream into the forecast are key. Generally, forecasters will refrain from second-guessing what lies beyond their field of expertise, such as exceptional natural phenomena, changes in the course of macroeconomic policy compared to what had been promised, and so forth. Thus, when an earthquake occurs, as in 1995 in Kobe (Japan), or when terrorists strike, as on 11 September 2001 in the United States, the forecast is clearly invalidated. But this reflects the limitations of economic science rather than any extraordinary incompetence on the part of forecasters.

Second, while accuracy is obviously important, it is not a sufficient, nor always an indispensable, condition for a valuable forecast. Other desirable features include the overall coherence of the forecast, but also its timeliness, the relevance of the variants accompanying the central scenario and more generally the quality of the analysis offered to policymakers. Crucially, a good forecast furthers the understanding of how the economy operates – and using accurate forecasting techniques is a prerequisite – but good 'story-telling' is of uppermost importance as a basis for sound decision-making.

# 12
# Using the Forecasts

Demand for forecasts obviously arises from a need to form a view on the future.[1] A government, for example, when preparing next year's budget, has to rely on a forecast of activity in order to quantify the foreseeable tax receipts. Social partners have to refer to some forecast of inflation when negotiating wage increases. Firms contemplating investment in new factories try to anticipate demand for the corresponding output. In fact, in virtually all walks of economic life, agents regularly use forecasts as inputs into their decisions. That said, forecast accuracy is far from perfect, as discussed in Chapter 11, and preferences and constraints along with forecasts matter in framing decisions.

This chapter therefore starts with a general overview of forecasts' virtues and limitations (Section 12.1). It then turns to the role of forecasts in the conduct of economic policy, particularly fiscal and monetary policy (Section 12.2). It ends with a discussion of the role forecasts play in other fora (Section 12.3).

## 12.1 Economic forecasts' virtues and limitations

### 12.1.1 The value added by forecasts

The rationale for economic forecasts stems from four basic facts: the existence of lags; the complexity of economic links; the irreversibility of many decisions; and uncertainty.

First, forecasts help assess the full impact of decisions taken today, which materialises with a lag. For example, when a central bank cuts or raises its policy rate, it expects inflation to be affected with a lag, with the bulk of the impact coming only one to two years down the road. Even inaction is a decision and warrants evaluating what the implications are going forward. And forecasts are a way to reduce, or at least to better circumscribe the uncertainties surrounding the future.

Second, economies are complex systems, with many interactions. While common sense may grasp economic mechanisms taken individually, it is harder to take a synthetic view of the combined picture that emerges from aggregating

---

[1] In this chapter and the next, the term 'forecast' will be used throughout even when 'projection' might be more appropriate (on the difference between the two, see Chapter 1).

numerous interactions. Forecasts make sense of the flow of economic news by integrating it in a consistent view of the economic outlook.

Third, many decisions are largely irreversible. For example, the outlays enshrined in the Budget law will in principle be disbursed even if growth departs from what was foreseen in the macroeconomic forecast underpinning the Budget. Indeed, in practice, governments have only limited means to freeze some spending or to add extra spending in reaction to evolving circumstances during the execution of the Budget. Likewise for wages paid by firms, even if the environment has changed since the last wage negotiation, though part of compensation may be contingent on firms' fortunes – witness the bonus system in Japan. In a nutshell, some decisions have very persistent effects owing to institutional mechanisms such as the automatic renewal of part of public spending commitments, or the fact that bargaining generally takes place over wage increases, as opposed to wage levels.

Lastly, interactions and lags are not only complex but also uncertain. The degree of overall economic uncertainty varies over time. It increases considerably following unforeseen shocks, when it is difficult to promptly assess all the reverberations and to anticipate agents' reactions. Moreover, the most important shocks are also the ones for which the consequences are most difficult to quantify (oil shocks, German unification, Asian crisis, 11 September 2001 terrorist attacks).

Again, a forecast offers a structured framework to address these four basic needs. It does not eliminate risks but provides a way to identify and rank them to assess the likelihood of alternative scenarios and to quantify the impact of various possible courses of action. A forecast thus helps make 'robust' choices, meaning choices that do not depend on too specific a set of assumptions (see Box 12.1).

### 12.1.2   How forecasts fit into decision-making processes

Different economic agents obviously have different forecasting needs. The government requires a comprehensive picture, including both the overall trends and a fair amount of detail. In contrast, a portfolio manager, say, is more focused on the variables affecting financial markets. And in manufacturing, business executives are mostly interested in sector-specific developments.

The type of forecast needed also varies. Some users are only looking for numbers, while others are more interested in explanations. Some agents only need a central scenario, for example if they are risk-neutral (as opposed to risk-averse), while others ask for a quantified risk analysis.

Furthermore, some users are after an unconditional forecast, notably when they cannot influence events but rather seek to adapt to circumstances. Others, notably the authorities, request conditional forecasts, based on assumptions regarding the measures they can take *ex ante* to shape the environment. Moreover, depending on the desired type of forecast, one or the other forecasting method is most suitable.

Not all users are equally reliant on forecasts. In growing order of importance, forecasts can be:

- Treated as one input among many others, provided mainly as background information;

- Set apart from the other pieces of information as one important ingredient for decision-making;
- Accompanied by more or less explicit recommendations, possibly based on alternative scenarios;
- Directly linked to operational decisions through some formalised procedure.

This last possibility is sometimes encountered in firms (for instance for inventory management as a function of forecasted demand), but rarely if ever in economic policy-making. Indeed, policymakers generally do not wish to tie their hands in advance by transferring their prerogatives to the technicians who build the forecasts.

---

**Box 12.1   Decision-making under uncertainty**

The framework for analysing decisions in an uncertain environment is that of 'decision theory', which stipulates that agents are characterised by a loss function spelling out the loss associated with each decision in each future state of nature. Let $L(d,y)$ denote the loss, where $d$ stands for the decision and $y$ for the state of nature. The latter is random and may in general depend on $d$. A decision rule then has to be defined. The usual criterion is the minimisation of the expected loss: $Min_d\, E_y(L(d,y))$.*

The decision thus selected generally leads to a relatively favourable, or at least not too unfavourable, result, in most of the possible states of nature. Such a decision is called 'robust' because it delivers acceptable results under a variety of circumstances. In contrast, decisions that would only be profitable under a small number of states of nature would be rejected.

By way of illustration, consider an investment project that would be profitable if the average forecast is realised but not in a fairly large number of less favourable scenarios. If overall it appears unduly risky, the project may be abandoned. Alternatively, the project may be shelved until more information becomes available allowing a better assessment of the associated risks.

This illustrates the fact that the forecaster should not confine his attention to the central forecast, but should carefully analyse the risks. In practice, however, it may be difficult to explain this to users, as the latter often tend to focus on one scenario in which they believe (see Chapter 13).

In fact, this attitude may not be irrational. In some cases, knowing the average scenario is sufficient to take the optimal decision (as defined by the above criterion). This is true in particular when the loss function is quadratic, for instance when $L(d,y) = -Ay^2 + B(d)y$. In that very specific case, the so-called certainty equivalence principle applies: the optimal decision, defined as the one minimising the average expected losses across all the states of nature, is also the one minimising the loss for the average state of nature $E(y)$: $Min_d\, L(d,E(y))$.

In practice, however, this condition is rarely met, not least because loss functions are not necessarily quadratic. In fact, loss functions may not even be symmetric, if agents dislike a given loss more than they like a gain of the same amount. Hence, analysing the risks surrounding the central forecast is normally a key part of the forecasting exercise.

---

* Another criterion would be the minimisation of the maximum loss, if the agent is particularly risk averse.

More generally, two sets of considerations rule out a direct link between forecast and decision:

- On the one hand, forecasts generally cover only part of the relevant information. For example, a central bank's macroeconomic forecast will assist it when setting policy interest rates but is less useful to analyse systemic risk (regarding the stability of the financial system for instance), which a central bank also cares about. Hence, policymakers have to take on board information other than that contained in the forecast itself.
- On the other hand, even a forecast that would build in all relevant information would not necessarily dictate what should be decided in a deterministic way, if only because preferences may differ across policymakers. This is noted in the case of monetary policy by Budd (1998), who stresses that agreement amongst members of the Monetary Policy Committee of the Bank of England on a given collective forecast does not preclude different votes on the interest rate decision.

The role of the forecast is therefore generally to highlight the existing constraints facing policymakers, leaving it to the latter to pursue their objectives, or those they are mandated to work towards. Granted, when forecasts suggest that an objective is unrealistic and thereby embarrass policymakers, they can be either ignored or otherwise disparaged. Nonetheless, forecasters for their part are expected to present their results as clearly and informatively as possible, so as to make sure that users properly grasp all the constraints (see Chapter 13).

In the end, the influence of the forecasts remains difficult to establish, even in specific cases. The policymaker himself may not be fully aware of it. The rationale officially provided for decisions may not say much in this respect since it does not always coincide with the real reasons. In the realm of public policy, where the social or political consequences of decisions are hotly debated, the role of economic forecasts is sometimes overlooked.

### 12.1.3   Forecasts' alleged shortcomings

Two criticisms are often levied against forecasts. One is that given their limited accuracy, they at best offer no more than broad trends, which can be derived at lower cost using simple extrapolations or just common sense. More sophisticated methods only complicate matters, the argument goes, or even serve to divert attention from real problems. The other criticism is that forecasts are instruments for interventionist policies.

*Excessive sophistication*

Regarding the first criticism, how sensible is it to devote considerable resources to setting up sophisticated forecasts? An alternative approach would rely largely on informal judgements and intuition, drawing on forecasts only as strictly necessary, and would use basic extrapolation algorithms (assuming for example that growth will equal the average observed over the last $x$ years), while remaining alert to incoming anecdotal or statistical information.

Such scepticism *vis-à-vis* formalised approaches is not entirely groundless. The cost of certain forecasting tools (such as macroeconomic models) could indeed seem high in view of their limited accuracy. In addition, models are sometimes seen as black boxes, the workings of which are obscure not only for the general public but even at times for the economists who use them. Worse still, economists may be too busy running the models to pay sufficient attention to reality. Refining the forecasting tools may thus come at the expense of observing the facts, leading to a belated recognition of cyclical developments and unrealistic assumptions, in particular those used to assess the impact of economic policy measures. In that case, sophistication would not just be costly but plain harmful.

These worries highlight the risks stemming from too mechanical a use of quantitative tools. But the latter also have a number of irreplaceable virtues. Indeed, formalised methods impose welcome discipline. They make it necessary to think through the underlying assumptions, which can be explained to users and discussed with them; in contrast, mere intuition lends itself less readily to such scrutiny and dialogue. More generally, making explicit assumptions and forecasts helps structure discussions, and facilitates the convergence of views, or at least clarifies the reasons for divergence. The forecast functions like a common language enabling the parties involved to understand each other better. Moreover, the complexity of economic systems is such that the raw information coming out every day often sends mixed and confusing signals. Forecasting tools make it possible to sift through this maze of indicators and to organise that information properly, while keeping track of past mistakes and learning from them.

Lastly, the notion that models would distract one from the observation of the facts should at the very least be nuanced. Historically, statistical data and tools have been developed jointly with macroeconomic models. One of the very purposes of the models is to help interpret cyclical developments (see Chapter 6). And models sometimes help to cast doubts on preliminary data which then are indeed subsequently revised.

### An excuse for interventionism?

Turning to the second sort of criticism, economic forecasts and the use of alternative scenarios are sometimes viewed as fostering the illusion that the authorities can control economic developments, thereby encouraging interventionist attitudes. In fact, prudence is called for when basing policy recommendations on forecasts. For one thing, forecasts do not eliminate uncertainty, neither as regards future shocks nor as concerns the impact of policy measures, as illustrated in the 1970s with the disappointing results of 'stop and go' policies. There is also a risk that forecasts simply serve to rationalise politically motivated initiatives: governments may use them to engage in unduly expansionary policies, hoping to benefit in the near term in the polls, but at the expense of longer-run stability and growth. These problems, however, are to be blamed less on the forecasters than on those who misuse their work, even though they should remind forecasters that modesty is called for when they present their results.[2]

Overall, forecasts are useful when they are not used naïvely, when the assumptions are spelled out transparently and rigorously, and when the robustness of the ensuing policy recommendations is adequately tested.

## 12.2   Forecasts and macroeconomic policy

### 12.2.1   Macroeconomic stabilisation policy

*Challenges and constraints*

Macroeconomics as a field developed based on the notion that policy could steer aggregate demand. In this perspective, forecasting plays a key role in the identification of imbalances and formulation of remedial measures. Smoothing the cycle at high frequencies ('fine tuning') would, however, be over-ambitious, given the uncertainty regarding where exactly the economy is in the cycle and what the impact of policy measures would be. In addition to recognition and decision lags, the lags with which these measures affect the economy are also uncertain and vary over time: hence, policy initiatives intended as counter-cyclical might produce their effects with such a lag that they turn out to be pro-cyclical, thus aggravating rather than reducing macroeconomic volatility.

A further complication is that in some cases stabilisation might not be desirable. Demand management is an inappropriate tool when permanent supply shocks hit (say, oil price shocks). In that event, the optimal policy response may even be not to try to offset the consequences for growth and inflation.

Counter-cyclical policies are therefore difficult to get right. Consider for instance an economy at full employment facing an unanticipated shock that is expected to reduce activity (say, a sudden drop in foreign demand). Before deciding how to react, the authorities should weigh the gains associated with offsetting measures (the reduction in slack) with the costs, including the uncertainty about the impact of the measures under consideration.

In such a situation, it may well be that the optimal policy reaction is to 'under-react' by taking stimulus measures that can be expected to reduce the slack but not to eliminate it entirely, as famously pointed out by Brainard (1967). Imagine yourself driving a car: sometimes when you turn the steering wheel, it barely responds; at other times, slightly adjusting the steering wheel produces a sharp change of direction. How should you drive? Very cautiously, according to the Brainard principle. In monetary policy terms, this translates into the recommendation for a central bank to calculate the optimal interest rate as if it faced no uncertainty, and then to move the policy rate in that direction, but only part of the way (Blinder, 1998).

However, there may also be a case for 'overreaction', notably if the authorities' loss function is asymmetric, for instance if they are more eager to avoid underemployment than overheating. To pursue the analogy, suppose you are driving

---

[2] Some economists go much further and propose to conduct policy solely on the basis of rules and not to rely on forecasts. This is discussed below.

that same unpredictable car along a narrow ridge, buffeted by gusting winds. Should you respond cautiously if a blast suddenly pushes the car towards the edge? No, since you might be pushed over the edge if the car fails to respond when you turn the wheel slightly. Better to risk over-steering. In the realm of monetary policy, for instance, there may be cases where aggressive interest rate movements are called for to avoid a major economic disruption (Giannoni, 2002). In fact, this rationale has been invoked by US Federal Reserve officials during the downturn at the beginning of the 2000s to justify rapid and deep interest rate cuts: deflation was seen as a scenario carrying a low probability but high costs, calling for the Federal Reserve to act more pre-emptively and more aggressively than usual (Bernanke, 2002).

### Choosing the right instruments

Against this background, choosing the appropriate policy instrument is not straightforward. Traditional models *à la* Mundell-Fleming suggest that monetary and fiscal policy have similar effects in a closed economy but not in an open economy, due to different exchange rate implications. A canonical result is that when capital mobility is high (as is the case in most advanced economies today), fiscal policy is more effective than monetary policy under fixed exchange rates and vice versa with floating exchange rates. While such models have clear pedagogical merits, they cannot be relied on in practice, as they abstract from numerous real world complications. For one thing, the link between monetary policy and exchange rates is far more complex in reality than in those models.

Nevertheless, a dominant view nowadays is that macroeconomic management should rely principally on monetary policy. In this perspective, fiscal policy typically only offers passive support, through the operation of the 'automatic stabilisers'.[3] A strong argument supporting this view is that monetary policy is agile: short-term interest rates can be changed overnight by the central bank. In contrast, fiscal policy decisions go through long gestation periods. Some of them may even never see the light of day, if Parliament refuses to endorse the measures proposed by the government. In addition, there is the fear that fiscal policy be mobilised for counter-cyclical purposes only during downturns, fiscal tightening during upturns being much harder to carry out. Furthermore, the room for fiscal manoeuvring may be limited if public debt is already high to start with, or if there are rules capping expenditure (such as the US Budget Enforcement Act during the 1990s) or the deficit (such as the Stability and Growth Pact in Europe).[4]

---

[3] This term refers to the cushioning role played by public finances over the cycle: during a downturn, for instance, tax receipts tend to decline more than activity, which helps sustain agents' disposable income and offsets the impact of the slowdown, while some components of public spending, such as unemployment benefit outlays, rise, thus working in the same direction (see Section 9.7). These are 'automatic' stabilisers to the extent that they operate without any need for discretionary government action.

[4] That said, the scope for monetary policy action may also be limited, in particular when short-term interest rates have come down to zero, as in Japan in the first part of the 2000s (although monetary stimulus can then still be engineered through other means, such as injections of liquidity).

These arguments do not close the debate, however. While fiscal policy decisions have longer lead times, their effects could be quicker and more powerful. The impact of monetary policy action is usually slower in coming and harder to gauge. In practice, central banks change interest rates more often than governments alter the fiscal stance, but when governments do, the injection or withdrawal of stimulus often has stronger effects. Obviously, fiscal and monetary policy can be used simultaneously to support activity: witness the massive policy stimulus in the United States during the downturn in the early 2000s, in the form of swift reductions in interest rates coupled with large tax cuts.

### Rule-based approaches

One strand of the economic literature goes further in the criticism of macroeconomic stabilisation policies. It claims that almost any discretionary move on the part of the authorities is destabilising, and suggests basing policy decisions on strict compliance with some basic rules. Such rules relate to variables that are deemed to be fairly directly controlled by the authorities. One is that the budget should balance at all times, another that some monetary aggregate should grow at a constant rate, or that the exchange rate should be fixed. The idea is that instead of having the authorities assess when to adjust policies, based on forecasts of the evolution of such variables as growth and inflation, their primary goal should be to ensure the stability of some instrument(s) or intermediate objective(s).

The great advantage of rules, the argument goes, is that policy-making is then 'depoliticised', which avoids the temptations mentioned above. In addition, the proponents of rules claim that these are required for institutions to function properly, even if politicians are not opportunistic.[5] Indeed, according to this line of thinking, rules foster credibility and thereby stabilise agents' expectations. Uncertainty thus diminishes, increasing the effectiveness of economic agents' decisions. For example, abiding by a fiscal rule helps anchor long-run expectations as regards public finances, with pleasant implications for interest rates (see Section 9.7).

In its most radical rendition, this view implies that forecasts have no practical purpose: policy decisions should be taken in accordance with the rules and without speculating about the business cycle. Monitoring can be restricted to that of the instruments featuring in the rules. For example, a central bank noting that money grows less than what the rule prescribes should automatically ease policy. Likewise, the emergence of a fiscal deficit during the execution of the budget should immediately prompt corrective measures.

In practice, however, implementing rules is greatly facilitated by using forecasts (Burns, 1986). The likelihood that the budget will remain balanced at all times will be increased if the authorities do not just look at incoming fiscal data but also try

---

[5] Seminal references in this vein include Kydland and Prescott (1977) and Barro and Gordon (1983), which assumed that policymakers suffered from an inflation bias. But more recent work points out that even in the absence of such a bias, rules may help (Clarida *et al.*, 1999).

to predict receipts and outlays, taking into account both past experience and the available information on the business cycle: once the deficit has been recorded, it is too late to correct it. The same holds for monetary aggregates, which do not react immediately to interest rate changes and can be predicted to some extent using business cycle information.

More importantly still, believing that economic policy can be set simply by obeying a few simple rules is naïve. However sound the rule, no rule is fit for all circumstances. But once the door to exceptions is ajar, where do they stop? Strict adherence to the type of rules discussed above is questionable in normal times but becomes particularly undesirable when catastrophes occur (such as stock market crashes or exchange rate crises). In such cases, discretionary action on the part of the authorities is essential to restore agents' shattered confidence. In fact, rigid rules can themselves cause crises, as illustrated by the collapse of some fixed exchange rate regimes.

Lastly, the notion that abiding by some rules is a necessary condition for credibility and a good reputation is misguided. These can equally or even better be built up by following a more flexible strategy, which takes into account changes in the economic environment without losing sight of a set of well-defined ultimate objectives.

### 12.2.2 Fiscal policy

The preparation, discussion and execution of budgets require forecasts for the main public finance aggregates, which generally draw on a broader set of macroeconomic and financial forecasts. The quality of these forecasts is key for sound management of public finances, since budgetary choices need to be consistent with macroeconomic constraints. The forecasts also provide a basis to assess proposed policy options. Hence, they help structure budgets in the public sector, be it at the level of general government, local governments or social security.

The forecasts and the associated macroeconomic framework allow the influence of the business cycle on budget constraints to be factored in.[6] Various channels are important here (and were discussed in more detail in Chapter 9), including:

- Tax receipts are very dependent on the evolution of the corresponding base, which itself depends on developments in activity and its components. For example, the growth (and distribution) of incomes affects direct tax receipts, that of domestic demand matters crucially for indirect tax receipts and that of the wage bill has a direct bearing on social contributions.
- Some categories of public outlays are quite cyclical, for example unemployment benefits, which fluctuate with labour market conditions.
- Recorded or forecasted inflation affects public sector wages, some tax bases and more broadly the size of total budget appropriations.

---

[6] The budget itself also influences the economic outlook and this has to be taken into account as well. In practice, the forecasts are prepared jointly and iteratively, and in the end the scenario underpinning the budget is supposed to reflect all the important feedbacks effects stemming from the budgetary decisions.

- Financial conditions – interest rates in particular – affect the cost of public borrowing, be it for the roll-over of existing debt or for the funding of today's deficit.

Properly framing the budget bolsters the credibility of fiscal policy. A plausible macroeconomic forecast offers a sound basis for evaluating how much can be spent, given the expected evolution of revenue and the target for the fiscal balance. The forecast thus delineates the contours of what is feasible. In some cases, it will highlight that there is room for manoeuvre, in others it will force policymakers to make choices and prioritise. The macroeconomic framework is also a coordination tool. It is used to help decide on the distribution of total expenditure across sectors, and ensures that various governmental departments or bodies use sensible and consistent assumptions, for example as regards deflators. Indeed, making good use of the forecasts requires substantial resources and expertise, as well as good coordination between the involved parties.

The forecasts needed for fiscal policy purposes are not confined to the coming fiscal year, but also encompass the medium or even the long run. In many countries nowadays, fiscal policy is embedded in some kind of 'medium-term' framework. Objectives are set for a period of several years, and some of the longer-run implications of today's choices are also considered. One reason to focus more on the medium run is to avoid opportunistic measures that would benefit politicians in the short run but at a cost further out. Another is the disenchantment with fine-tuning. A third reason is that in many OECD countries ageing populations will put enormous pressures on pension and health-care spending, casting doubts on the sustainability of current policies.

### 12.2.3   Monetary policy

Economic forecasts are also a key ingredient of monetary policy. Base money or money market interest rates do influence its final objectives, but with variable lags and potency, meaning that central banks have to anticipate future developments, instead of simply reacting to incoming data. Hence the need for forecasts.

Practitioners generally consider that the bulk of the impact on prices and activity of changes in policy-controlled interest rates occurs one to two years down the road, although they can also have significant effects in the nearer term and continue to work their way through beyond the two-year horizon. Therefore, the forecast should cover at least the current year and the following one, if not a bit more.

Undertaking forecasts enables the central bank to form a view on some key questions, such as: how exchange rate movements will affect import prices and inflation, how the fiscal deficit will affect long-term interest rates, and how growth and unemployment will evolve, since this has indirect implications for inflation and may even be part and parcel of the central bank's direct mandate (witness the US Federal Reserve, which has two legislated goals, price stability and full employment).

In many countries nowadays, central banks enjoy a fair degree of independence from politicians in the conduct of monetary policy, have price stability as their primary although not necessarily as their only objective, and pilot short-term money market rates on a day-to-day basis. In this context, the role of the forecasts depends on their specific operational framework. Simply put, there are three types of regime:

- Monetarist frameworks rest on a target for the growth of a monetary aggregate (typically M2 or M3), and rely relatively less on forecasts. They were in vogue in the 1980s but have since fallen into disrepute, due to often unstable relationships between monetary aggregates and inflation.
- Eclectic frameworks, such as those of the US Federal Reserve of the ECB, rely more heavily on forecasts, but there is no clear and explicit link between forecasts and decisions.
- Inflation targeting regimes, which have become increasingly popular,[7] assign the most prominent role to forecasts. In fact, they are often referred to as 'inflation forecast targeting' regimes, since the central bank takes its interest rate decisions so as to ensure that forecasted inflation coincides with its objective.

As in the case of fiscal policy, effective use of forecasts requires considerable technical and organisational expertise, as illustrated *a contrario* by the somewhat hectic beginnings of inflation targeting in some transition countries. Usually, the central bank conditions its forecasts on an assumption regarding its own policy actions. A first forecast is often based on the simple and not always realistic assumption of unchanged interest rates or of the interest rate path expected by financial market participants.[8] An alternative forecast is then built, in which the interest rate is adjusted so that the central bank's inflation objective is met. Forecasts are thus key since they help calibrate the desirable interest rate moves: even when it seems clear which way they should move, it is important for the central bank to get the size and timing of the interest rate adjustments right. In addition, forecasts also help factor in the lagged impact of past monetary policy decisions.[9]

Three sets of factors, however, tend to limit the role of forecasts in monetary policy: namely, central banks' imperfect knowledge of transmission mechanisms, their propensity to smooth interest rates and their systemic responsibilities with respect to the stability of the financial system. First, the transmission channels of monetary policy are numerous and tend to work differently across countries and time, so that the impact of monetary policy decisions is difficult to assess, especially *ex ante*. The main channels include the direct impact of changes in the policy rate on household and enterprise spending, their impact on asset prices and thereby agents' wealth, the rationing of credit by banks and the effects on the exchange rate and thereby on imported inflation and the trade balance.

---

[7] Among OECD countries, inflation targeting has been adopted successively by New Zealand, Canada, the United Kingdom, Sweden, Australia, the Czech Republic, South Korea, Poland, Mexico, Switzerland, Norway, Iceland and Hungary.

[8] The implicit assumption in this example is that the central bank's main instrument is the short-term interest rate.

[9] For further discussion, see Amato and Laubach (2000).

Second, central banks generally try to smooth interest rates over time, implying more gradual policy moves than would be optimal in light of the forecast. This reflects the desire not to surprise market participants with unduly brisk interest rate changes and in particular to avoid frequent shifts in direction, which could hurt central bank credibility. If forecasts and decisions are well explained, however (see Chapter 13), there is less of a need to smooth interest rates.

Lastly, central banks also worry about financial system stability. When systemic risks loom large, this objective comes to dominate and the central bank may inject massive amounts of liquidity, for example to save a large bank or to safeguard the operation of the payment system (as happened following the 11 September 2001 terrorist attacks). Under such circumstances, forecasts play a limited role, if any.

## 12.3   Private sector uses

Firms, business and trade unions, as well as households (both as economic agents and as voters) also rely on forecasts for various purposes. To some extent, these agents produce their own forecasts, tailored to their specific concerns. They also rely on published forecasts, including government forecasts, which may serve as a benchmark.

### 12.3.1   Firms

Firms tend to use three types of forecasts:

- Operational forecasts, for day-to-day management purposes. In the very short run, the stock of capital is fixed, but the firm needs to plan how much it can sell and at what price, and to optimise its inventory levels. Such forecasts are frequently updated, possibly in *ad hoc* fashion, although more formalised methods can also be used, in particular to plan for seasonal and calendar day fluctuations.
- More elaborate procedures are normally used for annual budget planning purposes. Forecasts for sales, production, prices and costs are put together in a more systematic way. This allows firms to form a broader view and to take decisions, if needed, in response to changes in their environment. This type of exercise is increasingly carried out in the course of the year as well, especially in larger firms, not least to keep shareholders and other stakeholders well informed.
- Economic forecasts are also used for medium-term development plans, in particular when firms ponder investment decisions. Such forecasts typically have a macroeconomic dimension and a sectoral one. They also include financial components in order to assess investment returns (not unlike in the case of the public investment projects discussed in Box 9.1). In addition, firms usually set medium-term growth and profitability objectives which are contingent on macroeconomic developments.

In all three cases, firm managers are influenced by the prevailing mood and by the macroeconomic outlook. In good times, managers will be more inclined to take risks, while in more difficult times, they will be cautious and may reject or abandon projects that had earlier looked viable. Macroeconomic forecasts are also particularly useful for firms which operate in a variety of sectors and/or countries. They allow to ensure that the assumptions used are consistent across firms' units.

One sector is very sensitive to movements in overall economic activity, and produces vast quantities of forecasts itself: the financial sector. Indeed, lending and portfolio allocation decisions are heavily influenced by forecasts, as are insurance decisions, and their profitability depends quite directly on the accuracy of these forecasts.

### 12.3.2   Business and trade unions

Business and trade unions also rely a lot on forecasts, in particular in the context of wage negotiations, which take into account forecasts of inflation, productivity growth, the evolution of the share of wages and profits in total income, and the labour market. Trend labour productivity is an important indicator to assess real wages: if both increase at the same pace, the wage share remains constant. The prospective labour market situation is one of the determinants of employers' and employees' bargaining power.

When wage negotiations are decentralised (at the level of the firm or even of the plant), sectoral forecasts matter most, even if macroeconomic forecasts continue to play some role, notably with respect to inflation. Conversely, in countries where wage negotiations are traditionally centralised, such as in northern Europe, macroeconomic forecasts play the leading role. Branch-level negotiations lie somewhere in between. In Germany, for instance, the wage increases negotiated by the metalworkers' trade union IG Metall have long tended to guide agreements in the other sectors, and analysts therefore are inclined to compare them with macroeconomic rather than sectoral forecasts.

### 12.3.3   Households

Household decisions also rely on economic forecasts, although somewhat more implicitly than explicitly. While relative positions may vary considerably across households at any given point in time, the way each personal situation is perceived is very much coloured by how overall economic conditions appear. For example, households' expectations as regards future income depend heavily on the overall outlook for wages and employment. Changes in household confidence, which are related to their perception of the business cycle but also to non-economic factors, may influence changes in consumption, not least on durables. In the specific and important case of a real estate purchase, the decision is in principle based on a forecast of future income and spending, of the evolution of the housing market, and of nominal as well as real interest rates. Households further rely on financial forecasts when deciding how to invest their savings. And they need to have a sense of the future tax burden and of future social benefits, since that conditions how much they should work and save today.

As voters, households need to assess politicians' economic programmes and promises. Forecasts can play a prominent role in this context too. In the Netherlands, for example, the Central Planning Bureau is tasked to quantify the economic consequences of the proposals set forth by each of the main parties during the run-up to general elections. Elsewhere, this role is more typically fulfilled by economic think tanks and the press. The validity of any forecasts in the context of electioneering is of course somewhat questionable, but they can nonetheless contribute to structuring the debate. Insofar as they do help improve households' understanding of the economic issues at stake, they can promote democracy. Cutting through the technicalities and caveats to clearly explain forecasts to the general public is, however, quite a communication challenge.

# 13
# Communication Challenges

Forecasts need to be explained both to policymakers and to other clients, but also to a wider public. This raises communication issues. First, some of the technical subtleties are difficult to explain in a simple way, not least as regards the uncertainties surrounding the forecast (Section 13.1). Second, there is the question of how much transparency is desirable: to what extent should governments and central banks publish their forecasts or keep them confidential (Section 13.2)? Lastly, in the case of official forecasts, it is important to acknowledge their ambivalent status: they are both a technical and a political exercise, and this raises tensions that need to be addressed (Section 13.3).

## 13.1 Explaining the technicalities

Forecasts are prepared by technicians but destined for an audience that usually lacks familiarity with the underlying methodological issues. Users are mainly interested in some of the salient features of the forecast, and much less in the caveats. Over-simplification or even misunderstandings can thus arise, which is a source of frustration for the technicians.

### 13.1.1 Numeric ambiguities

Numbers can be misleading if improperly presented or if the recipient does not have the necessary background to interpret them correctly.

At the most basic level, economic statistics are frequently quoted with insufficient context or rigour, notably by the media. For example, a newspaper article will report that 'US GDP soared by 8.2 per cent in the third quarter of 2003'. Precluding any ambiguity would have required to specify that this referred to the increase in real GDP from the second to the third quarter, expressed at a seasonally adjusted and annualised rate, and to the preliminary – as opposed to the advance or final – official estimate. Some European readers might otherwise read the statement in the same way as they read Eurostat press releases, which express growth rates on a non-annualised (albeit seasonally adjusted) basis.[1] Similarly, a newspaper

---

[1] Other unspecified technical aspects include working-day adjustments or the absence thereof.

article saying 'consumer price inflation in September declined and stood at only 0.1 per cent, while analysts expected 0.2 per cent' leaves open the question of which measure of inflation is being described. It could be the month-on-month rate, in which case it is hard to interpret if not deseasonalised, or it could be the 12-month rate (September over September of the previous year).

Such ambiguities can be amplified in the absence of relevant benchmarks. For example, commentators often focus on relatively small differences, of a few decimal points, when comparing official and private-sector growth forecasts, overlooking the fact that in light of the average forecast error and of the degree of precision of national accounts data, these differences are rather insignificant. Such seemingly different forecasts often mask a similar assessment of the cycle, although in some cases they may indeed reflect diverging views. Likewise, when forecasts are updated, too much attention is sometimes paid to minor adjustments which do not alter the overall assessment.

A more delicate issue has to do with carry-over effects (see Section 3.1). When news reports focus on average annual growth rates, they may give a seriously distorted picture of the expected growth dynamics. Suppose that, looking ahead at next year from December of the current year, growth is about to pick up strongly following very weak or negative developments in recent quarters. Then annual average growth for the coming year will be very modest, despite the acceleration in activity. A naïve reading of the forecast would ignore the imminent recovery. Presenting quarter-on-quarter forecasts alongside the annual ones can dispel such misunderstandings, although communication can then become somewhat top-heavy.

### 13.1.2   Keep it simple but not simplistic

Many forecast users are after just a few key statistics such as GDP growth and inflation, looking for a simple story that fits with their own view of the economy. In contrast, forecasters normally try to work taking into account a wide range of variables and possibilities. Hence, there is a tension between the need to present a concise and comprehensible story to a broad audience and the need to take on board a wealth of detailed information, some of which is complex and potentially confusing. Simple stories are fine, indeed they are desirable, but only as long as they are not misleading.

The public's perception of the global outlook may differ from that of the forecaster because it can be shaped by events in some specific sectors or regions. Rural audiences for instance may tend to look at the overall outlook through the lens of the harvest and put a lot of weight on weather conditions and animal diseases, even when the fortunes of agriculture do not have a significant bearing on nationwide macroeconomic aggregates.

Another complication has to do with lags. Employment, for example, is known to react with a lag of several months to slowdowns or accelerations in output. Therefore, a recovery may be under way but households may not perceive it until a year later. Conversely, activity may have started to slump without households yet realising it. This can contribute to a feeling that forecasters misconstrue reality.

### 13.1.3   Misunderstandings

In addition, the meaning of forecasts is often misunderstood. Official forecasts are frequently seen as objectives set by politicians, which they may be in some ways, as discussed below, but not primarily. At the same time, the distinction between conditional and unconditional forecasts is rarely made explicit and is frequently lost on the audience (Don, 2001). Users tend to assume that the forecasts are unconditional and that they reflect the assumptions that the forecaster deems most plausible.

For example, in the autumn of 1998, the exchange rate assumption used in the draft Budget Law for 1999 in France was harshly criticised by the press. As usual, the assumption was that the exchange rate would remain at the level recorded during the first few months of 1998. But the dollar depreciated sharply in the weeks preceding the presentation of the draft (in connection *inter alia* with the Russian crisis in August), and commentators ridiculed the assumption as totally obsolete, forgetting about its status – which was that of a technical hypothesis rather than an attempt to second-guess financial market developments. Ironically, the dollar rebounded in 1999 and *ex post* the assumption turned out to under- rather than to overestimate the strength of the US currency.

### 13.1.4   How to describe the uncertainties

Conveying a clear understanding of the uncertainty surrounding a forecast is difficult. The public often underestimates this uncertainty, or on the contrary is too sceptical of forecasters' ability to provide any guidance.

Some telling examples drawn from the press illustrate this (Coyle, 2001). The typesetting software used by the newspaper *The Independent* does not enable journalists to write '$2\frac{1}{2}$ per cent' with a fraction, to highlight the approximation involved. It has to be a spuriously precise '2.5 per cent', or at best 'around 2.5 per cent'. But 'around' is likely to get subbed out in order to save a line of print. News editors are also allergic to words such as 'probably', 'might' and 'approximately': if it's only worth a 'might', it probably isn't a story, is their line of thinking. Another example is that journalists are encouraged to use superlatives even when none apply, for example to write about economists 'slashing' their growth forecasts, say, from 1.5 to 1.3 per cent. Obviously, this is not propitious terrain to introduce notions of probability distribution, variance and margin of error.

How can the degree of uncertainty be made clear? One traditional approach is to identify the most significant risks (for example regarding oil prices or exchange rates) and to present alternative scenarios assuming that they materialise, or to present the consequences of different policy options. In a way, this is what is done in the Netherlands for budget purposes, where official growth forecasts come in pairs, with one 'favourable' and one 'prudent' scenario. This approach is fairly intuitive and can be well understood, provided the number of variants is limited, and that they are sufficiently differentiated without being extreme. One drawback is that users may tend to favour one scenario and to abstract from the other(s). Another disadvantage is that one cannot infer where the scenarios lie in the complete distribution of possible outcomes: for some users, 'favourable' sounds like 'pie in the sky' and 'prudent' like 'doom and gloom', while for others the terms rather refer to moderately optimistic and pessimistic variants (Wallis, 2003).

A different approach is to present forecasts in the form of ranges rather than point estimates, as done for example by the UK Treasury in its budget documentation, or by the ECB in its regular forecasts. The ranges usually correspond to statistical confidence intervals: for instance, a 95 per cent interval means that the probability that the outcome would fall outside that range is 5 per cent. Such intervals widen as the horizon stretches out, reflecting higher uncertainty as to the more distant future. The intervals need not always be symmetric, as the balance of risks around the central forecast may well be skewed.

In general, such ranges can be generated in two ways:

- Directly from the statistical model used in the forecast. This is only feasible when relatively small systems of linear equations are being used for the forecast, without any *ad hoc* adjustment. In contrast, when large-scale econometric models are used, non-linearities arise and stochastic simulation methods are required to calculate the distribution of estimated outcomes.
- On the basis of past forecast errors. If the sample of past errors is assumed to be normally distributed, its mean and standard error can be readily derived (a non-zero mean denoting a systematic error, or bias). This method requires fewer assumptions and is relatively straightforward to implement.

Showing confidence intervals has tended to become more popular in recent years (see the survey by Tay and Wallis, 1999). A very complete way to describe uncertainty is the plotting of the density forecast, as done since 1996 by the Bank of England in its quarterly *Inflation Report*, both for inflation (Figure 13.1) and for growth (not shown).[2] This is called a 'fan chart' because the dispersion of the distribution increases and the intervals 'fan out' as the forecast horizon lengthens. Technically, the fan chart is based on a two-piece normal distribution, with a common mode but different standard errors, on the upside and on the downside of the forecast. This is a convenient way to represent departures from the symmetry of the normal distribution, while with suitable scaling the probability calculations can still be carried out using standard normal tables. The published density forecast pictures the subjective assessment of inflationary pressures by the members of the Bank's Monetary Policy Committee (MPC): although the prevailing level of uncertainty is initially assessed based on past forecast errors, the final calibration of the distribution embodies the Committee's collective judgement. Its degree of skewness in particular displays its view of the balance of risks on the upside and downside of the forecast.

---

[2] The Swedish central bank, the CBO in the United States and the NIESR also use this device to present some of their forecasts. Market analysts extract density forecasts of future interest rates and exchange rates from the prices of traded options and futures contracts, which help interpret market sentiment and assess policy credibility. For further analysis on how central banks present their projections, see Fracasso *et al.* (2003).

***Figure 13.1*** **Fan chart for inflation forecast***
(based on market interest rate expectations)

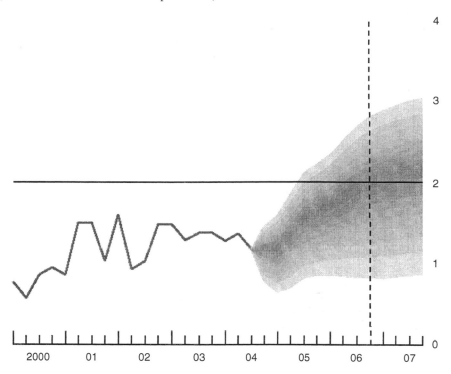

*Note:*
* Percentage increase in the consumer price index on a year earlier. The target is 2 per cent.
*Source*: Bank of England.

An alternative way to describe the uncertainty surrounding the forecast is to use a histogram. The oldest example in macroeconomics is the quarterly Survey of Professional Forecasters published by the Federal Reserve Bank of Philadelphia.[3] A sample of around 30 forecasters are each asked to provide a stylised distribution of their growth and inflation forecasts for the US economy, based on a given set of intervals. These responses are then averaged (Table 13.1).

***Table 13.1*** **Density forecast of US growth**
(mean probability attached to an *x* per cent increase in real GDP in 2005)

| Growth rate | $x < -2$ | $-2 \le x < -1$ | $-1 \le x < 0$ | $0 \le x < 1$ | $1 \le x < 2$ | $2 \le x < 3$ | $3 \le x < 4$ | $4 \le x < 5$ | $5 \le x < 6$ | $x \ge 6$ |
|---|---|---|---|---|---|---|---|---|---|---|
| Probability | 0.3 | 0.1 | 0.4 | 1.9 | 5.7 | 18.7 | 46.0 | 21.5 | 4.2 | 1.2 |

*Source*: Philadelphia Federal Reserve Bank, November 2004 Survey.

While density forecasts are attractive, there are some limitations. From a practical standpoint, it would be fastidious to produce and present them for all variables. Even

---

[3] This survey started in 1968, as the ASA-NBER survey. Its methodology is discussed by Diebold *et al.* (1999).

when this is done only for a few key indicators, it is not easy to construct intervals that are consistent across variables. More fundamentally, fan charts do not allow rigorous portrayal of how uncertainty varies as circumstances evolve (for instance, if a major shock hits, this will not translate directly into a re-estimation of the size of the risks), even if this can be done *ex post* in an *ad hoc*, heuristic, fashion. Histograms based on survey responses may be better instruments in that case. However, in neither case is there an explicit link between causes and consequences, in the form of an explanation of how economic events drive the degree of uncertainty attached to the forecasts. Hence, in contrast with the traditional scenario approach, using density forecasts in order to gauge potential policy decisions is difficult.

## 13.2   Transparency

### 13.2.1   A context conducive to transparency

As societies grow richer and more democratic, information demands increase. This trend is particularly conspicuous in financial markets, where participants act instantly on incoming information and penalise opacity (by charging risk premia). Central banks have been gaining more autonomy, as politicians disengaged from day-to-day management of monetary policy to set a framework within which technicians can be in charge. But the granting of greater independence to central banks has gone hand in hand with new obligations to be more transparent and accountable. Few central banks nowadays continue to take decisions based on undisclosed internal forecasts.

More generally, while government intervention in the economic sphere has been retreating in several ways in recent decades, the authorities' role in providing information and guiding expectations has tended to increase. Undoubtedly, the resources available to government bodies to collect and treat economic information enable them to play a key role, and indeed private-sector forecasters use government figures as a benchmark.

Last, but not least, new means of communication facilitate the dissemination of forecasts. In addition to the traditional media such as the economic and financial press, the internet provides rapid and low-cost access to a wide variety of publications, including forecasts and the attendant documentation.

### 13.2.2   The costs of transparency

Transparency, however, also entails costs. Certainly, preserving some secrecy has in the past been deemed critical to ensure the efficiency of policy decisions. A classic but not so relevant rationale is that in some circumstances the authorities may want to create and exploit a surprise. But it is difficult to cheat everybody all the time, not least because of the expansion of other sources of forecasts over the past few decades. More importantly, as the importance of credibility and reputation increases, the authorities prefer to avoid rather than to engineer surprises. From this perspective, the cost of transparency should not be exaggerated.

Two other costs of transparency can, however, be highlighted. The first is that forecast errors hurt the authorities' credibility, even when the same errors are made by private-sector economists as well, and can cast doubts on the appropriateness of the policies in place. When this highlights genuine policy deficiencies, this is welcome. But in some cases, sound policies may be abandoned prematurely as a result (Burns, 2001).

The second cost is that by publishing their forecasts, which at least implicitly reveal policy intentions, the authorities tie their hands. If an unexpected shock occurs, they face an uncomfortable trade-off: either they implement the policies embedded in their forecasts, which are no longer optimal, or they change course, at the risk of being judged inconsistent with their earlier commitments.

### 13.2.3 The benefits of transparency

But transparency also offers many benefits. In particular, the regular publication of forecasts including a cogent exposition of the underlying assumptions and of the risks surrounding the central scenario has three virtues. First, many of the above arguments in favour of confidentiality rest on the hypothesis that the audience does not understand the limitations of a forecast. This is questionable in any event, but especially so in a context where greater dissemination of economic information should improve the public's familiarity with economic issues.

Second, transparency promotes accountability. By making it clear what underpins policy decisions, it facilitates their objective assessment *ex post*, notably after the appearance of surprises. The sources of the forecast errors can more easily be traced and explained. Instead of the somewhat defensive concept of credibility referred to earlier (don't take the risk of error), a more reasonable and sophisticated one is to recognise that some developments are beyond the authorities' control, whilst others are not. Accountability would only extend to what policymakers actually exert some leverage over.

Lastly, transparency facilitates coordination and consensus-building. It reduces the uncertainty regarding the authorities' intentions and the reasons to suspect that figures are being massaged. Transparency therefore helps anchor agents' expectations, not least in the case of monetary policy, where it plays an important role in enabling the central bank to guide financial markets (see Geraats, 2002).

In short, transparency reinforces the credibility of sound policies. And credibility in turn provides policymakers with the flexibility required to react to unexpected events without undermining public trust. Besides, much of the debate on transparency also applies to the private sector, particularly to banks. *A priori*, they might seem to have an interest in keeping their forecasts confidential in order to profit in the financial markets from the associated insights. But in practice, they have to deal with their clients, who legitimately push for them to disclose their views and forecasts. Hence, many of the banks nowadays publish their forecasts and even explain how they are produced.

## 13.3 Science or politics?

### 13.3.1 Forecasts rarely come in isolation

Forecasting is both a technical and a politically charged activity, at least in the case of official forecasts. The attention given to leaks of government forecasts illustrates how sensitive these can be. Indeed, government forecasts usually are part of political documents such as the budget bill or medium-term fiscal orientations, and serve to justify or support politicians' claims and measures.

Behind a more technical facade, the same holds for central banks, whose decisions also have a political dimension, if only because of their implications for fiscal policy, but also more generally because of their influence on the outlook and on the relative position of debtors and creditors. A vivid illustration here is the speculation surrounding the decisions of the Federal Reserve in the United States during the run-up to presidential elections, when commentators fret whether the central bank will give the incumbent party a hand, or be inhibited to act for fear of appearing partisan.

A key factor is that within official organisations, forecasting activities can hardly be completely separated from policymaking advice. In fact, the very same tools used by the forecasters for projecting the outlook are also mobilised to simulate and predict the impact of policy measures. In this regard, a telling episode was the fate of a proposal floated in the early 1990s within the British Treasury to outsource forecasting to the private sector: a feasibility study rejected the proposal, noting that given the intimate relationship between forecasting and advising policymakers, outsourcing was out of the question (Smith, 1998).

### 13.3.2   Prediction or objective?

In these circumstances, official projections inevitably come to resemble policy objectives. This is certainly not fully correct insofar as the published forecasts usually do not depart significantly from what the experts who prepared them really concluded (notwithstanding the dressing-up discussed below).

At the same time, however, these forecasts are also policy objectives, to the extent that they embody the authorities' favourite scenario. Indeed, the underlying assumptions include the implementation of the announced policies. If the forecast fails to materialise, and in particular if it turns out to have been too optimistic, it may be that the policies were not put in place, or that they were less effective than hoped for.

Even when under-performance can be ascribed to exogenous events, say, to a deterioration of the international environment, the responsibility of the public authorities cannot be fully denied. Forecast errors, for instance, can be seen as a failure of the policies conducted elsewhere, or as the result of a lack of international economic policy coordination, or simply as a sign of the inability to appreciate the international constraints and risks at the time of the preparation of the forecast.

### 13.3.3   Dressing up the forecast

The wish to have the forecast reflect policymakers' objectives can lead to dressing up the numbers produced by the technicians, and to the publication of only the adjusted forecast. Some non-public institutions could also be tempted to bias their forecasts in accordance with their political preferences (think tanks) or their strategic plans (private investors). Another and perhaps more benign motive may be to smooth revisions, for instance if the new forecast involves a sharp downward revision but it is preferred to recognise this only gradually, say for credibility purposes.

In most government forecasts, any dressing-up will usually translate into a somewhat prettier outlook, where performance is a bit better than was actually forecasted. This may reflect a desire to preserve or boost confidence, in the hope that agents will then be more inclined to spend, which in turn will lead to higher growth – though how much hope policymakers can in practice pin on wished-for self-fulfilling prophecies remains a subject of debate. Or the intention may be to delay the announcement of unpleasant but necessary measures, say tax increases that could appear necessary if the technical forecasts point to a widening budget shortfall.

In other cases, dressing up the forecast can bias it downwards. Regarding government forecasts, one reason can be prudence, so as to preserve margins for fiscal policy, or political strategy, say in order to be able to show that the situation *ex post* was better than expected thanks to the policies implemented thereafter. Turning to central banks, they often prefer to err on the side of caution, by underestimating growth prospects and putting somewhat more emphasis on the risks to price stability (be they excessive inflation or deflation). For instance, they might be inclined to show a slightly lower growth forecast so as to try and influence agents' expectations, with a view to fostering wage moderation.

The extent of such normative adjustments should not be exaggerated, however. Official forecasts are generally not suffering from a systematic bias, nor do the forecasts of other institutions. Usually, the adjustments are far smaller than the uncertainty surrounding the forecast, while any significant modification would be so obvious that it might badly affect decision-makers' future credibility. Dressing up the forecast can thus often be considered as a self-serving 'rounding' of the technicians' numbers rather than blatant manipulation.

### 13.3.4  Who takes responsibility?

Forecast errors cast doubts on the credibility of the forecaster and of those who have commissioned the forecasts, especially policymakers. They tend to prompt defensive reactions, with sometimes the temptation for the technician to blame the decision-maker and vice versa. When the international environment deteriorates more than anticipated, the policymaker can fairly easily justify a change in course. At the same time, the forecaster may not be too embarrassed, as he or she typically stakes more credibility on successfully predicting domestic behaviour, based on relatively exogenous assumptions about international developments. An example would be a surge in oil prices: in most cases, the forecaster can convincingly argue that it was not foreseeable.

But often the responsibility for the forecast error is shared, and can be ascribed both to the forecaster, for an inaccurate assessment of the cycle and/or of the effect of policies, and to the decision-maker, for instance for having dressed up the technician's forecast a bit too complacently or for having altered policy unwisely. In the absence of an exogenous scapegoat, the forecaster and the policymaker may then be inclined to engage in denial and to blame each other for the error.

In fact, given that the fragility of any forecast is well known, such reactions may seem a bit futile. Technicians and decision-makers are usually well aware of this, with the former repeatedly highlighting the risks associated with the forecast and the latter trying to avoid staking their reputation on a particular forecast. Some policymakers even try to distance themselves very explicitly from the forecast, presenting it as their staff's rather than their own. This is the case at the ECB for instance, where the forecast is presented to the Governing Council but not endorsed by them (ECB, 2001b), in contrast to the practice at the Bank of England, where the forecast is prepared by the staff but then amended by the MPC, which takes responsibility for the published forecast (Bean, 2001).[4]

### 13.3.5   Forecasting ethics

In sum, the division of labour should be as follows: the technician presents the central scenario and the relevant variants based on different policy options to the policymaker, and the latter then decides. In practice, however, tensions may arise when the policymaker's objectives are not consistent with what the forecast shows as being feasible, but the policymaker still wants to use the forecast to justify his choices. The fact that any projection comes with sizeable margins of uncertainty is in fact an invitation to the policymaker to request that the technician adjusts the original forecast so that it fits the policymaker's needs. Hence, the forecast (both the central scenario and the variants) are often subject to some negotiation (Mahmoud *et al.*, 1992). The forecaster's bargaining strength depends on his or her status. If the forecaster is seen as a mere number-cruncher, the policymaker may massage the forecast without much restraint. If instead the forecaster is closely involved in policymaking, or conversely has more independence, this will be less of a risk. This risk can be even lessened further if the significance of the forecasts is transparent to all.

---

[4] To what extent the broader public perceives such subtle differences, and whether it cares, remains questionable.

# 14
# A Tour of the Forecasting Institutions

Myriad public, semi-public and private bodies are engaged in regular or occasional forecasting. Users are also very diverse. On the supply side of the market for forecasts, some producers are driven by profit motives, while others offer a public good. The demand side includes policymakers – especially finance ministers and central bank governors – but also a broader public, say, the readers of the financial press. The product itself is far from homogeneous: many forecasts cover only the short run, but some extend over longer horizons, and quality is very uneven. It is also a market with fads, as some forecasters' reputation rides high when they surf on a run of successful predictions, but can suddenly collapse when they fail to foresee some major turning point. Lastly, price-setting is rather opaque in this market, since cross-subsidisation is rife, including in the private sector.

Against this background, this chapter tours some of the main forecasting institutions, a subset of which is listed in Table 14.1. First, a general typology is laid out (Section 14.1). Then the role of forecasting in some of the main public international institutions is described (Section 14.2). Lastly, a selection of national institutions in some of the largest OECD countries are presented (Section 14.3).[1]

## 14.1 Types of forecasters

There are three main types of forecasters:

- Public international institutions: they produce forecasts that ensure some degree of global consistency, for purposes of multilateral cooperation.
- Public or semi-public national bodies: either they are directly involved in fiscal or monetary policy (economics departments of ministries of finance and central banks) or they have more of a general information role aimed at a broader public (statistical offices where they are engaged in forecasting, publicly sponsored institutes).

---

[1] The tour is clearly far from exhaustive, as it misses out on many interesting countries and publications.

*Table 14.1* **Forecasting institutions***

| International | | Website |
|---|---|---|
| IMF | *World Economic Outlook*, Article IV consultations | www.imf.org |
| OECD | *Economic Outlook*, country surveys | www.oecd.org |
| World Bank | *Global Economic Prospects* | www.worldbank.org/prospects |
| European Commission | *Economic Forecasts* | www.europa.eu.int/comm/economy_finance |
| ECB | *Monthly Bulletin* | www.ecb.int |
| ECRI | | www.businesscycle.com |
| CEPR | EuroCOIN | www.cepr.org/data/eurocoin |
| Panels | *Consensus forecasts*, … | www.consensuseconomics.com |
| Global Insight | | www.globalinsight.com |
| NIESR | *National Institute Economic Review* | www.niesr.ac.uk |
| OEF | | www.oef.com |
| **United States** | | |
| Federal Reserve Board | *Monetary Policy Report to the Congress* | www.federalreserve.gov |
| CEA | *Economic Report of the President* | www.whitehouse.gov/cea |
| OMB | Budget and economic outlooks | www.whitehouse.gov/omb/ |
| CBO | Economic and budget projections | www.cbo.gov |
| NBER | Business Cycle Dating Committee memos, … | www.nber.org |
| Conference Board | *Business Cycle Indicators* | www.conference-board.org |
| Philadelphia Fed | Survey | www.phil.frb.org/econ/spf/ |
| **Japan** | | |
| Cabinet office | Economic and Fiscal Policy Management publications | www.cao.go.jp/index-e.html |
| ESRI | | www.esri.go.jp/index-e.html |
| Bank of Japan | *Outlook for Economic Activity and Prices* | www.boj.or.jp/en |
| JCER | Short-, medium- and long-run forecasts | www.jcer.or.jp/eng |
| DIR | Research reports | www.dir.co.jp |

**United Kingdom**

| | | |
|---|---|---|
| Bank of Eng and | *Inflation Report* | www.bankofengland.co.uk |
| Treasury | *Budget* and *Pre-Budget Report* | www.hm-treasury.gov.uk |
| IFS | *Green Budget* | www.ifs.org.uk |
| CBI | *Economic Bulletin* | www.cbi.org.uk |

**Germany**

| | | |
|---|---|---|
| Ministry of Economics and Labour | *Jahreswirtschaftsbericht* | www.bmwa.bund.de |
| Deustche Bundesbank | *Monthly Report* | www.bundesbank.de/index.en.php |
| Ministry of Finance | Budget documents and forecasts | www.bundesfinanzministerium.de |
| Council of Economic Experts | *Annual Report* | www.sachverstaendigenrat-wirtschaft.de/ |
| IFO | *IFO Schnelldienst* | www.cesifo.de |
| DIW | *Economic Bulletin* | www.diw.de/english |
| IfW | *Business Cycle Forecast* | www.uni-kiel.de/ifw/homeeng.htm |
| HWWA | *Economic Trends* | www.hwwa.de/hwwa_engl.html |
| RWI | *Konjonkturbericht* | www.rwi-essen.de |
| IWH | *Economy in Change* | www.iwh.uni-halle.de |

**France**

| | | |
|---|---|---|
| Ministry of Finance | Budget documents and forecasts | www.minefi.gouv.fr/dgtpe |
| INSEE | *Note de conjoncture, …* | www.insee.fr/en/home/home_page.asp |
| Banque de France | | www.banque-france.fr |
| OFCE | *Monthly Digest* | www.ofce.sciences-po.fr/index_uk.php |
| CEPII | *Revue de l'OFCE* | www.cepii.fr/anglaisgraph/news/accueilengl.htm |

* Some institutions present their most popular forecasts in their flagship publications, others issue them in a variety of formats (not all listed here).

- Private and other entities: economics departments in large financial institutions or enterprises in other sectors, and think tanks attached to business or trade unions, or to political parties.

In practice, the delineation is not that clear-cut. Some think tanks straddle the academic and policymaking worlds even as they produce forecasts for clients in the private sector. Moreover, there is the special case of forecasting panels, which pool existing forecasts.[2]

### 14.1.1   Public international institutions

Public international institutions are themselves of three sorts: some are involved in multilateral surveillance activities; others have less of a macroeconomic focus and are less prominent as forecasters; and others still serve economic/monetary unions.

The main multilateral surveillance organisations include the Bretton Woods institutions (International Monetary Fund (IMF), and World Bank) the Organisation for Economic Co-operation and Development (OECD), and the Bank for International Settlements (BIS). The first three were created in the wake of the Second World War to promote reconstruction and strengthen economic cooperation, so as to avoid a repeat of the *débâcle* of the 1930s. Their global reach and considerable human resources account for their influence and prestige. Their forecasts are milestones in the calendar of the forecasting profession and serve as benchmarks in international fora, but also domestically, especially in the smaller member countries, where national forecasting resources are more limited. They also foster the harmonisation of economic statistics across countries.

While the IMF, the World Bank and the OECD are inter-governmental bodies, the BIS is a central banking institution, set up in 1930 in the context of the payment of German reparations following the First World War. The BIS brings together the central banks of the advanced economies and of selected emerging markets. It monitors global financial developments and hosts several committees in charge of various aspects of financial stability, some of which have regulatory powers. The BIS also monitors economic developments but is not strictly speaking involved in macroeconomic forecasting.

The second group of international organisations is more varied and also less directly implicated in the type of forecasting covered in this book. It includes the International Energy Agency (IEA), which is a semi-autonomous body of the OECD and forecasts energy sector developments, and some United Nations bodies. The latter encompass its own Department of Economic and Social Affairs, its regional economic commissions, the United Nations Development Programme (UNDP),

---

[2] Related to, yet distinct from, forecasting is futures research, which investigates how the world may change over the coming decades, and is produced by the Club of Rome (www.clubofrome.org), the Rand Pardee Center (www.rand.org/pardee), the Hudson Institute (www.hudson.org), the Institute for the Future (www.iftf.org), the Institute for Alternative Futures (www.altfutures.com), SRI International (www.sri.com) and the World Future Society (www.wfs.org), among others.

which in particular is in charge of elaborating regular Human Development Reports (see Section 2.4), the United Nations Conference on Trade and Development (UNCTAD), which deals with general issues related to trade and development and, more specifically, analyses trends in foreign direct investment, the International Labour Organisation (ILO), the World Trade Organisation (WTO) and more.

The third group, which serves economic/monetary unions, engages in multilateral surveillance but with a focus on economic policymaking in the areas where sovereignty has been pooled. Examples include the European Union (EU) or, on a more restricted basis, the franc zone in Africa.

### 14.1.2 Public domestic institutions

At the national level, the most important forecasting bodies are usually those attached directly to policymakers, namely the national government or central bank, who most need forecasts and economic advice, have sufficient resources at their disposal and are in a position to disseminate forecasts as a public good. They may also be attached to parliament or to subnational governments.

Other public institutions are more independent from the national authorities even if in some cases they have close links with or are part of the government administration, as is the case of the French statistical office (INSEE) or the Dutch Bureau for Economic Policy Analysis (previously CPB). Their forecasts are typically less normative, insofar as they can more easily depart from official policy assumptions.

There are also a host of publicly sponsored institutions that are further removed from government and play an important role in forecasting, such as the well-known six institutes in Germany or many of the think tanks in the United States and the United Kingdom. Their forecasts are even less normative. A number of them are associated with universities and cooperate in networks, such as the European Forecasting Network (which includes *inter alia* Cambridge University's Department of Applied Economics, the French CEPII, the German IWH, the Italian IGIER and the Spanish IFL). Often, they also cooperate with and receive support from international institutions, notably the European Commission.

### 14.1.3 The private sector

Though it is not their main activity, some of the large private firms engage in economic forecasting, typically of the sector-specific sort (for instance on the oil or automobile market). Private financial institutions – notably investment banks such as Goldman Sachs, Lehman Brothers, JP Morgan and Morgan Stanley – carry out more macroeconomic forecasting activities, both for internal purposes (to inform their traders and fund managers in particular) and for outside clients, not least with a view to enhancing their reputation. Part of the forecasts are sold very expensively to select customers, and part are disseminated free of charge. In many cases, the staff in charge of economic forecasts have transferred from central banks, ministries or international institutions. Even in their new capacity, they continue to be in touch with policymakers in various fora where prospects and policies are discussed.

There are also private firms whose main activity is to provide economic forecasts. A number of autonomous businesses sell data, forecasts and analyses to governments or firms, such as Global Insight (formerly DRI-WEFA). In a similar vein, rating agencies (such as Standard and Poor's or Moody's) also undertake economic forecasts. Some other firms are specialised in sectoral forecasts or *ad hoc* economic analysis, in particular for local authorities. Lastly, political parties or trade unions in some countries have outfits engaging in certain forms of forecasting.

### 14.1.4  Panels

Yet another approach is that of pooling existing forecasts in a panel. This is done by governments (the British Treasury for example), research institutes (such as the Association for Economic Planning in Japan), magazines (*The Economist* in particular), or specialised firms. The most prominent among the latter is Consensus Economics, which follows a somewhat more systematic and thorough approach than the media in assembling such information in its monthly publication *Consensus Forecasts*. While the average forecast appearing there is influential – to the point that it becomes news itself – it tends to be somewhat behind the curve, particularly around turning points, not least because some of the members of the panel may be slower than others to update their forecast. Finally, the role played by news agencies (such as Reuters) has become increasingly important. They provide on a timely basis the forecasts of key short-term economic indicators – say, monthly US industrial production. These forecasts are usually made by economists working closely with traders, and appear to be highly influential, as financial markets have shown an increased tendency to react to economic 'surprises', understood as the difference between outcomes and consensus expectations.

## 14.2  International institutions

### 14.2.1  The IMF

The IMF, headquartered in Washington, DC, counts 184 member countries (in 2005), each with a voice in decision-making that depends on their economic weight. It is the central institution of the international monetary system, tasked with preventing crises by encouraging countries to adopt sound economic policies, and with lending to members requiring temporary financing to address balance of payments problems. More specifically, the IMF's statutory purposes include promoting international economic cooperation, the balanced expansion of world trade, real incomes and employment, the stability of exchange rates and in particular the avoidance of competitive currency devaluations, and the orderly correction of countries' balance of payments problems. To this end, the IMF monitors economic and financial developments and policies, both in member countries and at the global level, and gives policy advice, including technical assistance to governments and central banks. IMF lending takes place in the context of adjustment programmes negotiated with the country in question and endorsed by the IMF Board.

Since the shift to floating exchange rates in the 1970s, and with the development of international capital markets, IMF lending has mainly been confined to troubled developing and emerging market countries. But multilateral surveillance of all member countries' policies has become increasingly important. Alongside the active promotion of statistical harmonisation and dissemination, this surveillance takes two forms:

- One is the monitoring and forecasting of national and global economic trends, in the *World Economic Outlook* (WEO), which normally comes out twice a year, in April/May and September/October. The WEO's main forecasts extend two years ahead, but are accompanied by some medium-run projections. The forecasts are more detailed for the advanced economies than for the rest, although not as much as the OECD forecasts for the former (only annual forecasts are provided). The WEO also contains extensive analysis, including the simulation of variants using the IMF's macroeconomic model, MULTIMOD.
- The second modality of surveillance are the regular country-specific examinations under the heading of the so-called Article IV consultations (in reference to the related Article of Agreement of the Fund). Originally, these reports remained confidential, on the grounds that this allowed them to be more outspoken. But since the late 1990s, many of these reports are published, in response to demands for greater transparency.[3] The reports are usually very thorough, contain useful data (sometimes hard to find in national sources) and constitute important reference material for forecasters.

Overall, IMF forecasts play an important role. That said, tensions can arise between the IMF's role as an analyst and its role as a lender. For example, IMF staff may have concerns with respect to the policies of a country involved in an IMF programme, and may doubt that programme objectives will be met. Yet, public criticism on the part of the staff, or the publication of forecasts inconsistent with the programme, might undermine the latter's credibility. The IMF also has to beware of the way it discloses market-sensitive information: drawing attention to or underlining a country's difficulties can send a disquieting signal and prompt capital outflows, whilst failing to react pre-emptively to worrying developments might mislead economic agents or even give rise to moral hazard risks.

## 14.2.2 The OECD

The forerunner of the OECD was the Organisation for European Economic Co-operation (OEEC), formed in 1948 to administer American and Canadian aid under the Marshall Plan for the reconstruction of Europe. Since it took over from the OEEC in 1961, the OECD's mandate has been to help strengthen its member country economies, expand free trade and contribute to development *lato sensu*.

---

[3] The decision to publish or not rests with the authorities of the country being examined. Not publishing can avoid the dissemination of sensitive or embarrassing information, but may well arouse suspicion and translate into higher risk premia on the country's international bond issues.

The OECD's membership is restricted to 30 of the most advanced economies (as of 2005), but many of the OECD's activities have a more global reach, especially through its Development Centre (which focuses on the emerging and developing economies of Africa, Asia and Latin America). Unlike the Bretton Woods institutions, the OECD does not lend money. It is best known for its publications and data, covering a great variety of fields, including macroeconomics, trade, agriculture, energy, education, the environment, development, and science and innovation; in this context, the OECD actively promotes statistical harmonisation and dissemination. Finally, the OECD also produces internationally agreed instruments, decisions and recommendations to promote rules of the game in areas such as taxation and corporate governance. OECD work is conducted in the context of specialised committees.

OECD economic surveillance, as at the IMF, takes place both at a global level and on a country-by-country basis. It involves business cycle monitoring, forecasting and policy analysis to identify and promote best practice, both in the macroeconomic and structural arenas. The forecasts are published twice a year, in April/May and November/December, in the OECD's *Economic Outlook*, accompanied by a global assessment plus country-specific ones. The main projections extend two years ahead, with the quarterly detail shown for the key variables. They are complemented by some medium-run projections. Alternative scenarios are often laid out, using the OECD's INTERLINK model.[4] The draft projections are discussed by the Short-Term Economic Prospects working party, where official forecasters from all member plus some non-member countries meet. They are then amended and updated, to be presented to the Economic Policy Committee, together with the OECD staff's assessment.[5] Moreover, the OECD regularly updates its quarterly GDP forecasts and every month it publishes leading economic indicators for the main economies.

The OECD also produces detailed country surveys, which are published at a one-to-two-year frequency. They resemble IMF Article IV reports but with a heavier focus on structural problems and in a more integrated and polished format. Unlike the IMF reports, which are endorsed by the Board but reflect the views of the staff, the OECD surveys are published under the authority of the so-called Economic and Development Review Committee, which has to reach a consensus on the basis of the draft produced by the staff. The OECD surveys receive extensive press coverage and constitute useful reference material.

### 14.2.3  The World Bank

The World Bank, located across the street from the IMF, now has as its main mission fighting poverty and promoting development.[6] In addition to providing

---

[4] The OECD also carries out long-run and sectoral projections.

[5] Two other working parties are attached to this committee: WP1, where high-level technicians from capitals discuss cross-country economic analysis, and WP3, where very high-level representatives of the G10 countries discuss economic policy.

[6] Besides the original International Bank for Reconstruction and Development (IBRD), the World Bank Group now includes the International Development Association (IDA), the

technical assistance in various fields, it finances specific projects or more general sectoral or even economy-wide programmes. The first type of lending involves extensive project analysis (see Section 9.4). The second type of activity requires forecasting sectoral and macroeconomic developments. The World Bank annually publishes detailed forecasts and analyses in its *Global Economic Prospects*, a key reference on developing countries and international capital flows.

While some of the World Bank's analytical work overlaps with the IMF's, it focuses more than the IMF on subjects like commodity markets and especially on the structural aspects of development. The World Bank maintains a number of valuable databases covering these areas in great detail.

### 14.2.4   European institutions

The most prominent institutions engaged in forecasting in a context of pooled sovereignty are the European Commission – which is the executive body of the European Union and one of its five constituting institutions – and the European Central Bank (ECB). Forecasts are needed at the aggregate level, to set common policies – most importantly monetary policy. They are also required on a national basis, since domestic policies have externalities which need to be taken into account. For example, a deterioration of the fiscal position of the largest euro area countries may lead to higher interest rates for all members, including those who pursue more disciplined fiscal policies.

Besides its important role in statistical harmonisation and data dissemination (through Eurostat),[7] the Commission plays a key role in multilateral policy surveillance, along three main dimensions:

- The Commission publishes aggregate and country-specific forecasts twice a year, at about the same time as the OECD, and following a similar format. Variants are also presented, using the in-house QUEST model. Furthermore, the Commission publishes short-run GDP quarterly forecasts on a regular basis.
- The Commission is also the guardian of the Stability and Growth Pact, which complements the Maastricht Treaty to set fiscal policy rules. In its original form, the Pact embodied a medium-run objective of budgets close to balance or in surplus in each of the member states. It also contained a mechanism that could lead to financial sanctions when the general government deficit durably exceeds 3 per cent of GDP (absent exceptional circumstances). Though the concrete

---

International Finance Corporation (IFC), the Multilateral Investment Guarantee Agency (MIGA) and the International Centre for Settlement of Investment Disputes (ICSID). There are also independent regional development banks, which carry out similar functions but in a specific region only, among which the Asian Development Bank (ADB), the Interamerican Development Bank (IADB), the African Development Bank (ADB) and the more recent European Bank for Reconstruction and Development (EBRD).

[7] Making sure statistics are comparable across countries has very concrete implications: one type of member state contributions to the European budget, for example, is indexed on GNP.

application of the Pact remains a matter of debate, its main consequence is that the Commission is clearly in charge of fiscal policy surveillance in the European Union. In particular, member states have each year to submit multi-year fiscal 'stability' (for euro area members) or 'convergence' (for other countries) programmes, including a description of the envisaged policy measures and scenario analysis. These plans are scrutinised by the Commission and endorsed or amended by the European Council, which is the EU's main decision-making body and represents the member states – in this case, the Council has its specific configuration devoted to economic and financial affairs (ECOFIN). To a large extent, all this information is published.

- Every year, the Commission also issues *Broad Economic Policy Guidelines*, which are subsequently adopted by the ECOFIN Council. These Guidelines pull together business cycle assessments and analysis and policy recommendations in the macroeconomic as well as in the structural areas (which are discussed, respectively, in the EU's Economic and Financial Committee and Economic Policy Committee).[8]

Monetary policy in the euro area requires euro-area-wide forecasts. These are produced twice a year by the staff of the Eurosystem (the ECB and the national central banks of the member countries), and subsequently published in the June and December issues of the ECB's *Monthly Bulletin* (ECB, 2001b). In between these forecasting rounds, ECB staff alone produces lighter quarterly updates, which remained confidential – notwithstanding the occasional leak – until 2004 but are now published. Although the ECB only sparingly discusses national policies and trends in its publications, it closely monitors country-specific developments as well.

Besides the Commission and ECB, there are also European-wide academic institutions, such as the Centre for Economic Policy Research (CEPR), a network of some 450 researchers based in universities, research institutes, central bank research departments and international organisations. It is in many ways the European equivalent of the US NBER (presented below) and indeed has set up its own Euro Area Business Cycle Dating Committee. The CEPR publishes policy-oriented macroeconomic analysis but also EuroCOIN, a coincident indicator of the euro area business cycle.

## 14.3   Forecasting bodies in selected countries

While an exhaustive presentation of the institutions producing forecasts is beyond the scope of this book, a selective tour covering the main ones in the United States, Japan, the United Kingdom, Germany and France illustrates the great variety of approaches in this area.

---

[8] When the subject matter concerns members of the euro area only, the ECOFIN and the Economic and Financial Committee gather in the Eurogroup formation, which excludes the United Kingdom, Sweden, Denmark and the ten new EU members.

## 14.3.1 United States

Like that of statistics, the production of forecasts in the United States is not dominated by a single institution. Besides government agencies, Congress, the central bank, academia and the private sector all play an important role, reflecting the system of checks and balances characterising US society.

In the executive branch, forecasting activities are mainly driven by the budgetary process. At the start of each calendar year, the US President tables a budget proposal for the coming fiscal year, which starts in October. The underlying macroeconomic forecast is prepared by the Council of Economic Advisors (CEA), which is a small department attached to the White House, and appears in the *Economic Report of the President*, published around early February.[9] It contains short- and longer-run forecasts, an analysis of economic developments and of some important policy-related issues, as well as a useful statistical compendium. The forecasts are not very detailed, however. Two departments of the administration, endowed with a much larger staff, work at a more disaggregated level: the Treasury, which monitors domestic and international developments, and the Office of Management and Budget (OMB), which twice a year publishes detailed budget forecasts extending over the next five years. In addition, several units in charge of producing statistical information (for example the Bureau of Economic Analysis, which releases national accounts estimates) also have some forecasting expertise. As a result, the production of economic forecasts is highly coordinated within the administration. However, the scope of such forecasts is rather limited compared with other countries: the international context is given short shrift (admittedly in part because the United States are not a small open economy), and the fiscal projections pertain only to the federal government level (including social security), leaving out state and local government finances.

The legislative branch of the US government is served in forecasting matters by the Congressional Budget Office (CBO), created in the mid-1970s as an agency independent from the executive branch. The CBO's mission is to provide the objective, timely and non-partisan analyses needed for economic and budget decisions as well as the information and estimates required for the legislative budget process.[10] The CBO does not make any explicit policy recommendations. It conducts a forecasting exercise similar to the OMB's, though on a longer (10-year) time frame. The CBO's budget projections and its cost estimates for the bills under consideration enable the House and Senate Budget committees to measure the effects of proposed changes in tax and spending laws – both the President's and their own.[11] The CBO often testifies before congressional committees on the economic and budget outlook as well as on specific fiscal matters.

---

[9] CEA chairmen since its creation in 1946 have included such figures as A. Burns, A. Okun, A. Greenspan, M. Feldstein, J. Stiglitz and G. Mankiw.

[10] Congress has two other support agencies in the economic field: the Congressional Research Service and the General Accounting Office. In addition, the Joint Economic Committee produces economic analyses as well as regular economic outlook assessments (*Current Economic Conditions and Outlook*).

[11] For most tax legislation, the CBO uses estimates provided by the Joint Committee on Taxation, a separate congressional analytic group that works closely with Congress's two tax-writing committees.

The Federal Reserve continuously monitors economic developments and publishes forecasts twice a year. It is independent from the executive branch and accountable to Congress. The Federal Reserve System, created in 1913, includes 12 regional federal reserve banks plus the Board, located in Washington, DC. The regional banks are to some extent specialised: the one in New York is actively involved in financial market supervision while the ones in Chicago and Philadelphia have developed widely used tools to closely follow economic fluctuations (see the latter's Survey of Professional Forecasters described in Section 13.1). The Board, with a large staff of highly qualified economists, produces (mostly internal) forecasts, statistics (such as the industrial production index and the flow of funds), and research. Two publications are of special interest:

- The so-called *Beige Book*, released eight times a year, a fortnight before the meeting of the body deciding on interest rates, the Federal Open Market Committee (FOMC). This *Summary of Commentary on Current Economic Conditions by Federal Reserve District* synthesises the anecdotal information on economic conditions collected by the regional banks.
- The *Monetary Policy Report to the Congress*, presented in February and July by the Chairman of the Board, in accordance with the 1978 Full Employment and Balanced Growth Act (or Humphrey-Hawkins Act). It contains the only published Federal Reserve forecasts. These cover a limited number of key variables, over a relatively short horizon, and in the form of ranges.

Alongside these three official pillars, there are a wealth of other institutions engaged in forecasting. The Business Cycle Dating Committee of the National Bureau of Economic Research (NBER) closely monitors the US cycle and is the arbiter of recessions. Every month, the Conference Board publishes leading, coincident, and lagging indicators of the cycle. The Survey Research Center at the University of Michigan puts out a well-known monthly index of consumer confidence. Numerous think tanks produce forecasts, be they general or more specialised. So do firms, notably financial institutions, whose economists are mostly located in New York City.

### 14.3.2 Japan

In Japan, economic forecasting is dominated by the government and the central bank. Within the government, economic analysis resources are somewhat dispersed, as is the production of economic statistics. Japan is the only large advanced economy where several official demand and supply-side estimates of activity coexist (in particular GDP data and the all-industry index), which are produced by different bodies, with at times significantly divergent results. As regards forecasting *stricto sensu*, however, responsibilities are more clearly defined. The Cabinet Office of the Prime Minister publishes the macroeconomic forecasts underpinning the budget as well as longer-run ones. The forecasts are prepared by the Economic and Social Research Institute (ESRI), which is attached to the Cabinet Office and pulls together the contributions of the relevant ministries. The ESRI also carries out surveys, compiles the national accounts, and establishes business cycle peaks and troughs, alongside policy-oriented research work. Of particular interest are the Cabinet Office's comprehensive *Annual Report on the Japanese Economy and Public Finance* and its *Monthly Economic Report*, which assesses current economic conditions.

The Bank of Japan is the other main pole of economic analysis and forecasting. It produces some of the business cycle indicators, notably in the context of its quarterly Tankan survey, and some statistics, including monetary aggregates, the balance of payments and several producer price indices. It publishes a useful *Monthly Report of Recent Economic and Financial Developments*. The Bank of Japan does not disclose its forecasts but twice a year, the ranges of all members' forecasts are published in its *Outlook for Economic Activity and Prices*.

Outside government, several institutions are playing an increasingly important role in forecasting. One is the Japan Center for Economic Research (JCER), which publishes short-, medium- and long-run forecasts. Financial institutions are also active in this area, both domestic ones such as the Daiwa Institute of Research (DIW) and foreign ones with offices in Tokyo.

### 14.3.3  United Kingdom

Her Majesty's Treasury and the Bank of England regularly release forecasts, with a remarkable emphasis on transparency.[12] To a large extent, the underlying models are public information, and the forecasts themselves are quite detailed.

Specifically, the Treasury publishes economic and budget forecasts twice a year, in March/April in the context of the report on the forthcoming Budget and then mid-way through the fiscal year or so, in the context of the *Pre-Budget Report*. Accompanying the short-run forecasts are long-run projections extending three decades out, with a focus on sustainability and inter-generational fairness.

On the monetary side, the Bank of England publishes a detailed *Inflation Report* four times a year. The forecasts therein represent a key pillar of the Bank's inflation targeting policy, in terms of both credibility and communication. By presenting the inflation and growth forecasts in the form of fan charts, it provides far more information than most other central banks on the risks surrounding the forecast (see Section 13.1). More generally, the Bank goes to great lengths to explain the minutiae of the forecast, both in the report and during the press conference held when it is released. It also assesses its forecasting record on a regular basis and in a transparent way.

Outside the public sector narrowly defined, quite a few institutions produce reputable forecasts. Banks in the City play far more of a role in this respect than in most other countries. Their forecasts are actually collated every month by the Treasury in *Forecasts for the UK Economy*. The main employers' organisation, the

---

[12] While transparency in the United Kingdom is high by international standards, there can be a gap between rhetoric and practice. In the case of fiscal policy, some observers have pointed to frequent changes in definitions, recourse to off-balance sheet operations and a lack of candour about tax policy (Heald, 2003). Others have expressed the concern that too much emphasis on transparency might at some point restrain policymakers' room for manoeuvre.

Confederation of British Industry (CBI), conducts its own surveys and publishes forecasts as well. The National Institute of Economic and Social Research (NIESR) maintains a model of the UK economy as well as a well-known international model, NiGEM. It also publishes a monthly GDP estimate. Likewise, Oxford Economic Forecasting (OEF) regularly publishes highly regarded forecasts, using a global macroeconomic model. And the Institute for Fiscal Studies (IFS) is a key actor in public finances forecasts. Against this background, the exchanges of views between the various players are particularly lively and useful.

### 14.3.4   Germany

In Germany, the government plays a relatively limited role in economic analysis and forecasting, with the central bank and a series of institutes more prominent than elsewhere, reflecting a will to restrain the influence of the central state following the Second World War and the federal structure of the country.

The Federal Ministry of Economics and Labour prepares a fairly detailed macroeconomic forecast which is presented in the Federal Government's *Annual Economic Report*, published in January. It also publishes a *Monthly Report on the Economic Situation in Germany* as well as medium-term 'trend forecasts' on a less regular basis. In collaboration with the Ministry of Economics and Labour, the Ministry of Finance produces an update of the main elements of these forecasts as the budget process unfolds, notably in spring and autumn in the context of the estimation of tax receipts, and in the summer, when the annual draft budget *Bundeshaushalt* and the medium-term fiscal outlook *Finanzplan des Bundes* are unveiled. These forecasts of the German administration, however, do not have a very high profile. One of several reasons is that, within a federal structure, much of the fiscal action takes place at the level of the *Länder* rather than at the national level. In fact, the budget process involves substantial forecasting input from outside the central government: biannually, a working group tasked with estimating the tax receipts for the ongoing and the next year meets, bringing together national and subnational administrations, the central bank and the institutes; besides this, a Financial Planning Council – including representatives of the federal, state and local governments – meets annually to prepare medium-run budget projections.

The Deutsche Bundesbank ('Buba') enjoys a good reputation, not least because in the view of the general public it contributed so importantly to Germany's economic renaissance following the Second World War. The Buba's *Monthly Report* is very authoritative, as are its statistical publications, including as regards the national accounts, where the central bank overshadows a comparatively weak Federal Statistical Office. The Buba's forecasts, however, remain confidential, although it does publish an early estimate of GDP growth for the elapsed quarter.

Economic forecasting and analysis largely takes place in a number of publicly subsidised institutes. Most famous, and long-established for some of them, are the following six: the Institut für Wirtschaftsforschung (IFO), in Munich, known for its business climate surveys; the more Keynesian-oriented Deutsche Institut für Wirtschaftsforschung (DIW) in Berlin, which produces its own national accounts data; the more neoclassical-oriented Institut für Weltwirtschaft (IfW) in Kiel; the

Hamburgische Welt-Wirtschafts-Archiv (HWWA), best known for its monitoring of commodity prices; the Rheinisch-Westfälisches Institut für Wirtschaftsforschung (RIW) in Essen, which focuses mainly on social issues; and the Institut für Wirtschaftsforschung (IWH) in Halle (former East Germany). Twice a year, and despite their different backgrounds, the six institutes jointly publish a common set of forecasts, including some detailed analysis and recommendations. Divergences in views amongst the institutes can be highlighted in the report, however. There are also many other institutes, especially those working closely with business and trade unions and the academic community.

Furthermore, Germany has a Council of Economic Experts which since 1963 brings together a handful of respected academics. They publish an annual report in November, including forecasts as well as policy advice. The tone is typically quite critical, reflecting the independence of the members of the Council.

Lastly, as elsewhere, the private sector and the large German banks (Deutsche Bank, Dresdner Bank, Commerzbank and others) also produce forecasts.

### 14.3.5 France

In contrast with Germany, forecasting in France is dominated by the central government, even if the landscape has become less polarised over the past few decades. This has reflected the traditional influence of the French administration in economic activity, which was very apparent during the post-Second World War period. Two bodies under the umbrella of the Ministry of Finance play a key role: the Direction Générale du Trésor et de la Politique Économique (DGTPE) and the Institut National de la Statistique et des Études Économiques (INSEE), the latter enjoying a fair degree of independence. The DGTPE prepares the short-run forecasts underpinning the budget bill as well as the medium-run forecasts appearing in the multi-year stability programmes submitted to the European Commission in the context of EU multilateral surveillance of fiscal policy (see above). The short-run forecasts are updated twice yearly: the spring forecasts are published in *Perspectives Économiques* and the autumn forecasts in the *Rapport Économique, Social et Financier* (attached to the budget bill). They are discussed in a meeting of the Commission Économique de la Nation, where government officials debate with outside experts. At the same time, the DGTPE plays a crucial role in the preparation of economic policy decisions, not least when evaluating the costs and benefits of alternative measures. The INSEE produces almost all economic statistics, including the national accounts, but also analyses and forecasts, unlike its German counterpart. Very short-run forecasts are published quarterly, in the *Notes de Conjoncture*. Though INSEE's forecasts do not commit the government, the INSEE and the DGTPE cooperate in many ways, including by sharing information and producing joint work.

Three other public sector institutions deserve mention. The Banque de France monitors economic developments, including via its own surveys. It regularly undertakes forecasts, at the national level and in the context of the Eurosystem exercises. However, its role in this area is less prominent than that of the Buba or the Federal Reserve. The Commissariat Général au Plan, which played an important role after the Second World War, still elaborates medium- and long-run projections, but they have long since become illustrative rather than normative. The Conseil d'Analyse Économique (CAE), created in 1997, differs from its US homonym, not least in that it has less of an operational function. It brings together some 35 economists, mostly from academia and the private sector, who discuss and publish reports on a great variety of economic topics. Attached to the CAE is a panel of experts watching the business cycle. Finally, Parliament has also developed some forecasting exercises, often in collaboration with external institutions.

Several independent think tanks also engage in economic forecasting. The Observatoire Français des Conjonctures Économiques (OFCE) regularly publishes detailed forecasts and analyses. The Centre d'Études Prospectives et d'Informations Internationales (CEPII) has less of a forecasting and more of an international focus. The private sector is represented as well, with the Centre d'Observation Économique of the Paris Chamber of Commerce and Industry, Rexecode, an institute attached to the main employer's federation, the Bureau d'Informations et de Prévisions Économiques (BIPE), which specialises in sectoral forecasts on demand, and large French and foreign financial institutions.

# Epilogue

A British Chancellor of the Exchequer who suffered more than others from the major forecasting errors made under his watch decided to take revenge on the technicians and declared in his Budget statement:

> Like long-term weather forecasts, they [economic forecasts] are better than nothing ... but their origin lies in the extrapolation from a partially known past, through an unknown present, to an unknowable future according to theories about the causal relationships between certain economic variables which are hotly disputed by academic economists and may in fact change from country to country or from decade to decade (Healy, 1990).

Granted, economic forecasting is an art almost as much as a science, and is eminently fallible. The very etymology of the word 'forecast' combines a reassuring 'fore' – 'in advance' – and a more disquieting 'cast' – as in 'cast the dice'. In fact, even the best forecasters cannot beat what Knight called uncertainty (as opposed to risk), namely, what we don't know we don't know.[1] Hence, calculated confidence intervals may not properly measure actual forecast uncertainty. Equally disturbing, the best forecasting models may be outperformed by cruder ones, or by merely pooling the forecasts lying around in the marketplace. The reason for this paradox is that any model is at best a simplified representation of reality as observed in the past, and that economies evolve, are hit by unpredictable shocks and undergo sudden shifts.

That said, the past does say a lot about the future and is ignored at one's peril. Models can cope more successfully with measurable uncertainty than a Chancellor's or anyone else's intuition can. While individual future shocks are unpredictable, they can be expected to average out to some extent. If they turn out to be broadly similar, on average, to those witnessed in the past, and if there are no overlooked structural breaks, the model-based projection should be on track.

Forecasting techniques have improved a lot in recent decades and are playing a more important role than ever. The statistical infrastructure has become far more elaborate, a wealth of empirical evidence has accumulated, econometric tools are now much more sophisticated and the role of forecasts in decision-making has been clarified. Despite their shortcomings, economic forecasts are thus used routinely in the public as well as in the private sector and beyond. Governments, central banks and other official agencies heavily rely on them, as do private firms, citizens and others, both for decisions pertaining to the near term and for ones that have longer-run implications.

Going forward, the conceptual challenge for forecasters is not to strive for impossibly complex and accurate models: on the contrary, some large-scale econometric models might benefit from radical streamlining and from the incorporation of the most robust features of the simpler models. As to the practical challenge, it remains that of adapting swiftly when mistakes are discovered, so as to avoid repeated failure, and of communicating effectively with users and broader audiences.

---

[1] Knight (1921) famously contrasted quantifiable risk (randomness with measurable probabilities, which forecasters can cope with), and uncertainty (randomness with unknowable probabilities).

# Bibliography

Akritidis L. (2002) Accuracy Assessment of National Accounts Statistics, *Economic Trends*, No. 589.

Allard-Prigent C., Audenis C., Berger K., Carnot N., Duchêne S. and Pesin F. (2002) Présentation du modèle MÉSANGE: Modèle économétrique de simulation et d'analyse générale de l'économie, Ministère de l'Économie, des Finances et de l'Industrie, Direction de la Prévision, Document de Travail No. 05/2002.

Altissimo F., Bassanetti A., Cristadoro R., Forni M., Lippi M., Hallin M., Reichlin L. and Veronese G. (2001) EuroCOIN: A Real Time Coincident Indicator of the Euro Area Business Cycle, CEPR Discussion Paper No. 3108.

Altissimo F., Siviero S. and Terlizzese D. (2002) How Deep are the Deep Parameters?, *Annales d'Économie et de Statistique*, No. 67–8.

Amato J. and Laubach T. (2000) The Role of Forecasts in Monetary Policy, *Federal Reserve Bank of Kansas City Economic Review*, Second Quarter.

Anand S. and Sen A. (1994) Human Development Index: Methodology and Measurement, UNDP Occasional Paper No. 12.

Andersson E., Bock D. and Frisén M. (2004) Detection of Turning Points in Business Cycles, *Journal of Business Cycle Measurement and Analysis*, Vol. 1, No. 1.

Ando A. and Modigliani F. (1963) The 'Life Cycle' Hypothesis of Saving: Aggregate Implications and Tests, *American Economic Review*, Vol. 53, No. 1.

Ang A., Piazzesi M. and Wei M. (2004) What Does the Yield Curve Tell Us about GDP Growth?, NBER Working Paper No. 10672.

Ariga K. and Matsui K. (2003) Mismeasurement of the CPI, NBER Working Paper No. 9436.

Artis M., Bladen-Hovell R. and Zhang W. (1995) Turning Points in the International Business Cycle: An Analysis of the OECD Leading Indicators for the G-7 Countries, *OECD Economic Studies*, No. 24.

Artis M. and Taylor M. (1995) Misalignment, Debt Accumulation and Fundamental Equilibrium Exchange Rates, *National Institute Economic Review*, No. 153.

Ashworth P. and Davis P. (2001) Some Evidence on Financial Factors in the Determination of Aggregate Business Investment for the G7 countries, NIESR Discussion Paper No. 187.

Auerbach A., Kotlikoff L. and Leibfritz W. (eds) (1999) *Generational Accounting Around the World*, Chicago: University of Chicago Press.

Azevedo J., Koopman S. and Rua A. (2003) Tracking Growth and the Business Cycle: A Stochastic Common Cycle Model for the Euro Area, Tinbergen Institute Discussion Paper No. TI 2003-069/4.

Baffigi A., Golinelli R. and Parigi G. (2004) Bridge Models to Forecast the Euro Area GDP, *International Journal of Forecasting*, Vol. 20, No. 3.

Ball L. and Mankiw G. (2002) The NAIRU in Theory and Practice, *Journal of Economic Perspectives*, Vol. 16, No. 4.

Banca d'Italia (1986) Modello trimestrale dell'economia italiana, Temi di discussione No. 80.

Bandholz H. and Funke M. (2003) In Search of Leading Indicators of Economic Activity in Germany, *Journal of Forecasting*, Vol. 22, No. 4.

Banerjee A., Marcellino M. and Masten I. (2003) Leading Indicators for Euro Area Inflation and GDP Growth, IGIER Working Paper No. 235.

Bank of England (1999) *Economic Models at the Bank of England*, London: Bank of England.

Barrell R., Dury K., Hurst I. and Pain N. (2001) Modelling the World Economy: The NIESR model NiGEM, presented at an ENEPRI workshop, Paris, July.

Barro R. and Gordon D. (1983) A Positive Theory of Monetary Policy in a Natural Rate Model, *Journal of Political Economy*, Vol. 91, No. 4.

Bartelmus P. (1999) Greening the National Accounts: Approach and Policy Use, United Nations, DESA Discussion Paper No. 3.

Batini N. and Turnbull K. (2002) A Dynamic Monetary Conditions Index for the UK, *Journal of Policy Modeling*, Vol. 24, No. 3.

Baxter M. and King R. (1999) Measuring Business Cycles: Approximate Band-Pass Filters for Economic Time Series, *Review of Economics and Statistics*, Vol. 81, No. 4.

Bean C. (2001) The Formulation of Monetary Policy at the Bank of England, *Bank of England Quarterly Bulletin*, Winter.

Belli P., Anderson J., Barnum H., Dixon J. and Tan J. (1997) *Handbook on Economic Analysis of Investment Operations*, World Bank, Operations Policy Department.

Benati L. (2001) Band-Pass Filtering, Cointegration and Business Cycle Analysis, Bank of England Working Paper No. 142.

Berg A. and Patillo C. (1999) Are Currency Crises Predictable? A Test, *IMF Staff Papers*, Vol. 46, No. 2.

Bernanke B. (2002) Deflation: Making Sure 'It' Doesn't Happen Here, Remarks before the National Economists Club, Washington, DC, 21 November.

Bernanke B., Boivin J. and Eliasz P. (2004) Measuring the Effects of Monetary Policy: A Factor-Augmented Vector Autoregressive (FAVAR) Approach, NBER Working Paper No. 10220.

Beveridge S. and Nelson C. (1981) A New Approach to Decomposition of Economic Time Series into Permanent and Transitory Components with Particular Attention to Measurement of the 'Business Cycle', *Journal of Monetary Economics*, Vol. 7, No. 2.

Beveridge S. and Oickle C. (1994) A Comparison of Box-Jenkins and Objective Methods for Determining the Order of a Non-Seasonal ARMA Model, *Journal of Forecasting*, Vol. 13, No. 5.

Biart M. and Praet P. (1986) Forecasting Aggregate Demand Components With Opinions Surveys in the Four Main EC Countries – Experience with the BUSY Model, European Commission Economic Papers, No. 46.

Blades D. and Roberts D. (2002) Measuring the Non-Observed Economy, *OECD Statistics Brief*, No. 5.

Blanchard O. (1990) Suggestions for a New Set of Fiscal Indicators, OECD Economics Department Working Paper No. 79.

Blanchard O. and Katz L. (1999) Wage Dynamics: Reconciling Theory and Evidence, *American Economic Review*, Vol. 89, No. 2.

Blanchard O. and Quah D. (1989) The Dynamic Effects of Aggregate Demand and Supply Disturbances, *American Economic Review*, Vol. 79, No. 4.

Blinder A. (1990) *Inventory Theory and Consumer Behavior*, Ann Arbor, MI: University of Michigan Press.

Blinder A. (1998) *Central Banking in Theory and Practice*, Cambridge, MA: MIT Press.

Bloem A., Dippelsman R. and Mæhle N. (2001) *Quarterly National Accounts Manual: Concepts, Data Sources and Compilation*, Washington, DC: IMF.

Bonin H. and Patxot C. (2004) Generational Accounting as a Tool to Assess Fiscal Sustainability: An Overview of the Methodology, IZA Discussion Paper No. 990.

Boone L., Girouard N. and Wanner I. (2001) Financial Market Liberalisation, Wealth and Consumption, OECD Economics Department Working Paper No. 308.

Bouthevillain C., Cour-Thimann P., Van den Dool G. *et al.* (2001) Cyclically Adjusted Budget Balances: An Alternative Approach, ECB Working Paper No. 77.

Bowman C. and Husain A. (2004) Forecasting Commodity Prices: Futures Versus Judgment, IMF Working Paper No. 04/41.

Box G. and Jenkins A. (1976) *Time Series Analysis: Forecasting and Control*, San Francisco, CA: Holden Day.

Brainard W. (1967) Uncertainty and the Effectiveness of Policy, *American Economic Review*, Vol. 57, No. 2.

Brunnermeier M. (2001) *Asset Pricing under Asymmetric Information: Bubbles, Crashes, Technical Analysis and Herding*, Oxford: Oxford University Press.

Budd A. (1998) Economic Policy, With and Without Forecasts, *Bank of England Quarterly Bulletin*, November.

Burniaux J.-M., Duval R. and Jaumotte F. (2003) Coping with Ageing: A Dynamic Approach to Quantify the Impact of Alternative Policy Options on Future Labour Supply in OECD Countries, OECD Economics Department Working Paper No. 371.

Burns T. (1986) The Interpretation and Use of Economic Predictions, *Proceedings of the Royal Society of London*, Series A, Vol. 407.

Burns T. (2001) The Costs of Forecast Errors, in D. Hendry and N. Ericsson (eds) *Understanding Economic Forecasts*, Cambridge, MA: MIT Press.

Burns A. and Mitchell W. (1946) *Measuring Business Cycles*, New York: NBER.

Byrne J. and Davis E. (2003) Disaggregate Wealth and Aggregate Consumption: An Investigation of Empirical Relationships for the G7, *Oxford Bulletin of Economics and Statistics*, Vol. 65, No. 2.

Case K., Quigley J. and Shiller R. (2003) Comparing Wealth Effects: The Stock Market versus the Housing Market, Berkeley University, Program on Housing and Urban Policy Working Paper No. W01-004.

Casey B., Oxley H., Whitehouse E., Antolin P., Duval R. and Leibfritz W. (2003) Policies for an Ageing Society: Recent Measures and Areas for Further Reform, OECD Economics Department Working Paper No. 369.

Cashin P. and McDermott J. (2002) The Long-Run Behavior of Commodity Prices: Small Trends and Big Variability, *IMF Staff Papers*, Vol. 49, No. 2.

CBO (Congressional Budget Office) (2003) *CBO's Economic Forecasting Record*, Washington, DC.

CBO (2004a) *A Summary of Alternative Methods for Estimating Potential GDP*, Washington, DC.

CBO (2004b) *The Cyclically Adjusted and Standardized Budget Measures: Updated Estimates*, Washington, DC.

Charpin F. (2002) Un indicateur de croissance à court terme de la zone euro, *Revue de l'OFCE*, No. 83.

Cheung Y.-W. and Chinn M. (2001) Currency Traders and Exchange Rate Dynamics: A Survey of the US Market, *Journal of International Money and Finance*, Vol. 20, No. 4.

Chirinko R. (1993) Business Fixed Investment Spending: Modeling Strategies, Empirical Results, and Policy Implications, *Journal of Economic Literature*, Vol. 31, No. 4.

Christiano L. and Fitzgerald T. (2003) The Band Pass Filter, *International Economic Review*, Vol. 44, No. 2.

Claessens S. and Forbes C. (eds) (2001) *International Financial Contagion*, Boston, MA: Kluwer Academic Publishers.

Clarida R., Gali J. and Gertler M. (1999) The Science of Monetary Policy: A New Keynesian Perspective, *Journal of Economic Literature*, Vol. 37, No. 4.

Claus I. and Li K. (2003) New Zealand's Production Structure: An International Comparison, New Zealand Treasury Working Paper No. 03/16.

Cohen D. and Follette G. (forthcoming) Forecasting Government Taxes and Spending in the United States : An Overview, in M. Artis, J. Perez and J. Toro (eds) *Conference Proceedings: Forecasting Fiscal Policy*, Sevilla, Spain: centrA.

Cook L. (2004) Revisions to Statistics: Their Role in Measuring Economic Progress, *Economic Trends*, No. 603.

Corsetti G., Pesenti P. and Roubini N. (1999) What Caused the Asian Currency and Financial Crisis?, *Japan and the World Economy*, Vol. 11, No. 3.

Côté D., Kuszczak J., Lam J.-P., Liu Y. and St-Amant P. (2003) A Comparison of Twelve Macroeconomic Models of the Canadian Economy, Bank of Canada Technical Report No. 94.

Cotis J.-P., Méary R. and Sobzack N. (1998) Le chômage d'équilibre: une évaluation, *Revue de l'OFCE*, Vol. 49, No. 3.

Cotis J.-P., Elmeskov J. and Mourougane A. (2005) Estimates of Potential Output: Benefits and Pitfalls from a Policy Perspective, in L. Reichlin (ed.) *The Euro Area Business Cycle: Stylized Facts and Measurement Issues*, London: CEPR.

Coyle D. (2001) Making Sense of Published Economic Forecasts, in D. Hendry and N. Ericsson (eds) *Understanding Economic Forecasts*, Cambridge, MA: MIT Press.

CPB (Central Planning Bureau) (2003) JADE: A Model for the Joint Analysis of Dynamics and Equilibrium, CPB Document No. 30, Netherlands.

Croushore D. (2004) Do Consumer Confidence Indexes Help Forecast Consumer Spending in Real Time?, University of Richmond, mimeo.

Cummins J., Hassett K. and Hubbard G. (1996) Tax Reforms and Investment: A Cross-Country Comparison, *Journal of Public Economics*, Vol. 62, No. 1–2.

Dalsgaard T. and de Serres A. (2001) Estimating Prudent Budgetary Margins, in A. Brunila, M. Buti and D. Franco (eds) *The Stability and Growth Pact: The Architecture of Fiscal Policy in EMU*, Basingstoke: Palgrave.

Dalsgaard T., André C. and Richardson P. (2001) Standard Shocks in the OECD INTERLINK Model, OECD Economics Department Working Paper No. 306.

Darby J., Ireland J., Leith C. and Wren Lewis S. (1999) COMPACT: A Rational Expectations, Intertemporal Model of the United Kingdom Economy, *Economic Modelling*, Vol. 16, No. 1.

Davidson J., Hendry D., Srba F. and Yeo S. (1978) Econometric Modelling of the Aggregate Time Series Relationship between Consumers' Expenditure and Income in the United Kingdom, *Economic Journal*, Vol. 88, No. 352.

De Masi P. (1997) IMF Estimates of Potential Output: Theory and Practice, IMF Working Paper No. 97-177.

Denis C., McMorrow K. and Röger W. (2002) Production Function Approach to Calculating Potential Growth and Output Gaps – Estimates for the EU Member States and the US, European Commission Economic Papers, No. 176.

Denton F. (1971) Adjustment of Monthly or Quarterly Series to Annual Totals: An Approach Based on Quadratic Minimisation, *Journal of the American Statistical Association*, Vol. 66, No. 333.

Detken C., Dieppe A., Henry J., Smets F. and Marin C. (2002) Determinants of the Effective Real Exchange Rate of the Synthetic Euro: Alternative Methodological Approaches, *Australian Economic Papers*, Vol. 41, No. 4.

Deutsche Bundesbank (1994) *Macro-Econometric Model of the German Economy*, Frankfurt am Main.

Devarajan S. and Robinson S. (2002) The Influence of Computable General Equilibrium Models on Policy, International Food Policy Research Institute, TMD Discussion Paper No. 98.

Diebold F., Tay A. and Wallis K. (1999) Evaluating Density Forecasts of Inflation: The Survey of Professional Forecasters, in R. Engle and H. White (eds) *Cointegration, Causality, and Forecasting: A Festschrift in Honour of Clive W.J. Granger*, Oxford: Oxford University Press.

Dixon J. and Hamilton K. (1996) Expanding the Measure of Wealth, *Finance and Development*, Vol. 33, No. 4.

Don F. (2001) Forecasting in Macroeconomics : A Practitioner's View, *De Economist*, Vol. 149, No. 2.

Doz C. and Lenglart F. (2001) Dynamic Factor Analysis: Estimation and Test with an Application to European Business Surveys, presented at a CEPR/Banca d'Italia Conference, Rome, September.

Dua P. and Banerji A. (2001) An Indicator Approach to Business and Growth Rate Cycles: The Case of India, *Indian Economic Review*, Vol. 36, No. 1.

Durlauf S. and Fafchamps M. (2004) Social Capital, NBER Working Paper No. 10485.

Dynan K. and Elmendorf D. (2001) Do Provisional Estimates of Output Miss Economic Turning Points?, Federal Reserve Board Finance and Economics Discussion Series, No. 2001-52.

ECB (European Central Bank) (2001a) Assessment of General Economic Statistics for the Euro Area, *Monthly Bulletin*, April.

ECB (2001b) *A Guide to Eurosystem Staff Macroeconomic Projection Exercises*, June.

ECB (2004) The Impact of the Number of Working Days on Euro Area GDP in 2004, *Monthly Bulletin*, June.

Edwards R. and Magee J. (2001) *Technical Analysis of Stock Trends*, 8th edn, Boca Raton, FL: St Lucie Press.

Engen E. and Hubbard R. (2004) Federal Government Debt and Interest Rates, NBER Working Paper No. 10681.

Estrella A. and Fuhrer J. (2003) Monetary Policy Shifts and the Stability of Monetary Policy Models, *Review of Economics and Statistics*, Vol. 85, No. 1.

Estrella A., Rodrigues A. and Schich S. (2003) How Stable Is the Predictive Power of the Yield Curve? Evidence from Germany and the United States, *Review of Economics and Statistics*, Vol. 85, No. 3.

European Commission (1999) Generational Accounting in Europe, *European Economy*, No. 6.

Fagan G., Henry J. and Mestre R. (2001) An Area-Wide Model (AWM) for the Euro Area, ECB Working Paper No. 42.

Faust J., Rogers J. and Wright J. (2000) News and Noise in G-7 GDP Announcements, Federal Reserve Board International Finance Discussion Papers, No. 690.

Faust J., Rogers J. and Wright J. (2003) Exchange Rate Forecasting: The Errors We've Really Made, *Journal of International Economics*, Vol. 60, No. 1.

Filardo A. (2004) The 2001 US Recession: What Did Recession Prediction Models Tell Us?, BIS Working Paper No. 148.

Findley D., Monsell B., Bell W., Otto M. and Chen B. (1998) New Capabilities and Methods of the X-12-ARIMA Seasonal Adjustment Program, *Journal of Business and Economic Statistics*, Vol. 16, No. 2.

Fintzen D. and Stekler H. (1999) Why Did Forecasters Fail to Predict the 1990 Recession?, *International Journal of Forecasting*, Vol. 15, No. 3.

Forni M., Hallin M., Lippi M. and Reichlin L. (2001) Coincident and Leading Indicators for the Euro Area, *Economic Journal*, Vol. 111, No. 471.

Fracasso A., Genberg H. and Wyplosz C. (2003) *How do Central Banks Write? An Evaluation of Inflation Reports by Inflation Targeting Central Banks*, Geneva Reports on the World Economy Special Report No. 2, CEPR.

Friedman M. (1957) *A Theory of the Consumption Function*, Princeton, NJ: Princeton University Press.

Gallo G., Granger C. and Jeon Y. (2002) Copycats and Common Swings: The Impact of the Use of Forecasts in Information Sets, *IMF Staff Papers*, Vol. 49, No. 1.

Gauthier C., Graham C. and Liu Y. (2004) Financial Condition Indexes in Canada, Bank of Canada Working Paper No. 2004-22.

Geraats P. (2002) Central Bank Transparency, *Economic Journal*, Vol. 112, No. 483.

Giannoni M. (2002) Does Model Uncertainty Justify Caution? Robust Optimal Monetary Policy in a Forward-Looking Model, *Macroeconomic Dynamics*, Vol. 6, No. 1.

Giorno C., Richardson P., Roseveare D. and van den Noord P. (1995) Estimating Potential Output, Output Gaps and Structural Budget Balances, OECD Economics Department Working Paper No. 152.

Granger C. (1996) Can We Improve the Perceived Quality of Economic Forecasts?, *Journal of Applied Econometrics*, Vol. 11, No. 5.

Grasmann P. and Keereman F. (2001) An Indicator-Based Short-Term Forecast for Quarterly GDP in the Euro Area, European Commission Economic Papers, No. 154.

Greer M. (2003) Directional Accuracy Tests of Long-Term Interest Rate Forecasts, *International Journal of Forecasting*, Vol. 19, No. 2.

Gregoir S. and Lenglart F. (2000) Measuring the Probability of a Business Cycle Turning Point by Using a Multivariate Qualitative Hidden Markov Model, *Journal of Forecasting*, Vol. 19, No. 2.

Griliches Z. (1994) Productivity, R&D and the Data Constraint, *American Economic Review*, Vol. 84, No. 1.

Hall S. (1995) Macroeconomics and a Bit More Reality, *Economic Journal*, Vol. 105, No. 431.

Hamilton J. (1989) A New Approach to the Economic Analysis of Nonstationary Time Series and the Business Cycle, *Econometrica*, Vol. 57, No. 2.

Hamilton J. (1994) *Time Series Analysis*, Princeton: Princeton University Press.

Hamilton J. (2003) What Is an Oil Shock?, *Journal of Econometrics*, Vol. 113, No. 2.

Harding D. and Pagan A. (2002) Dissecting the Cycle: A Methodological Investigation, *Journal of Monetary Economics*, Vol. 49, No. 2.

Harrison R., Nikolov K., Quinn M., Ramsay G., Scott A. and Thomas R. (2005) *The Bank of England Quarterly Model*, Bank of England.

Harvey A. (1985) Trends and Cycles in Macroeconomic Time Series, *Journal of Business and Economic Statistics*, Vol. 3, No. 3.

Harvey C. (1991) The Term Structure and World Economic Growth, *Journal of Fixed Income*, Vol. 1, No. 1.

Heald D. (2003) Fiscal Transparency: Concepts, Measurement and UK Practice, *Public Administration*, Vol. 81, No. 4.

Healy D. (1990) *The Time of my Life*, London: Penguin.

Healy T. and Côté S. (2001) *The Well-being of Nations: The Role of Human and Social Capital*, Paris: OECD.

Helbling T. and Terrones M. (2003) When Bubbles Burst, in IMF, *World Economic Outlook*, April.

Hendershott P. and White M. (2000) The Rise and Fall of Housing's Favored Investment Status, *Journal of Housing Research*, Vol. 11, No. 2.

Hendry D. and Clements H. (2002) Pooling of Forecasts, Nuffield College, University of Oxford, Economics Papers, No. 2002-W9.

Heravi S., Osborn D. and Birchenhall C. (2004) Linear versus Neural Network Forecasts for European Industrial Production Series, *International Journal of Forecasting*, Vol. 20, No. 3.

Herring R. and Wachter S. (2003) Bubbles in Real Estate Markets, in W. Hunter, G. Kaufman and M. Pomerleano (eds) *Asset Price Bubbles: The Implications for Monetary, Regulatory, and International Policies*, Cambridge MA: MIT Press.

Hertveldt B. and Lebrun I. (2003) MODTRIM II: A Quarterly Model for the Belgian Economy, Federal Planning Bureau Working Paper No. 6-2003.

HM Treasury (Her Majesty's Treasury) (2001) *Pre-Budget Report*, London, November.

HM Treasury (2002) *Trend Growth: Recent Developments and Prospects*, London, April.

Hodrick R. and Prescott E. (1980) Postwar U.S. Business Cycles: An Empirical Investigation, Discussion Paper No. 451, Carnegie Mellon University, reprinted in *Journal of Money, Credit and Banking*, Vol. 29, No. 1, 1997.

Hooper P., Johnson K. and Marquez J. (2000) *Trade Elasticities for the G7 Countries*, Princeton Studies in International Economics, No. 87.

IEA (International Energy Agency) (2004) *World Energy Outlook*, Paris.

IMF (International Monetary Fund) (2000) The Impact of Higher Oil Prices on the Global Economy, Research Department, December.

IMF (2004) GEM: A New International Macroeconomic Model, Research Department, January.

Isard P. (2000) The Role of MULTIMOD in the IMF's Policy Analysis, IMF Policy Discussion Paper No. 00/5.

Islam N. (2003) What Have We Learnt from the Convergence Debate?, *Journal of Economic Surveys*, Vol. 17, No. 3.

Ito T. (1990) Foreign Exchange Rate Expectations: Micro Survey Data, *American Economic Review*, Vol. 80, No. 3.

Jorgenson D. (1997) *Tax Policy and the Cost of Capital*, Cambridge, MA: MIT Press.

Juhn G. and Loungani P. (2002) Further Cross Country Evidence on the Accuracy of the Private Sector's Output Forecasts, *IMF Staff Papers*, Vol. 49, No. 1.

Kaashoek J. and van Dijk H. (2003) Neural Networks: An Econometric Tool, in D. Giles (ed.) *Computer-Aided Econometrics*, New York, Basel: Marcel Dekker.

Kaldor N. (1961) Capital Accumulation and Economic Growth, in F. Lutz and D. Hague (eds) *The Theory of Capital*, New York: St Martin's Press.

Keynes J.M. (1936) *General Theory of Employment, Interest and Money*, London: Macmillan.

Kim C.-J. and Nelson C. (1999) Friedman's Plucking Model of Business Fluctuations: Tests and Estimates of Permanent and Transitory Components, *Journal of Money, Credit and Banking*, Vol. 31, No. 3, Part 1.

Kim C.-J., Morley J. and Piger J. (2005) Nonlinearity and the Permanent Effects of Recessions, *Journal of Applied Econometrics*, Vol. 20, No. 2.

Klein L. (1950) *Economic Fluctuations in the United States: 1921–1941*, New York: Wiley.

Knight F. (1921) *Risk, Uncertainty and Profit*, Boston, MA: Houghton and Mifflin.

Koen V. and van den Noord P. (2005) Fiscal Gimmickry in Europe: One-off Measures and Creative Accounting, OECD Economics Department Working Paper No. 417.

Kopits G. (2001) Fiscal Rules: Useful Policy Framework or Unnecessary Ornament?, IMF Working Paper No. 01/145.

Koutsogeorgopoulou V. (2000) A Post-Mortem on Economic Outlook Projections, OECD Economics Department Working Paper No. 274.

Kranendonk H. (2003) The Cyclically Adjusted Budget Balance: Some Recommendations for Brussels, *CPB Report*, No. 2003/3.

Krugman P. (1979) A Model of Balance-of-Payments Crises, *Journal of Money, Credit and Banking*, Vol. 11, No. 3.

Krugman P. (1999) Balance Sheets, the Transfer Problem, and Financial Crises, in P. Isard, A. Razin and A. Rose (eds) *International Finance and Financial Crises – Essays in Honor of Robert P. Flood*, Kluwer Academic Publishers and IMF.

Kydland F. and Prescott E. (1977) Rules Rather than Discretion: the Inconsistency of Optimal Plans, *Journal of Political Economy*, Vol. 85, No. 3.

Lafrance R. and St-Amant P. (1999) Real Exchange Rate Indexes for the Canadian Dollar, *Bank of Canada Review*, Autumn.

Landefeld J., Moulton B. and Vojtech C. (2003) Chained-Dollar Indexes Issues, Tips on Their Use, and Upcoming Changes, *Survey of Current Business*, Vol. 83, No. 11.

Laster D., Bennett P. and Geoum I. (1999) Rational Bias in Macroeconomic Forecasts, *Quarterly Journal of Economics*, Vol. 114, No. 1.

Laubach T. (2003) New Evidence on the Interest Rate Effects of Budget Deficits and Debt, Federal Reserve Board Finance and Economics Discussion Series, No. 2003-12.

Laxton D., Isard P., Faruqee H., Prasad E. and Turtelboom B. (1998) *MULTIMOD Mark III: The Core Dynamic and Steady-State Models*, IMF Occasional Paper No. 164.

Layard R., Nickell S. and Jackman R. (1991) *Unemployment: Macroeconomic Performance and the Labour Market*, Oxford: Oxford University Press.

Lebow D. and Rudd J. (2003) Measurement Error in the Consumer Price Index: Where Do We Stand?, *Journal of Economic Literature*, Vol. 41, No. 1.

Leontief W. (1941) *The Structure of the American Economy, 1919–1929*, Cambridge, MA: Harvard University Press.

Lequiller F. (2001) The New Economy and the Measurement of GDP Growth, INSEE Working Paper No. G2001-01.

L'Horty Y. and Rault C. (2003) Why is French Equilibrium Unemployment so High? An Estimation of the WS-PS Model, *Journal of Applied Economics*, Vol. 6, No. 1.

Lin J.-L. and Liu T.-S. (2002) Modeling Lunar Calendar Holiday Effects in Taiwan, US Bureau of Census, mimeo.

Lindh T. and Malmberg B. (2002) Demography and Housing Demand – What Can we Learn from Residential Construction Data?, mimeo, May.

Loungani P. (2001) How Accurate are Private Sector Forecasts? Cross-Country Evidence from Consensus Forecasts of Output Growth, *International Journal of Forecasting*, Vol. 17, No. 3.

Loungani P. (2002) 'There Will Be Growth in the Spring': How Credible are Forecasts of Recovery?, *World Economics*, Vol. 3, No. 1.

Lucas R. (1976) Econometric Policy Evaluation: a Critique, *Carnegie-Rochester Conference Series on Public Policy*, Vol. 1.

Ludwig A. and Sløk T. (2004) The Relationship between Stock Prices, House Prices and Consumption in OECD Countries, *Topics in Macroeconomics*, Vol. 1, No. 1.

Maddison A. (2001) *The World Economy : A Millennium Perspective*, Paris: OECD Development Centre.

Maeso-Fernandez F., Osbat C. and Schnatz B. (2002) Determinants of the Euro Real Effective Exchange Rate: A BEER/PEER Approach, *Australian Economic Papers*, Vol. 41, No. 4.

Mahmoud E., DeRoeck R., Brown R. and Rice G. (1992) Bridging the Gap between Theory and Practice in Forecasting, *International Journal of Forecasting*, Vol. 8, No. 2.

Malinvaud E. (1983) *Essais sur la théorie du chômage*, Paris: Calmann-Lévy.

Mankiw N., Romer D. and Weil D. (1992) A Contribution to the Empirics of Economic Growth, *Quarterly Journal of Economics*, No. 107, No. 2.

Marcellino M. (forthcoming) Leading Indicators: What Have We Learned? in G. Elliot, C. Granger and A. Timmermann (eds) *Handbook of Economic Forecasting*, North Holland: Elsevier.

McCarthy J. and Peach R. (2002) Monetary Policy Transmission to Residential Investment, Federal Reserve Bank of New York, *Economic Policy Review*, Vol. 8, No. 1.

McKibbin W. and Sachs J. (1989) The McKibbin-Sachs Global Model: Theory and Specification, NBER Working Paper No. 3100.

McMorrow K. and Röger W. (2001) Potential Output: Measurement Methods, 'New' Economy Influences and Scenarios for 2001–2010 – A Comparison of the EU15 and the US, European Commission Economic Papers, No. 150.

McMorrow K. and Röger W. (2004) *The Economic and Financial Market Consequences of Global Ageing*, New York: Springer-Verlag.

Meese R. and Rogoff K. (1983) Empirical Exchange Rate Models of the Seventies: Do They Fit out of Sample?, *Journal of International Economics*, Vol. 14, No. 1.

Miles D. (2003) *The UK Mortgage Market: Taking a Longer-Term View*, Interim Report, London.

Monsell B., Aston J. and Koopman S. (2003) Toward X-13? US Census Bureau, mimeo.

Morley J., Nelson C. and Zivot E. (2003) Why Are the Beveridge-Nelson and Unobserved-Components Decompositions of GDP so Different?, *Review of Economics and Statistics*, Vol. 135, No. 2.

Murata K. and Saitou T. (2004) The CAO Short-Run Macroeconometric Model of Japanese Economy (2004 version): Basic Structure, Multipliers, and Economic Policy Analyses, ESRI Discussion Paper No. 122.

Musso A. and Phillips S. (2002) Comparing Projections and Outcomes of IMF-Supported Programs, *IMF Staff Papers*, Vol. 49, No. 1.

Nardo M. (2003) The Quantification of Qualitative Survey Data: A Critical Assessment, *Journal of Economic Surveys*, Vol. 17, No. 5.

Neftçi S. (1982) Optimal Prediction of Cyclical Downturns, *Journal of Economic Dynamics and Control*, Vol. 4, No. 4.

Neftçi S. (1984) Are Economic Time Series Asymmetric over the Business Cycle? *Journal of Political Economy*, Vol. 92, No. 2.

Nilsson C. (2002) Rixmod – The Riksbank's Macroeconomic Model for Monetary Policy Analysis, *Economic Review*, No. 2.

Nilsson R. (1987) OECD Leading Indicators, *OECD Economic Studies*, No. 9.

Obstfeld M. (1994) The Logic of Currency Crises, NBER Working Paper No. 4640.

OECD (Organisation for Economic Co-operation and Development) (2002) *Measuring the Non-Observed Economy: A Handbook*, Paris.

OEF (Oxford Economic Forecasting) (2000) The Oxford World Macroeconomic Model: An Overview, mimeo, Oxford.

Oliveira Martins J. and Scarpetta S. (2002) Estimation of the Cyclical Behaviour of Mark-Ups: A Technical Note, *OECD Economic Studies*, No. 34.

OMB (Office of Management and Budget) (2004) *Analytical Perspectives, Budget of the United States Government, Fiscal Year 2005*, Washington, DC.

Osborn D., Sensier M. and van Dijk D. (2005) Predicting Growth Regimes for European Countries, in L. Reichlin (ed.), *The Euro Area Business Cycle: Stylized Facts and Measurement Issues*, London: CEPR.

Palumbo M., Rudd J. and Whelan K. (2002) On the Relationships between Real Consumption, Income and Wealth, Federal Reserve Board, Finance and Economics Discussion Series, No. 2002-38.

Phillips A. (1958) The Relationship between Unemployment and the Rate of Change of Money Wage Rates in the United Kingdom, 1861–1957, *Economica*, Vol. 25, No. 100.

Pichette L. and Tremblay D. (2004) Are Wealth Effects Important for Canada?, *Bank of Canada Review*, Spring.

Pons J. (2000) The Accuracy of IMF and OECD Forecasts for G7 Countries, *Journal of Forecasting*, Vol. 19, No. 1.

Poterba J. (2000) Stock Market Wealth and Consumption, *Journal of Economic Perspectives*, Vol. 14, No. 2.

Powell A. and Murphy C. (1997) *Inside a Modern Macroeconometric Model – A Guide to the Murphy Model*, 2nd edn, Berlin: Springer.

Qi M. (2001) Predicting US Recessions With Leading Indicators and Neural Network Models, *International Journal of Forecasting*, Vol. 17, No. 3.

Rae D. and Turner D. (2001) A Small Global Forecasting Model, OECD Economics Department Working Paper No. 286.

Ramsey F. (1928) A Mathematical Theory of Saving, *Economic Journal*, Vol. 38, No. 152.

Razzak W. (2001) Business Cycle Asymmetries: International Evidence, *Review of Economic Dynamics*, Vol. 4, No. 1.

Reserve Bank of New Zealand (2003) An Introduction to the Forecasting and Policy System at the Reserve Bank of New Zealand, mimeo.

Reifschneider D., Tetlow R. and Williams J. (1999) Aggregate Disturbances, Monetary Policy, and the Macroeconomy: The FRB/US Perspective, *Federal Reserve Bulletin*, January.

Richardson P., Visco I. and Giorno C. (1999) Predicting the Evolution and Effects of the Asia Crisis from the OECD Perspective, *Economic Notes*, Vol. 28, No. 3.

Roeger W. and in't Veld J. (1997) QUEST II – A Multi-Country Business Cycle and Growth Model, *European Economy*, Economic Papers, No. 123.

Romer D. (2001) *Advanced Macroeconomics*, 2nd edn, New York: McGraw-Hill.

Sakellaris P. and Vijselaar F. (2004) Capital Quality Improvement and the Sources of Growth in the Euro Area, ECB Working Paper No. 368.

Santero T. and Westerlund N. (1996) Confidence Indicators and their Relationship to Changes in Economic Activity, OECD Economics Department Working Paper No. 170.

Sauvy A. (1984) *Histoire économique de la France entre les deux guerres*, Paris: Economica.

Schnatz B., Vijselaar F. and Osbat C. (2004) Productivity and the Euro–Dollar Exchange Rate, *Weltwirtschaftliches Archiv*, Vol. 140, No. 1.

Sédillot F. and Pain N. (2003) Indicator Models of Real GDP Growth in Selected OECD Countries, OECD Economics Department Working Paper No. 364.

Sensier M., Artis M., Osborn D. and Birchenhall C. (2004) Domestic and International Influences on Business Cycle Regimes in Europe, *International Journal of Forecasting*, Vol. 20, No. 2.

Simpson P., Osborn D. and Sensier M. (2001) Modelling Business Cycle Movements in the UK Economy, *Economica*, Vol. 68, No. 270.

Sims C. (1980) Macroeconomics and Reality, *Econometrica*, Vol. 48, No. 1.

Sims C. (1992) Interpreting the Macroeconomic Time Series Facts: The Effects of Monetary Policy, *European Economic Review*, Vol. 36, No. 5.

Smith R. (1998) Emergent Policy-Making with Macroeconometric Models, *Economic Modelling*, Vol. 15, No. 3.

Solow R. (1956) A Contribution to the Theory of Economic Growth, *Quarterly Journal of Economics*, Vol. 70, No. 1.

Stalder P. (2001) Un modèle macroéconométrique pour la Suisse, Banque Nationale Suisse, *Bulletin Trimestriel*, No. 2.

Stein J. (1994) The Natural Exchange Rate of the US Dollar and Determinants of Capital Flows, in J. Williamson (ed.) *Estimating Equilibrium Exchange Rates*, Washington, DC: Institute for International Economics.

Stock J. and Watson M. (1989) New Indexes of Coincident and Leading Economic Indicators, in O. Blanchard and S. Fischer (eds) *NBER Macroeconomics Annual*, Cambridge, MA: MIT Press.

Stock J. and Watson M. (1999) A Comparison of Linear and Non-Linear Univariate Models for Forecasting Macroeconomic Time Series, in R. Engle and H. White (eds) *Cointegration, Causality and Forecasting: A Festschrift in Honor of Clive W.J. Granger*, Oxford: Oxford University Press.

Stock J. and Watson M. (2002) Macroeconomic Forecasting Using Diffusion Indices, *Journal of Business Economics and Statistics*, Vol. 20, No. 2.

Stone R. (1986) Nobel Memorial Lecture 1984: The Accounts of Society, *Journal of Applied Econometrics*, Vol. 1, No. 1.

Svensson L., Houg K., Solheim H. and Steigum E. (2002) An Independent Review of Monetary Policy and Institutions in Norway, Centre for Monetary Economics.

Tay A. and Wallis K. (1999) Density Forecasting: A Survey, *Journal of Forecasting*, Vol. 19, No. 4.

Taylor J. (1993) Discretion versus Policy Rules in Practice, *Carnegie-Rochester Conference Series on Public Policy*, Vol. 39.

Temple J. (1998) Robustness Tests of the Augmented Solow Model, *Journal of Applied Econometrics*, Vol. 13, No. 4.

Thomakos D. and Guerard J. (2004) Naïve, ARIMA, Nonparametric, Transfer Function and VAR Models: A Comparison of Forecasting Performance, *International Journal of Forecasting*, Vol. 20, No. 1.

Tinbergen J. (1939) *Statistical Testing of Business Cycle Theories*, Geneva: League of Nations.

Triplett J. (2001) Hedonic Indexes and Statistical Agencies, Revisited, *Journal of Economic and Social Measurement*, Vol. 27, No. 3/4.

Turner C., Boone L., Giorno C., Meacci M., Richardson P. and Rae D. (2001) Estimating the Structural Rate of Unemployment for the OECD Countries, *OECD Economic Studies*, No. 33.

Vaccara B. and Zarnowitz V. (1978) Forecasting with the Index of Leading Indicators, NBER Working Paper No. 244.

van den Noord, P. (2002) The Size and Role of Automatic Stabilisers in the 1990s and Beyond, in M. Buti, J. von Hagen and C. Martinez-Mongay (eds) *The Behaviour of Fiscal Authorities – Stabilisation, Growth and Institutions*, Basingstoke: Palgrave.

Van Dijk D., Teräsvirta T. and Franses P. (2002) Smooth Transition Autoregressive Models – A Survey of Recent Developments, *Econometric Reviews*, Vol. 21, No. 1.

Wallis K. (2003) Forecast Uncertainty, its Representation and Evaluation, *Boletin Inflacion y Analisis Macroeconomico*, No. 100.

Wallis K. (2004) Comparing Empirical Models of the Euro Economy, *Economic Modelling*, Vol. 21, No. 5.

Watson M. (1986) Univariate Detrending Methods with Stochastic Trends, *Journal of Monetary Economics*, Vol. 18, No. 1.

Whitley J. (1994) *A Course in Macroeconomic Modelling and Forecasting*, London: Harvester Wheatsheaf.

Williamson C. (2002) The Global Purchasing Managers' Index, *World Economics*, Vol. 3, No. 3.

Williamson J. (1983, revised 1985) *The Exchange Rate System*, Washington, DC: Institute of International Economics.

Wilson D. and Purushothaman R. (2003) Dreaming with BRICs: The Path to 2050, Goldman Sachs Global Economic Paper No. 99.

Wilson K. (2005) The Architecture of the System of National Accounts: A Three-way Country Comparison, Canada, Australia and United Kingdom, NBER Working Paper No. 11106.

World Bank (2000) *World Development Report 2000/2001: Attacking Poverty*, Washington, DC.

Wößmann L. (2003) Specifying Human Capital, *Journal of Economic Surveys*, Vol. 17, No. 3.

Wren-Lewis S. (2003) Estimates of Equilibrium Exchange Rates for Sterling Against the Euro, in HM Treasury, *UK Membership of the Single Currency: An Assessment of the Five Economic Tests*, London.

York R. and Atkinson P. (1997) The Reliability of Quarterly National Accounts in Seven Major Countries: A User's Perspective, OECD Economics Department Working Paper No. 171.

Zarnowitz V. (1986) The Record and Improvability of Economic Forecasting, *Economic Forecasts: A Worldwide Survey*, Vol. 3, No. 12.

# Index